How Motivation Affects Cardiovascular Response

How Motivation Affects Cardiovascular Response

Mechanisms and Applications

Edited by
Rex A. Wright and Guido H. E. Gendolla

American Psychological Association • Washington, DC

Published by
American Psychological Association
750 First Street, NE
Washington, DC 20002
www.apa.org

To order
APA Order Department
P.O. Box 92984
Washington, DC 20090-2984
Tel: (800) 374-2721; Direct: (202) 336-5510
Fax: (202) 336-5502; TDD/TTY: (202) 336-6123
Online: www.apa.org/pubs/books
E-mail: order@apa.org

In the U.K., Europe, Africa, and the Middle East, copies may be ordered from
American Psychological Association
3 Henrietta Street
Covent Garden, London
WC2E 8LU England

Typeset in Goudy by Circle Graphics, Inc., Columbia, MD

Printer: United Book Press, Baltimore, MD
Cover Designer: Mercury Publishing Services, Rockville, MD

The opinions and statements published are the responsibility of the authors, and such opinions and statements do not necessarily represent the policies of the American Psychological Association.

Library of Congress Cataloging-in-Publication Data

How motivation affects cardiovascular response : mechanisms and applications / edited by Rex A. Wright and Guido H.E. Gendolla.
    p. cm.
Includes index.
ISBN-13: 978-1-4338-1026-8
ISBN-10: 1-4338-1026-3
1. Heart—Physiology. 2. Motivation (Psychology)—Physiological aspects. 3. Heart—Pathophysiology. I. Wright, Rex A. II. Gendolla, Guido H. E.
QP111.4.H69 2011
612.1'71—dc22
                                    2011006294

British Library Cataloguing-in-Publication Data

A CIP record is available from the British Library.

Printed in the United States of America
First Edition

DOI: 10.1037/13090-000

CONTENTS

CONTRIBUTORS

Mustafa al'Absi, PhD, University of Minnesota Medical School, Duluth

Richard W. Backs, PhD, CPE, Department of Psychology, Center for Driving Evaluation, Education, and Research, Central Michigan University, Mount Pleasant

Patricia Barreto, MA, Department of Psychology, University of Alabama at Birmingham

Gary G. Berntson, PhD, Department of Neuroscience, Ohio State University, Columbus

Stephan Bongard, PhD, Department of Psychology, Goethe-University Frankfurt am Main, Frankfurt, Germany

Jack W. Brehm, PhD, Department of Psychology, University of Kansas, Lawrence

Kerstin Brinkmann, PhD, Geneva Motivation Lab, Department of Psychology, University of Geneva, Geneva, Switzerland

John T. Cacioppo, PhD, Department of Psychology, University of Chicago, Chicago, IL

Rémi L. Capa, PhD, Department of Cognitive Sciences, University of Liège, Liège, Belgium

Douglas Carroll, PhD, School of Sport and Exercise Sciences, University of Birmingham, Birmingham, England

Nicholas Cassavaugh, PhD, Center for Driving Evaluation, Education, and Research, Central Michigan University, Mount Pleasant

Nicholas J. S. Christenfeld, PhD, Department of Psychology, University of California, San Diego

Richard J. Contrada, PhD, Department of Psychology, Rutgers, The State University of New Jersey, Piscataway

Hugo D. Critchley, DPhil, Clinical Imaging Sciences Centre, Brighton and Sussex Medical School; University of Sussex, Falmer, Brighton, England

Jenny M. Cundiff, MA, Department of Psychology, University of Utah, Salt Lake City

A. Courtney DeVries, PhD, Department of Neuroscience, Ohio State University, Columbus

Daniel R. Evans, MS, Department of Psychology, University of Kentucky, Lexington

Craig K. Ewart, PhD, Department of Psychology, Syracuse University, Syracuse, NY

Stephen H. Fairclough, PhD, School of Natural Sciences and Psychology, Liverpool John Moores University, Liverpool, England

Guido H. E. Gendolla, PhD, Geneva Motivation Lab, Department of Psychology, University of Geneva, Geneva, Switzerland

Marcus A. Gray, PhD, Psychiatry and Clinical Imaging Sciences Centre, Brighton and Sussex Medical School, University of Sussex, Brighton, East Sussex, England; School of Psychology and Psychiatry, Faculty of Medicine, Nursing, and Health Sciences, Monash University, Clayton, Victoria, Australia

Jaime K. Hardy, MS, Department of Psychology, University of Kentucky, Lexington

Louise Hawkley, PhD, Department of Psychology, University of Chicago, Chicago, IL

Robert M. Kelsey, PhD, Department of Pediatrics, Division of Cardiology, University of Tennessee Health Science Center, Memphis

Sylvia D. Kreibig, PhD, Department of Psychology, Stanford University, Stanford, CA

Britta A. Larsen, MA, Department of Psychology, University of California, San Diego

John Lenneman, PhD, Center for Driving Evaluation, Education, and Research, Central Michigan University, Mount Pleasant

William R. Lovallo, PhD, Department of Psychiatry and Behavioral Sciences, University of Oklahoma Health Sciences Center and Veterans Administration Medical Center, Oklahoma City

Anca M. Miron, PhD, Department of Psychology, University of Wisconsin, Oshkosh

L. J. M. Mulder, PhD, Department of Psychology, University of Groningen, Groningen, The Netherlands

Greg J. Norman, PhD, Department of Psychology, University of Chicago, Chicago, IL

Anna C. Phillips, PhD, School of Sport and Exercise Sciences, University of Birmingham, Birmingham, England

Michael Richter, PhD, Geneva Motivation Lab, Department of Psychology, University of Geneva, Geneva, Switzerland

Suzanne C. Segerstrom, PhD, Department of Psychology, University of Kentucky, Lexington

Nicolas Silvestrini, PhD, Geneva Motivation Lab, Department of Psychology, University of Geneva, Geneva, Switzerland

Timothy W. Smith, PhD, Department of Psychology, University of Utah, Salt Lake City

Justin E. Stanley, BA, CBIS, Department of Psychology, Rutgers, The State University of New Jersey, Piscataway

Christopher C. Stewart, PhD, Department of Neurology, Division of Neuropsychology, Medical College of Wisconsin, Milwaukee

Bert N. Uchino, PhD, Department of Psychology, University of Utah, Salt Lake City

Natalie F. Winters, BA, Department of Educational Psychology, University of Houston, Houston, TX

Rex A. Wright, PhD, Department of Psychology, University of Alabama at Birmingham

PREFACE

This book is a product of discussions between the editors that began a number of years back. When the discussions began, we both were highly involved in motivationally based cardiovascular research and knew of many others who were as well. However, we were struck by how relatively isolated different motivationally based research programs were, chiefly because they tended to be carried out in different scientific quarters (e.g., neuroscience vs. ergonomics). The relative isolation was problematic for a variety of reasons. Most notably, it interfered with communication among laboratories and the appreciation of common theoretical themes and points of disagreement. It also masked the level of motivationally based research activity and made it difficult for outsiders to see the utility of a motivational approach. One way to counter this kind of isolation is to bring together a sampling of relevant investigators under a single literary "roof." Thus, this is what we set out to do. The process of selecting contributors, securing commitments from them, and then actually getting chapters from them was not abbreviated. It also was not always simple. Most book editors will confirm that working with independent-minded academics can be a bit like herding cats. But we have no complaints. We were fortunate to obtain chapters from a truly stellar group of investigators who were cheerful for the most part and at least tolerated our various annoyances (e.g., regarding deadlines and page limits).

In the way of acknowledgment, we would like to thank Maureen Adams of the American Psychological Association's Books Department for her helpful suggestions and patience in dealing with our sometimes naïve concerns and questions. We also would like to thank Klaus Scherer for providing early counsel on the project, and friends, family members, and colleagues who suffered politely when they were inconvenienced by our involvement in it. Special thanks go to members of our laboratories, who were likely most affected, and of course to all authors who made this book possible.

There was one great sadness associated with the book's preparation. In August 2009, one of the authors—Jack Brehm—died. Jack was not only a major figure in psychology but also a dear friend and mentor. He had an incalculable influence on our research programs and lives. We are still coming to terms with the reality of his loss and, with it in mind, dedicate the book to his memory. To our knowledge, Jack's chapter with Anca Miron will be his last publication. We are deeply honored to include it.

How
Motivation
Affects
Cardiovascular
Response

INTRODUCTION

REX A. WRIGHT AND GUIDO H. E. GENDOLLA

The field of motivation is concerned with action—its selection, preparation, and execution. Put differently, it is concerned with why organisms move in the directions they do and why they do so with different degrees of persistence and vigor (McClelland, 1985). Outside of classic behaviorism (e.g., Hull, 1943), traditional conceptions of motivation (e.g., Lewin, 1935) have assumed that motivation has subjective feeling components that prompt individuals to act. Thus, for example, hungry people seek food because they experience an increased desire for it. Similarly, they seek to escape danger because they experience a "push" of fear. Because motivation is generally believed to have crucial feeling components, its formal study can be viewed as a part of the broader study of affective science.

Interest in motivational processes has waxed and waned across the history of psychology (for early theories, see Ach, 1935; Freud, 1966; James, 1884; Lewin, 1935). It waned especially during a period running from the mid 1960s through the 1980s due chiefly to the rise and temporary dominance of cognitive science. However, in the decade that followed, the interest regained force, being seen most often in discussions of effort, emotion, goals, and desire (Brehm, 1999; Brehm & Self, 1989; Carver & Scheier, 1998; Damasio, 1994; Deci & Ryan, 1985; Frijda, 1986; H. Heckhausen & Gollwitzer, 1987; Kuhl

& Beckmann, 1994; LeDoux, 1996; Locke & Latham, 1990). Interest in motivational processes continued to grow in the new millennium, and the field of motivation is currently among the most active areas of scientific study.

The level of contemporary interest in motivation is indicated in part by the veritable flood of books dealing with motivation that have appeared recently (Brewer & Hewstone, 2004; Deci & Ryan, 2002; Dreikurs-Ferguson, 2000; Dweck, 2000; Elliot, 2008; Elliot & Dweck, 2005; Forgas, Williams, & Laham, 2005; J. Heckhausen & H. Heckhausen, 2010; Higgins & Kruglanski, 2000; Morsella, Bargh, & Gollwitzer, 2009; Moskowitz & Grant, 2009; Ryan, 2011; Sander & Scherer, 2009; Shah & Gardner, 2008). It also is indicated by recent developments in the psychology research community. Included among these are (a) the revitalization of the journal *Motivation and Emotion;* (b) the emergence of new dedicated motivation research outlets, such as the motivation section of the journal *Social and Personality Psychology Compass;* (c) the formation of motivation research centers at major universities, such as Columbia University (Motivation Science Center) and the University of Geneva (Swiss Center for Affective Sciences); and (d) the establishment of the Society for the Study of Motivation, which held its first conference in May 2008. The establishment of the Society for the Study of Motivation is especially noteworthy. Properly guided, it should increase the visibility of motivation as a subdiscipline of psychology, improve the already active exchange of motivation ideas, and promote the development of motivation research and training programs at universities around the world.

It is in this context of heightened interest in motivation that we offer the present edited volume concerned with motivation influence on cardiovascular (CV) response, that is, adjustment in CV function. The volume is made up of chapters prepared by emerging as well as established research scientists and is international, including contributions from Belgium, Germany, the Netherlands, Switzerland, the United Kingdom, and the United States. Its central purposes are multifold. One is to increase awareness of the amount and diversity of motivationally based CV response research that is currently being conducted. Much of this work is being carried out in distinct quarters ("silos") of psychological science, such as those concerned with neuroscience, psychophysiology, social processes, and health. As a result, many scholars, investigators, and practitioners may be unaware of its extent and character. A second purpose is to facilitate relevant cross-disciplinary communication as well as comparison and contrast of guiding theoretical propositions and assumptions. Because scholars, investigators, and practitioners tend to work in distinct professional quarters, they tend not to communicate as much as they should with the broader range of their peers. This lack of communication works against the identification of crosscutting themes, complementarities, and points of conflict but can be countered by endeavors such as the present one to draw members of disparate groups together. A third purpose of the volume is practical—specifically, to illustrate how useful motivational approaches can be in informing us about CV responses in social, work, and achievement circumstances and highlighting conditions under which they might have implications for health.

MOTIVATION AND CARDIOVASCULAR RESPONSE:
A BRIEF HISTORY

Research scientists who take a motivational approach to understanding CV response are ones who think in terms of goal pursuit, considering the roles of motivational variables such as effort, needs, and rewards. Although psychologists have long suspected linkages between motivational variables and CV responses (Cannon, 1927, 1929; Duffy, 1951), formal study of these linkages was limited for many years. An early research pioneer was Albert Ax (1953), who explored the possibility that anger (associated with motive to attack) had different CV correlates than fear (associated with motive to escape). Later pioneers included John and Beatrice Lacey (e.g., Lacey, Kagan, Lacey, & Moss, 1963) and Rogers Elliott (1965, 1969, 1972). The Laceys made the case that phasic (very-short-term) heart rate (HR) responses decrease when people work to absorb environmental stimuli and increase when people work to shut out such stimuli. This perspective was motivational because—like the Ax perspective—it tied CV adjustment to the character of goal pursuit, specifically, the aims to take in and reject. Elliott (e.g., 1972) took issue with the Lacey view, proposing instead that HR is controlled by the instigation, anticipation, and initiation of behavioral responses and the presence of incentives. Elliott's incentive perspective was elaborated a decade later by Don Fowles (e.g., Fowles, Fisher, & Tranel, 1982; Tranel, Fisher, & Fowles, 1982), who concluded that HR varies in direct proportion to the magnitude (value) of performance incentives (see also Fowles, 1980, 1982).

Among the most influential motivational voices of the 20th century was that of Paul Obrist. Like Elliott, Obrist had difficulty with the Lacey "intake versus rejection" proposal. His early research explored the possibility that HR findings cited in support of the proposal in fact reflected cardiac–somatic coupling, that is, decreased motor activity during the performance of "intake" tasks and increased motor activity during performance of "rejection" tasks (Obrist, 1968). The research was predicated on two ideas that seem obvious in retrospect but went largely against the intellectual grain in psychology at the time. One was that the CV system is a biological system that functions chiefly to perfuse tissue in proportion to its need. The other was that perfusion requirements vary with the level of behavior. These ideas were fresh because most people investigating CV correlates of motivational variables assumed, at least implicitly, that the variables generated CV outcomes directly. Psychologists also tended to think little about metabolism in accounting for CV adjustments.

Later studies investigated when CV responses may become somatically uncoupled, that is, dissociated from movement (Obrist et al., 1978; Obrist, Webb, Sutterer, & Howard, 1970). Obrist's interest in cardiac–somatic uncoupling led in time to what currently is considered his most significant scientific contribution: his reasoning regarding *active* and *passive* coping (Obrist, 1976, 1981). Obrist proposed that active coping involves effortful action on the environment, whereas passive coping involves docile endurance of some environmental condition. He proposed further that the two types of coping are associated with distinct CV outcomes and possibly distinct health outcomes. Specifically, active (i.e., effortful) coping leads to beta-adrenergic sympathetic stimulation of the heart and potentially pathological tissue overperfusion, that is, perfusion in excess of that which is required metabolically. Passive coping, by contrast, leads to alpha-adrenergic stimulation of the vasculature and tissue perfusion scaled to metabolic requirements. Obrist's thoughts regarding active and passive coping have had a profound impact on CV psychophysiology. Many of the research programs discussed in this volume, including those in our own laboratories, can be traced back to them.

A special comment might be made about a friend and colleague of Obrist's, Jasper Brener. Drawing both on theory about the mobilization and expenditure of energy (Duffy, 1951; Germana, 1972) and on Obrist's ideas pertaining to active coping, Brener proffered a number of hypotheses concerning the conditions under which tissues will become overperfused. A construct of central focus was behavioral uncertainty. Brener (e.g., 1987) observed that energy consumption (i.e., metabolic activity) and CV responses commonly fall across experimental trial periods even though performance outcomes improve over the periods. By way of explanation, he suggested that energy mobilization is positively correspondent to behavioral uncertainty, whereas performance tends to improve as behavioral uncertainty is reduced. Brener reasoned that it is functional for metabolic rates to be elevated under conditions of behavioral uncertainty because organisms need to be prepared to carry out the most difficult behavior that may be required. Once some lesser action is required, a reduced metabolic rate can follow. An implication is that tissue overperfusion may be especially likely where behavioral uncertainty is high.

ORGANIZATION OF THIS BOOK

Motivation perspectives in this volume draw from and build on past views. They vary in multiple respects, including level of analysis, assumptions regarding mediating mechanisms, and emphasis on process versus application.

Because of this, they do not lend themselves to easy organization. However, they are sufficiently thematic to have allowed us to break the volume into two major parts—mechanisms and applications—with distinctive subsections.

Part I: Mechanisms

Part I includes chapters that address relationships between motivational variables and CV outcomes, sometimes assuming direct links and at other times assuming indirect mediation. Where indirect mediation is assumed, it most frequently is tied to effort. The first subsection begins with a chapter by Gray and Critchley (Chapter 1) that discusses neural integrative processes that underlie CV adjustments in performance contexts. It continues with two chapters concerned with effort as a direct CV response determinant. The first, by Kelsey (Chapter 2), follows strongly in the Obrist tradition by addressing cardiac pre-ejection period as an index of effort-related beta-adrenergic adjustment. The second, by Fairclough and Mulder (Chapter 3), follows in the Obrist tradition as well but takes a broader psychophysiological perspective and considers in greater detail underlying effort processes.

The second subsection offers new discussions pertaining to reward influence on CV response and the possibility that CV response patterns may be motive specific. Richter (Chapter 4) considers past and present reward ideas and evidence relevant to them, attending especially to the possibility that reward effects might be by-products of effort, that is, present only insofar as reward affects the degree to which performers become task-engaged. Kreibig (Chapter 5) examines motivation influence in light of a contemporary analysis that holds that emotions are associated with distinct autonomic activation patterns. As noted previously, emotions can be conceptualized as motivational states, that is, states in which people are impelled to pursue particular goals. Thus, the implication is that different motives may be associated with different autonomic themes that presumably have functional utility.

The third subsection of Part I focuses on affect and stress associated with motivational conflict. Miron and Brehm (Chapter 6) discuss possible CV implications of a theory of emotion to which Brehm devoted the bulk of his professional attention during the last decade of his life. The theory links emotion intensity to factors that oppose emotions and the behaviors they promote. In doing so, it presents the possibility that the same "deterrence" factors may affect CV responses in complex, but identifiable, ways. Gendolla, Brinkmann, and Silvestrini (Chapter 7) consider mood and depression influence on CV response. Taking the perspective of Gendolla's mood–behavior model (Gendolla, 2000), they conclude that mood and depression effects are multifaceted and mediated by their impact on people's evaluations of task demand and the value of success. Stanley and Contrada (Chapter 8) observe that people can experience opposing inclinations, orientations, and presses in action circumstances and review theory and research that links that experience to CV responsivity.

Part I concludes with a subsection concerned with fatigue, defined as depletion of a replenishable resource within a performance system. The first fatigue chapter, by Segerstrom, Hardy, Evans, and Winters (Chapter 9), addresses self-regulatory fatigue, that is, depletion generated by effortful control of thoughts, actions, and emotions. Based largely on neural process reasoning relevant to that discussed by Gray and Critchley, it links self-regulatory strength and the self-regulatory process to parasympathetically mediated cardiac adjustments. The second chapter in this subsection, by Wright and Stewart (Chapter 10), addresses fatigue more generally, making the case that fatigue CV influence might best be understood in terms of fatigue's impact on task difficulty appraisals and the effort effects that flow from them.

Part II: Applications

Part II includes chapters that involve application, with focuses on health and goal pursuit in different life circumstances. Those in the first subsection address the common assumption that CV responses mark or cause CV disease development. Bongard, al'Absi, and Lovallo (Chapter 11) discuss evidence relevant to the assumption, considering in the process the roles of motivational variables such as effort and task difficulty. Carroll, Phillips, and Lovallo (Chapter 12) take a contrarian view, arguing that blunted CV reactions associated with motivational variables might sometimes yield negative health outcomes.

The second subsection is concerned with social motives. Ewart (Chapter 13) starts with a discussion of his work on CV correlates of two types of striving, one oriented toward controlling others (agonistic) and the other oriented toward controlling oneself (transcendence), making the case that the former type of striving may be associated with greater health risk. Smith, Cundiff, and Uchino (Chapter 14) follow with a chapter that pursues a related theme. Their chapter explores broadly the control or agency dimension of social behavior, considering CV and health consequences of a range of agentic strivings, such as those to acquire status and influence others. Norman, DeVries, Hawkley, Cacioppo, and Berntson (Chapter 15) discuss social interaction influence on social strivings and their associated psychophysiological responses, including CV responses. Larsen and Christenfeld (Chapter 16) consider CV effects of social stress, attending especially to social situations in which goals are ambiguous and associated with no clear measures of success (indeterminate). The subsection closes with a chapter concerned with sex differences in CV response. Wright and Barreto (Chapter 17) contend that progress can be made in understanding these and health outcomes that may follow from them by considering sex influence on critical motivational variables such as appraisals of goal value and the impact that these variables have on effort.

The third subsection of Part II is concerned with work behavior and achievement. Backs, Lenneman, and Cassavaugh (Chapter 18) review human factors and ergonomics research concerned with CV responses in work settings, attending especially to the use of CV outcomes as indices of mental workload—a construct with obvious motivational implications. Capa (Chapter 19) takes a fresh look at achievement motivation, deriving some new effort hypotheses and arguing for the use of CV measures in the assessment of achievement striving.

AN OVERARCHING FRAMEWORK

Although the perspectives represented in this volume are diverse, a sizable portion of them use in some fashion a conceptual analysis that has long guided work in our laboratories (Gendolla, Wright, & Richter, in press; Wright, 1996). Many others address variables related to the analysis and discuss evidence that comports with it. These considerations hold out the possibility that the analysis might provide an overarching framework from which general lessons about motivation influence might be derived. With this possibility in mind, we end our introduction by outlining some elements of this conceptual analysis and identifying potential lessons that we see and consider to be important. Readers will find additional depictions of the analysis in later chapters and can access elaborations with full literature reviews elsewhere (e.g., Gendolla et al., in press). We include a description here to encourage readers to consider the lessons from the first chapter forward.

Core Components, Assumptions, and Suggestions

As has been noted in many previous publications (e.g., Wright, 1996, 1998), the conceptual analysis begins with Obrist's active coping hypothesis, that is, the hypothesis that beta-adrenergic CV adjustments vary with effort or task engagement. It continues by applying a theory of motivation intensity by Brehm that specifies conditions under which performers will be more and less task-engaged (Brehm & Self, 1989). One assumption of Brehm's formulation is that the motivational system is oriented toward resource conservation, which suggests that performers should expend effort (a) only to the degree that it is required and (b) only when doing so yields a sufficiently important benefit in terms of the attainment of something attractive or the avoidance of something aversive. A further assumption of the formulation is that effort is required to the degree that instrumental (i.e., approach or avoidant) behavior is difficult. This in combination with the conservation principle suggests that effort should first rise and then fall sharply as difficulty rises, with the fall occurring where success is viewed as impossible or excessively difficult considering the importance of the outcome that it can yield. Because effort should bear a nonmonotonic (sawtooth) relation to difficulty, so should effort-related CV responses.

Ability (Efficacy)

Presumably, difficulty appraisals are determined in part by the nature of behavioral challenges with which performers are confronted. However, they also should be affected by performers' ability (efficacy) in regard to the challenges, with less able performers viewing success at any given objective difficulty level as harder than more able performers. This means that although effort and associated CV responses should first rise and then fall with difficulty for both low- and high-ability performers, these outcomes should be consistently stronger for low-ability performers so long as those performers view instrumental behavior as possible and worthwhile. In addition, the outcomes should drop at a lower difficulty level for low-ability performers because those performers should reach more quickly the difficulty level at which success appears impossible or excessively difficult. When an instrumental act calls for more than even high-ability performers can or will do, then effort and associated CV responses should be low for both ability groups.

When Difficulty Is Unknown

The difficulty of instrumental behavior is not always apparent. Consider, for example, untested soldiers caught suddenly in confusing crossfire. They would know that something needs to be done but could be at a loss as to what it might be. Brehm asserted that in such situations engagement should be proportional to (i.e., rise with) the perceived importance of the outcome that might be attained or avoided up to the point that the engagement attains its peak. Once people have reached the point beyond which they can engage no further, outcome importance should have no effect. Thus, in the soldiers' case, engagement should rise with the perception of what is at stake until it can rise no more. Because engagement should bear this relationship to outcome importance, so should effort-related CV responses.

Potential Lessons

What might these ideas tell us generally about the influence of motivation on CV response? We see at least five potential lessons. One is that a particular—and widely studied—class of CV adjustments might not derive from goals per se but rather from the effort that they engender. According to this view, goals such as those to attack, acquire status, or refrain from giving in to a behavioral impulse only create potential for CV responsivity. Whether that potential is realized depends on whether the goals translate into action, that is, engagement. Further, the extent to which it is realized depends on the degree of action generated.

A second potential lesson is that the conversion of goals into engagement and CV response can be anticipated by the application of relatively simple heuristics. When difficulty is known, effort and associated CV responses should (a) correspond to it so long as success is perceived as possible and worthwhile and (b) be low if success is perceived as impossible or excessively difficult, given the importance of the contingent outcome. When difficulty is unknown, effort and associated CV responses should correspond to the importance of the contingent outcome up to the point that performers can try no harder. Application of these heuristics could be enormously useful for interpreting and integrating studies concerned with goal pursuit. Application also could be useful for identifying conditions under which certain goals (e.g., those to achieve and control) may be associated with health risk.

A third potential lesson is that variables that determine the importance of outcomes being pursued might affect CV responses only indirectly via their impact on effort. Further (and relatedly), they might enhance these responses only under some conditions. As discussed previously, the ideas that we have outlined suggest that goals—no matter how important—convert into CV responses only insofar as they engender effort. The ideas also highlight conditions under which importance variables should and should not affect effort and associated CV responses. In theory, importance variables should affect effort and associated CV responses in two circumstances: (a) where difficulty is known and the variables determine whether effort requirements are justified and (b) where difficulty is not known and a performer's upper engagement limit has not been reached. By contrast, they should not affect these outcomes where difficulty is known and they do not determine whether effort requirements are justified. Nor should they affect the outcomes where difficulty is known and success is viewed as impossible. Richter (Chapter 4) addresses this lesson in detail when considering CV effects of one importance variable: reward. Other importance variables to consider are performers' need for available incentives, their expectancy of incentive attainment given successful execution of instrumental behavior (i.e., their outcome expectancy), and their expectancy of incentive attainment given unsuccessful execution of instrumental behavior.

A fourth potential lesson is that ability and variables that determine it might also affect CV responses only indirectly via their impact on effort and, further, should bear different relations to CV response under different performance conditions. In theory, low ability should lead to improved effort and CV response so long as success is seen as possible and worthwhile. However, it should (a) lead to disengagement and reduced CV activity when it causes success to be viewed as excessively difficult or impossible and (b) have no effort or CV impact when it leaves unaltered an existing belief that success is excessively difficult or impossible. This lesson is most obviously relevant to the present research programs concerned with fatigue, because fatigue commonly is associated with reduced ability. However, it also is relevant to other research programs such as that by Gendolla et al. concerned with CV correlates of mood and depressive affect (Chapter 7) and that by Carroll et al. concerned with relatively blunted CV responses in depressed and obese individuals (Chapter 12).

The fifth potential lesson that we see is that indeterminate and conflicting goals (motives) might exert their CV impact largely through their association with behavioral uncertainty and its influence on effort. It seems true almost by definition that performers who have ambiguous and opposing aims should also have uncertainty about what they need to do to in the moment. Insofar as this is the case and performers believe that immediate action is in fact called for, the implication is that their engagement and CV response levels should reflect the importance of the outcomes that hang in the balance up to the point that they can engage no further.

Apart from this, we might add that the ideas suggest an interesting possibility related to Obrist's distinction between active and passive coping. As discussed earlier, Obrist proposed that active (i.e., effortful) coping leads to potentially pathological tissue overperfusion whereas passive coping leads to tissue perfusion scaled to metabolic requirements. Although this certainly is possible, it also could be that active coping is associated with overperfusion only so long as performers experience some uncertainty about what they need to do. Both task characteristics and personal resources are sometimes ambiguous. When they are, one might expect difficulty to be unclear and effort to approximate that which is needed, but also to be affected by the importance of outcomes that are contingent on success, with the latter influence sometimes yielding perfusion that exceeds that which ultimately will be required. Presumably, perfusion would scale to metabolic demand once difficulty became clear. This suggestion is, of course, similar to Brener's suggestion regarding energization and behavioral uncertainty (see historical review), differing mainly in terms of the role it includes for the importance of contingent outcomes. If the suggestion is borne out in further research, an implication might be that active coping health risk varies with the degree of uncertainty in action circumstances.

CONCLUDING THOUGHTS

This volume concerns how motivation influences CV response. It includes diverse perspectives that are representative of work being carried out in different quarters of psychological science. Broad lessons can be drawn taking into account the determinants and CV consequences effort. However, it would be hard to explain all of the discussed influences (e.g., character of goal pursuit, passive coping) in effort terms. There are many processes to be explored and findings to be reconciled. We will be well pleased if our effort to bring the perspectives together helps to inspire even a few readers to continue or take on new scholarship along these lines.

REFERENCES

Ach, N. (1935). *Analyse des willens* [Analysis of the will]. Berlin, Germany: Urban & Schwarzenberg.

Ax, A. F. (1953). The physiological differentiation between fear and anger in humans. *Psychosomatic Medicine, 15*, 433–442.

Brehm, J. W. (1999). The intensity of emotion. *Personality and Social Psychology Review, 3*, 2–22. doi:10.1207/s15327957pspr0301_1

Brehm, J. W., & Self, E. (1989). The intensity of motivation. *Annual Review of Psychology, 40*, 109–131. doi:10.1146/annurev.ps.40.020189.000545

Brener, J. (1987). Behavioral energetics: Some effects of uncertainty on the mobilization and distribution of energy. *Psychophysiology, 24*, 499–512. doi:10.1111/j.1469-8986.1987.tb00326.x

Brewer, M. B., & Hewstone, M. (2004). *Emotion and motivation*. Oxford, England: Blackwell.

Cannon, W. B. (1927). The James-Lange theory of emotion: A critical examination and an alternative theory. *The American Journal of Psychology, 39*, 106–124. doi:10.2307/1415404

Cannon, W. B. (1929). *Bodily changes in pain, hunger, fear, and rage*. New York, NY: D. Appleton-Century.

Carver, C. S., & Scheier, M. F. (1998). *On the self-regulation of behavior*. New York, NY: Cambridge University Press.

Damasio, A. (1994). *Descartes' error: Emotion, reason, and the human brain*. New York, NY: Penguin Putnam.

Deci, E. L., & Ryan, R. M. (1985). *Intrinsic motivation and self-determination in human behavior*. New York, NY: Plenum Press.

Deci, E. L., & Ryan, R. M. (2002). *Handbook of self-determination research*. Rochester, NY: University of Rochester Press.

Dreikurs-Ferguson, E. (2000). *Motivation: A biosocial and cognitive integration of motivation and emotion*. New York, NY: Oxford University Press.

Duffy, E. (1951). The concept of energy mobilization. *Psychological Review, 58*, 30–40. doi:10.1037/h0054220

Dweck, C. S. (2000). *Self-theories: Their role in motivation, personality, and development*. Philadelphia, PA: Psychology Press.

Elliot, A. J. (2008). *Handbook of approach and avoidance motivation*. New York, NY: Psychology Press.

Elliot, A. J., & Dweck, C. S. (2005). *Handbook of competence and motivation*. New York, NY: Guilford Press.

Elliott, R. (1965). Reaction times and heart rates as functions of magnitude of incentive and probability of success. *Journal of Personality and Social Psychology, 2*, 604–609. doi:10.1037/h0022470

Elliott, R. (1969). Tonic heart rate: Experiments on the effects of collative variables lead to a hypothesis about its motivational significance. *Journal of Personality and Social Psychology, 12*, 211–228. doi:10.1037/h0027630

Elliott, R. (1972). The significance of heart rate for behavior: A critique of Lacey's hypothesis. *Journal of Personality and Social Psychology, 22*, 398–409. doi:10.1037/h0032832

Forgas, J. P., Williams, K. D., & Laham, S. M. (2005). *Social motivation: Conscious and unconscious processes*. New York, NY: Cambridge University Press.

Fowles, D. C. (1980). The three-arousal model: Implications of Gray's two-factor theory for heart rate and electrodermal activity and psychopathology. *Psychophysiology, 17*, 87–104. doi:10.1111/j.1469-8986.1980.tb00117.x

Fowles, D. C. (1982). Heart rate as an index of anxiety: Failure of a hypothesis. In J. T. Cacioppo & R. E. Petty (Eds.), *Perspectives in cardiovascular psychophysiology* (pp. 93–126). New York, NY: Guilford Press.

Fowles, D. C., Fisher, A. E., & Tranel, D. T. (1982). The heart beats to reward: The effect of monetary incentive on heart rate. *Psychophysiology, 19*, 506–513. doi:10.1111/j.1469-8986.1982.tb02577.x

Freud, S. (1966). *Introductory lectures on psychoanalysis* (J. Strachey, Trans.). New York, NY: Norton.

Frijda, N. H. (1986). *The emotions: Studies in emotion and social interaction*. Cambridge, England: Cambridge University Press.

Gendolla, G. H. E. (2000). On the impact of mood on behavior: An integrative theory and a review. *Review of General Psychology, 4*, 378–408. doi:10.1037/1089-2680.4.4.378

Gendolla, G. H. E., Wright, R. A., & Richter, M. (in press). Effort intensity: Some answers from the cardiovascular system. In R. Ryan (Ed.), *The Oxford handbook of motivation*. New York, NY: Oxford University Press.

Germana, J. (1972). Response uncertainty and autonomic–behavioral integration. *Annals of the New York Academy of Sciences, 193,* 185–188. doi:10.1111/j.1749-6632.1972.tb27834.x

Heckhausen, H., & Gollwitzer, P. M. (1987). Thought contents and cognitive functioning in motivational versus volitional states of mind. *Motivation and Emotion, 11,* 101–120. doi:10.1007/BF00992338

Heckhausen, J., & Heckhausen, H. (2010). *Motivation and action.* New York, NY: Cambridge University Press.

Higgins, E. T., & Kruglanski, A. W. (2000). *Motivation science: Social and personality perspectives.* Ann Arbor, MI: Taylor & Francis.

Hull, C. L. (1943). *Principles of behavior.* New York, NY: Appleton-Century-Crofts.

James, W. (1884). What is emotion? *Mind, 9,* 188–205.

Kuhl, J., & Beckmann, J. (1994). *Volition and personality: Action versus state orientation.* Seattle, WA: Hogrefe.

Lacey, J. I., Kagan, J., Lacey, B. C., & Moss, H. A. (1963). The visceral level: Situational determinants and behavioral correlates of autonomic response patterns. In P. H. Knapp (Ed.), *Expression of emotions in man* (pp. 161–196). New York, NY: International Universities Press.

LeDoux, J. (1996). *The emotional brain: The mysterious underpinnings of emotional life.* New York, NY: Simon & Schuster.

Lewin, K. (1935). *A dynamic theory of personality: Selected papers.* New York, NY: McGraw-Hill.

Locke, E. A., & Latham, G. P. (1990). *A theory of goal setting and performance.* Englewood Cliffs, NJ: Prentice Hall.

McClelland, D. C. (1985). *Human motivation.* New York, NY: Cambridge University Press.

Morsella, E., Bargh, J. A., & Gollwitzer, P. M. (Eds.). (2009). *Oxford handbook of human action.* New York, NY: Oxford University Press.

Moskowitz, G. B., & Grant, H. (Eds.). (2009). *The psychology of goals.* New York, NY: Guilford Press.

Obrist, P. A. (1968). Heart rate and somatic–motor coupling during classical aversive conditioning in humans. *Journal of Experimental Psychology, 77,* 180–193. doi:10.1037/h0025814

Obrist, P. A. (1976). The cardiovascular–behavioral interaction as it appears today. *Psychophysiology, 13,* 95–107. doi:10.1111/j.1469-8986.1976.tb00081.x

Obrist, P. A. (1981). *Cardiovascular psychophysiology: A perspective.* New York, NY: Plenum Press.

Obrist, P. A., Gaebelein, C. J., Teller, E. S., Langer, A. W., Grignolo, A., Light, K. C., & McCubbin, J. A. (1978). The relationship among heart rate, carotid dp/dt, and blood pressure in humans as a function of type of stress. *Psychophysiology, 15,* 102–115. doi:10.1111/j.1469-8986.1978.tb01344.x

Obrist, P. A., Webb, R. A., Sutterer, J. R., & Howard, J. L. (1970). The cardiac–somatic relationship: Some reformulations. *Psychophysiology, 6,* 569–587. doi:10.1111/j.1469-8986.1970.tb02246.x

Ryan, R. (Ed.). (2011). *The Oxford handbook of motivation.* New York, NY: Oxford University Press.

Sander, D., & Scherer, K. R. (Eds.). (2009). *Oxford companion to emotion and the affective sciences.* New York, NY: Oxford University Press.

Shah, J. Y., & Gardner, W. L. (Eds.). (2008). *Handbook of motivation science.* New York, NY: Guilford Press.

Tranel, D. T., Fisher, A. E., & Fowles, D. C. (1982). Magnitude of incentive effects on heart rate. *Psychophysiology, 19,* 514–519. doi:10.1111/j.1469-8986.1982.tb02578.x

Wright, R. A. (1996). Brehm's theory of motivation as a model of effort and cardiovascular response. In P. M. Gollwitzer & J. A. Bargh (Eds.), *The psychology of action: Linking cognition and motivation to behavior* (pp. 424–453). New York, NY: Guilford Press.

Wright, R. A. (1998). Ability perception and cardiovascular response to behavioral challenge. In M. Kofta, G. Weary, & G. Sedek (Eds.), *Control in action: Cognitive and motivational mechanisms* (pp. 197–232). New York, NY: Plenum Press.

I
MECHANISMS

A. NEURAL INTEGRATION AND DIRECT EFFECTS OF EFFORT

1

INTEGRATION OF CARDIAC FUNCTION WITH COGNITIVE, MOTIVATIONAL, AND EMOTIONAL PROCESSING: EVIDENCE FROM NEUROIMAGING

MARCUS A. GRAY AND HUGO D. CRITCHLEY

Mental activity, notably cognitive, emotional, and executive processing, interacts with the control of internal physiological state. In most situations, this coherence between mind and body is thought to allow flexible and effective responding to a dynamic and changing environment; that is, it facilitates adaptive behavior. The relationship is likely to reflect evolutionary advantages of both evaluative cognitive processes and reactive physiological readiness to facilitate successful avoidance of predators and threats. Motivational states can be conceptualized as a hierarchy. At the bottom are homeostatic emotions; motivational states that are directly tied to physiological needs (i.e., thirst, hunger, cold) represent an efficient means of motivating behaviors that satisfy homeostatic demands. Evolutionary development within social environments may underlie the further development of this motivational hierarchy, extending initially to threats posed by predators and later to social and cognitive challenges. Complex emotions may hold motivational value because they can anticipate potential social, emotional, and cognitive challenges with relevance to long-term prospects for mating and longevity. These associations may be mediated by factors such as self-esteem and social status.

A hierarchy of motivational states that developed from a homeostatic origin may then explain why the neural circuits that underpin cognitive and emotional activity are bound with those regulating bodily physiology, including cardiovascular function. Beyond overtly survival-related responses, this integration is also demonstrable in a subtler context, where bodily state alters in accordance with emotional state during interpersonal exchanges or with mental state while carrying out complex cognitive activity. The capacity for the body to adjust to internal perturbations through single-channel homeostatic reflexes is limited. Sustained control requires coordinated responses across different systems and anticipation, ultimately behavioral responses driven by feelings and thoughts (i.e., allostasis). Thus, cognitive and emotional processing is influenced dynamically by feedback concerning the ongoing state of the body.

In this chapter, we focus on the integration of emotion, cognition, and cardiovascular function, which underlie motivational influences on cardiology. Modern neuroimaging techniques allow opportunities to explore how the interplay between cardiovascular status, cognitive–emotional functioning, and environmental demands are realized within the central and peripheral nervous systems. Research involving healthy people during experimental paradigms evoking stress and effort, studies of patients with existing cardiovascular or autonomic dysfunction, and observations in patients with damage or lesions within circumscribed neural regions provide valuable insight into the mechanisms that underpin this integration. We first consider the system in overview, outlining the range of environmental influences on cardiovascular function, the neural centers within the cortex, midbrain, and brainstem with important roles in mediating these influences, and the functional consequences and potential pathological end states that result from these mechanisms. We then consider evidence from neuroimaging research that implicates the anterior cingulate, amygdala, and insula in cardiovascular regulation and supports models of a centralized command for cardiovascular function. Next, we consider the importance of afferent feedback of physiological and cardiovascular arousal and its impact on cognitive, emotional, or cardiovascular function in patients with cardiovascular or autonomic disorders. Finally, we highlight how recognition of the motivational integration of cognition, emotion, and cardiovascular function is becoming increasingly recognized in neuroscientific research and directly tested in neural and statistical models of coordinated neural and cardiovascular function.

SYSTEM OVERVIEW

Salient environmental stimuli may motivate alterations in cardiovascular function, beyond physiological motivators such as physical stress, exercise, fainting, or hemorrhaging. The range of these specific environmental (or experimental) situations that can affect cardiovascular state is extremely large, reflecting both primary and learned challenges that ultimately evoke mental and physiological stress. Associations are apparent at the population level between environmental stressors and adverse cardiac outcomes such as acute coronary syndromes or sudden cardiac death. For example, the major earthquakes in Los Angeles (Leor, Poole, & Kloner, 1996) and the Kobe region of Japan (Suzuki et al., 1997) were both followed by significantly increased hospital admissions for acute myocardial infarction (Bhattacharyya & Steptoe, 2007).

Similar research suggests that war, terrorist acts, industrial disasters, and even sporting events are associated with higher rates of infarction, disruption of normal cardiac rhythm, and sudden cardiac death. More predictable is the increased hospitalization of cardiac patients during Christmas (Reedman, Allegra, & Cochrane, 2008), New Year's Eve (Phillips, Jarvinen, Abramson, & Phillips, 2004), and on Mondays (Barnett & Dobson, 2005), further highlighting associations between times of potential psychosocial stress and cardiovascular dysfunction. Specific emotional states are particularly associated with increased risk of clinically significant cardiac events (see Bhattacharyya & Steptoe, 2007). Acute episodes of anger (Mittleman et al., 1995), stress (Vlastelica, 2008), or depression (Chapter 7, this volume) are significantly over-reported in cardiac patients prior to admission, suggesting that negative emotions may trigger adverse cardiac events. Likewise, longer term exposure to stress may also increase cardiac risk (Bhattacharyya, Perkins-Porras, Wikman, & Steptoe, 2010; Dimsdale, 2008).

Neuroimaging research suggests that emotional and cognitive stress, either occurring naturally or induced during experimental tasks, increases activity within a matrix of brain regions encompassing specific cortical, subcortical, and brainstem centers. The result is coordinated patterns of activity expressed through peripheral changes in sympathetic and parasympathetic branches of the autonomic nervous system, hormonal, and neuroendocrine systems. Fixed patterns of cardiovascular response, observable in precollicular decerebrate experimental animals (Dick, Baekey, Paton, Lindsey, & Morris, 2009), may be differentially selected and modified by cortical and midbrain activity during cognitive and emotional processing. Parasympathetic efferents from the nucleus ambiguous and the dorsal motor nucleus of the vagus nerve alter both the heart contractility and heart rate. Likewise, sympathetic efferents from the rostroventrolateral medulla innervate the sinoatrial and atrioventricular nodes of the heart, influencing the speed and force of cardiac contractions. These efferent neural influences on the heart are accompanied and shaped by neuroendocrine and inflammatory stress responses that affect barosensitive, thermosensitive, and glucosensitive cardiac reflexes to modify cardiovascular functioning during acute stress (Dampney, Horiuchi, & McDowall, 2008;

Grippo & Johnson, 2009). Further, the balance of vasoconstriction and vasodilation in splanchnic, cutaneous, and skeletal muscle vascular beds contributes to the regulation of arterial blood pressure, cardiac output, and heart rate. Finally, dynamic adjustments of the baroreceptor set point during acute stress may shift the operating range of baroreceptor reflexes in a similar manner to those observed during exercise (Gallagher et al., 2006).

Although the integration of cognitive, emotional, and cardiovascular function typically facilitates effective behavioral responding to environmental challenges where these challenges occur in the context of preexisting cardiovascular disease, acute cardiovascular change may translate into adverse cardiac events, such as acute myocardial infarction, arrhythmias, unstable angina, or sudden cardiac death. Mechanistically, this translation frequently involves rupture of the fibrous cappings of coronary plaques and subsequent development of a thrombus (Schoenhagen, McErlean, & Nissen, 2000; see Figure 1.1). Neuroimaging has begun to inform a more complete understanding of how brain regions, specifically including the anterior cingulate, amygdala, and insula, regulate midbrain and brainstem cardiovascular circuitry and mediate adaptive and pathological changes in the cardiovascular system.

CARDIOVASCULAR FUNCTION AND CORTICOLIMBIC ACTIVITY: ANTERIOR CINGULATE, INSULA, AND AMYGDALA

Modern neuroimaging techniques, established during the 1980s and 1990s, include positron emission tomography (PET) and functional magnetic resonance imaging (fMRI). These provide the valuable opportunity to explore in vivo in humans neural activity associated with actions and sensations, thoughts and feelings, and the central regulation of the cardiovascular system. Neuroscientific investigations of a plethora of different cognitive and emotional processes typically use tasks that evoke activation within the anterior cingulate cortex (ACC). This commonality in findings across studies suggests there may be features of different experimental paradigms that are shared across studies. Paus, Koski, Caramanos, and Westbury (1998) investigated these commonalities in a meta-analysis of 107 PET neuroimaging studies published between 1990 and 1995 and coded each in terms of type and rate of input and output, cognitive process type, and task difficulty. They observed that task difficulty clearly distinguished studies that reported activation peaks within the ACC. Further, task difficulty differentially affected ACC activity, with greater increases observed within the supracallosal ACC, smaller increases within the ventral or limbic part of this gyrus, and little association within the subcallosal ACC (see Figure 1.2a). Additional variance in ACC activations also observed relating to the presence of memory components and

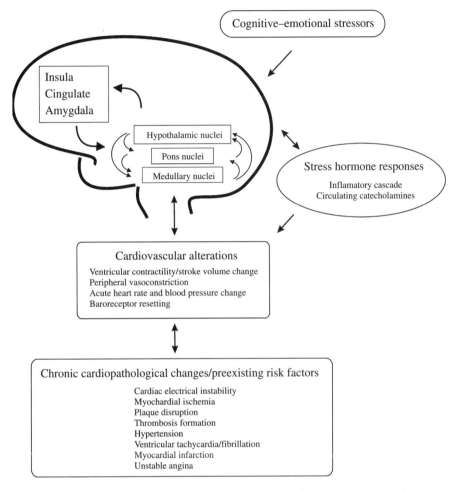

Motivational influences
(experimental or environmental)

Cognitive–emotional stressors

Insula
Cingulate
Amygdala

Hypothalamic nuclei

Pons nuclei

Medullary nuclei

Stress hormone responses

Inflamatory cascade
Circulating catecholamines

Cardiovascular alterations

Ventricular contractility/stroke volume change
Peripheral vasoconstriction
Acute heart rate and blood pressure change
Baroreceptor resetting

Chronic cardiopathological changes/preexisting risk factors

Cardiac electrical instability
Myochardial ischemia
Plaque disruption
Thrombosis formation
Hypertension
Ventricular tachycardia/fibrillation
Myocardial infarction
Unstable angina

Figure 1.1. Motivational influences alter cardiovascular function through an integrated system mediating cognitive–emotional and cardiovascular "sympathy."

response reaction time are also likely to correlate with degree of task difficulty. A key consideration here is the well-recognized association between task difficulty and cardiovascular arousal and reactivity (Richter, Friedrich, & Gendolla, 2008; Wright & Kirby, 2001).

Although task difficulty and increased arousal may frequently be correlated, other findings, such as those by Teves, Videen, Cryer, and Powers (2004), demonstrate that a visceral challenge (i.e., hypoglycemia induced by arterial injection of insulin) that induces widespread increases in autonomic arousal without cognitive or emotional stress also strongly activates the ACC. These findings were highlighted by Critchley (2004), who offered a challenge to simple "cognitive–emotional" theories of ACC function, which frequently assign autoregulatory control only to subcortical "reptilian" regions (MacLean, 1973) while separating these from cortical activity underlying cognitive and emotional processing.

These separations are opposed by recent theories that emphasize the integration of cognition and emotion with bodily states of arousal (Damasio, 1999). Critchley suggested a primary role of the ACC was in the integration of autonomic responses with processes mediated in neighboring prefrontal, insula, and striatal regions. Thus, activation of different subregions of the ACC reflects the corresponding sensorimotor, cognitive, or emotional processes supported nearby and their translation into adaptive states of bodily arousal (see Figure 1.2b). Thus, caudal ACC is associated with arousal during pain or physical effort, dorsal supragenual ACC with arousal accompanying cognitive processes, genual ACC with arousal accompanying reward-based emotional motivational processing, and subgenual ACC with parasympathetic, or antisympathetic, "vegetative" autonomic response. These proposed differentiations are broadly consistent with known connectivity of the ACC, with bidirectional connectivity with virtually all areas of the frontal cortex (Barbas, 1995) as well as connectivity with autonomic nuclei in the hypothalamus, pons, and medulla, which exert powerful control over cardiovascular function (Barbas, Saha, Rempel-Clower, & Ghashghaei, 2003). Further, direct stimulation of ACC evokes a range of autonomic and cardiovascular responses in both humans and animals (Kaada, 1951; Pool & Ransohoff, 1949).

The importance of ACC activity to cardiovascular function is further highlighted by additional neuroimaging research. Critchley and colleagues (2003) had six control subjects perform, under easy and hard conditions, alternating 2-min blocks of isometric exercise and a working memory task while fMRI data were collected. In addition, three patients with lesions encompassing the ACC underwent neuropsychological and autonomic testing and performed slightly different cognitive and isomeric exercise tests allowing comparison with normative results collected from an additional 147 healthy control participants. Heart rate variability (HRV) measures during scanning tasks were calculated for control participants, providing a measure of both sympathetic and parasympathetic cardiovascular regulation. Both sympathetic and parasympathetic power were correlated with neural activity within the ACC (see Figure 1.2c.i & 1.2c.ii). Although patients with lesions performed well behaviorally during neuropsychological testing, they displayed abnormal autonomic and cardiovascular activity (see Figure 1.2c.iii–v). In addition, in a separate study using the same cognitive and exercise stress tasks (Critchley, Corfield, Chandler, Mathias, & Dolan, 2000), increased cardiovascular arousal

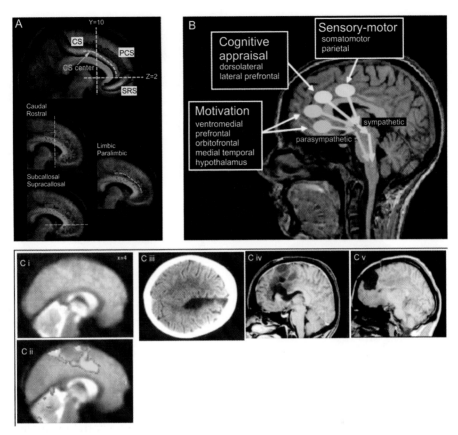

Figure 1.2. Anterior cingulate cortex activity and cognitive–emotional stress. (A) Meta-analysis of neuroimaging research reveals cingulate activity within the anterior cingulate cortex is associated with task difficulty, particularly within supracallosal regions. CS = cingulate sulcus; PCS = paracingulate sulcus; SRS = superior rostral sulcus. Adapted from "Regional Differences in the Effects of Task Difficulty and Motor Output on Blood Flow Response in the Human Anterior Cingulate Cortex: A Review of 107 PET Activation Studies," by T. Paus, L. Koski, Z. Caramanos, and C. Westbury, 1998, *Neuroreport, 9,* p. R39. Copyright 1998 by Wolters Kluwer Health. Adapted with permission. (B) Activity within cingulate regions reflects cardiovascular responses associated with behavioral, cognitive, and emotional responding. Adapted from "The Human Cortex Responds to an Interoceptive Challenge," by H. D. Critchley, 2004, *Proceedings of the National Academy of Sciences of the United States of America, 101,* p. 6333. Copyright 2004 by the National Academy of Sciences. Adapted with permission. (C) Cardiovascular arousal, indexed by sympathetic and parasympathetic cardiovascular response, which are reflected by cingulate activity in healthy participants (C.i and C.ii) is disturbed in patients with lesions of the cingulate cortex (C.iii–C.v). Adapted from "Human Cingulate Cortex and Autonomic Control: Converging Neuroimaging and Clinical Evidence," by H. D. Critchley, C. J. Mathias, O. Josephs, J. O'Doherty, S. Zanini, B. K. Dewar, L. Cipolotti, T. Shallice, and R. J. Dolan, 2003, *Brain, 126,* pp. 2144–2145. Copyright 2003 by Oxford University Press. Adapted with permission.

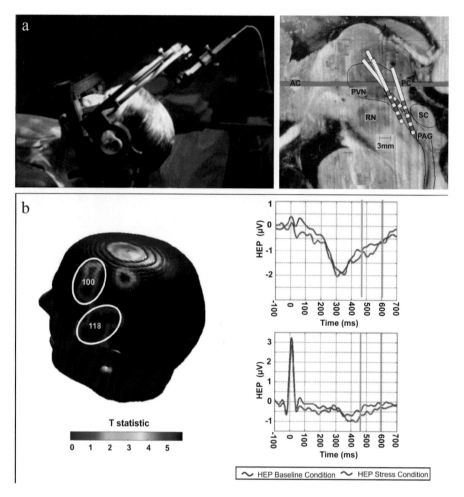

Figure 1.3. Central command and cortical representations of afferent cardiac feedback. (a) Deep brain stimulation through electrodes located within the periaqueductal grey matter and hypothalamus directly influences cardiovascular function. AC = anterior commissure; PAG = periaqueductal gray matter; PC = posterior commissure; PVG = paraventricular gray; RN = red nucleus; SC = superior colliculus. Adapted from "Identification of Neurocircuitry Controlling Cardiovascular Function in Humans Using Functional Neurosurgery: Implications for Exercise Control," by A. L. Green and D. J. Paterson, 2008, *Experimental Physiology, 93,* p. 1024. Copyright 2008 by The Physiological Society. Adapted with permission. (b) Within cardiovascular patients, the functional activity of the heart is reflected in cortical activity overlying the insula cortex. HEP = heartbeat evoked potential. Adapted from "A Cortical Potential Reflecting Cardiac Function," by M. A. Gray et al., 2007, *Proceedings of the National Academy of Sciences of the United States of America, 104,* p. 6820. Copyright 2007 by the National Academy of Sciences. Adapted with permission.

indexed by increased mean arterial pressure (MAP) in six healthy control participants was associated with increased PET measures of functional activity within the ACC. These imaging findings collectively highlight the importance of ACC activity in integrating effective cardiovascular regulation during acute experimental stressors.

In addition to the ACC, the insula cortex has also emerged from neuro-imaging research as a critical cortical site for the integration of cognitive–emotional and cardiovascular functioning. Here, hemispheric laterality may be particularly important. The insula cortex is reciprocally connected to the ACC and amygdala and also has extensive connections with midbrain and pontine–medullary structures regulating cardiovascular function (Augustine, 1996). A number of studies with rats have demonstrated a close correspondence between the functioning of the insula cortex and the heart (see Oppenheimer, 2007). Direct electrical stimulation of the left insula cortex over 8 hr significantly alters the cardiac QRS complex, progressively depressing the ST segment and increasing QT length until complete cardiac and death in asystole occurs (Oppenheimer, Wilson, Guiraudon, & Cechetto, 1991). Stimulation of the right insula cortex increases sympathetic cardiac activity indexed by HRV analysis and decreases baroreceptor reflex gain while leaving heart rate and blood pressure unchanged (Oppenheimer, Zhang, & Boekholdt, 1998). These results suggest a differential influence of the left versus right insular cortices. Further evidence of laterality is observed after lesioning insula cortex in rats. Although lesions in the anterior insula in either hemisphere did not influence baroreceptor gain, in the posterior insula left hemisphere lesions significantly increased baroreceptor gain, whereas right hemisphere lesions increased heart rate and blood pressure while leaving baroreceptor gain unaltered (Zhang, Rashba, & Oppenheimer, 1998).

Clinical and neuroimaging research with human participants further confirms a correspondence between insula and cardiac function. Direct stimulation of the insular cortex was possible in five patients who were undergoing temporal lobectomy for intractable seizures. In patients who received stimulation of the right anterior insula, increased heart rate or blood pressure was observed, effects that were not evident following stimulation of the left anterior insula cortex (Oppenheimer, Gelb, Girvin, & Hachinski, 1992). Again, these findings suggest a lateralized influence on cardiovascular function, with sympathetic cardiovascular effects associated with the right insula cortex. Laowattana et al. (2006) provided further evidence of lateralized cardiovascular influences in their examination of clinical outcomes (i.e., cardiac death, myocardial infarction, angina, and heart failure) 1 year after strokes that disrupted either the left insula (32 patients) or other noninsular regions (84 patients). Left insula stroke was associated with a significantly poorer clinical outcome and with decreased cardiac wall motion. These effects were more pronounced in patients without symptomatic coronary artery disease (SCAD), a feature that may be attributable to the protective effects of beta-blockers in patients with SCAD (Laowattana et al., 2006).

In addition to the importance of ACC and insula activity to integrated cardiovascular regulation, neuroimaging research has also frequently identified the amygdala as being functionally associated with cardiovascular change. Like the ACC and insula, the amygdala expresses reciprocal connections with pontine and medullary cell groups critical for cardiovascular control (Lowey & McKellar, 1980). Individual neurons within the amygdala also respond to activation of baro- and chemoreceptors governing cardiovascular reflex activity (Cechetto & Calaresu, 1984). Conversely, cardiovascular and ventrolateral medullary function is directly influenced by electrical stimulation of amygdala neurons (Gelsema, Agarwal, & Calaresu, 1989).

Functional brain imaging studies also frequently identify amygdala activity during tasks that induce alterations in cardiovascular function. Gianaros et al. (2005) had nine women and 11 men complete a demanding Stroop Color–Word Interference task (Stroop, 1935) that was titrated on an individual basis to keep performance at 60% accuracy. Blood pressure monitored during each of the 16 task blocks was used to calculate MAP throughout the experimental session. Increased MAP was associated with increases in activity within two regions of the ACC, bilateral insula, thalamus, periaqueductal gray matter (PAG), and within a lentiform region extending into the amygdala (see Figure 1.2). Gianaros et al. (2007) extended this research by examining the degree of change in mean arterial blood pressure (MAP), or blood pressure reactivity. Blood pressure reactivity during emotional or cognitive stress is a recognized indicator of risk of hypertension, ventricular hypertrophy, and premature atherosclerosis (Krantz & Manuck, 1984; Treiber et al., 2003).

Using fMRI scanning optimized to detect amygdala activity, 32 healthy participants completed the same titrated Stroop task (Stroop, 1935), with blood pressure recorded at baseline and repeatedly during the experimental task (Gianaros et al., 2008). During the more difficult incongruent condition, change in MAP was positively associated with change in bilateral amygdala activity. Furthermore, volumetric analysis of participants structural MRI scans revealed that gray matter volume within the amygdala was negatively correlated with MAP reactivity. This same pattern (i.e., positive activation MAP correlation and negative volume MAP correlation) was also observed within the genual ACC. Finally, these findings were associated with activity within pontine nuclei governing lower-level cardiovascular control. They observed that the greater the degree of MAP reactivity during the experimental stress task, the greater the degree of functional connectivity between activity within the pons and activity within both the left and the right amygdala.

Gianaros et al. (2009) explored carotid artery intima–media thickness (IMT) ultrasonographically in 36 adults as an indicator of atherosclerosis and a risk factor for a range of cardiovascular diseases including angina, myocardial infarction, and stroke (Lorenz, Markus, Bots, Rosvall, & Sitzer, 2007). Amygdala reactivity was probed with a facial expression matching task while fMRI data was collected. Dorsal amygdala reactivity was positively correlated with carotid IMT. Further, the greater the carotid IMT, the greater the positive correlation between functional activity within the amygdala and functional activity within the ACC. These results add further support for the notion of a cortical network including the amygdala, insula, and ACC through which cognitive–emotional stressors are translated into changes in cardiovascular function. Moreover, they suggest a pattern whereby exaggerated amygdala responses to emotional stressors are linked to cardiovascular damage as a direct consequence of excessive reactivity to stress (Gianaros et al., 2009).

CENTRAL COMMAND AND CORTICAL AFFERENT REPRESENTATIONS

Many of these findings are consistent with a top-down model for cardiovascular control, whereby cognitive and emotional processing within cortical and limbic regions initiate and control cardiovascular nuclei within the pons and medulla. This idea has been termed the *cortical radiation* (Krogh & Lindhard, 1913) or *central command* theory of cardiovascular control (Waldrop, Eldridge, Iwamoto, & Mitchell, 1996). In practice, the control of cardiovascular responses involves two-way traffic with important regulatory influences arising from afferent cardiovascular feedback as well as central command processes. Next, we briefly consider neuroimaging findings that illustrate both central command and afferent feedback aspects in the regulation of cardiovascular function during cognitive and emotional stress.

As is outlined in many textbooks of physiology, cardiovascular function is tightly regulated by nuclei within the pons and medulla. In addition to these nuclei, cardiovascular function is regulated to meet cognitive and emotional demands through a nested hierarchy, including important regulatory input from the PAG and hypothalamus. In 1995, Jansen illustrated the potential for neurons within the hypothalamus to regulate both systemic catecholamine and direct cardiovascular function by injecting rats with two transneuronal labeling viruses, one in the adrenal medulla and another in the stellate ganglion, mediating sympathetic innervation of the heart. Later immunohistochemical analysis revealed double labeled neurons within regions including the PAG and hypothalamus (Jansen, Nguyen, Karpitskiy,

Mettenleiter, & Loewy, 1995), which allows for the generation of coordinated sympathetic responses.

Influences on cardiovascular function are also clearly demonstrated by the eloquent experimental and surgical work of Green and Paterson, who have used direct electrophysiological recordings and electrical stimulation in the intact human brain known as *deep brain stimulation* (DBS). DBS, a therapeutic intervention which has been used to treat Parkinson's disease, Tourette's syndrome, obsessive–compulsive disorder, and chronic neuropathic pain refractory to medical therapies involves the insertion of electrodes into the human brain to enable direct electrical stimulation (Green & Paterson, 2008). This work illustrated a range of influences on cardiovascular function following stimulation of the hypothalamus and PAG, including sustained reduction of hypertension (Pereira et al., 2010) and acute alterations in blood pressure, baroreflex sensitivity, and HRV measures of sympathetic cardiac regulation (Green et al., 2006) and clearly demonstrated central command activity associated with the hypothalamus and PAG (Green et al., 2007; see Figure 1.3a). An important question at this stage is whether cortical regions are also associated with motivational central command processing, integrating cognitive–emotional and cardiovascular function.

Williamson, McColl, Mathews, Ginsburg, and Mitchell (1999) investigated central cardiovascular command activity within cortical regions by examining heart rate, blood pressure, perceived effort, and single-photon-emission computed tomography (SPECT) measures of brain activity while 18 participants performed exercise conditions ranging in intensity (i.e., isometric hand grip or cycling). They reported increased bilateral insula activity during increased intensity of exercise, increases which in the right hemisphere also correlated with perceived effort and blood pressure change. Although these initial findings provided some support for conscious intentional (i.e. central command) modulation by the insula, they may also reflect secondary changes in hemodynamic measures of insula activity that follow from differing exercise load.

Attempts to better isolate intentional aspects of cardiovascular modulation were made in a second paper by this group (Williamson et al., 2001) in which hypnosis was used to alter the perception of effort made during exercise, independently from the actual force produced. This allowed separation of afferent impulses arising from working skeletal muscles. Williamson et al. (2001) screened volunteers with the Harvard Group Scale of Hypnotic Susceptibility (Shor & Orne, 1962) and selected six participants who were highly susceptible to hypnotic suggestion. It was suggested to these participants that the final 5 min of an exercise bike condition would seem to be like cycling either uphill or downhill (i.e., greater or lesser effort sense), as opposed to the first 10 min, which would be flat cycling. In reality, following injection with a radioisotope, all participants cycled at a constant load, after which brain activity was assessed with SPECT. They found that an increased effort sense increased heart rate, blood pressure, and functional activity within the right insula cortex and thalamus, whereas decreased effort sense decreased activity within the ACC and left insula without altering heart rate or blood pressure. Cortical activity within the hand and leg motor regions, however, remained constant across hypnotic conditions. These findings go some way toward demonstrating a central command role for regions of the insula and ACC in the context of exercise-associated cardiovascular change.

Williamson et al. (2002) advanced these findings by exploring central command without simultaneous exercise. They also used hypnotic suggestion, selecting five high and four low susceptible participants. All participants were asked to perform an isometric handgrip exercise at 30% of maximum effort and in a second condition to imagine performing the same exercise while heart rate, blood pressure, forearm electromyography (EMG), and SPECT measures of cerebral blood flow were recorded. All participants showed increased blood pressure and heart rate during exercise; however, highly suggestible participants also showed increases during imagined exercise and an increase in perceived effort, despite no increases in forearm EMG. These participants also showed increased ACC and insula activity during imagined exercise, relative to participants with low hypnotic suggestibility.

Williamson, McColl, and Mathews (2003) next sought to identify central command activity within the insula, which was independent of muscle metaboreflex activation and blood pressure elevations. To dissociate blood pressure, an arm cuff was used to maintain exercise induced increases in blood pressure after exercise had ceased. Eight participants were administered a radioisotope, after which they performed an isometric hand grip exercise, increasing blood pressure by 15 mmHg, an increase maintained for approximately 2 min after exercise by occlusion of the arm. Activity within both the ACC and insula cortices reflected the central initiation of exercise, independently from blood pressure. By dissociating peripheral blood pressure from exercise, these findings provided further support for central command processes within the ACC and insula cortices.

Neuroimaging research has also demonstrated an important role for cortical structures in representing ongoing feedback of bodily status and cardiovascular function in cognitive–emotional and visceral integration. Jackson (1875) proposed cortical afferent representations and suggested that not only voluntary movements but also the movement of the arteries and viscera and the function of all lower nervous centers are represented by functional units or "convolutions" of the cerebral cortex (Hoff, Kell, & Carrol, 1963). Cardiac afferent feedback within the baroreceptor reflex supports continuous control of arterial pressure in response to orthostatic volume shifts. The brainstem sites responsible for this mechanism are well characterized in animals and involve baroreceptor afferents to the nucleus of the solitary tract (NTS) that modulate efferent autonomic pressor tone generated and maintained within the rostral ventrolateral medulla.

Neuroimaging correlates of central responses to blood pressure manipulations have been examined in both animals and humans. In anaesthetized cats, decreases in blood pressure (induced by sodium nitroprusside) evoked fMRI signal decreases in the medullary/NTS pathway and also in the cerebellum, pons, and right insula (Henderson et al., 2004). The same regions responded to increases in arterial pressure induced by phenylephrine, supporting interpretations of cortical representations of afferent cardiac signals. In humans, baroreceptor reflex activity can be induced experimentally using lower body negative pressure, an orthostatic stressor that reduces venous return and cardiac filling pressure, causing baroreceptor-mediated elevations in heart rate supporting homeostatic maintenance of arterial blood pressure. Kimmerly, O'Leary, Menon, Gati, and Shoemaker (2005) manipulated the baroreflex in an fMRI experiment with eight healthy male participants through lower body negative pressure induced in sealed pressure trousers. The fMRI measures of neural function revealed the induction of baroreflex responses evokes enhanced activity in posterior insula and lateral prefrontal cortex, whereas activity in genual (not dorsal) ACC, amygdala, and anterior insula decreases, suggesting these latter areas suppress, or are suppressed by, sympathoexcitatory tone at rest.

Natural baroreceptor activation gates the efferent sympathetic nerve traffic to vessels supplying skeletomusculature (muscle sympathetic nerve activity; MSNA). This effect also modulates the bodily reactions to painful somatosensory stimulation: The conjunction of electrical shock to skin and cardiac systole inhibits MSNA (Donadio, Kallio, Karlsson, Nordin, & Wallin, 2002). In an fMRI study, combining triggered shock delivery at systole and diastole with beat-to-beat blood pressure monitoring, natural baroreceptor activation at systole inhibited blood pressure reactions to pain delivery, an effect associated with differences in evoked activity within right insula, amygdala, and dorsal pons/PAG (Gray, Rylander, Harrison, Wallin, & Critchley, 2009). Individual differences in resting and evoked parasympathetic tone further predicted the magnitude of these baroreceptor effects in the brain. This study has direct relevance to understanding blood pressure and cardiovascular control, particularly in reaction to aversive physical stimulation. The findings also have broader relevance because the brain regions implicated are also sensitive to cognitive and emotional stress. Further, baroreceptor gating of pain may lead to sustained hypertension; attenuation of experiential and physical reactions to pain by increased blood pressure and increased baroreceptor activation (Dworkin et al., 1994) may lead to conditioning (i.e., associative learning) whereby hypertension results in an analgesic state, particularly in the context of hypersensitive negative emotional states such as stress (Rau & Elbert, 2001).

In addition, the presence of preexisting cardiac disease may be an amplifying factor whereby afferent feedback of abnormal cardiac responses during stress contributes to disordered central regulation of cardiovascular function. An electroencephalographic (ECG) study tested this notion by first identifying a signature of afferent cardiac activity (i.e., a heartbeat evoked potential) that reflected the integrity of effective cardiac function during mental arithmetic in heart patients who varied in the degree to which they could mount an effective cardiac output response to the stress challenge. Significant overlap was observed in the spatial distribution and related features of this potential and the ECG-derived proarrhythmic changes induced by stress (Gray et al., 2007). The observation that a central representation of stress-induced cardiac response also predicts proarrhythmic state highlights the dynamic relationship between peripheral and central factors in mechanisms underpinning the risk of stress-induced cardiac sudden death (see Figure 1.3b).

Feedback of autonomic and cardiovascular function also influences emotional experience. Patients with peripheral denervation of autonomic efferents (i.e., pure autonomic failure; PAF) are unable to generate normal sympathetic arousal responses. Functional neuroimaging while these patients completed cognitive and exercise stressor tasks revealed greater activation of pons nuclei and the ACC (Critchley, Mathias, & Dolan, 2001). Unlike in healthy controls, cardiovascular arousal was absent in PAF patients, and increases within pons and ACC are consistent with exaggerated attempts to generate normal arousal responses. Significantly reduced anxiety amongst PAF patients during PET scanning may represent a subtle influence of absent cardiovascular arousal on emotional experience. Further evidence for emotional influences of cardiac arousal are provided during false feedback experiments. Valins (1966) demonstrated that providing false auditory feedback of a racing heart can influence ongoing emotional judgments. Extending this with fMRI, Gray, Harrison, Wiens, and Critchley (2007) observed an increase in attributed emotional intensity of neutral facial expressions when participants were led to believe they were aroused. Neuroimaging data revealed increases in anterior insula activity, consistent with attempts to integrate actual cardiovascular afferent signals with false feedback of arousal, which directly reflected alterations in behavioral ratings, suggesting afferent cardiovascular information is integrated into consciously experienced emotional attributions.

A FUNCTIONALLY INTEGRATED SYSTEM

We have outlined the motivational integration of cognitive–emotional and cardiovascular function, providing examples from recent neuroimaging research that highlight neural systems important in mediating these relationships. At a general level, this research provides insight into brain–body interactions that promote broader understandings of health and disease, consistent with known risk factors for adverse cardiac events including depression, anxiety, and psychosocial triggers. More specifically, we have endeavored to highlight the importance of cortical activity in cognitive–emotional and cardiovascular integration. ACC activity is recurrently observed during cognitive and emotional experimental paradigms and also has a demonstrated role in cardiovascular regulation accompanying cognitive and emotional processing, consistent with a role as "visceromotor" cortex. Likewise, insula cortex activity is important in both the regulation and representation of cardiovascular function and may be conceptualized as a "viscerosensory" cortical region (see Craig, 2005). Activity here may assist the integration of visceral and emotional processing, facilitating the coloring of emotional experience by concomitant cardiovascular and visceral activity. Further, the amygdala demonstrates a functional correspondence with stress and emotion effects in the heart and vasculature in addition to its demonstrated contributions to processing emotional and salient stimuli. Activity within these regions may regulate hypothalamic, pons, and medullary circuits responsible for coordinated sympathetic regulation of the heart. Recent methodological advances in neuroimaging (i.e., moderation analysis) allow for the construction of statistical models that directly assess the degree to which neural change during stressor tasks mediate cardiovascular changes also accompanying stressor tasks (Wager et al., 2009). The continuing development of functional neuroimaging techniques that allow the simultaneous investigation of neural and psychophysiological activity in vivo (Gray, Minati, et al., 2009) promise further advances in delineating the integration of cardiac function with cognitive and emotional processing.

REFERENCES

Augustine, J. R. (1996). Circuitry and functional aspects of the insular lobe in primates including humans. *Brain Research Reviews, 22,* 229–244. doi:10.1016/S0165-0173(96)00011-2

Barbas, H. (1995). Anatomic basis of cognitive–emotional interactions in the primate prefrontal cortex. *Neuroscience and Biobehavioral Reviews, 19,* 499–510. doi:10.1016/0149-7634(94)00053-4

Barbas, H., Saha, S., Rempel-Clower, N., & Ghashghaei, T. (2003). Serial pathways from primate prefrontal cortex to autonomic areas may influence emotional expression. *BMC Neuroscience, 4,* 25. doi:10.1186/1471-2202-4-25

Barnett, A. G., & Dobson, A. J. (2005). Excess in cardiovascular events on Mondays: A meta-analysis and prospective study. *Journal of Epidemiology and Community Health, 59,* 109–114. doi:10.1136/jech.2003.019489

Bhattacharyya, M. R., Perkins-Porras, L., Wikman, A., & Steptoe, A. (2010). The long-term effects of acute triggers of acute coronary syndromes on adaptation and quality of life. *International Journal of Cardiology, 138*, 246–252. doi:10.1016/j.ijcard.2008.08.014

Bhattacharyya, M. R., & Steptoe, A. (2007). Emotional triggers of acute coronary syndromes: Strength of evidence, biological processes, and clinical implications. *Progress in Cardiovascular Diseases, 49*, 353–365. doi:10.1016/j.pcad.2006.11.002

Cechetto, D. F., & Calaresu, F. R. (1984). Units in the amygdala responding to activation of carotid baro- and chemoreceptors. *American Journal of Physiology, 246*, R832–R836.

Craig, A. D. (2005). Forebrain emotional asymmetry: A neuroanatomical basis? *Trends in Cognitive Sciences, 9*, 566–571. doi:10.1016/j.tics.2005.10.005

Critchley, H. D. (2004). The human cortex responds to an interoceptive challenge. *Proceedings of the National Academy of Sciences of the United States of America, 101*, 6333–6334.

Critchley, H. D., Corfield, D. R., Chandler, M. P., Mathias, C. J., & Dolan, R. J. (2000). Cerebral correlates of autonomic cardiovascular arousal: A functional neuroimaging investigation in humans. *The Journal of Physiology, 523*, 259–270. doi:10.1111/j.1469-7793.2000.t01-1-00259.x

Critchley, H. D., Mathias, C. J., & Dolan, R. J. (2001). Neuroanatomical basis for first- and second-order representations of bodily states. *Nature Neuroscience, 4*, 207–212. doi:10.1038/84048

Critchley, H. D., Mathias, C. J., Josephs, O., O'Doherty, J., Zanini, S., Dewar, B. K., . . . Dolan, R. J. (2003). Human cingulate cortex and autonomic control: Converging neuroimaging and clinical evidence. *Brain, 126*, 2139–2152. doi:10.1093/brain/awg216

Damasio, A. R. (1999). *The feeling of what happens: Body and emotion in the making of consciousness*. New York, NY: Harcourt.

Dampney, R. A., Horiuchi, J., & McDowall, L. M. (2008). Hypothalamic mechanisms coordinating cardiorespiratory function during exercise and defensive behavior. *Autonomic Neuroscience: Basic & Clinical, 142*, 3–10. doi:10.1016/j.autneu.2008.07.005

Dick, T. E., Baekey, D. M., Paton, J. F., Lindsey, B. G., & Morris, K. F. (2009). Cardio–respiratory coupling depends on the pons. *Respiratory Physiology & Neurobiology, 168*, 76–85. doi:10.1016/j.resp.2009.07.009

Dimsdale, J. E. (2008). Psychological stress and cardiovascular disease. *Journal of the American College of Cardiology, 51*, 1237–1246. doi:10.1016/j.jacc.2007.12.024

Donadio, V., Kallio, M., Karlsson, T., Nordin, M., & Wallin, B. G. (2002). Inhibition of human muscle sympathetic activity by sensory stimulation. *The Journal of Physiology, 544*, 285–292. doi:10.1113/jphysiol.2002.019596

Dworkin, B. R., Elbert, T., Rau, H., Birbaumer, N., Pauli, P., Droste, C., & Brunia, C. H. (1994). Central effects of baroreceptor activation in humans: Attenuation of skeletal reflexes and pain perception. *Proceedings of the National Academy of Sciences of the United States of America, 91*, 6329–6333. doi:10.1073/pnas.91.14.6329

Gallagher, K. M., Fadel, P. J., Smith, S. A., Strømstad, M., Ide, K., Secher, N. H., & Raven, P. B. (2006). The interaction of central command and the exercise pressor reflex in mediating baroreflex resetting during exercise in humans. *Experimental Physiology, 91*, 79–87. doi:10.1113/expphysiol.2005.032110

Gelsema, A. J., Agarwal, S. K., & Calaresu, F. R. (1989). Cardiovascular responses and changes in neural activity in the rostral ventrolateral medulla elicited by electrical stimulation of the amygdala of the rat. *Journal of the Autonomic Nervous System, 27*, 91–99. doi:10.1016/0165-1838(89)90091-X

Gianaros, P. J., Derbyshire, S. W., May, J. C., Siegle, G. J., Gamalo, M. A., & Jennings, J. R. (2005). Anterior cingulate activity correlates with blood pressure during stress. *Psychophysiology, 42*, 627–635. doi:10.1111/j.1469-8986.2005.00366.x

Gianaros, P. J., Hariri, A. R., Sheu, L. K., Muldoon, M. F., Sutton-Tyrrell, K., & Manuck, S. B. (2009). Preclinical atherosclerosis covaries with individual differences in reactivity and functional connectivity of the amygdala. *Biological Psychiatry, 65*, 943–950. doi:10.1016/j.biopsych.2008.10.007

Gianaros, P. J., Jennings, J. R., Sheu, L. K., Greer, P. J., Kuller, L. H., & Matthews, K. A. (2007). Prospective reports of chronic life stress predict decreased grey matter volume in the hippocampus. *NeuroImage, 35*, 795–803. doi:10.1016/j.neuroimage. 2006.10.045

Gianaros, P. J., Sheu, L. K., Matthews, K. A., Jennings, J. R., Manuck, S. B., & Hariri, A. R. (2008). Individual differences in stressor-evoked blood pressure reactivity vary with activation, volume, and functional connectivity of the amygdala. *The Journal of Neuroscience, 28*, 990–999. doi:10.1523/JNEUROSCI.3606-07.2008

Gray, M. A., Harrison, N. A., Wiens, S., & Critchley, H. D. (2007). Modulation of emotional appraisal by false physiological feedback during fMRI. *PLoS ONE, 2*, e546. doi:10.1371/journal.pone.0000546

Gray, M. A., Minati, L., Harrison, N. A., Gianaros, P. J., Napadow, V., & Critchley, H. D. (2009). Physiological recordings: Basic concepts and implementation during functional magnetic resonance imaging. *NeuroImage, 47*, 1105–1115. doi:10.1016/j.neuroimage.2009.05.033

Gray, M. A., Rylander, K., Harrison, N. A., Wallin, B. G., & Critchley, H. D. (2009). Following one's heart: Cardiac rhythms gate central initiation of sympathetic reflexes. *The Journal of Neuroscience, 29*, 1817–1825. doi:10.1523/JNEUROSCI. 3363-08.2009

Gray, M. A., Taggart, P., Sutton, P. M., Groves, D., Holdright, D. R., Bradbury, D., . . . Critchley, H. E. (2007). A cortical potential reflecting cardiac function. *Proceedings of the National Academy of Sciences of the United States of America, 104*, 6818–6823. doi:10.1073/pnas.0609509104

Green, A. L., & Paterson, D. J. (2008). Identification of neurocircuitry controlling cardiovascular function in humans using functional neurosurgery: implications for exercise control. *Experimental Physiology, 93,* 1022–1028. doi:10.1113/expphysiol.2007.039461

Green, A. L., Wang, S., Owen, S. L., Xie, K., Bittar, R. G., Stein, J. F., . . . Aziz, T. Z. (2006). Stimulating the human midbrain to reveal the link between pain and blood pressure. *Pain, 124,* 349–359. doi:10.1016/j.pain.2006.05.005

Green, A. L., Wang, S., Purvis, S., Owen, S. L., Bain, P. G., Stein, J. F., . . . Paterson, D. J. (2007). Identifying cardiorespiratory neurocircuitry involved in central command during exercise in humans. *The Journal of Physiology, 578,* 605–612. doi:10.1113/jphysiol.2006.122549

Grippo, A. J., & Johnson, A. K. (2009). Stress, depression, and cardiovascular dysregulation: A review of neurobiological mechanisms and the integration of research from preclinical disease models. *Stress, 12,* 1–21. doi:10.1080/10253890802046281

Henderson, L. A., Richard, C. A., Macey, P. M., Runquist, M. L., Yu, P. L., Galons, J. P., & Harper, R. M. (2004). Functional magnetic resonance signal changes in neural structures to baroreceptor reflex activation. *Journal of Applied Physiology, 96,* 693–703. doi:10.1152/japplphysiol.00852.2003

Hoff, E. C., Kell, J. F., Jr., & Carrol, M. N., Jr. (1963). Effects of cortical stimulation and lesions on cardiovascular function. *Physiological Reviews, 43,* 68–114.

Jackson, J. (1875). *Clinical and physiological researches on the nervous system: Vol. I. On the anatomical and physiological localization of movements in the brain.* London, England: Low, Churchill.

Jansen, A. S., Nguyen, X. V., Karpitskiy, V., Mettenleiter, T. C., & Loewy, A. D. (1995, October 27). Central command neurons of the sympathetic nervous system: Basis of the fight-or-flight response. *Science, 270,* 644–646. doi:10.1126/science.270.5236.644

Kaada, B. R. (1951). Somato-motor, autonomic, and electrocorticographic responses to electrical stimulation of rhinencephalic and other structures in primates, cat, and dog: A study of responses from the limbic, subcallosal, orbito-insular, piriform and temporal cortex, hippocampus-fornix, and amygdala. *Acta Physiologica Scandinavica. Supplementum, 24,* 1–262.

Kimmerly, D. S., O'Leary, D. D., Menon, R. S., Gati, J. S., & Shoemaker, J. K. (2005). Cortical regions associated with autonomic cardiovascular regulation during lower body negative pressure in humans. *The Journal of Physiology, 569,* 331–345. doi:10.1113/jphysiol.2005.091637

Krantz, D. S., & Manuck, S. B. (1984). Acute psychophysiologic reactivity and risk of cardiovascular disease: A review and methodologic critique. *Psychological Bulletin, 96,* 435–464. doi:10.1037/0033-2909.96.3.435

Krogh, A., & Lindhard, J. (1913). The regulation of respiration and circulation during the initial stages of muscular work. *The Journal of Physiology, 47,* 112–136.

Laowattana, S., Zeger, S. L., Lima, J. A. C., Goodman, S. N., Wittstein, I. S., & Oppenheimer, S. M. (2006). Left insular stroke is associated with adverse cardiac outcome. *Neurology, 66,* 477–483. doi:10.1212/01.wnl.0000202684.29640.60

Leor, J., Poole, W. K., & Kloner, R. A. (1996). Sudden cardiac death triggered by an earthquake. *The New England Journal of Medicine, 334*, 413–419. doi:10.1056/NEJM199602153340701

Loewy, A. D., & McKellar, S. (1980). The neuroanatomical basis of central cardiovascular control. *Federation Proceedings, 39*, 2495–2503.

Lorenz, M. W., Markus, H. S., Bots, M. L., Rosvall, M., & Sitzer, M. (2007). Prediction of clinical cardiovascular events with carotid intima-media thickness: A systematic review and meta-analysis. *Circulation, 115*, 459–467. doi:10.1161/CIRCULATIONAHA.106.628875

MacLean, P. D. (1973). Man's reptilian and limbic inheritance. In T. J. Boag & D. Campbell (Eds.), *A triune concept of brain and behavior* (pp. 6–22). Toronto, Canada: University of Toronto Press.

Mittleman, M. A., Maclure, M., Sherwood, J. B., Mulry, R. P., Tofler, G. H., Jacobs, S. C., . . . Muller, J. E. (1995). Triggering of acute myocardial infarction onset by episodes of anger. Determinants of myocardial infarction onset study investigators. *Circulation, 92*, 1720–1725.

Oppenheimer, S. (2007). Cortical control of the heart. *Cleveland Clinic Journal of Medicine, 74*(Suppl. 1), S27–S29. doi:10.3949/ccjm.74.Suppl_1.S27

Oppenheimer, S. M., Gelb, A., Girvin, J. P., & Hachinski, V. C. (1992). Cardiovascular effects of human insular cortex stimulation. *Neurology, 42*, 1727–1732.

Oppenheimer, S. M., Wilson, J. X., Guiraudon, C., & Cechetto, D. F. (1991). Insular cortex stimulation produces lethal cardiac arrhythmias: A mechanism of sudden death? *Brain Research, 550*, 115–121. doi:10.1016/0006-8993(91)90412-O

Oppenheimer, S. M., Zhang, Z. H., & Boekholdt, M. (1998). Electrical stimulation of the right posterior insular cortex increases cardiac sympathetic tone in the rat. *Society for Neuroscience Abstracts, 24*, 1134.

Paus, T., Koski, L., Caramanos, Z., & Westbury, C. (1998). Regional differences in the effects of task difficulty and motor output on blood flow response in the human anterior cingulate cortex: A review of 107 PET activation studies. *Neuroreport, 9*, R37–R47. doi:10.1097/00001756-199806220-00001

Pereira, E. A., Wang, S., Paterson, D. J., Stein, J. F., Aziz, T. Z., & Green, A. L. (2010). Sustained reduction of hypertension by deep brain stimulation. *Journal of Clinical Neuroscience, 17*, 124–127. doi:10.1016/j.jocn.2009.02.041

Phillips, D. P., Jarvinen, J. R., Abramson, I. S., & Phillips, R. R. (2004). Cardiac mortality is higher around Christmas and New Year's than at any other time: The holidays as a risk factor for death. *Circulation, 110*, 3781–3788. doi:10.1161/01.CIR.0000151424.02045.F7

Pool, J. L., & Ransohoff, J. (1949). Autonomic effects on stimulating rostral portion of cingulate gyri in man. *Journal of Neurophysiology, 12*, 385–392.

Rau, H., & Elbert, T. (2001). Psychophysiology of arterial baroreceptors and the etiology of hypertension. *Biological Psychology, 57*, 179–201. doi:10.1016/S0301-0511(01)00094-1

Reedman, L. A., Allegra, J. R., & Cochrane, D. G. (2008). Increases in heart failure visits after Christmas and New Year's Day. *Congestive Heart Failure, 14*, 307–309. doi:10.1111/j.1751-7133.2008.00021.x

Richter, M., Friedrich, A., & Gendolla, G. H. (2008). Task difficulty effects on cardiac activity. *Psychophysiology, 45*, 869–875. doi:10.1111/j.1469-8986.2008.00688.x

Schoenhagen, P., McErlean, E. S., & Nissen, S. E. (2000). The vulnerable coronary plaque. *The Journal of Cardiovascular Nursing, 15*, 1–12.

Shor, R. E., & Orne, E. C. (1962). *Harvard Group Scale of Hypnotic Susceptibility. Form A*. Palo Alto, CA: Consulting Psychologists Press.

Stroop, J. R. (1935). Studies of interference in serial verbal reactions. *Journal of Experimental Psychology, 18*, 643–662. doi:10.1037//0096-3445.121.1.15

Suzuki, S., Sakamoto, S., Koide, M., Fujita, H., Sakuramoto, H., Kuroda, T., . . . Matsuo, T. (1997). Hanshin-Awaji earthquake as a trigger for acute myocardial infarction. *American Heart Journal, 134*, 974–977. doi:10.1016/S0002-8703(97)80023-3

Teves, D., Videen, T. O., Cryer, P. E., & Powers, W. J. (2004). Activation of human medial prefrontal cortex during autonomic responses to hypoglycemia. *Proceedings of the National Academy of Sciences of the United States of America, 101*, 6217–6221. doi:10.1073/pnas.0307048101

Treiber, F. A., Kamarck, T., Schneiderman, N., Sheffield, D., Kapuku, G., & Taylor, T. (2003). Cardiovascular reactivity and development of preclinical and clinical disease states. *Psychosomatic Medicine, 65*, 46–62.

Valins, S. (1966). Cognitive effects of false heart-rate feedback. *Journal of Personality and Social Psychology, 4*, 400–408. doi:10.1037/h0023791

Vlastelica, M. (2008). Emotional stress as a trigger in sudden cardiac death. *Psychiatria Danubina, 20*, 411–414.

Wager, T. D., van Ast, V. A., Hughes, B. L., Davidson, M. L., Lindquist, M. A., & Ochsner, K. N. (2009). Brain mediators of cardiovascular responses to social threat, Part II: Prefrontal-subcortical pathways and relationship with anxiety. *NeuroImage, 47*, 836–851. doi:10.1016/j.neuroimage.2009.05.044

Waldrop, T. G., Eldridge, F. L., Iwamoto, G. A., & Mitchell, J. H. (1996). Central neural control of respiration and circulation during exercise. In L.B. Rowell & J. T Shepperd (Eds.), *Handbook of physiology: Section 12. Exercise: Regulation and integration of multiple systems* (pp. 333–380). Bethesda, MD: American Physiological Society.

Williamson, J. W., McColl, R., & Mathews, D. (2003). Evidence for central command activation of the human insular cortex during exercise. *Journal of Applied Physiology, 94*, 1726–1734.

Williamson, J. W., McColl, R., Mathews, D., Ginsburg, M., & Mitchell, J. H. (1999). Activation of the insular cortex is affected by the intensity of exercise. *Journal of Applied Physiology, 87*, 1213–1219.

Williamson, J. W., McColl, R., Mathews, D., Mitchell, J. H., Raven, P. B., & Morgan, W. P. (2001). Hypnotic manipulation of effort sense during dynamic exercise:

Cardiovascular responses and brain activation. *Journal of Applied Physiology, 90,* 1392–1399.

Williamson, J. W., McColl, R., Mathews, D., Mitchell, J. H., Raven, P. B., & Morgan, W. P. (2002). Brain activation by central command during actual and imagined handgrip under hypnosis. *Journal of Applied Physiology, 92,* 1317–1324.

Wright, R. A., & Kirby, L. D. (2001). Effort determination of cardiovascular response: An integrative analysis with applications in social psychology. In M. P. Zanna (Ed.), *Advances in experimental social psychology* (Vol. 33, pp. 255–307). San Diego, CA: Academic Press.

Zhang, Z. H., Rashba, S., & Oppenheimer, S. M. (1998). Insular cortex lesions alter baroreceptor sensitivity in the urethene-anesthestized rat. *Brain Research, 813,* 73–81. doi:10.1016/S0006-8993(98)00996-2

2

BETA-ADRENERGIC CARDIOVASCULAR REACTIVITY AND ADAPTATION TO STRESS: THE CARDIAC PRE-EJECTION PERIOD AS AN INDEX OF EFFORT

ROBERT M. KELSEY

The primary function of the cardiovascular system is to ensure an adequate distribution of blood flow throughout the body to meet the energy demands of active tissues, muscles, and organs. Behavior requires energy and thus imposes demands on the cardiovascular system (Berne & Levy, 1981; Brener, 1987; Obrist, 1981). However, the cardiovascular system does not merely respond to peripheral feedback from active tissues, muscles, and organs; it also responds to efferent signals from the central nervous system to anticipate and prepare for action. Accordingly, motivational and emotional processes underlying behavior can exert an impact on cardiovascular function. This impact is largely mediated by the sympathetic and parasympathetic divisions of the autonomic nervous system.

Psychophysiological research has identified a number of behavioral and psychological factors and conditions that elicit changes in cardiovascular function. The term *cardiovascular reactivity* is commonly used when referring to these changes. Two important dimensions that have emerged from this research are those of *active versus passive coping* (Bandler, Price, & Keay, 2000; Obrist, 1981) and *novelty/uncertainty versus familiarity* (Brener, 1987; Kelsey, 1993; Kelsey et al., 1999; Kelsey, Soderlund, & Arthur, 2004; Obrist, 1981).

Active coping applies to circumstances in which there is some possibility of escape from a stressful situation or some degree of actual or perceived control over the outcome of events. Conversely, *passive coping* applies to circumstances in which there is little or no possibility of escape from, or control over, stressful events. The fight–flight response is the prototype for active coping, whereas the conservation–withdrawal response is the prototype for passive coping. Accordingly, active coping is characterized by sympathetic activation and mobilization of resources for action and engagement, whereas passive coping is characterized by sympathetic inhibition, immobility, and disengagement (Bandler et al., 2000). A large body of research has shown that cardiovascular reactivity, especially cardiac reactivity, is greater during active than passive coping (Kelsey, Ornduff, McCann, & Reiff, 2001; Lovallo et al., 1985; Obrist, 1981; Obrist, Light, James, & Strogatz, 1987; Saab et al., 1992; Sherwood, Allen, Obrist, & Langer, 1986; Sherwood, Dolan, & Light, 1990). Obrist (1981) argued that cardiac and somatic activity are tightly coupled over a broad range of conditions, including resting conditions and those involving passive coping, and that the heart is primarily under parasympathetic vagal control during such conditions. In contrast, beta-adrenergic sympathetic effects on the heart predominate during conditions that involve active efforts to cope with environmental demands (Obrist, 1981; Sherwood et al., 1986).

Extending this perspective, Brener (1987) argued that sympathetic influences on the heart are most evident when environmental conditions and stressors are novel, unpredictable, or high in uncertainty. Indeed, research has shown that cardiovascular reactivity, particularly beta-adrenergic sympathetic cardiac reactivity, declines significantly with repeated exposure to the same or similar tasks and environmental conditions (Brenner, Beauchaine, & Sylvers, 2005; Kelsey, 1991, 1993; Kelsey et al., 1999, 2000, 2004; Light & Obrist, 1983; Obrist, 1981; Sherwood et al., 1986). Thus, sympathetic effects on the heart are most likely to emerge during active coping under conditions of high environmental and behavioral uncertainty (Brener, 1987; Kelsey et al., 1999, 2001, 2004; Lovallo et al., 1985; Obrist, 1981). The model of arousal, activation, and effort proposed by Pribram and McGuinness (1975) brings together these dimensions of active–passive coping and novelty/uncertainty–familiarity. According to their model, an arousal system controls phasic physiological responses to environmental stimuli (i.e., perceptual input; "what is it?"), whereas an activation system controls a tonic physiological readiness to respond (i.e., motor readiness; "what to do?"). An effort system coordinates and integrates the arousal and activation systems to formulate effective responses to meet environmental demands, implying that physiological responses to environmental demands change as a result of familiarity and experience.

In this chapter, I review research from my laboratory and others indicating that the cardiac pre-ejection period (PEP) is a viable index of effort. This research shows that PEP is a reliable and valid measure of beta-adrenergic sympathetic effects on the heart, responds primarily to environmental conditions that require effortful active coping, and is sensitive to both environmental and behavioral uncertainty.

MEASURES OF CARDIOVASCULAR REACTIVITY

Blood pressure (BP) and heart rate (HR) are the most commonly used measures in cardiovascular psychophysiology. These measures have proved useful for many purposes, but they have limited utility for disentangling sympathetic and parasympathetic influences on cardiovascular function. BP is influenced by beta-adrenergic sympathetic effects on the heart and by counteracting beta-adrenergic vasodilatory and alpha-adrenergic vasoconstrictive sympathetic effects on vascular resistance (Berne & Levy, 1981; Obrist, 1981). Chronotropic cardiac measures such as HR and its inverse, heart period (HP), are under both sympathetic and parasympathetic control; thus, increases in HR (or decreases in HP) may result from increased beta-adrenergic sympathetic drive and/or decreased parasympathetic vagal restraint on the heart (Berne & Levy, 1981; Obrist, 1981). In contrast, inotropic measures of myocardial contractility such as the cardiac PEP are controlled primarily by beta-adrenergic sympathetic influences on the left ventricle of the heart (Newlin & Levenson, 1979; Obrist, 1981; Sherwood, Allen, et al., 1990).

As the systolic time interval between the onset of ventricular depolarization (represented by the Q-wave of the QRS-complex of the electrocardiogram [ECG]) and the onset of left ventricular ejection into the aorta, PEP includes the time during which left ventricular contractile force is generated (Newlin & Levenson, 1979; Sherwood, Allen, et al., 1990). Consequently, increases in myocardial contractility are reflected in decreases in PEP. The traditional method of measuring PEP requires an ECG to determine the Q-wave (onset of ventricular depolarization), a phonocardiogram to determine the second heart sound (S2, denoting aortic valve closure and end of systole), and a peripheral pulse wave to determine ejection time (upstroke to dicrotic notch). The measure of ejection time is then subtracted from the Q–S2 interval (electromechanical systole) to determine PEP. Unfortunately, this indirect method is vulnerable to movement artifact and inflated measurement error resulting from the detection of four different waveform points (Sherwood, Allen, et al., 1990). Impedance cardiography offers a more direct method for measuring PEP and other systolic time intervals, as well as a useful method for measuring relative changes in cardiac output (CO) and total peripheral vascular resistance (TPR; Kelsey & Guethlein, 1990; Sherwood, Allen, et al., 1990).

The dZ/dt waveform of the impedance cardiogram includes inflections that are associated with (a) the onset of left ventricular ejection and aortic valve opening (the B-point) and (b) the end of ejection and aortic valve closure (the X-point). Accordingly, PEP is defined as the interval between the Q-wave of the ECG and the B-point of the dZ/dt waveform, whereas left ventricular ejection time (LVET) is defined as the interval between the B-point and the X-point of the dZ/dt waveform (Kelsey & Guethlein, 1990; Sherwood, Allen, et al., 1990). Given that there is little variation of interest in the interval between the Q-wave and the R-wave of the ECG (Mezzacappa, Kelsey, & Katkin, 1999), a useful abbreviated measure of PEP can be calculated as the interval between the peak of the R-wave and the B-point of the dZ/dt waveform (the R–B interval; Kelsey & Guethlein, 1990; Kelsey et al., 1998; Mezzacappa et al., 1999; Sherwood, Allen, et al., 1990). This abbreviated PEP capitalizes on the ease and accuracy of detecting the large R-wave as compared with the subtle Q-wave of the ECG, thereby reducing measurement error without impairing validity.

PRE-EJECTION PERIOD AS AN INDEX OF BETA-ADRENERGIC SYMPATHETIC EFFECTS ON THE HEART

Several studies have evaluated the reliability and validity of impedance cardiographic measures, including PEP (Sherwood, Allen, et al., 1990). Studies in our laboratory have demonstrated that these measures have high internal consistency (Kelsey, Ornduff, & Alpert, 2007) and interrater reliability (Kelsey et al., 1998), as well as good concurrent validity across different averaging and scoring methods (Kelsey & Guethlein, 1990; Kelsey et al., 1998). Other researchers have reported good test–retest reliability for PEP and other impedance cardiographic measures (Burleson et al., 2003; McGrath & O'Brien, 2001; Saab et al., 1992).

Substantial evidence shows that PEP is a sensitive index of beta-adrenergic sympathetic activation (Newlin & Levenson, 1979; Sherwood, Allen, et al., 1990). McCubbin, Richardson, Langer, Kizer, and Obrist (1983) reported that plasma concentrations of epinephrine correlated inversely with PEP during cognitive stress and poststress recovery periods, whereas plasma concentrations of norepinephrine correlated inversely with PEP at the onset of stress. Overall, correlations with catecholamine concentrations were more consistent for PEP than for HR or BP. Consistent with these findings, experimental studies have shown that beta-adrenergic receptor stimulation with agonists, including norepinephrine, epinephrine, and isoproterenol, causes a significant shortening of PEP (Mezzacappa et al., 1999; Newlin & Levenson, 1979; Schächinger, Weinbacher, Kiss, Ritz, & Langewitz, 2001). Mezzacappa et al. (1999) used impedance cardiography to measure cardiovascular responses to a bolus injection of either epinephrine or saline in undergraduate men. Epinephrine had the greatest impact on PEP, yielding an effect size of $\eta = 0.84$, whether measured from the peak of the Q-wave or the peak of the R-wave of the ECG. Epinephrine had progressively smaller effects on CO ($\eta = 0.81$), TPR ($\eta = 0.75$), HP ($\eta = 0.61$), systolic BP ($\eta = 0.52$), and diastolic BP ($\eta = 0.44$), and no significant effects on either LVET or the Q–R interval of the ECG.

Other studies have shown that beta-adrenergic receptor blockade with antagonists (beta blockers) eliminates the shortening of PEP during isoproterenol stimulation and active coping (Berntson et al., 1994; Newlin & Levenson, 1979; Sherwood et al., 1986) and lengthens PEP during rest and passive coping (Berntson et al., 1994; Cacioppo et al., 1994; Schächinger et al., 2001; Sherwood et al., 1986). It is important to note that these studies have shown that vagal blockade has little or no impact on PEP (Berntson et al., 1994; Cacioppo et al., 1994; Newlin & Levenson, 1979).

We recently completed a large genetic association study of cardiovascular reactivity to cold and psychological stress in young Black Americans that included an evaluation of genetic variants in the β_1- and β_2-adrenergic receptor genes (Kelsey, Alpert, Dahmer, Krushkal, & Quasney, 2010). The β_1-adrenergic receptor subtype is located primarily in the heart, where it mediates increases in rate and contractility when stimulated by norepinephrine or epinephrine; the β_2-adrenergic receptor subtype is located primarily in blood vessels, where it mediates vasodilation when stimulated by epinephrine (Brodde, 2008). We found a significant association between PEP reactivity to stress and a common, functional polymorphism in the β_1-adrenergic receptor gene that involves a change from arginine (Arg) to glycine (Gly) at amino acid position 389 (Arg389Gly, rs1801253); this change results in a loss of receptor function. The decrease in PEP during stress was significantly smaller in males who were homozygous for the lower functioning Gly389 variant (M ± SEM = −1.5 ± 0.4 ms) than in males who carried one or two copies of the higher functioning Arg389 variant of the receptor (M ± SEM = −3.4 ± 0.3 ms and −3.1 ± 0.4 ms, respectively). Curiously, this association did not appear in females. The β_1-adrenergic receptor polymorphism was not associated with other measures of cardiovascular reactivity or cardiovascular baseline measures. Moreover, there were no significant associations between PEP reactivity and genetic variants in the β_2-adrenergic receptor. These findings further substantiate the link between PEP reactivity and beta-adrenergic sympathetic activation and provide new evidence indicating that the β_1-adrenergic receptor is the specific subtype involved in PEP reactivity, at least in males.

Although these studies provide strong evidence that decreases in PEP result primarily from increases in beta-adrenergic sympathetic effects on the heart, other mechanisms may cause changes in PEP (Newlin & Levenson, 1979; Sherwood, Allen, et al., 1990). Decreases in PEP may result from autoregulatory mechanisms involving increases in preload (left ventricular filling) or decreases in afterload (aortic diastolic pressure). Fortunately, these autoregulatory influences tend to be minimal under many circumstances, especially when body posture is stable (Berntson et al., 1994; Cacioppo et al., 1994; Kelsey, 1991; Kelsey et al., 1999, 2000, 2004; Obrist et al., 1987).

PRE-EJECTION PERIOD REACTIVITY
AND ADAPTATION TO STRESS

We have argued that PEP reactivity is a sensitive index of the fight–flight response and the mobilization of effort in preparation for action (Kelsey, 1991; Kelsey et al., 1999, 2000, 2001, 2004), with beta-adrenergic sympathetic activation providing the mediating mechanism (Berntson et al., 1994; Kelsey et al., 2010; McCubbin et al., 1983; Mezzacappa et al., 1999; Sherwood et al., 1986). Epinephrine is likely to play a key role because it is the quintessential hormone of the fight–flight response, as well as a crucial component of the physiological response to novelty, uncertainty, mental work, and effortful active coping (Frankenhaeuser, 1971; Kaji et al., 1989; McCubbin et al., 1983). Our program of research on cardiovascular reactivity and adaptation to stress has evaluated PEP and other cardiovascular measures during active and passive coping conditions and during recurrent mental arithmetic stress. The results of these studies support the utility of PEP as a measure of beta-adrenergic sympathetic activation and effortful active coping.

Effects of Active and Passive Coping

We have evaluated cardiovascular reactivity during active coping with a 3-min video game task (with monetary performance incentives during the last minute) and passive coping with a 3-min forehead cold pressor task in two studies with Black and White adolescents and young adults (Kelsey et al., 2007). Previous studies of active and passive coping have used similar tasks (Obrist, 1981; Obrist et al., 1987; Saab et al., 1992; Sherwood et al., 1986). In our studies, both video game and cold pressor evoked increases in systolic and diastolic BP, but the video game alone elicited a significant decrease in PEP (i.e., an increase in myocardial contractility). Thus, PEP reactivity was uniquely associated with active as opposed to passive coping. The video game and cold pressor tasks clearly differed on a number of dimensions besides active and passive coping, including appetitive and aversive aspects and degree of sensory intake and rejection. These other characteristics might have confounded some of the effects of active–passive coping. With some notable exceptions (e.g., Kelsey et al., 2001; Lovallo et al., 1985; Obrist, 1981; Sherwood, Dolan, et al., 1990), this sort of "apples and oranges" comparison is a common weakness of many studies of the active–passive coping dimension.

Our initial study of the psychophysiological characteristics of narcissism (Kelsey et al., 2001) provided a clearer test of the effects of active and passive coping on cardiac reactivity. We measured HR, PEP, and skin conductance response frequency (SCR; a measure of cholinergic sympathetic activation) in undergraduate men at rest and during active and passive anticipatory coping tasks. Each of these tasks involved five trials of a 27-s visual countdown from nine to one presented on a computer display. In the passive coping condition, an unavoidable aversive tone occurred 1 s after the end of the countdown period. In the active coping condition, the participant could avoid the aversive tone by making a simple motor response within this 1-s interval. Thus, the active and passive conditions differed only in the availability of control over the occurrence of an aversive stimulus, thereby providing a pure manipulation of active and passive coping. The tasks were presented in counterbalanced order, and measures of reactivity were calculated in the usual manner by subtracting mean values during pretask baseline rest periods from values during the corresponding task period.

As expected, PEP decreased significantly more during active coping (M ± SEM = −2.0 ± 0.5 ms) than passive coping (M ± SEM = 0.2 ± 0.5 ms). In fact, PEP differed significantly from baseline only during the active condition. In contrast, HP lengthened to a similar degree in both conditions (M ± SEM = 11.4 ± 6.5 ms and 13.7 ± 9.1 ms, respectively). Mirroring the pattern for PEP, SCR frequency increased more during active coping (M ± SEM = 1.0 ± 0.1 response) than passive coping (M ± SEM = 0.4 ± 0.1 response), although the increases were significantly above baseline in both conditions. The results for PEP and SCR reactivity indicate greater sympathetic activation during active than passive coping, whereas the results for HP reactivity suggest parasympathetic inhibition of HR with cardiac–somatic coupling and vigilant attention (Obrist, 1981). The picture is a bit more complex, however, because the differential effects of active and passive coping on PEP and SCR reactivity emerged primarily when the active task occurred first; that is, when the environment and aversive stimulus were relatively novel. Thus, our findings indicate that PEP reactivity occurs primarily during active coping under conditions of high environmental uncertainty. Other studies have found similar order effects on cardiac reactivity (Kelsey, 1991, 1993) and significant reductions in cardiac reactivity as a result of prior experience with an aversive stimulus (Obrist, 1981).

Effects of Task Difficulty

An increase in task demand due to an increase in task difficulty would generally be expected to increase active coping effort and cardiovascular reactivity (Light & Obrist, 1983; Obrist, 1981). Accordingly, an early study in our laboratory showed that decreases in PEP and increases in HR and CO were significantly greater when undergraduate men counted backward aloud by 13 s than when they counted forward aloud by 1 s (Kelsey, 1991). The impact of task difficulty on PEP reactivity was maintained throughout a 5-min task period, whereas the impact on HR and CO dissipated over time. Nevertheless, we found no significant effects of arithmetic task difficulty on cardiovascular reactivity in a subsequent study, although arithmetic performance varied with difficulty as expected (Kelsey, 1993; Kelsey et al., 1999, Experiment 1). Two studies have confirmed a predicted curvilinear relationship between task difficulty and PEP reactivity (Light & Obrist, 1983; Richter, Friedrich, & Gendolla, 2008). Light and Obrist (1983) found larger decreases in PEP during easy and difficult versions of an appetitive reaction time task than during an impossible version. Parallel but weaker effects occurred for BP increases but not for HR increases. Richter et al. (2008) found that decreases in PEP and increases in systolic blood pressure (SBP) were progressively larger across easy, moderately difficult, and highly difficult versions of a memory task but were greatly attenuated during an impossible version. The difficulty effect was stronger for PEP reactivity than for SBP reactivity, and was not significant for HR reactivity.

Overall, these studies provide further support for an association between active coping effort and beta-adrenergic sympathetic cardiac reactivity as indexed by PEP. These findings also suggest that it may be useful to conceptualize the effect of task difficulty on PEP reactivity in terms of outcome uncertainty rather than task demand. That is, PEP reactivity may be greater when behavioral performance outcomes are uncertain, as with difficult active coping tasks, than when outcomes are more predictable, as with easy or impossible tasks.

Effects of Prior Experience

We have investigated the effects of novelty and experience on cardiovascular reactivity during active coping with repeated mental arithmetic stress (Kelsey, 1991, 1993; Kelsey et al., 1999, 2000, 2004). These studies have shown consistently that cardiac reactivity, but not necessarily vascular reactivity, declines with repeated exposure to stress. In fact, PEP reactivity actually returns to baseline during the performance of successive tasks (Kelsey, 1991; Kelsey et al., 1999, 2004). Conversely, significant cardiac reactivity occurs in anticipation of task performance during pretask instruction periods (Kelsey, 1991).

We conducted a pair of experiments to evaluate the effects of prior exposure to stress on cardiovascular reactivity (Kelsey et al., 1999). After an initial baseline rest period, participants were randomly assigned to groups that either (a) performed an arithmetic pretest task (repeated exposure groups) involving vocal serial subtractions by threes or sevens or (b) continued resting (delayed exposure groups). After a final baseline rest period, all participants performed an arithmetic test task involving vocal serial subtractions from a new four-digit number by sevens. The results of these two experiments were very similar. In both cases, there was a small but significant rise in resting levels of PEP and TPR over baseline periods. In the repeated exposure groups, cardiovascular reactivity declined over tasks and time, whereas arithmetic performance improved. During the test task, the naïve delayed exposure groups showed greater cardiac reactivity, but not vascular reactivity, than the experienced repeated exposure groups.

Figure 2.1 shows the results for PEP and HR reactivity in the second experiment (Kelsey et al., 1999). As in our earlier work (Kelsey, 1991), PEP reactivity in the repeated exposure group peaked during the first minute of the pretest task and then declined toward baseline, showing some spontaneous recovery at the start of the test task before declining further. In fact, PEP reactivity returned to baseline during the test task in this group. HR reactivity showed a similar pattern during repeated exposure, although it remained above baseline during both tasks, presumably because of respiratory and/or motor effects associated with vocal task performance (i.e., cardiac–somatic coupling). The shortening of PEP and the elevation of HR during the test task were significantly greater in the naïve delayed exposure group than in the experienced repeated exposure group, despite a significantly higher arithmetic answer rate in the experienced group (12 answers per minute) than in the naive group (nine answers per minute).

These experiments indicate that prior experience attenuates beta-adrenergic sympathetic cardiac reactivity without necessarily affecting sympathetic vascular reactivity. The concurrent attenuation in cardiac reactivity and improvement in task performance with experience are consistent with a centrally integrated adaptation process (cf. Brener, 1987). The increase in resting levels of PEP and TPR over baseline periods suggests a general decline in beta-adrenergic sympathetic arousal, resulting in reductions in contractility and vasodilation, as a simple function of time. Together, these results indicate that PEP alone was responsive to both the specific effects of repeated exposure to stress and the general effects of time in the environment, suggesting that it is uniquely sensitive to both behavioral uncertainty ("what to do?") and environmental uncertainty ("what is it?" cf. Brener, 1987; Pribram & McGuinness, 1975).

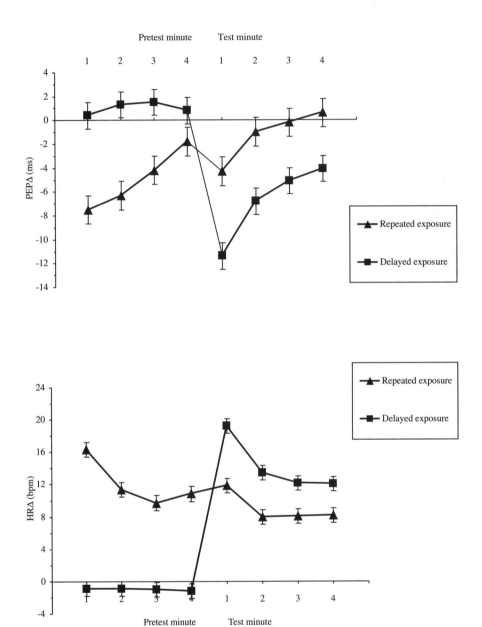

Figure 2.1. Means and standard errors for pre-ejection period (PEPΔ) and heart rate (HRΔ) reactivity (changes from baseline) during 4-min pretest and test periods in repeated exposure and delayed exposure groups. Adapted from "Cardiovascular Reactivity and Adaptation to Recurrent Psychological Stress: Effects of Prior Task Exposure," by R. M. Kelsey, J. Blascovich, J. Tomaka, C. L. Leitten, T. R. Schneider, and S. Wiens, 1999, *Psychophysiology, 36,* p. 825. Copyright 2003 by John Wiley and Sons. Reprinted with permission.

Effects of Evaluative Observation

The typical psychophysiology experiment exposes participants to a relatively novel environment and a considerable degree of monitoring and observation (e.g., audio and video surveillance, physiological monitoring), which may engender uncertainty and threat. Moreover, active coping tasks often are rather novel and include evaluative aspects that may further increase uncertainty and threat. The dissipation of this uncertainty and threat over the course of an experiment may contribute to the attenuation of cardiovascular reactivity during repeated exposure to stress. We conducted two experiments to determine whether obtrusive evaluative observation would disrupt cardiovascular adaptation to recurrent stress, thereby restoring beta-adrenergic sympathetic cardiovascular reactivity (Kelsey et al., 2000, 2004). In both experiments, we manipulated evaluative observation by presenting a set of evaluative instructions and obtrusively videotaping participants while they performed a mental arithmetic task. We assessed cardiovascular reactivity in the usual manner by subtracting mean pretask baseline values from values during the corresponding task. We also assessed arithmetic performance (number of answers and errors) and cognitive appraisals of stress. The stress appraisals were based on reliable five-item scales that assessed participants' perceptions of threat, demand, stressfulness, coping ability, and performance ability before and after each task.

In the first experiment (Kelsey et al., 2000), undergraduate men and women were randomly assigned to three groups that performed a series of three mental arithmetic tasks (vocal serial subtractions by sevens from different four-digit numbers): (a) a control group that performed all three tasks without evaluative observation, (b) an experimental group that was exposed to evaluative observation only during the second task, and (c) another experimental group that was exposed to evaluative observation only during the third task. There were no significant group differences in cardiovascular reactivity, task performance, or stress appraisals during the initial task, but the introduction of evaluative observation during the subsequent tasks disrupted the normal patterns of adaptation. Evaluative observation during the second and third tasks increased cardiac reactivity in the observed group as compared with the other two groups. Further analysis revealed that the effect of evaluative observation was primarily attributable to group differences in PEP reactivity. Evaluative observation also increased stress appraisals but had inconsistent effects on task performance.

The second experiment (Kelsey et al., 2004) assessed cardiovascular reactivity, task performance, and stress appraisals in undergraduate men and women during a series of four mental arithmetic tasks (vocal serial subtraction by sevens from different four-digit numbers). The manipulation of evaluative observation took place during the third task, with random assignment of participants to either an observed experimental group or an unobserved control group. The results showed that evaluative observation during the third task disrupted cardiovascular adaptation, restoring PEP and HR reactivity but not TPR reactivity. As shown in Figure 2.2, PEP and HR reactivity declined over tasks in the control group as expected, with PEP hovering near baseline during the third and fourth tasks. In contrast, evaluative observation temporarily disrupted the decline in cardiac reactivity in the observed group, resulting in significant cubic trends for both PEP and HR reactivity. This effect was stronger for PEP than for HR. Further analysis of reactivity during the critical third task revealed that the observed and control groups differed significantly in PEP reactivity but only marginally in HR reactivity. Thus, evaluative observation exerted a stronger effect on PEP than on HR. As expected, stress appraisals declined over tasks, but evaluative observation during the third task momentarily disrupted the decline in the observed group. In contrast, evaluative observation had no impact on arithmetic performance, which improved linearly over tasks in both groups. Arithmetic performance correlated consistently with stress appraisals for all tasks but did not correlate with cardiac reactivity. Stress appraisals correlated weakly with cardiac reactivity, and regression analyses confirmed that the effects of evaluative observation on PEP reactivity were independent of appraisals.

Other investigators have found similar effects of evaluative observation on PEP reactivity during active coping (Blascovich, Mendes, Hunter, & Salomon, 1999; Bosch et al., 2009; Christian & Stoney, 2006). As in our studies, Bosch et al. (2009) and Christian and Stoney (2006) found that evaluative observation had a greater impact on PEP reactivity than on other measures of cardiovascular reactivity.

Given that our manipulation of evaluative observation involved a change in environmental context rather than a change in task parameters, and given that this manipulation disrupted cardiac adaptation without affecting task performance, our findings suggest that environmental uncertainty is a critical determinant of PEP reactivity. After considering various alternative theoretical perspectives, we concluded that the pattern of cardiac reactivity and adaptation to recurrent stress and the transient disruptive effect of evaluative observation were best explained by independent processes of habituation and sensitization (Kelsey et al., 2000, 2004), as postulated by dual process theory (Groves & Thompson, 1970). According to this interpretation, the decline in cardiac reactivity with repeated exposure to stress resulted from a process of habituation, most likely involving a decrease in beta-adrenergic sympathetic activation, whereas the temporary disruption of this cardiac adaptation by evaluative observation resulted from a transient process of sensitization superimposed on the ongoing habituation process. This transitory sensitization

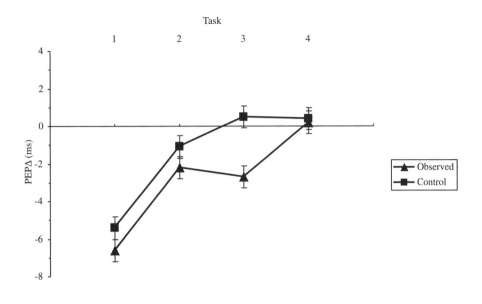

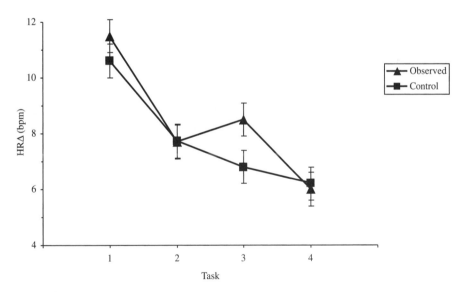

Figure 2.2. Means and standard errors for pre-ejection period (PEPΔ) and heart rate (HRΔ) reactivity (changes from baseline) during four mental arithmetic tasks in two evaluative observation conditions (observed vs. control). The manipulation of evaluative observation occurred during the third task. Adapted from "Cardiovascular Reactivity and Adaptation to Recurrent Psychological Stress: Replication and Extension," by R. M. Kelsey, K. Soderlund, and C. M. Arthur, 2004, *Psychophysiology, 41,* p. 930. Copyright 2004 by John Wiley and Sons. Reprinted with permission.

presumably involved a state of activation stemming from central motivational systems (Groves & Thompson, 1970), which rekindled beta-adrenergic sympathetic effects on the heart. Removal of evaluative observation unmasked the ongoing habituation process to reveal further cardiac adaptation during the final task.

Effects of Monetary Incentives

Several studies have evaluated the effects of monetary incentives for task performance on PEP reactivity (Brenner et al., 2005; Richter & Gendolla, 2009; Seery, Weisbuch, & Blascovich, 2009; Waldstein, Bachen, & Manuck, 1997). Three of these studies found enhanced PEP shortening when monetary incentives were at stake (Brenner et al., 2005; Richter & Gendolla, 2009; Seery et al., 2009), whereas one study failed to find this effect (Waldstein et al., 1997). Brenner et al. (2005) found significant PEP reactivity only during reward, not during extinction (nonreward), and Richter and Gendolla (2009) found that PEP reactivity alone was sensitive to the magnitude of monetary reward. With one exception (Richter & Gendolla, 2009), these studies also support Fowles's (1988) work showing a positive association between HR reactivity and rewards. In our work with Black and White youth (Kelsey et al., 2007), we observed similar effects of monetary performance incentives on PEP and other measures of cardiovascular reactivity during video game tasks.

CONCLUSION

Our research supports the use of PEP as a sensitive index of beta-adrenergic sympathetic effects on the heart. We and others have shown that PEP reactivity occurs primarily during conditions that involve effortful active coping with environmental demands. Both evaluative observation and monetary incentives enhance PEP reactivity during active coping. With repeated exposure to the same or similar conditions, PEP reactivity habituates, returning to baseline levels despite ongoing behavioral performance. This response is remarkably different from patterns of HR and BP adaptation to repeated stress. Moreover, PEP is particularly sensitive to the disruptive effects of a change in environmental context and demands. Such changes result in a resurgence of PEP reactivity, presumably mediated by a sensitization process that rekindles beta-adrenergic sympathetic drive on the myocardium. Together these findings suggest that PEP, more than any other cardiovascular measure, is sensitive to the combined influences of environmental uncertainty ("what is it?"), behavioral uncertainty ("what to do?"), and outcome uncertainty ("will that succeed?"). Therefore, we propose that PEP reactivity provides a peripheral index of central interactions among the arousal, activation, and effort control systems that are critical for the development of effective responses for coping with environmental demands (Bandler et al., 2000; Brener, 1987; Pribram & McGuinness, 1975). Finally, we expect that PEP reactivity will be associated with traits and dimensions of individual differences that are sensitive to the confluence of these forms of uncertainty and are predisposed toward active (fight–flight) rather than passive (conservation–withdrawal) modes of coping (Kelsey, 1991; Kelsey et al., 2001).

REFERENCES

Bandler, R., Price, J. L., & Keay, K. A. (2000). Brain mediation of active and passive emotional coping. In E. A. Mayer & C. B. Saper (Eds.), *Progress in brain research* (Vol. 22, pp. 333–349). Amsterdam, The Netherlands: Elsevier Science.

Berne, R. M., & Levy, M. N. (1981). *Cardiovascular physiology* (4th ed.). Saint Louis, MO: Mosby.

Berntson, G. G., Cacioppo, J. T., Binkley, P. F., Uchino, B. N., Quigley, K. S., & Fieldstone, A. (1994). Autonomic cardiac control. III. Psychological stress and cardiac response in autonomic space as revealed by pharmacological blockades. *Psychophysiology, 31,* 599–608. doi:10.1111/j.1469-8986.1994.tb02352.x

Blascovich, J., Mendes, W. B., Hunter, S. B., & Salomon, K. (1999). Social "facilitation" as challenge and threat. *Journal of Personality and Social Psychology, 77,* 68–77. doi:10.1037/0022-3514.77.1.68

Bosch, J. A., de Geus, E. J., Carroll, D., Goedhart, A. D., Anane, L. A., van Zanten, J. J., & Edwards, K. M. (2009). A general enhancement of autonomic and cortisol responses during social evaluative threat. *Psychosomatic Medicine, 71,* 877–885. doi:10.1097/PSY.0b013e3181baef05

Brener, J. (1987). Behavioral energetics: Some effects of uncertainty on the mobilization and distribution of energy. *Psychophysiology, 24,* 499–512. doi:10.1111/j.1469-8986.1987.tb00326.x

Brenner, S. L., Beauchaine, T. P., & Sylvers, P. D. (2005). A comparison of psychophysiological and self-report measures of BAS and BIS activation. *Psychophysiology, 42,* 108–115. doi:10.1111/j.1469-8986.2005.00261.x

Brodde, O. E. (2008). β-1 and β-2 adrenoceptor polymorphisms: Functional importance, impact on cardiovascular diseases, and drug responses. *Pharmacology & Therapeutics, 117,* 1–29. doi:10.1016/j.pharmthera.2007.07.002

Burleson, M. H., Poehlmann, K. M., Hawkley, L. C., Ernst, J. M., Berntson, G. G., Malarkey, W. B., & Cacioppo, J. T. (2003). Neuroendocrine and cardiovascular reactivity to stress in mid-aged and older women: Long-term temporal consistency of individual differences. *Psychophysiology, 40,* 358–369. doi:10.1111/1469-8986.00039

Cacioppo, J. T., Berntson, G. G., Binkley, P. F., Quigley, K. S., Uchino, B. N., & Fieldstone, A. (1994). Autonomic cardiac control. II. Noninvasive indices and basal response as revealed by autonomic blockades. *Psychophysiology, 31*, 586–598. doi:10.1111/j.1469-8986.1994.tb02351.x

Christian, L. M., & Stoney, C. M. (2006). Social support versus social evaluation: Unique effects on vascular and myocardial response patterns. *Psychosomatic Medicine, 68*, 914–921. doi:10.1097/01.psy.0000244023.20755.cf

Fowles, D. C. (1988). Psychophysiology and psychopathology: A motivational approach. *Psychophysiology, 25*, 373–391. doi:10.1111/j.1469-8986.1988.tb01873.x

Frankenhaeuser, M. (1971). Behavior and circulating catecholamines. *Brain Research, 31*, 241–262. doi:10.1016/0006-8993(71)90180-6

Groves, P. M., & Thompson, R. F. (1970). Habituation: A dual-process theory. *Psychological Review, 77*, 419–450. doi:10.1037/h0029810

Kaji, Y., Ariyoshi, K., Tsuda, Y., Kanaya, S., Fujino, T., & Kuwabara, H. (1989). Quantitative correlation between cardiovascular and plasma epinephrine response to mental stress. *European Journal of Applied Physiology, 59*, 221–226. doi:10.1007/BF02386191

Kelsey, R. M. (1991). Electrodermal lability and myocardial reactivity to stress. *Psychophysiology, 28*, 619–631. doi:10.1111/j.1469-8986.1991.tb01005.x

Kelsey, R. M. (1993). Habituation of cardiovascular reactivity to psychological stress: Evidence and implications. In J. Blascovich & E. S. Katkin (Eds.), *Cardiovascular reactivity to psychological stress and disease* (pp. 135–153). Washington, DC: American Psychological Association.

Kelsey, R. M., Alpert, B. S., Dahmer, M. K., Krushkal, J., & Quasney, M. W. (2010). Beta-adrenergic receptor gene polymorphisms and cardiovascular reactivity to stress in Black adolescents and young adults. *Psychophysiology, 47*, 863–873.

Kelsey, R. M., Blascovich, J., Leitten, C. L., Schneider, T. R., Tomaka, J., & Wiens, S. (2000). Cardiovascular reactivity and adaptation to recurrent psychological stress: The moderating effects of evaluative observation. *Psychophysiology, 37*, 748–756. doi:10.1111/1469-8986.3760748

Kelsey, R. M., Blascovich, J., Tomaka, J., Leitten, C. L., Schneider, T. R., & Wiens, S. (1999). Cardiovascular reactivity and adaptation to recurrent psychological stress: Effects of prior task exposure. *Psychophysiology, 36*, 818–831. doi:10.1111/1469-8986.3660818

Kelsey, R. M., & Guethlein, W. (1990). An evaluation of the ensemble averaged impedance cardiogram. *Psychophysiology, 27*, 24–33. doi:10.1111/j.1469-8986.1990.tb02173.x

Kelsey, R. M., Ornduff, S. R., & Alpert, B. S. (2007). Reliability of cardiovascular reactivity to stress: Internal consistency. *Psychophysiology, 44*, 216–225. doi:10.1111/j.1469-8986.2007.00499.x

Kelsey, R. M., Ornduff, S. R., McCann, C. M., & Reiff, S. (2001). Psychophysiological characteristics of narcissism during active and passive coping. *Psychophysiology, 38*, 292–303. doi:10.1111/1469-8986.3820292

Kelsey, R. M., Reiff, S., Wiens, S., Schneider, T. R., Mezzacappa, E. S., & Guethlein, W. (1998). The ensemble averaged impedance cardiogram: An evaluation of scoring methods and interrater reliability. *Psychophysiology, 35*, 337–340. doi:10.1017/S0048577298001310

Kelsey, R. M., Soderlund, K., & Arthur, C. M. (2004). Cardiovascular reactivity and adaptation to recurrent psychological stress: Replication and extension. *Psychophysiology, 41*, 924–934. doi:10.1111/j.1469-8986.2004.00245.x

Light, K. C., & Obrist, P. A. (1983). Task difficulty, heart rate reactivity, and cardiovascular responses to an appetitive reaction time task. *Psychophysiology, 20*, 301–312. doi:10.1111/j.1469-8986.1983.tb02158.x

Lovallo, W. R., Wilson, M. F., Pincomb, G. A., Edwards, G. L., Tompkins, P., & Brackett, D. J. (1985). Activation patterns to aversive stimulation in man: Passive exposure versus effort to control. *Psychophysiology, 22*, 283–291. doi:10.1111/j.1469-8986.1985.tb01602.x

McCubbin, J. A., Richardson, J. E., Langer, A. W., Kizer, J. S., & Obrist, P. (1983). Sympathetic neuronal function and left ventricular performance during behavioral stress in humans: The relationship between plasma catecholamines and systolic time intervals. *Psychophysiology, 20*, 102–110. doi:10.1111/j.1469-8986.1983.tb00910.x

McGrath, J. J., & O'Brien, W. H. (2001). Pediatric impedance cardiography: Temporal stability and intertask consistency. *Psychophysiology, 38*, 479–484. doi:10.1111/1469-8986.3830479

Mezzacappa, E. S., Kelsey, R. M., & Katkin, E. S. (1999). The effects of epinephrine administration on impedance cardiographic measures of cardiovascular function. *International Journal of Psychophysiology, 31*, 189–196. doi:10.1016/S0167-8760(98)00058-0

Newlin, D. B., & Levenson, R. W. (1979). Pre-ejection period: Measuring beta-adrenergic influences upon the heart. *Psychophysiology, 16*, 546–552. doi:10.1111/j.1469-8986.1979.tb01519.x

Obrist, P. A. (1981). *Cardiovascular psychophysiology: A perspective*. New York, NY: Plenum Press.

Obrist, P. A., Light, K. C., James, S. A., & Strogatz, D. S. (1987). Cardiovascular responses to stress: I. Measures of myocardial response and relationships to high resting systolic pressure and parental hypertension. *Psychophysiology, 24*, 65–78. doi:10.1111/j.1469-8986.1987.tb01864.x

Pribram, K. H., & McGuinness, D. (1975). Arousal, activation, and effort in the control of attention. *Psychological Review, 82*, 116–149. doi:10.1037/h0076780

Richter, M., Friedrich, A., & Gendolla, G. H. (2008). Task difficulty effects on cardiac activity. *Psychophysiology, 45*, 869–875. doi:10.1111/j.1469-8986.2008.00688.x

Richter, M., & Gendolla, G. H. (2009). The heart contracts to reward: Monetary incentives and preejection period. *Psychophysiology, 46*, 451–457. doi:10.1111/j.1469-8986.2009.00795.x

Saab, P. G., Llabre, M. M., Hurwitz, B. E., Frame, C. A., Reineke, L. J., Fins, A. I., . . . Schneiderman, N. (1992). Myocardial and peripheral vascular responses to behavioral challenges and their stability in Black and White Americans. *Psychophysiology, 29*, 384–397. doi:10.1111/j.1469-8986.1992.tb01712.x

Schächinger, H., Weinbacher, M., Kiss, A., Ritz, R., & Langewitz, W. (2001). Cardio-vascular indices of peripheral and central sympathetic activation. *Psychosomatic Medicine, 63*, 788–796.

Seery, M. D., Weisbuch, M., & Blascovich, J. (2009). Something to gain, something to lose: The cardiovascular consequences of outcome framing. *International Journal of Psychophysiology, 73*, 308–312. doi:10.1016/j.ijpsycho.2009.05.006

Sherwood, A., Allen, M. T., Fahrenberg, J., Kelsey, R. M., Lovallo, W. R., & van Doornen, L. J. (1990). Committee report: Methodological guidelines for imped-ance cardiography. *Psychophysiology, 27*, 1–23.

Sherwood, A., Allen, M. T., Obrist, P. A., & Langer, A. W. (1986). Evaluation of beta-adrenergic influences on cardiovascular and metabolic adjustments to phys-ical and psychological stress. *Psychophysiology, 23*, 89–104. doi:10.1111/j.1469-8986.1986.tb00602.x

Sherwood, A., Dolan, C. A., & Light, K. C. (1990). Hemodynamics of blood pres-sure responses during active and passive coping. *Psychophysiology, 27*, 656–668. doi:10.1111/j.1469-8986.1990.tb03189.x

Waldstein, S. R., Bachen, E. A., & Manuck, S. B. (1997). Active coping and cardiovas-cular reactivity: A multiplicity of influences. *Psychosomatic Medicine, 59*, 620–625.

3

PSYCHOPHYSIOLOGICAL PROCESSES OF MENTAL EFFORT INVESTMENT

STEPHEN H. FAIRCLOUGH AND L. J. M. MULDER

There is general agreement that stress, fatigue, and mental workload exert significant influence on the quality of human performance (Hancock & Desmond, 2001). Research into this triad is united by the need to understand and predict changes in performance under conditions of challenge or duress. The appraisal of threat and the derivation of compensatory strategies to protect performance are described by a dynamic cycle of behavioral adaptation (Hancock & Warm, 1989). Hockey (1993, 1997) proposed a model of this process wherein an upper executive was associated with a controlled, effortful mode of cognitive processing that was slow but capable of dealing with novelty and uncertainty. This upper loop is related to compensatory effort and processes of goal setting. By contrast, the lower performance loop was responsible for effort investment into task-specific cognitive demand (i.e., task-related effort).

This process of effort regulation is fundamental to the study of stress, fatigue, and mental workload. All three states constitute potential threats to

The authors wish to thank Dick de Waard for his stimulating comments on earlier versions of the manuscript.

performance quality and psychological well-being. All three provoke cycles of appraisal and adaptation to protect performance and preserve the personal goals of the individual. The main proposition of the current chapter is that mental workload, stress, and fatigue engage a common mechanism of effortful adaptation to (a) preserve the quality of performance and (b) protect the personal goals of the individual.

The trigger for mental effort investment has been described as cognitive or compensatory in nature (Mulder, 1986). In the case of the former, mental effort is invested in response to changing task demands (e.g., increased working memory load). Compensatory mental effort is important to protect performance under demanding conditions, such as sustained task activity or extraneous biological stressors (e.g., sleep deprivation, drugs). In both cases, mental effort investment represents an adaptation to external or internal stimuli. This adaptive facility of effort may be better understood in relation to four central hypotheses (Pashler, 1998) that encapsulate core themes associated with mental effort derived from different theoretical traditions:

- The investment of mental effort will improve or sustain the quality of cognitive performance. This first hypothesis is obvious; however, there are many situations where effort and performance are not closely related to one another. This distinction was captured by Eysenck (1997), who characterized the efficiency of performance as the relationship between covert effort investment and overt performance quality.
- There are finite limits on mental effort investment. This hypothesis is derived from resource theory (Kahneman, 1973), and it takes one of two forms. One hypothesis states that finite mental effort may be shared only between concurrent activities in a limited fashion dependent on input modalities, sensory codes, and outputs (Wickens, 2002). The second form concerns finite limitations on effort investment with respect to time, such as vigilance tasks (Davies & Parasuraman, 1982).
- Mental effort investment is associated with costs. The investment of mental effort is coupled with changes in central nervous system (CNS) activity and associated variables such as subjective mood. These changes have been characterized as "costs" to the individual (Hockey, 1993, 1997). Concurrent costs represent instantaneous changes in mood and CNS activity that occur as a direct consequence of performance. See also the mood-behavior model (Gendolla, 2000) for a similar concept.
- The investment of mental effort is associated with volition. The purpose of effort investment (in a narrow sense) is the attain-

ment and maintenance of task goals that are inherently desirable, such as "good" performance (e.g., low error frequency, efficient task completion). In this sense, effort has strong ties to broad constructs such as willpower (James, 1890), volition (Baars, 1993), goal regulation (Locke & Latham, 1990), and potential motivation (Brehm & Self, 1989).

These four hypotheses encapsulate an adaptive mechanism of mental effort that responds to increased workload, fatigue, or stress. This mechanism is associated with volition and changes in mood and may only be deployed for a limited period of time.

In this chapter, we address the psychophysiological processes of mental effort investment and related measures in the laboratory and the field with reference to existing research. First, we briefly consider several studies of energy mobilization at cerebral sites. Then, we describe the influence of mental effort investment on the cardiovascular system, detailing the relationship between blood pressure regulation and heart rate variability.

THE PROCESS OF MENTAL EFFORT INVESTMENT

The process of mental effort investment may be identified by energy expenditure at cerebral sites. This connection is simple (Beatty, 1986) but also intuitive because the brain requires a continuous supply of glucose and oxygen from the bloodstream. Both are required to generate adenosine triphosphate, which acts as the primary source of cellular energy at cerebral sites. In addition, the energy requirements of the brain are considerable, accounting for approximately 20% to 30% of the body's resting metabolic rate (Saravini, 1999). Despite these high requirements, the brain has only a limited capacity to store energy substrates, and cerebral metabolism is dependent on the supply of glucose and oxygen from the bloodstream. The process of mental effort investment may be identified with catabolic activity at cerebral sites or with the transport of energy substrates to the brain.

The process of energy transport to the brain has been studied directly through the use of transcranial Doppler sonography to monitor blood velocity in the middle cerebral artery. Changes in blood flow have been associated with vigilance performance over sustained periods only (Helton et al., 2007; Warm & Parasuraman, 2007) and with changes in electroencephalogram (EEG) activity (Szirmai, Amrein, Palvolgyi, Debreczeni, & Kamondi, 2005). With respect to measuring energy substrates directly, there is evidence that raised glucose levels (through ingestion) enhanced cognitive performance for effortful tasks but not for tasks that were less demanding (i.e., a glucose drink improved performance on a serial sevens task but not a serial threes task; Kennedy & Scholey, 2000). Similarly, when participants performed either a demanding or an easy version of the Stroop task (Stroop, 1935) over 40 min, blood glucose levels fell at a higher rate during an effortful task relative to an effortless activity (Fairclough & Houston, 2004). In the following sections, we focus on changes associated with mental effort investment at cerebral sites (electrocortical activation) and autonomic modes of energy mobilization that influence the cardiovascular system.

The use of neuroimaging techniques, such as positron emission tomography and functional magnetic resonance imaging, has made the measurement of energy consumption the norm in cognitive neuroscience research (e.g., Cabeza & Nyberg, 2000). With respect to brain areas and circuits associated with mental effort, meta-analyses of the n-back working memory paradigm (an effortful activity) identified robust activation over a number of regions, particularly the dorsolateral and ventrolateral prefrontal cortex, as well as the medial and lateral posterior parietal cortex (Owen, McMillan, Laird, & Bullmore, 2005).

Early research on EEG activity and mental effort indicated that high levels of visual demand reduced alpha activity in parietal and occipital locations while augmenting theta activity in left frontal areas (Gundel & Wilson, 1992). The source of the frontal midline theta rhythm has been localized to the anterior cingulate cortex (ACC; Gevins, Smith, McEvoy, & Yu, 1997) and the bilateral medial prefrontal cortex (Ishii et al., 1999). These findings were replicated in further studies with respect to levels of working memory load (Gevins et al., 1998) and the effects of practice on effortful performance (Smith, McEvoy, & Gevins, 1999). The same pattern of theta augmentation at frontal midline sites and alpha suppression in occipital areas was apparent using applied tasks such as operating the Multi-Attribute Test Battery (i.e., a simulation of multi-tasking in an aviation environment; Smith, Gevins, Brown, Karnik, & Du, 2001). This pattern of EEG activity may be characteristic of task-related mental effort investment. Interested readers are advised to read available summaries of this research (Gevins & Smith, 2003, 2006).

MENTAL EFFORT AND THE CARDIOVASCULAR SYSTEM

As described in the introductory portion of this chapter, mental effort may be invested in response to task-related changes, such as increased cognitive complexity (computational effort), and to protect performance when the person is fatigued (compensatory effort; Mulder, 1986). It is argued that both categories of effort investment have specific effects on the cardiovascular system. When mental effort is invested, there are a number of characteristic changes in the cardiovascular system, such as increased heart rate (HR) and blood pressure (BP) in combination with a more regular heart rate (i.e., decreased heart rate variability [HRV]). This pattern is associated with the investment of computational effort in response to increased task difficulty (i.e., increased mental workload). In those cases where effort is invested to compensate for a nonoptimal physiological state (e.g., fatigue), cardiovascular state changes are less consistent and strongly dependent on the specifics of the state (e.g., stress, fatigue, sustained performance, sleep deprivation). This depends mainly on the individual's response pattern related to short-term BP control (baroreflex).

Autonomic activation influences HR and other effector subsystems of short-term BP control, such as contraction force of the heart, (peripheral) resistance of the arteries, filling of the large veins of the body (venous volume, venous return to the heart). All these subsystems work in concert to control heart function and levels of BP to optimize performance for the present mental state (i.e., to provide appropriate energetical resources to the brain). The level of BP is monitored by baroreceptors in the large body arteries (Karemaker, 1987), and these receptors provide information to a specific "team of nuclei" in the brainstem that could be considered to be the cardiovascular control center; members of this team include the nucleus tractus solitarius (NTS; integration of incoming information), nucleus ambiguous (NA; vagal control) and the rostral ventrolateral medulla (RVLM; sympathetic control). Sympathetic activation is further supported by motor neurons situated in the intermediolateral cell column (IML) of the spine. This complete subsystem is crucial in the regulation of sympathetic and parasympathetic activation to the heart and encompasses the negative feedback loop of the baroreflex (see Figure 3.1).

To achieve effective cybernetic control, it is important to know that BP (and not, for instance, blood supply to the brain) is the controlled variable in this system. This category of BP control is achieved through the baroreflex (Guyton, 1980; Julius, 1988). Therefore, we may expect that observed changes in one effector subsystem, such as HR, have a function in relation to the control of short-term BP. During periods of task-related effort investment, HR will be influenced by the activity of cortical centers that project to NA, RVLM, IML, NTS, or related areas in the limbic system and higher brain areas, such as the ACC, the hypothalamic area, the locus coeruleus, the amygdalae, and the prefrontal cortex. The latter group serves a main function in regulating state control, emotional functioning, general activation of brain and body, and task performance (e.g., decision making, planning). The equilibrium between these state-regulating mechanisms for BP control and task-related autonomic activity determines the precise pattern of cardiovascular responses that is observed during mental effort investment.

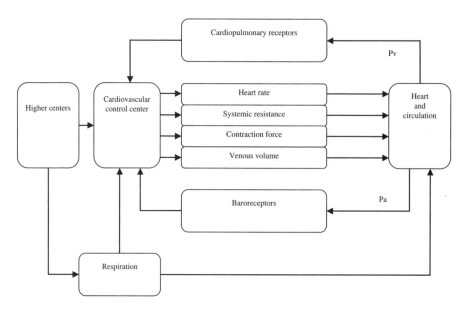

Figure 3.1. Mechanisms of short-term blood pressure control. Pa = arterial pressure; Pv = venous pressure.

This description begs a question regarding the relationship between HRV and these regulating mechanisms in the brain. A main source of HRV is the so-called 10-s or Mayer-Hering rhythm (0.1 Hz component), whose amplitude decreases during mental effort investment (Mulder & Mulder, 1981). Wesseling and Settels (1985) used a simulation model of the baroreflex to demonstrate that this rhythmicity can be seen as an "eigenrhythm" of the baroreflex and that it explains more than half of HRV. The frequency of this rhythm is determined by a combination of time constants and time delays in the effector systems described in Figure 3.1. Van Roon, Mulder, Althaus, and Mulder (2004) extended this model to demonstrate that the magnitudes of these waves were strongly determined by the level and balance of autonomic activation. For instance, a 50% reduction of HRV in this frequency range (which is typical of increased computational effort) can be explained by a combination of vagal inhibition (about 40%) and increased sympathetic activation (about 25%).

Changes in BP control are not the only way to influence the pattern of HRV during mental effort investment. Respiratory sinus arrhythmia (RSA) is another source of HRV that is related to respiration. During inspiration HR increases and returns to the previous level at the end of expiration (Grossman & Taylor, 2007). The main factor underlying these changes is vagal inhibition: During inspiration a vagal reduction of approximately 30% occurs. In general, respiratory frequency (i.e., breathing rate) is between nine and 21 cycles per minute (0.15 Hz–0.35 Hz). This means that in many cases RSA is well separated from the 0.10 Hz rhythm. However, this does not hold for situations such as strong relaxation or meditation where breathing rate can come down to the frequency region of the 0.10 Hz rhythm (six cycles per minute). In this case, a kind of synchronization occurs between both rhythms called *entrainment*.

The RSA magnitude is dependent on both respiratory depth and frequency (Grossman & Taylor, 2007). The level of RSA is highest when breathing rate is around 0.10 Hz, whereas it decreases continuously to about 30% of this level at about 0.40 Hz. RSA is also larger with deeper respiration than with more superficial breathing, and the difference in magnitude can be large, around a factor of two during normal respiration (Angelone & Coulter, 1964; Hirsh & Bishop, 1981). Knowing that the sympathetic system is too slow to induce HRV changes in a frequency area higher than 0.15 Hz, HRV reductions during task performance in this area are considered to be related to vagal inhibition (Saul, Berger, Chen, & Cohen, 1991). A third source of HRV can be found in the lower frequency range, roughly below 0.06 Hz. HRV fluctuations in this range are supposed to be related to either slow adaptations to the task demands or body temperature changes. Although connections with sympathetic activation can be expected, origins of HRV changes in this frequency area are too variable in general to be useful in experimental research (Mulder & Mulder, 1981).

HRV indices can be derived either in the time or the frequency domain. Time domain measures are based on the durations of cardiac intervals (IBI, interbeat interval times) and include standard deviations (or variance) as well as succeeding differences in IBIs (Berntson et al., 1997). Frequency domain measures, such as the power in several frequency bands, can either be based on IBI sequences or on HR variations. Spectral measures have the advantage that results can be better connected to underlying physiological mechanisms than time domain measures. IBI spectra, in general, are obtained by using fast Fourier transform algorithms, whereas HR spectra are obtained by applying a discrete Fourier analysis algorithm (Rompelman, 1980). The choice between IBI or HR measures is dependent on both practical and theoretical arguments (Rompelman, 1980). It must be realized that IBI-based and HR-based variability measures do not give the same results, unless normalization to the mean is applied (Akselrod et al., 1981; Mulder, 1992). If such a normalization is not applied, spectral HRV measures are heavily dependent on mean HR in the analysis segment at hand (Stuiver & Mulder, 2009).

The spectral bands that are used for both HRV and other cardiovascular measures are dependent on the field of application (mental effort vs. medical/physiological/stress research) and on historical habits. In general, either low

(0.02–0.06 Hz), mid (0.07–0.14 Hz), and high (0.15–0.40 Hz) frequency bands are used (Mulder, 1992) or low (0.04–0.14) and high (0.15–0.40) frequency bands (Pagani, Rimoldi, & Maliani, 1992). In addition, a spectral band around the mean respiration frequency may be applied in special cases (Mulder, 1992). In general terms, HR increases and becomes more regular during mentally demanding performance compared with resting measurements and/or easy tasks (i.e., HRV) decreases as a function of invested mental effort. HRV herein is defined as the series of the beat-to-beat changes in time duration between successive heartbeats (IBI) or the equivalent changes in HR.

Several authors have shown the strong effects of mental effort investment on HRV, in particular for tasks in which working memory is heavily involved, such as mental arithmetic, memory search and counting, or planning (Aasman, Mulder, & Mulder, 1987; Kramer, 1991; Mulder & Mulder, 1981; Veltman & Gaillard, 1993). All these authors indicate that the mid-frequency band is most sensitive to manipulations of task load, whereas the pattern of changes is about the same for the other two frequency bands (low and high = RSA). Most of these results were confirmed over short periods (e.g., about 5 min) in laboratory tasks. Veltman and Gaillard (1998) indicated that differences in both HR and HRV measures in most cases are not consistent (or not large) enough to distinguish different levels of task load. This may be related to the sensitivity of these measures but is also connected to the fact that participants are not always motivated to perform tasks at a maximum level; therefore, they can regulate their effort investment over a wide range when conducting well-defined laboratory tasks without showing a significant decrease in task performance (de Waard, 1996; Hockey, 1997).

Although the HRV rest-task effect in the mid frequency band is fairly strong in the majority of participants, this effect may be magnified by increased breathing rhythm during task performance. This factor is particularly apparent when participants are breathing quite slowly (slower than eight or nine cycles per minute) during rest in comparison with faster breathing rates (e.g., > nine cycles per minute) during task performance. During rest, breathing rate is within the mid frequency range in such cases, whereas it is in the high frequency band during task performance (Althaus, Mulder, Mulder, van Roon, & Minderaa, 1998; Grossman & Taylor, 2007). However, Mulder and Mulder (1981) emphasized that the mid-frequency band is the most suitable index of mental effort because it is less affected by respiration than the high-frequency band. Some authors have proposed methods for (statistically) separating breathing-related HRV (= RSA) from other HR fluctuations (Althaus et al., 1998; Berntson, Cacioppo, & Grossman, 2007; Grossman & Taylor, 2007). The methods indicate that it is relevant to pay more attention to the interaction between effort-related effects on HRV and breathing-related effects. This holds in particular when respiration rate is at the boundaries of the defined frequency bands (mid and high band) or when respiration rate (and amplitude) is strongly different between conditions. It should be realized, however, that any change in respiratory pattern is not just a "mechanical" phenomenon; it is a relevant indication of a changed physiological state during task performance. In this respect, it is helpful to use measures of respiration frequency and depth and, if possible, a respiration-related frequency band of HRV in research on mental effort investment (Grossman & Taylor, 2007).

Aside from laboratory tasks, HRV is also applied in numerous workload studies in different applied situations. Effects of mental effort changes are difficult to study in daily working environments because of the enormous variations in mental work. In studies on simulated and real mental work (driving, flying, air traffic control), significant results show decreased HRV in the mid-frequency band with increasing levels of task complexity (De Rivecourt, Kuperus, Post, & Mulder, 2008; de Waard, Kruizinga, & Brookhuis, 2008; Veltman & Gaillard, 1996; Wilson & Fisher, 1991). Although finger BP and respiration changes (amplitude and frequency) are applied only occasionally in comparison with HR and HRV measurement, clear results have also been found in these measures, both in laboratory and simulated workload applications (Mulder et al., 2003). The overall cardiovascular pattern found can be characterized by increased BP, HR, and breathing frequency and decreased HRV, BP variability, baroreflex sensitivity, and breathing amplitude. Some authors have described this general pattern as a defensive reaction type (Mulder, Dijksterhuis, Stuiver, & de Waard, 2009).

The other aspect of effort investment is related to compensatory mechanisms when an operator is in a less than optimal physiological state, for instance, after sleep deprivation or when seriously fatigued after a long working day (Myles & Romet, 1987; Myrtek et al., 1994). In such situations, an operator must put additional effort into the task to counteract the deleterious effects of fatigue on performance. Experimental cardiovascular effects related to this aspect of effort investment are far less clear than those on task-related effort (Hockey, 1997). It is obvious that not only HR or HRV is relevant to compensatory effort but also that cardiovascular regulation has to be studied in connection to brain mechanisms and BP control. Knowing that BP is the regulated variable in this context (Julius, 1988), it is necessary to capture BP, BP variability, and the sensitivity of short-term BP control (baroreflex sensitivity) to get adequate information about cardiovascular state changes.

Van Roon et al. (2004) used a simulation model of the baroreflex to show that the effects on task-related effort can be explained by a strong decrease in vagal activity in combination with a moderate increase in sympathetic activation. The same model can be applied to study compensatory effort effects or to increase the knowledge about cortical influences on autonomic control. Before this stage is reached, however, more experimental results are necessary on compensatory effort investment. In many studies on natural or simulated working conditions, decreases of HR are observed as a function of time, for instance, during a working day. In several cases, this indicates the presence of fatigue, probably related to diminished invested effort during the day. It is questionable whether this is a correct interpretation. In many studies, task performance decrements are not found or are found only as a shift toward another task strategy at the end of a long working period (making more errors, faster reactions). Mulder et al. (2009) reported a disruption of the initial defense-type response pattern associated with mental effort investment already after only 5 or 10 min. According to these authors, this pattern can be characterized by an ongoing increase in BP in combination with decreased HR, increased baroreflex sensitivity, increased HRV, and increased BP variability (Mulder et al., 2003). According to van Roon's simulation model, this pattern is explained by a "recovery" of vagal activation to resting levels, whereas sympathetic activation gradually increases as a function of time.

It is striking that in some studies of simulated flight that required higher levels of motor activity relative to cognitive tasks, the baroreflex-mediated decrease of HR did not occur as a function of time (Wilson, 1993); in some cases, even a distinct increase was observed that may be connected to increased task complexity (De Rivecourt et al., 2008). Therefore, it may be concluded that response patterns of HR and HRV are situation (and task) dependent (Boucsein & Backs, 2000) in applied investigations. In addition, one must account for the effect of speaking, which has a large influence on both HR and HRV, which may diminish any other effects. In this context, it is recommended to carefully connect specific demanding task events to short segments of cardiovascular variables and to rule out disturbing artifacts (e.g., speaking; Mulder et al., 2009).

To summarize, the effects of demanding mental task performance on cardiovascular variables can be described as occurring in two basic patterns: (a) a defensive type reaction during short-lasting task performance and during initial phases of long-lasting work and (b) an increased reaction of the baroreflex as a means for limiting BP increases. During demanding longer lasting tasks, it may be expected that a mix of both patterns will occur continuously.

CONCLUSION

Mental effort is considered to be a psychophysiological process of energy mobilization. The goal of this process is to preserve acceptable levels of task performance under conditions of duress, such as increased task difficulty or sleep deprivation. The process is considered to be finite (i.e., it may not be sustained indefinitely), associated with a range of costs (e.g., changes in mood), and a manifestation of volitional activity. Research on EEG activity has identified a pattern of frontal theta activation coupled with a suppression of alpha activity. This research has focused primarily on working memory, although there is some evidence of this pattern being replicated on other tasks. It is not known whether this measure of computational mental effort will generalize to other stressors (e.g., sleep deprivation, sustained performance) or respond to motivational incentives. There is also a body of experimental evidence supporting the hypothesis that HRV, specifically the 0.1 Hz component, is sensitive to cognitive manipulation. It is argued that cardiovascular responses to increased mental effort are assessed in the context of BP control. At the time of writing, little research has sought to characterize mental effort mobilization in terms of both EEG activity and the cardiovascular response. It is suggested that mental effort represents a unitary process in which autonomic variables respond to the need to transport energy substrates to the brain, and cerebral measures capture spatial and temporal correlates of effortful activity in the brain. Further research is required to reconcile both categories of psychophysiological processes as part of the same mechanism.

REFERENCES

Aasman, J., Mulder, G., & Mulder, L. J. M. (1987). Operator effort and the measurement of heart rate variability. *Human Factors, 29,* 161–170.

Akselrod, S., Gordon, D., Ubel, F. A., Shannon, D. C., Berger, A. C., & Cohen, R. J. (1981, July 10). Power spectrum analysis of heart rate fluctuation: A quantitative probe of beat-to-beat cardiovascular control. *Science, 213,* 220–222. doi:10.1126/science.6166045

Althaus, M., Mulder, L. J. M., Mulder, G., van Roon, A. M., & Minderaa, R. B. (1998). The influence of respiratory activity on the cardiac response pattern to mental effort. *Psychophysiology, 35,* 420–430. doi:10.1111/1469-8986.3540420

Angelone, A., & Coulter, N. A. (1964). Respiratory sinus arrhythmia: A frequency dependent phenomenon. *Journal of Applied Physiology, 19,* 479–482.

Baars, B. J. (1993). Why volition is a foundation issue for psychology. *Consciousness and Cognition, 2,* 281–309. doi:10.1006/ccog.1993.1025

Beatty, J. (1986). Computation, control and energetics: A biological perspective. In G. R. J. Hockey, A. W. K. Gaillard, & M. G. H. Coles (Eds.), *Energetical states underlying task performance* (pp. 43–51). Dordrecht, The Netherlands: Martinus Nijhoff.

Berntson, G. G., Bigger, J. T., Eckberg, D. L., Grossman, P., Kaufmann, P. G., Malik, M., . . . van der Molen, M. W. (1997). Heart rate variability: Origins, methods, and interpretive caveats. *Psychophysiology, 34*, 623–648. doi:10.1111/j.1469-8986.1997.tb02140.x

Berntson, G. G., Cacioppo, J. T., & Grossman, P. (2007). Whither vagal tone. *Biological Psychology, 74*, 295–300. doi:10.1016/j.biopsycho.2006.08.006

Boucsein, W., & Backs, R. W. (2000). Engineering psychophysiology as a discipline: Historical and theoretical aspects. In W. Boucsein & R. W. Backs (Eds.), *Engineering psychophysiology: Issues and applications* (pp. 3–30). Mahwah, NJ: Erlbaum.

Brehm, J. W., & Self, E. A. (1989). The intensity of motivation. *Annual Review of Psychology, 40*, 109–131. doi:10.1146/annurev.ps.40.020189.000545

Cabeza, R., & Nyberg, L. (2000). Imaging cognition II: An empirical review of 275 PET and fMRI studies. *Journal of Cognitive Neuroscience, 12*, 1–47. doi:10.1162/08989290051137585

Davies, D. R., & Parasuraman, R. (1982). *The psychology of vigilance*. London, England: Academic Press.

De Rivecourt, M., Kuperus, M. N., Post, W. J., & Mulder, L. J. M. (2008). Heart rate and eye movement measures as indices for mental effort during simulated flight. *Ergonomics, 51*, 1295–1319. doi:10.1080/00140130802120267

de Waard, D. (1996). *The measurement of drivers' mental workload* (Doctoral dissertation, University of Groningen, Groningen, The Netherlands). Retrieved from http://home.zonnet.nl/waard2/mwl.htm

de Waard, D., Kruizinga, A., & Brookhuis, K.A. (2008). The consequences of an increase in heavy goods vehicles for passenger car drivers' mental workload and behaviour: A simulator study. *Accident Analysis and Prevention, 40*, 818–828.

Eysenck, M. W. (1997). *Anxiety and cognition: A unified theory*. Hove, England: Psychology Press.

Fairclough, S. H., & Houston, K. (2004). A metabolic measure of mental effort. *Biological Psychology, 66*, 177–190. doi:10.1016/j.biopsycho.2003.10.001

Gendolla, G. H. E. (2000). On the impact of mood on behaviour: An integrative theory and a review. *Review of General Psychology, 4*, 378–408. doi:10.1037/1089-2680.4.4.378

Gevins, A., & Smith, M. E. (2003). Neurophysiological measures of cognitive workload during human–computer interaction. *Theoretical Issues in Ergonomics Science, 4*(1–2), 113–131. doi:10.1080/14639220210159717

Gevins, A., & Smith, M. E. (2006). Electroencephalography (EEG) in neuroergonomics. In R. Parasuraman & A. A. Rizzo (Eds.), *Neuroergonomics: The brain at work* (pp. 15–31). New York, NY: Oxford University Press. doi:10.1093/acprof:oso/9780195177619.003.0002

Gevins, A., Smith, M. E., Leong, H., McEvoy, L., Whitfield, S., Du, R., & Rush, G. (1998). Monitoring working memory load during computer-based tasks with EEG pattern recognition models. *Human Factors, 40*(1), 79–91. doi:10.1518/001872098779480578

Gevins, A., Smith, M. E., McEvoy, L., & Yu, D. (1997). High-resolution EEG mapping of cortical activation related to working memory: Effects of task difficulty, type of processing, and practice. *Cerebral Cortex, 7*, 374–385. doi:10.1093/cercor/7.4.374

Grossman, P. & Taylor, E. W. (2007). Toward understanding respiratory sinus arrhythmia: Relations to cardiac vagal tone, evolution, and biobehavioral functions. *Biological Psychology, 74*, 263–285. doi:10.1016/j.biopsycho.2005.11.014

Gundel, A., & Wilson, G. F. (1992). Topographical changes in the ongoing EEG related to the difficulty of mental tasks. *Brain Topography, 5*(1), 17–25. doi:10.1007/BF01129966

Guyton, A. C. (1980). *Circulatory physiology III: Arterial pressure and hypertension.* Philadelphia, PA: W. B. Saunders.

Hancock, P. A., & Desmond, P. A. (2001). *Stress, workload, and fatigue.* Mahwah, NJ: Erlbaum.

Hancock, P. A., & Warm, J. S. (1989). A dynamic model of stress and sustained attention. *Human Factors, 31*, 519–537.

Helton, W. S., Hollander, T. D., Warm, J. S., Tripp, L. D., Parsons, K., Matthews, G., . . . Hancock, P.A. (2007). The abbreviated vigilance task and cerebral hemodynamics. *Journal of Clinical and Experimental Neuropsychology, 29*, 545–552. doi:10.1080/13803390600814757

Hirsh, J. A., & Bishop, B. (1981). Respiratory sinus arrhythmia in humans: How breathing pattern modulates heart rate. *The American Journal of Physiology, 241*, 620–629.

Hockey, G. R. J. (1993). Cognitive–energetical control mechanisms in the management of work demands and psychological health. In A. Baddeley & L. Weiskrantz (Eds.), *Attention: Selection, awareness, and control* (pp. 328–345). Oxford, England: Clarendon Press.

Hockey, G. R. J. (1997). Compensatory control in the regulation of human performance under stress and high workload: A cognitive-energetical framework. *Biological Psychology, 45*, 73–93. doi:10.1016/S0301-0511(96)05223-4

Ishii, R., Kazuhiro, S., Ukai, S., Inouye, T., Ishihara, T., Yoshimine, T., . . . Takeda, M. (1999). Medial prefrontal cortex generates frontal midline theta rhythm. *Neuroreport, 10*, 675–679. doi:10.1097/00001756-199903170-00003

James, W. (1890). *The principles of psychology.* New York, NY: Holt. doi:10.1037/10538-000

Julius, S. (1988). The blood pressure seeking properties of the central nervous system. *Journal of Hypertension, 6*, 177–185. doi:10.1097/00004872-198803000-00001

Kahneman, D. (1973). *Attention and effort.* Englewood Cliffs, NJ: Prentice Hall.

Karemaker, J. M. (1987). Neurophysiology of the baroreceptor reflex. In R. I. Kitney & O. Rompelman (Eds.), *The beat-by-beat investigation of cardiovascular function* (pp. 27–49). Oxford, England: Clarendon Press.

Kennedy, D. O., & Scholey, A. B. (2000). Glucose administration, heart rate, and cognitive performance: Effects of increasing mental effort. *Psychopharmacology, 149*, 63–71. doi:10.1007/s002139900335

Kramer, A. F. (1991). Physiological metrics of mental workload: A review of recent progress. In D. L. Damos (Ed.), *Multiple-task performance* (pp. 279–328). London, England: Taylor & Francis.

Locke, E. A., & Latham, G. P. (1990). *A theory of goal setting and task performance.* Englewood Cliffs, NJ: Prentice Hall.

Mulder, G. (1986). The concept and measurement of mental effort. In G. R. J. Hockey, A. W. K. Gaillard, & M. G. H. Coles (Eds.), *Energetical issues in research on human information processing* (pp. 175–198). Dordrecht, The Netherlands: Martinus Nijhoff.

Mulder, G., & Mulder, L. J. M. (1981). Task-related cardiovascular stress. In J. Long & A. Baddeley (Eds.), *Attention and performance IX* (pp. 591–606). Hillsdale, NJ: Erlbaum.

Mulder, L. J. M. (1992). Measurement and analysis methods of heart rate and respiration for use in applied environments. *Biological Psychology, 34*, 205–236. doi:10.1016/0301-0511(92)90016-N

Mulder, L. J. M., Dijksterhuis, C., Stuiver, A., & de Waard, D. (2009). Cardiovascular state changes during performance of a simulated ambulance dispatchers' task: Potential use for adaptive support. *Applied Ergonomics, 40*, 965–977. doi:10.1016/j.apergo.2009.01.009

Mulder, L. J. M., van Roon, A., Veldman, H., Laumann, K., Burov, A., Quispel, L., & Hoogeboom, P. J. (2003). How to use cardiovascular state changes in adaptive automation. In G. R. J. Hockey, A. W. K. Gaillard, & O. Burov (Eds.), *Operator functional state. The assessment and prediction of human performance degradation in complex tasks* (pp. 260–272). Amsterdam, The Netherlands: IOS Press.

Myles, W. S., & Romet, T. T. (1987). Self-paced work in sleep deprived subjects. *Ergonomics, 30*, 1175–1184. doi:10.1080/00140138708966006

Myrtek, M., Deutschmann-Janicke, E., Strohmaier, H., Zimmermann, W., Lawerenz, S., Brügner, G., & Müller, W. (1994). Physical, mental, emotional, and subjective workload components in train drivers. *Ergonomics, 37*, 1195–1203. doi:10.1080/00140139408964897

Owen, A. M., McMillan, K. M., Laird, A. R., & Bullmore, E. (2005). N-back working memory paradigm: A meta-analysis of normative functional neuroimaging studies. *Human Brain Mapping, 25*, 46–59. doi:10.1002/hbm.20131

Pagani, M., Rimoldi, O., & Maliani, A. (1992). Low-frequency components of cardiovascular variabilities as markers of sympathetic modulation. *Trends in Pharmacological Sciences, 13*, 50–54. doi:10.1016/0165-6147(92)90022-X

Pashler, H. E. (1998). *The psychology of attention.* Cambridge, MA: MIT Press.

Rompelman, O. (1980). The assessment of fluctuations in heart rate. In R. I. Kitney & O. Rompelman (Eds.), *The study of heart rate variability* (pp. 59–77). Oxford, England: Clarendon Press.

Saravini, F. (1999). Energy and the brain: Facts and fantasies. In E. Della Salla (Ed.), *Mind myths* (pp. 43–58). Chichester, England: Wiley.

Saul, J. P., Berger, R. D., Chen, M. H., & Cohen, R. (1991). Transfer function analysis of autonomic regulation II. Respiratory sinus arrythmia. *The American Journal of Physiology, 256,* 153–161.

Smith, M. E., Gevins, A., Brown, H., Karnik, A., & Du, R. (2001). Monitoring task loading with multivariate EEG measures during complex forms of human–computer interaction. *Human Factors, 43,* 366–380. doi:10.1518/001872001775898287

Smith, M. E., McEvoy, L., & Gevins, A. (1999). Neurophysiological indices of strategy development and skill acquisition. *Cognitive Brain Research, 7,* 389–404. doi:10.1016/S0926-6410(98)00043-3

Stroop, J. R. (1935). Studies of interference in serial verbal reactions. *Journal of Experimental Psychology, 18,* 643–661. doi:10.1037//0096-3445.121.1.15

Stuiver, A., & Mulder, L. J. M. (2009). Artefact-free real-time computation of cardiovascular measures. In C. Mühl, D. Heylen, & A. Nijholt (Eds.), *Affective Computing and Intelligent Interaction, 2,* 1–6.

Szirmai, I., Amrein, I., Palvolgyi, L., Debreczeni, R., & Kamondi, A. (2005). Correlation between blood flow velocity in the middle cerebral artery and EEG during cognitive effort. *Cognitive Brain Research, 24,* 33–40. doi:10.1016/j.cogbrainres.2004.12.011

van Roon, A. M., Mulder, L. J. M., Althaus, M., & Mulder, G. (2004). Introducing a baroreflex model for studying cardiovascular effects of mental workload. *Psychophysiology, 41,* 961–981. doi:10.1111/j.1469-8986.2004.00251.x

Veltman, J. A., & Gaillard, A. W. K. (1993). Indices of mental workload in a complex task environment. *Neuropsychobiology, 28,* 72–75. doi:10.1159/000119003

Veltman, J. A., & Gaillard, A. W. K. (1996). Physiological indices of workload in a simulated flight task. *Biological Psychology, 42,* 323–342. doi:10.1016/0301-0511(95)05165-1

Veltman, J. A., & Gaillard, A. W. K. (1998). Physiological workload reactions to increasing levels of task difficulty. *Ergonomics, 41,* 656–669. doi:10.1080/001401398186829

Warm, J. S., & Parasuraman, R. (2007). Cerebral hemodynamics and vigilance. In R. Parasuraman & M. Rizzo (Eds.), *Neuroergonomics: The brain at work* (pp. 146–158). New York, NY: Oxford University Press.

Wesseling, K. H., & Settels, J. J. (1985). Baromodulation explains short-term blood pressure variability. In J. F. Orlebeke, G. Mulder, & L. P. J. van Doornen (Eds.),

The psychophysiology of cardiovascular control (pp. 69–97). New York, NY: Plenum Press.

Wickens, C. D. (2002). Multiple resources and performance prediction. *Theoretical Issues in Ergonomics Science, 3,* 159–177. doi:10.1080/14639220210123806

Wilson, G. F. (1993). Air-to-ground training missions: A psychophysiological work-load analysis. *Ergonomics, 36,* 1071–1087. doi:10.1080/00140139308967979

Wilson, G. F., & Fisher, F. (1991). The use of cardiac and eye blink measures to determine flight segments in F-4 crews. *Aviation, Space, and Environmental Medicine, 62,* 959–962.

B. REWARD INFLUENCE
AND RESPONSE SPECIFICITY

4

CARDIOVASCULAR RESPONSE TO REWARD

MICHAEL RICHTER

There is no doubt that rewards have a strong impact on human behavior, at least not when one considers the frequent application of rewards in our society. In almost every field of life, rewards are used with the idea that they will shape behavior and enhance performance. In business, salary is seen as an incentive that increases the performance of the employee, and performance-related pay systems are justified by the performance-enhancing qualities of monetary rewards. In school and at university, outstanding students receive prizes to reward them for their past performance in the hope that this will also boost their future performance. Most parents educate their children on the basis of the fundamental idea of operant conditioning, which holds that reinforcing a behavior will increase the probability that the behavior is shown again. Given that the link between reward and human behavior is so prominent in everyday life, it is little wonder that it is also a topic of interest in cardiovascular psychophysiology. In this chapter, I discuss two prominent approaches that both focus on the relationship between reward and cardiovascular response but differ in their specific predictions.

REWARD VALUE AS A DIRECT DETERMINANT OF
CARDIOVASCULAR RESPONSE: THE APPROACH OF FOWLES

A large part of the research in the domain of cardiovascular psychophysiology is based on the more or less explicit assumption that cardiovascular response is a direct function of the magnitude of reward. Cardiovascular response should rise in a monotonic way with reward value: The higher the reward, the higher the cardiovascular response. Probably the most influential approach postulating an association between reward and cardiovascular response is Fowles's motivational theory (e.g., 1980, 1988). Fowles was especially interested in assessing the activity of the behavioral activation system (BAS) and the behavioral inhibition system (BIS)—the two major systems in Gray's (1982) first model of personality—by means of peripheral psychophysiological measures. Drawing on findings on cardio–somatic coupling (e.g., Obrist, Webb, Sutterer, & Howard, 1970) and on previous work on heart rate (HR) as an indicator of reward effects (e.g., Bélanger & Feldman, 1962; Elliot, 1969, 1974, 1975; Elliot, Bankart, & Light, 1970; Malmo & Bélanger, 1967), he postulated that HR changes in response to reward reflect BAS activity. The BAS should be stimulated by the presence of positive rewards and by situations that call for active behavior to avoid punishment (Fowles, 1980, 1988) and should underlie all active behavior—including both approach behavior and active avoidance behavior. In a nutshell, Fowles postulated that rewards stimulate the BAS and that BAS activity leads to increased HR.

In a series of studies, Fowles and colleagues demonstrated that reward value determines HR reactivity (i.e., the change from rest to task performance; e.g., Fowles, Fisher, & Tranel, 1982; Tranel, 1983; Tranel, Fisher, & Fowles, 1982). In a study by Tranel et al. (1982), participants had to press one of five buttons arranged in a semicircle. Each button was accompanied by a light. At the beginning of each trial, one light was turned on, and participants had to press the corresponding button to turn it off. Different groups of participants could earn 2 cents for every two correct responses, 5 cents for every two correct responses, 2 cents for every five correct responses, or 5 cents for every five correct responses. A fifth group of participants served as control group and could not win anything. As predicted, HR reactivity was positively associated with reward value. Participants in the control group did not show any HR increase compared with a baseline task performance. Participants who could earn 5 cents for correct responses showed a statistically significant higher HR reactivity than the control group. HR reactivity of participants who could earn 2 cents for correct responses was between the HR reactivity of the control group and the 5-cents groups. The number of correct responses required for the monetary reward—which determined the total amount of reward that participants could earn—had no statistically significant impact on HR reactivity. However, in a later experiment, Tranel (1983) showed that both the reward value and the total amount that participants can earn exert an effect on HR reactivity.

Drawing on the work of Fowles, several authors have used HR to assess the activity of the BAS (e.g., Brenner, Beauchaine, & Sylvers, 2005; Gomez & McLaren, 1997; Iaboni, Douglas, & Ditto, 1997; Sosnowski, Nurzynska, & Polec, 1991). For instance, Iaboni et al. (1997) used HR reactivity to examine BAS activity in a sample of children with attention-deficit/hyperactivity disorder (ADHD). Manipulating the presence and absence of rewards in a series of trials, they observed a faster habituation of HR responses to reward and a weaker HR response to reappearing rewards in children with ADHD compared with a control group. Iaboni et al. concluded that this indicates that the BAS is weak in children with ADHD. Using a similar design as Iaboni and colleagues, Brenner et al. (2005) replicated the finding that HR changes reliably predict the absence and presence of reward. However, they did not find a significant relationship between HR changes and BAS activity, assessed with the self-report scales of Carver and White (1994).

Beauchaine (2001) proposed a model of autonomic nervous system functioning that linked the BAS to the sympathetic nervous system. According to this model, myocardial sympathetic activity can be used to reliably assess BAS activity. It is noteworthy that this provides a qualitative extension of Fowles's model because Beauchaine's model includes specific predictions regarding the autonomic basis of BAS-related cardiac activity, which has significant implications for the cardiovascular measures that are supposed to indicate BAS activity. HR is affected by both the sympathetic and the parasympathetic branch of the autonomic nervous system. Increased sympathetic activity leads to increased HR; increased parasympathetic activity reduces HR. However, the interplay of both branches is complex: Changes in HR can be due to changes in sympathetic activity, changes in parasympathetic activity, or changes in both branches (e.g., Berntson, Cacioppo, & Quigley, 1991). For Fowles's model, this is of minor concern because he proposed HR as an indicator of BAS activity without making any specific predictions regarding the underlying autonomic mechanisms. However, HR does not constitute a satisfying indicator of BAS activity in Beauchaine's framework. According to Beauchaine, BAS activity is specifically linked to sympathetic impact on the heart. Given that HR is an ambiguous measure of sympathetic activity, HR is not the measure of choice in Beauchaine's model. He proposes pre-ejection period as a measure of myocardial sympathetic activity and thus BAS activity. *Pre-ejection period* (PEP) refers to the time interval between the onset of ventricular depolarization and the opening of the aortic valve. Empirical evidence suggests that this time interval constitutes a reliable and valid indicator of myocardial sympathetic (beta-adrenergic) activity under most conditions (e.g., Benschop et al., 1994; Harris, Schoenfeld, & Weissler, 1967; Newlin & Levenson, 1979; Obrist, Light, James, & Strogatz, 1987; Schächinger, Weinbacher, Kiss, Ritz, & Langewitz, 2001; Sherwood et al., 1990).

Supporting evidence for Beauchaine's model can be found in the Brenner at al. (2005) study cited previously. In this study, PEP reactivity showed the same pattern as HR reactivity: Changes in PEP reactivity indicated the absence and the presence of rewards. Furthermore, PEP reactivity was specifically associated with reward and did not change—as for instance did HR reactivity—during periods of extinction. Based on this finding and on the predictions of his model, Beauchaine and colleagues have recently started to assess BAS activity in different mental diseases by means of PEP reactivity (e.g., Beauchaine, 2002; Beauchaine, Katkin, Strassberg, & Snarr, 2001; Crowell et al., 2005).

REWARD VALUE AS AN INDIRECT DETERMINANT OF CARDIOVASCULAR RESPONSE: THE APPROACH OF WRIGHT

Wright (1996) formulated an integrative model that provides an alternative view of how reward may affect cardiovascular response. Like Fowles's approach, Wright's integrative model draws on Obrist's work. Wright was especially interested in Obrist's demonstration that cardiovascular responses are associated with task engagement in mental tasks (Light & Obrist, 1983; Obrist, 1976, 1981). Obrist and colleagues observed that beta-adrenergic (sympathetic) impact on the heart increases with task engagement, even if somatic activity is low (*cardiac–somatic uncoupling*). Integrating this finding with the ideas of Brehm's motivational intensity theory (Brehm & Self, 1989), Wright predicted that task difficulty and success importance determine cardiovascular reactivity in active coping tasks (i.e., when task outcome is linked to the performance of the individual). According to motivational intensity theory, human behavior is guided by a resource conservation principle: Humans try to avoid wasting energy. Drawing on this principle, Wright predicted that myocardial beta-adrenergic activity is a direct function of task demand if the difficulty of a task is fixed and known. Using the difficulty of a task to determine effort mobilization allows the individual to respect the resource conservation principle. Because task difficulty indicates the effort necessary for success, one will never invest too much energy. Success importance—which is influenced by needs, rewards, and task instrumentality—should exert only an indirect effect on cardiovascular response by limiting the difficulty–cardiovascular response relationship. Myocardial beta-adrenergic activity should thus rise with increasing task difficulty as long as success is possible and the necessary effort is justified. If the task is impossible or too difficult—because the necessary energy exceeds the energy justified by success importance—individuals should disengage, and cardiovascular response should be low. It follows that reward should have no direct impact on cardiovascular response if task difficulty is fixed and clear. Cardiovascular response should be a function of task demand; reward—as a determinant of success importance—should only set the upper limit of this relationship. Figure 4.1 summarizes these predictions.

These predictions only apply if the difficulty of a task is fixed to a certain performance standard and if task difficulty is clear (*fixed task difficulty*). If task difficulty is either unclear (*unclear task difficulty*) or not fixed to a performance standard (*unfixed task difficulty*), Wright predicts that cardiovascular response should be a direct function of reward: The higher the reward, the higher the cardiovascular response. The reasoning for tasks with fixed but unclear task difficulty is straightforward. If individuals have no information at hand about the difficulty of the upcoming task, they are in need of another indicator to guide their effort investment without violating the resource conservation principle. Success importance constitutes such an indicator. By investing as much effort as justified, individuals can be sure not to invest more than justified. Individuals may invest more energy than necessary, but the costs will never outweigh the benefits. The reasoning for tasks with an unfixed difficulty is slightly more complex and draws on a second assumption. To arrive at predictions for tasks that do not have a fixed performance standard, Brehm assumed that individuals strive for the best performance if they are free to perform at any level (e.g., Brehm & Self, 1989). It follows that individuals should invest the maximum effort that is justified in this kind of task. Even if the reasoning for unfixed and unclear tasks is different, the prediction is the

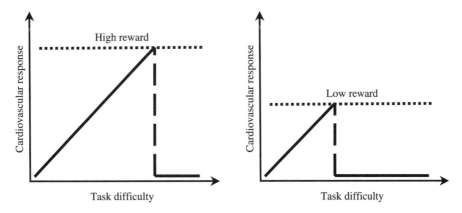

Figure 4.1. The predictions of Wright's integrative model for the joint impact of reward value and task difficulty on cardiovascular response under conditions of fixed and clear task difficulty.

same: Success importance should directly determine cardiovascular response. This implies that cardiovascular response should rise with increasing reward. This prediction is shown in Figure 4.2. In sum, Wright's integrative model predicts that reward should only have a direct impact on cardiovascular response if the difficulty of a task is either unfixed or unclear. If the difficulty is fixed and clear, reward should only set the upper limit of the relationship between task difficulty and cardiovascular response.

Support for Wright's predictions that cardiovascular response is a direct function of success importance if task difficulty is either unfixed or unclear comes from a series of studies. Most of them were concerned with the association of success importance and cardiovascular responses under conditions of unfixed task difficulty (e.g., Gendolla & Richter, 2005, 2006b; Gendolla, Richter, & Silvia, 2008; Wright, Killebrew, & Pimpalapure, 2002, Experiment 1; Wright, Tunstall, Williams, Goodwin, & Harmon-Jones, 1995). Success importance was manipulated in these studies by increasing self-awareness, presenting the task as a test that is predictive for study success, or by the presence of an observer. A more direct demonstration of how reward value can influence cardiovascular response can be found in a study of Wright's (Wright et al., 2002, Experiment 2). In this study, one group of participants performed a letter-scanning task in which they had to circle Es on pages full of different letters. One half of the participants could earn 1 cent for every two Es circled, the other half could earn 5 cents for every two Es circled. The participants were instructed to circle Es as long as the task performance period continued. As in most of the studies conducted to test Wright's predictions, cardiovascular response was assessed by determining systolic blood pressure (SBP), diastolic blood pressure, and HR during rest and task performance. Supporting

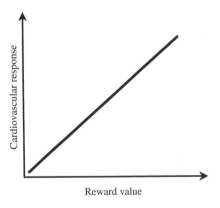

Figure 4.2. The predictions of Wright's integrative model for the impact of reward value on cardiovascular response under conditions of unfixed and unclear task difficulty.

the predictions of Wright's integrative model, SBP reactivity was significantly higher when participants could earn 5 cents for every two Es circled than when they could earn only 1 cent. HR reactivity showed the same pattern but the difference between both cells was not statistically significant.

Two studies addressed the relationship between reward and cardiovascular response in tasks with unclear difficulty (Richter & Gendolla, 2006, 2007). In the first article, Richter and Gendolla (2006) demonstrated that SBP reactivity during a memory task with a fixed but unclear performance standard is higher when participants can earn a valuable reward than when they can earn an unattractive reward or no reward. The second study (Richter & Gendolla, 2007) extended previous research by manipulating task reward across four levels. Participants performed a memory task without knowing the difficulty of the task in advance and could earn no reward, 10 Swiss francs, 20 Swiss francs, or 30 Swiss francs for a successful task performance. The results supported the predictions of Wright's integrative model: SBP reactivity increased with increasing monetary reward across the four levels. HR reactivity showed the same pattern, but the proportional relationship was less pronounced.

As noted, Wright's model assumes that effort mobilization is associated with myocardial beta-adrenergic activity. Because blood pressure and HR are not pure indicators of sympathetic impact on the heart, recent studies (Annis, Wright, & Williams, 2001; Richter, Friedrich, & Gendolla, 2008; Richter & Gendolla, 2009) have begun examining myocardial beta-adrenergic activity directly by assessing PEP (for a discussion, see Richter et al., 2008; Richter & Gendolla, 2009; Wright, 1996). As noted, PEP is a noninvasive indicator of myocardial beta-adrenergic activity. Most relevant to the discussion of reward effects on cardiovascular response is a study by Richter and Gendolla (2009). These authors assessed PEP reactivity of participants performing under either one of three levels of reward a delayed-matching-to-sample task with an unclear difficulty. The results provided strong support for Wright's hypothesis: PEP reactivity was low if participants could earn 1 Swiss franc by successfully performing the task, PEP reactivity was moderate if they could earn 15 Swiss francs, and PEP reactivity was high if they could earn 30 Swiss francs. SBP showed the same pattern, but the difference between both high reward cells was less pronounced.

In sum, there is plenty of evidence for the predicted relationship between success importance and cardiovascular response in the frame of Wright's integrative model. However, the findings of all the cited studies also fit with Fowles's approach. Most of the research could be explained by assuming that reward activates the BAS and that the resulting BAS activity is reflected by changes in HR, SBP, and PEP. However, the difference between Wright's model and Fowles's approach becomes apparent if one considers cardiovascular responses under conditions of clear and fixed task difficulty. Under this condition, Wright predicted that cardiovascular responses are a direct function of task difficulty as long as task difficulty is not too high, and the necessary effort is justified by success importance. It follows that reward should have no direct impact on cardiovascular response under these conditions. By determining success importance, reward should only set the upper limit of the task difficulty–cardiovascular response relationship.

The results of a number of studies support this prediction (e.g., Eubanks, Wright, & Williams, 2002; Gendolla & Richter, 2006a, 2006b; Wright, Dill, Geen, & Anderson, 1998; Wright, Shaw, & Jones, 1990). In the study by Eubanks et al. (2002), participants could earn chances for a $100 prize or $10 prize by attaining a 90% success rate in a Sternberg task (Sternberg, 1966). In this task, a target letter or a letter string was presented on the screen for 4 s. After a break of 1 s, a single letter appeared on the screen, and the participants had to decide whether this letter had appeared in the preceding letter string. Participants performed five difficulty levels of this Sternberg task. In the easiest version, a single letter was present as target. In the most difficult version the letter string included 13 letters. Eubanks and colleagues observed that HR reactivity increased across the first four difficulty levels for both reward groups. Furthermore, HR did not statistically differ between the $100 and the $10 groups on the first four difficulty levels. At the highest difficulty level, HR reactivity was high in the $100 group and low in the $10 group. Even if there were no significant effects on SBP, this example illustrated the interaction between task difficulty and reward value predicted by Wright's integrative model. Reward value has no direct impact; it only sets the upper limit for the reward–cardiovascular response relationship.

CONCLUDING REMARKS

It should be apparent that Wright's integrative model and the hypothesis that rewards have a direct effect on cardiovascular response have a lot in common. Both approaches predict that reward may have an effect on cardiovascular response. Furthermore, both approaches postulate that cardiovascular response may rise as a function of reward value. However, the two approaches differ in some important aspects. Wright's integrative model predicts that reward only exerts a direct effect on cardiovascular response in tasks that are characterized by either unfixed or fixed but unclear difficulty. If the difficulty of the task is fixed and clear, rewards should only set the upper limit of the difficulty–cardiovascular response relationship. It is obvious that research demonstrating a linear or a proportional relationship between reward value and cardiovascular response can easily be explained by Wright's integrative model by assuming that task difficulty was either unfixed or fixed but unclear in these studies. It is more difficult for approaches that rely on the assumption that reward exerts a direct effect on cardiovascular response to explain the results of studies conducted in the framework of Wright's integrative model. It is noteworthy that studies that have manipulated both task difficulty and reward value and that have found the interaction predicted by Wright's integrative model cannot be explained by the simple assumption that reward has a direct impact on cardiovascular response.

However, it should also be noted that both approaches aim to explain different phenomena. Wright used cardiovascular measures to test theory-derived predictions regarding effort mobilization. Fowles and Beauchaine proposed models that refer to the BAS and proposed cardiovascular measures that should be linked to BAS activity. Nevertheless, one could speculate that the BAS underlies effort mobilization and that any kind of effort mobilization should be associated with an increase in BAS activity. In this case, one would expect that variables that have an impact on effort mobilization also affect BAS activity. Given that research on Wright's integrative model has repeatedly shown that task difficulty is a main determinant of effort mobilization—at least if task difficulty is fixed and clear—changes in BAS activity could also be due to task difficulty effects. This implies that it may be problematic to use cardiovascular measures to infer reward responsiveness. Under certain conditions, increases in HR or PEP may not be due to reward effects but due to effects of task difficulty.

It is also noteworthy that the two approaches—at least the approaches of Wright and Fowles—differ in their specific predictions. Wright's integrative model is based on the assumption that myocardial beta-adrenergic activity is associated with effort mobilization. Fowles was concerned with HR changes as an indicator of BAS activity. This implies that the main dependent variables in research on Wright's integrative model are variables, such as PEP, that indicate myocardial beta-adrenergic activity, whereas the main variable in research on Fowles's model is HR. Furthermore, Wright predicted a specific physiologic mechanism that should underlie effort mobilization, whereas Fowles only specified the cardiovascular measure that should be associated with BAS activity.

In sum, there is accumulating evidence that shows that rewards may have an impact on cardiovascular responses. Research on Fowles's model—as well as on Beauchaine's model—has shown that the presence of rewards may increase HR and PEP reactivity. Research on Wright's integrative model has demonstrated that the effect of rewards on blood pressure and PEP reactivity is moderated by task difficulty and the type of task. Given that both approaches aim to explain different phenomena and have largely relied on different cardiovascular measures to test their predictions, a conclusive comparison of both approaches might be premature. However, given that Beauchaine

recently made predictions that refer to the same dependent variable—PEP—
as Wright's integrative model, future research may easily integrate and compare both models.

REFERENCES

Annis, S., Wright, R. A., & Williams, B. J. (2001). Interactional influence of ability
perception and task demand on cardiovascular response: Appetitive effects at
three levels of challenge. *Journal of Applied Biobehavioral Research, 6*, 82–107.
doi:10.1111/j.1751-9861.2001.tb00108.x

Beauchaine, T. (2001). Vagal tone, development, and Gray's motivational theory:
Toward an integrated model of autonomic nervous system functioning in psy-
chopathology. *Development and Psychopathology, 13*, 183–214. doi:10.1017/
S0954579401002012

Beauchaine, T. P. (2002). Autonomic substrates of heart rate reactivity in adolescent
males with conduct disorder and/or attention-deficit/hyperactivity disorder. In
S. P. Shohow (Ed.), *Advances in psychology research* (Vol. 18, pp. 83–95). New
York, NY: NOVA Science.

Beauchaine, T. P., Katkin, E. S., Strassberg, Z., & Snarr, J. (2001). Disinhibitory
psychopathology in male adolescents: Discriminating conduct disorder form
attention-deficit/hyperactivity disorder through concurrent assessment of multiple autonomic states. *Journal of Abnormal Psychology, 110*, 610–624. doi:10.1037/
0021-843X.110.4.610

Bélanger, D., & Feldman, S. M. (1962). Effects of water deprivation upon heart rate
and instrumental activity in the rat. *Journal of Comparative and Physiological Psychology, 55*, 220–225. doi:10.1037/h0042797

Benschop, R. J., Nieuwenhuis, E. E. S., Tromp, E. A. M., Godaert, G. L. R., Ballieux,
R. E., & van Doornen, L. J. P. (1994). Effects of fl-adrenergic blockade on
immunologic and cardiovascular changes induced by mental stress. *Circulation,
89*, 762–769.

Berntson, G. G., Cacioppo, J. T., & Quigley, K. S. (1991). Autonomic determinism:
The modes of autonomic control, the doctrine of autonomic space, and the laws
of autonomic constraints. *Psychological Review, 98*, 459–487. doi:10.1037/0033-
295X.98.4.459

Brehm, J. W., & Self, E. A. (1989). The intensity of motivation. *Annual Review of
Psychology, 40*, 109–131. doi:10.1146/annurev.ps.40.020189.000545

Brenner, S. L., Beauchaine, T. P., & Sylvers, P. D. (2005). A comparison of psychophysiological and self-report measures of BAS and BIS activation. *Psychophysiology, 42*, 108–115. doi:10.1111/j.1469-8986.2005.00261.x

Carver, C. S., & White, T. L. (1994). Behavioral inhibition, behavioral activation, and
affective responses to impending reward and punishment: The BIS/BAS scales.

Journal of Personality and Social Psychology, 67, 319–333. doi:10.1037/0022-3514.67.2.319

Crowell, S. E., Beauchaine, T. P., McCauley, E., Smith, C. J., Stevens, A. L., & Sylvers, P. (2005). Psychological, autonomic, and serotonergic correlates of para-suicide among adolescent girls. *Development and Psychopathology, 17,* 1105–1127. doi:10.1017/S0954579405050522

Elliott, R. (1969). Tonic heart rate: Experiment on the effects of collative variables lead to a hypothesis about its motivational significance. *Journal of Personality and Social Psychology, 12,* 211–228. doi:10.1037/h0027630

Elliott, R. (1974). The motivational significance of heart rate. In P. A. Obrist, A. H. Black, J. Brener, & L. V. DiCara (Eds.), *Cardiovascular psychophysiology* (pp. 505–537). Chicago, IL: Aldine.

Elliott, R. (1975). Heart rate, activity, and activation in rats. *Psychophysiology, 12,* 298–305. doi:10.1111/j.1469-8986.1975.tb01294.x

Elliott, R., Bankart, B., & Light, T. (1970). Differences in the motivational signifi-cance of heart rate and palmar conductance: Two tests of a hypothesis. *Journal of Personality and Social Psychology, 14,* 166–172. doi:10.1037/h0028686

Eubanks, L., Wright, R. A., & Williams, B. J. (2002). Reward influence on the heart: Cardiovascular response as a function of incentive value at five levels of task demand. *Motivation and Emotion, 26,* 139–152. doi:10.1023/A:1019863318803

Fowles, D. C. (1980). The three-arousal model: Implications of Gray's two-factor learning theory for heart rate, electrodermal activity, and psychopathy. *Psy-chophysiology, 17,* 87–104. doi:10.1111/j.1469-8986.1980.tb00117.x

Fowles, D. C. (1988). Psychophysiology and psychopathology: A motivational approach. *Psychophysiology, 25,* 373–391. doi:10.1111/j.1469-8986.1988.tb01873.x

Fowles, D. C., Fisher, A. E., & Tranel, D. T. (1982). The heart beats to reward: The effect of monetary incentive on heart rate. *Psychophysiology, 19,* 506–513. doi:10.1111/j.1469-8986.1982.tb02577.x

Gendolla, G. H. E., & Richter, M. (2005). Ego-involvement and mental effort: Cardio-vascular, electrodermal, and performance effects. *Psychophysiology, 42,* 595–603. doi:10.1111/j.1469-8986.2005.00314.x

Gendolla, G. H. E., & Richter, M. (2006a). Cardiovascular reactivity during perfor-mance under social observation: The moderating role of task difficulty. *International Journal of Psychophysiology, 62,* 185–192. doi:10.1016/j.ijpsycho.2006.04.002

Gendolla, G. H. E., & Richter, M. (2006b). Ego-involvement and the difficulty law of motivation: Effects on performance-related cardiovascular response. *Personality and Social Psychology Bulletin, 32,* 1188–1203. doi:10.1177/0146167206288945

Gendolla, G. H. E., Richter, M., & Silvia, P. J. (2008). Self-focus and task difficulty effects on effort-related cardiovascular reactivity. *Psychophysiology, 45,* 653–662. doi:10.1111/j.1469-8986.2008.00655.x

Gomez, R., & McLaren, S. (1997). The effects of reward and punishment on response disinhibition, moods, heart rate and skin conductance level during instrumental learning. *Personality and Individual Differences, 23*, 305–316. doi:10.1016/S0191-8869(97)00031-7

Gray, J. A. (1982). *The neuropsychology of anxiety: An enquiry into the functions of the septo-hippocampal system*. New York, NY: Oxford University Press.

Harris, W. S., Schoenfeld, C. D., & Weissler, A. M. (1967). Effects of adrenergic receptor activation and blockade on the systolic preejection period, heart rate, and arterial pressure in man. *The Journal of Clinical Investigation, 46*, 1704–1714. doi:10.1172/JCI105661

Iaboni, F., Douglas, V., & Ditto, B. (1997). Psychophysiological response of ADHD children to reward and extinction. *Psychophysiology, 34*, 116–123. doi:10.1111/j.1469-8986.1997.tb02422.x

Light, K. C., & Obrist, P. A. (1983). Task difficulty, heart rate reactivity, and cardiovascular responses to an appetitive reaction time task. *Psychophysiology, 20*, 301–312. doi:10.1111/j.1469-8986.1983.tb02158.x

Malmo, R. B., & Bélanger, D. (1967). Related physiological and behavioral changes: What are their determinants? *Research Publications—Association for Research in Nervous and Mental Disease, 45*, 288–318.

Newlin, D. B., & Levenson, R. W. (1979). Pre-ejection period: Measuring beta-adrenergic influences upon the heart. *Psychophysiology, 16*, 546–552. doi:10.1111/j.1469-8986.1979.tb01519.x

Obrist, P. A. (1976). The cardiovascular–behavioral interaction as it appears today. *Psychophysiology, 13*, 95–107. doi:10.1111/j.1469-8986.1976.tb00081.x

Obrist, P. A. (1981). *Cardiovascular psychophysiology: A perspective*. New York, NY: Plenum Press.

Obrist, P. A., Light, K. C., James, S. A., & Strogatz, D. S. (1987). Cardiovascular responses to stress: I. Measures of myocardial response and relationships to high resting systolic pressure and parental hypertension. *Psychophysiology, 24*, 65–78. doi:10.1111/j.1469-8986.1987.tb01864.x

Obrist, P. A., Webb, R. A., Sutterer, J. R., & Howard, J. L. (1970). The cardiac–somatic relationship: Some reformulations. *Psychophysiology, 6*, 569–587. doi:10.1111/j.1469-8986.1970.tb02246.x

Richter, M., Friedrich, A., & Gendolla, G. H. E. (2008). Task difficulty effects on cardiac activity. *Psychophysiology, 45*, 869–875. doi:10.1111/j.1469-8986.2008.00688.x

Richter, M., & Gendolla, G. H. E. (2006). Incentive effects on cardiovascular reactivity in active coping with unclear task difficulty. *International Journal of Psychophysiology, 61*, 216–225. doi:10.1016/j.ijpsycho.2005.10.003

Richter, M., & Gendolla, G. H. E. (2007). Incentive value, unclear task difficulty, and cardiovascular reactivity in active coping. *International Journal of Psychophysiology, 63*, 294–301. doi:10.1016/j.ijpsycho.2006.12.002

Richter, M., & Gendolla, G. H. E. (2009). The heart contracts to reward: Monetary incentives and pre-ejection period. *Psychophysiology, 46*, 451–457. doi:10.1111/j.1469-8986.2009.00795.x

Schächinger, H., Weinbacher, M., Kiss, A., Ritz, R., & Langewitz, W. (2001). Cardiovascular indices of peripheral and central sympathetic activation. *Psychosomatic Medicine, 63*, 788–796.

Sherwood, A., Allen, M. T., Fahrenberg, J., Kelsey, R. M., Lovallo, W. R., & van Doornen, L. J. P. (1990). Methodological guidelines for impedance cardiography. *Psychophysiology, 27*, 1–23. doi:10.1111/j.1469-8986.1990.tb02171.x

Sosnowski, T., Nurzynska, M., & Polec, M. (1991). Active–passive coping and skin conductance and heart rate changes. *Psychophysiology, 28*, 665–672. doi:10.1111/j.1469-8986.1991.tb01011.x

Sternberg, S. (1966, August 5). High speed scanning in human memory. *Science, 153*, 652–654.

Tranel, D. T. (1983). The effects of monetary incentive and frustrative non-reward on heart rate and electrodermal activity. *Psychophysiology, 20*, 652–657. doi:10.1111/j.1469-8986.1983.tb00933.x

Tranel, D. T., Fisher, A. E., & Fowles, D. C. (1982). Magnitude of incentive effects on heart rate. *Psychophysiology, 19*, 514–519. doi:10.1111/j.1469-8986.1982.tb02578.x

Wright, R. A. (1996). Brehm's theory of motivation as a model of effort and cardiovascular response. In P. M. Gollwitzer & J. A. Bargh (Eds.), *The psychology of action: Linking cognition and motivation to behavior* (pp. 424–453). New York, NY: Guilford Press.

Wright, R. A., Dill, J. C., Geen, R. G., & Anderson, C. A. (1998). Social evaluation influence on cardiovascular response to a fixed behavioral challenge: Effects across a range of difficulty levels. *Annals of Behavioral Medicine, 20*, 277–285. doi:10.1007/BF02886377

Wright, R. A., Killebrew, K., & Pimpalapure, D. (2002). Cardiovascular incentive effects where a challenge is unfixed: Demonstrations involving evaluation, evaluator status, and monetary reward. *Psychophysiology, 39*, 188–197. doi:10.1111/1469-8986.3920188

Wright, R. A., Shaw, L. L., & Jones, C. R. (1990). Task demand and cardiovascular response magnitude: Further evidence of the mediating role of success importance. *Journal of Personality and Social Psychology, 59*, 1250–1260. doi:10.1037/0022-3514.59.6.1250

Wright, R. A., Tunstall, A. M., Williams, B. J., Goodwin, J. S., & Harmon-Jones, E. (1995). Social evaluation and cardiovascular response: An active coping approach. *Journal of Personality and Social Psychology, 69*, 530–543. doi:10.1037/0022-3514.69.3.530

5

EMOTION, MOTIVATION, AND CARDIOVASCULAR RESPONSE

SYLVIA D. KREIBIG

Climbing stairs, working intensely on a cognitive task, or recalling a fight with one's spouse are events that can powerfully influence cardiovascular responding (CVR). The first two examples relate to physical and cognitive activities; the third example illustrates a case where emotion elicited by a personally significant event directs CVR.

These examples illustrate that emotion and CVR are not uniquely associated. Whereas we see changes in CVR under a majority of emotional conditions, changes in CVR need not indicate a change in emotion but may also be related to behavior or cognition. Emotion is believed to influence CVR only in a short moment from the onset of the emotion to the subsequent initiation of behavior. Thus, studying the relationship between emotion and CVR necessitates parsing the continuous stream of CVR into a narrowly defined time window in which emotion dominates over the other mental faculties. CVR hence precedes emotion, is a response component of

The author thanks Klaus Scherer and Tom Cochrane for helpful comments on earlier versions of this manuscript. This research was supported by the Swiss National Science Foundation (PBGEP1-125914) as well as by the National Center of Competence in Research (NCCR) Affective Sciences financed by the Swiss National Science Foundation (51NF40-104897) and hosted by the University of Geneva.

emotion, and persists after the occurrence of an emotion. A similar relation is true between emotion and motivation: Motivation can be seen as a cause of emotion, as one of its major aspects, and as one of its consequences (Frijda, 2000). How, then, can emotion, motivation, and CVR be integrated?

The present chapter examines the relation between emotion, motivation, and CVR from the perspective of autonomic emotion specificity. The specificity hypothesis suggests that different emotions are associated with distinct activation patterns of the autonomic nervous system (ANS; Stemmler, 1992), of which the cardiovascular system (CVS) is one prominent component. Scholars of emotion, starting with James (1884), have long speculated about the potential of emotion to organize ANS responding in ways that relate specifically to the type of elicited emotion. Still, there is no scientific consensus on whether autonomic emotion specificity exists or what its functions might be. Both notions of unspecific and highly specific response patterns in emotion can be found in the current literature (for a review, see Kreibig, 2010).

The chapter opens with a brief outline of the physical components of CVR in emotion. It then reviews theoretical positions on the organization of CVR in emotion and its motivational function. The chapter closes with considerations for a systematic integration of emotion, motivation, and CVR.

THE CARDIOVASCULAR SYSTEM

The CVS can be viewed as embedded within the ANS, which in turn, is integrated into the central nervous system. The CVS consists of the heart and vascular pathways that deliver oxygenated blood to the organs and tissues and return deoxygenated blood to the lungs. The CVS is controlled by the two branches of the ANS: the sympathetic nervous system (SNS) and parasympathetic nervous system (PNS).

Increased SNS activity leads to increased CVR, including heart rate (HR) acceleration, increased myocardial contractility (indicated by shortened cardiac pre-ejection period [PEP]), and increased blood pressure (BP). Increased PNS activity leads to decreased cardiac activity, such as HR deceleration and decreased contractile force, but it does not affect BP regulation. Because the heart is dually innervated, assessing functionally distinct cardiovascular measures allows investigators to parse the relative influence of the SNS and PNS on overall CVR. Whereas HR reflects the influence of both SNS and PNS, PEP is a relatively pure indicator of sympathetic influence on myocardial contractility; high-frequency HR variability (HRV), or respiratory sinus arrhythmia (RSA), has been used as an indicator of parasympathetic influence on the heart (Berntson, Cacioppo, & Quigley, 1991).

CARDIOVASCULAR RESPONSE ORGANIZATION IN EMOTION

The following review of models of CVR in emotion is structured according to conceptual levels, on which an organizing principle may operate. Conceptual levels span from the physiological over the behavioral to the psychological level, as summarized in Table 5.1.

Models on the peripheral physiological level see the organizing principle of CVR in emotion in the structure and functioning of the ANS or in the functioning of transmitter substances. Models on the brain–behavioral level view the organizing principle in the functioning of brain–behavioral systems and refined behavioral modes. Finally, models on the psychological level place particular emphasis on the functioning of appraisal modules as a general organizing principle of CVR in emotion. From a component view of emotion, models on the same conceptual level rival each other, whereas models on different levels have complementary value, because they address different levels of response organization.

Cardiovascular Response Organization in Emotion Based on Autonomic Nervous System Structure

The basic anatomical dichotomy of the sympathetic and parasympathetic divisions of the ANS has long inspired claims that certain groups of emotions are related to the dominant activation of one or the other autonomic branch, which differentially influence CVR.

Undifferentiated Sympathetic Activation

Cannon (1915) criticized the high degree of autonomic differentiation of emotion proposed by James (1884). Rather, he observed that

> any high degree of excitement in the central nervous system, whether felt as anger, terror, pain, anxiety, joy, grief, or deep disgust, is likely to break over the threshold of the sympathetic division and disturb the functions of all the organs which that division innervates. (Cannon, 1915, p. 279)

According to Cannon, CVR is the same in all emotions. This emphasis on the sympathetic–adrenal system as the physiological substrate of emotion led to the coining of the fight–flight reaction as the generic motivational outcome of all emotions. CVR in the fight–flight response is characterized by hypertension, tachycardia, visceral vasoconstriction, and muscle vasodilation.

TABLE 5.1
Conceptual Levels of Cardiovascular Response Organization in Emotion

Psychological level

Functioning of appraisal modules
Componential process model — Scherer (2009)
Motivational intensity theory — Gendolla (2004); Wright (1996, 1998)
Biopsychosocial model — Blascovich & Katkin (1993); Blascovich, Mendes, Tomaka, Salomon, & Seery (2003)

Brain–behavioral level

Functioning of behavioral systems
Behavioral coping — Obrist (1981); Schneiderman & McCabe (1989)
Dual-system models — Bradley & Lang (2000); Cloninger (1987); Davidson (1998)
Polyvagal theory — Porges (1995, 2007)
Reinforcement sensitivity theory — Beauchaine (2001); Fowles (1980); Gray (1982); Gray & McNaughton (2000)

Functioning of behavioral modes
Basic modes of defensive coping — Folkow (2000); Stemmler (2009)
Modes of defensive coping and environmental demands — Bandler & Shipley (1994); Keay & Bandler (2001)
Predator imminence model — Bradley & Lang (2000); Fanselow (1994)

Peripheral physiological level

Functioning of autonomic systems
Undifferentiated sympathetic activation — Cannon (1915)
Parasympathetic activation — Kling (1933); Vingerhoets (1985)
Sympathetic versus parasympathetic response dominance — Gellhorn (1964, 1970); Hess (1957)
Autonomic space — Berntson, Cacioppo, & Quigley (1991)
Functioning of transmitter substances
Catecholamine hypothesis — Ax (1953); Funkenstein, King, & Drolette (1954)
Receptor-types hypothesis — Stemmler (2003, 2009)

Note. Data from Kreibig (2010).

Parasympathetic Activation

Kling (1933) emphasized the involvement of the PNS in certain negative emotions. He maintained that parasympathetic activity might dominate under conditions of intense fear or depression and that this may serve as a differentiating aspect compared with other emotions, such as rage. He suggested "that the degree of fear corresponds somewhat to the degree of parasympathetic influence" (Kling, 1933, p. 369).

PNS activity in emotion has been suggested to occur particularly in such emotions that are characterized by action tendencies of passivity and helplessness (Vingerhoets, 1985). Accordingly, relaxation and depression are proposed to show PNS dominance and consequential inhibition of CVR due to the absence of any apparent need for the ANS to prepare the body for overt action. Fear has been suggested to involve a diphasic response (Vingerhoets, 1985) because this emotion is sometimes manifested in increased SNS activity and sometimes in increased PNS activity. The first phase of fear reflects anxiety, where action, such as the fight–flight response, is perceived as adequate. This motivational outcome is characterized by enhanced SNS activity. The second phase reflects the conservation–withdrawal response, where no active coping responses are viewed as available, and the individual feels as if he or she must surrender or give up. This motivational outcome is characterized by enhanced PNS activity, in particular a fall in BP and decrease in HR.

Sympathetic Versus Parasympathetic Response Dominance

Hess (1957) advanced a model according to which the sympathetic–ergotropic system functions to increase the body's preparedness for energetic activity as well as the organism's efficiency in interacting with the environment. The parasympathetic–trophotropic system, in contrast, has a protective function, which avoids exhaustion and produces conditions for an undisturbed recovery.

On the basis of this framework, Gellhorn (1964, 1970) suggested striated muscle tone as the crucial organizing principle of CVR in emotion. He argued that proprioceptive discharges from increased or decreased muscle tone can induce ergotropic and trophotropic excitation, respectively, via the hypothalamic system. CVR is thus here viewed as a by-product of the motoric emotion response. Rather than a distinction between pleasant and unpleasant emotions, emotions are divided into two major groups according to ergotropic or trophotropic system dominance. Thus, for example, sadness and postprandial happiness—two psychologically opposing states—were viewed as associated with muscular relaxation and trophotropic dominance, leading to decreased CVR. In contrast, the feeling of triumph and extreme happiness, as well as the state of rage and aggressiveness, were viewed as associated with high muscle tone and excitation of the ergotropic system, leading to increased CVR. Similarly, sudden fear was believed to elicit mainly trophotropic effects, whereas states of frustration and resentment were chiefly related to ergotropic effects. In spite of this postulated reciprocal inhibition, some intensive emotional states, such as anxiety, could still affect both the ergotropic and trophotropic systems, leading to sympathetic–parasympathetic coactivation of the heart.

Conceptual Implications of Autonomic Space

The majority of views thus far examined are based on a dichotomous conceptualization of an autonomic activation continuum, extending from sympathetic to parasympathetic dominance (Cannon, 1915). This doctrine of functional reciprocity has been superseded by the view that the SNS and PNS may function in coupled or uncoupled modes, as formalized in the model of autonomic space (Berntson et al., 1991). Coupled modes include the traditional view of reciprocal functioning as well as modes of coactivation and coinhibition. In uncoupled mode, the two autonomic divisions function independently. This conceptualization considerably extends the range of possible autonomic modes of CVR in both emotional and non-emotional conditions.

Alternate modes of autonomic control are proposed to be associated with distinct adaptive features and to entail different characteristic responses of the CVS. Reciprocal modes show high directional consistency, wide dynamic range, and high lability of the target organ response. Reciprocal modes can thus yield large, directionally stable shifts in the functional state of the CVS and may therefore be suited for well-defined adaptive adjustments to survival challenges. Cannon's (1915) observation of pervasive reciprocal sympathetic influence on CVR in the context of highly evocative survival challenges is an example of reciprocal mode. In contrast, organ responses under nonreciprocal modes are fundamentally variable in direction and have a restricted dynamic range and low lability. Nonreciprocal modes of CVR thus tend to preserve baseline functional states. To illustrate, coactivation of sympathetic and vagal controls maximizes cardiac contractility while minimizing increases in rate and thus yields increased stroke volume (SV) by a longer ventricular filling time (Koizumi, Terui, Kollai, & Brooks, 1982).

Cardiovascular Response Organization in Emotion
Based on Transmitter Substances

Various mediators of CVR, such as endocrine functioning, catecholaminergic neuromodulators, or receptors sensitive to specific neurotransmitters, have been related to CVR in emotion, particularly for the differentiation of anger and fear.

Catecholamine Hypothesis

Noradrenaline (NA) is the primary neurotransmitter of the SNS in the synaptic cleft, whereas adrenaline (A; as well as some NA) is released into the bloodstream from the adrenal medulla through sympathetic stimulation. Release of A reinforces sympathetic responses and reaches tissues not directly innervated by the SNS to execute additional functions (Benarroch, Daube, Flemming, & Westmoreland, 2008). Different effects of NA and A are mediated by different receptors. Both catecholamines have approximately the same potency at β_1-adrenergic receptors that regulate cardiac automatism, conduction, excitability, and contractility. Only A can activate β_2-adrenergic receptors that relax the smooth muscles of blood vessels in the heart and skeletal muscles (Benarroch et al., 2008). NA, in contrast, has greater affinity for alpha-adrenergic receptors, activation of which leads to vasoconstriction. Because arterioles in digestive organs and kidneys are equipped only with $\alpha 1$ receptors, combined NA and A discharge leads to a redistribution of blood away from the viscera to the heart and skeletal muscles, which can be viewed as preparing the body for action. Table 5.2 gives an overview of cardiovascular effects of A and NA.

Based on the differential effects of the catecholamines, CVR in fear has been associated with the effect of A, whereas anger has been associated with the joint effects of A and NA (Ax, 1953; Funkenstein, King, & Drolette, 1954). Differential effects between A and NA would be expected to be expressed in lower HR, lower SV and cardiac output (CO), and higher total peripheral resistance (TPR), diastolic BP (DBP), and finger temperature under NA (cf. Stemmler, 2009). Specific routes for activation of adrenal medullary A and NA secretion as well as sympathetic postganglionic NA secretion (Vollmer, 1996) form a physiological basis for such differential CVR and action preparation in anger and fear.

Receptor-Types Hypothesis

An alternative model of CVR in emotion refers to major receptor types of the CVS, such as alpha-adrenergic, beta-adrenergic, and cholinergic receptors mediating cardiovascular tonus (Stemmler, 2003, 2009). To integrate the observation of increased DBP in both fear and anger, Stemmler (2003) suggested a heightened alpha-adrenergic state in anger and a state of vagal withdrawal (i.e., decreased cholinergic cardiovascular tonus) in fear. A receptor types model has also been suggested for the differentiation of fear and sadness (see Kolodyazhniy, Kreibig, Roth, Gross, & Wilhelm, 2010).

TABLE 5.2

Effects of Adrenaline and Noradrenaline on the Cardiovascular System

Adrenaline	Noradrenaline
Source of excretion adrenal medulla	sympathetic ganglion neurons adrenal medulla
Target of excretion blood stream	synapses and blood stream

Receptors
  α-adrenergic
  β_1-adrenergic
  β_2-adrenergic
	α-adrenergic
	β_1-adrenergic

Autonomic responses
  ↑ HR
	↓ HR
	↑ cardiac vagal tonus
	  (via baroreceptor reflex)

↑ left ventricular
    contractility
  ↑ SV
  ↑ CO
  ↑ SBP
  ↓ DBP
  ↓ TPR
  ↓ FT (greater)
  ↑ perfusion of skeletal
    muscles
  ↓ perfusion of blood
    vessels in skin (greater)
	↑ left ventricular
	  contractility
	↔ SV
	↔ CO
	↑ SBP
	↑ DBP
	↑ TPR
	↓ FT (smaller)
	↓ perfusion of skeletal
	  muscles
	↓ perfusion of blood
	  vessels in skin (smaller)

Note. CO = cardiac output; DBP = diastolic blood pressure; FT = finger temperature; HR = heart rate; SBP = systolic blood pressure; SV = stroke volume; TPR = total peripheral resistance. Data from Stemmler (2009).

Conceptual Implications of Neurotransmission

Transmitter substances and receptor types further extend modes of autonomic functioning from SNS–PNS combinations to higher combinatorial space. Because only partial support has been found for the catecholamine hypothesis for CVR in fear and anger (cf. Stemmler, 2009), it can be evaluated as a good, albeit nonexhaustive, hypothesis. Yet further implications of mechanisms of autonomic neurotransmission remain to be explored, such as neuromodulators and their role in CVR in emotion. Neuromodulators may be particularly useful in explaining variance because these substances potentiate or dampen effects of primary neurotransmitters. The classic view of autonomic control suggests antagonistic actions of NA and acetylcholine (ACh) causing either constriction or relaxation, depending on the tissue. This view has been extended by the acknowledgment of nonadrenergic, noncholinergic autonomic neurotransmitters, such as neuropeptide Y (NPY), that moderate and modulate the effects of NA and ACh (Benarroch et al., 2008). Thus, the catecholamine hypothesis perhaps requires a revision in face of recent findings of cotransmission by NPY, coreleased in substantial amounts at high sympathetic–adrenal medullary stimulation rates (Folkow, 2000) and known to affect the emotional stress response (Zhou et al., 2008).

Cardiovascular Response Organization in Emotion Based on Brain–Behavioral Systems

Whereas the models discussed up to now draw heavily on physiological processes associated with the structure and functioning of the ANS, subsequent models rely particularly on higher brain centers and more abstract behavioral processes to explain CVR in emotion. Against this background, behavioral coping and general brain–behavioral systems have been introduced as explanatory constructs.

Behavioral Coping Approach to Cardiovascular Adjustments

CVR in emotion can be viewed as directionally appropriate with the manner in which an organism will attempt to cope with a situation that is perceived as significant to its survival and state of well-being (i.e., according to the actual or perceived challenge; Obrist, 1981). CVR is thus expected to follow anticipated behavior or—more specific—a dimension of active–passive coping (Obrist, 1981). Active coping occurs in situations where some overt or covert act is anticipated to result in effective coping. It evokes an excitation of CVR through reciprocal SNS activation, including tachycardia and increased myocardial force as well as increased CO and forearm muscle blood flow (see Table 5.3). This heightened beta-adrenergic state is viewed as an adaptive function, permitting the individual to be prepared for action.

Passive coping, however, occurs in situations in which no action appears to be viable and the individual feels helpless, resulting in disengagement and inactivity. Passive coping or behavioral immobilization is characterized by SNS/PNS coactivation that leads to an inhibition of myocardial activity, including bradycardia and decreased CO (see Table 5.3). Under conditions of passive coping, vagally mediated HR changes are viewed as directly related to somatomotor activity, such as HR deceleration due to somatic immobility (e.g., cessation of movements of the mouth, eyes, and head, as well as of postural changes and respiration). In contrast, sympathetically mediated HR acceleration and increased CO under active coping conditions are independent of concurrent somatic activity and are thus viewed as CVR in excess of metabolic requirements, constituting a cardiac–somatic uncoupling.

TABLE 5.3
Cardiovascular Adjustment Patterns of Active Coping, Passive Coping, and Relaxation

Active coping Active avoidance Defense	Inhibitory coping Passive avoidance Aversive vigilance	Relaxation
↑ HR	↓ HR	↓ HR ↓ SV

↑ CO
↑ myocardial
  contractility
↑ BP
  (primarily ↑ SBP)
	↓ CO
	↓ myocardial
	  contractility
	↑ BP
	  (primarily ↑ DBP)
	↑ TPR
		↓ CO
		↓ myocardial
		  contractility
		↓ BP

skeletal muscle
  vasodilation
	skeletal muscle
	  vasoconstriction	

↑ β_1-adrenergic
  activity
↑ SNS activity
↓ vagal tone
	↑ α-adrenergic
	  activity
	↑ SNS activity
	↑ vagal tone
		↓ β_1-adrenergic
		  activity
		↓ SNS activity
		↑ PNS activity

reciprocal SNS activation	SNS/PNS coactivation accentuated antagonism	reciprocal PNS activation

Note. BP = blood pressure; CO = cardiac output; DBP = diastolic blood pressure; HR = heart rate; PNS = parasympathetic nervous system; SNS = sympathetic nervous system; SV = stroke volume; TPR = total peripheral resistance. Data from Schneiderman and McCabe (1989).

A separate class of responses is constituted by relaxation (Schneiderman & McCabe, 1989; see Table 5.3). This is associated with reciprocal PNS activation, leading to decreased CO, SV, myocardial contractility, and BP.

Dual-System Models

Various dual-system models, defining dichotomous brain systems, have been proposed to underlie the organization of emotional behavior and CVR—for example, the behavioral approach and withdrawal systems (Davidson, 1998), the behavioral activation and inhibition systems (Cloninger, 1987), or the appetitive and aversive/defensive systems (Bradley & Lang, 2000).

The model advanced by Bradley and Lang (2000) is of particular relevance to the present discussion because it explicitly addresses CVR in emotion. According to this model, emotions are viewed as organized around a motivational base that can be exhaustively described by two motive features of behavior (its direction and strength), labeled *affective valence* (positive/negative) and *intensity of activation* (arousal). The valence dimension in affective expression is proposed to reflect two motivational brain systems—an appetitive and an aversive/defensive—with arousal representing activation (metabolic and neural) of either system (but see Carver & Harmon-Jones, 2009, for problems of equating positive affect with appetitive motivation and negative affect with aversive motivation). Emotions are defined as activation in one of these motive systems. CVR to affective stimuli is proposed to also reflect a predominant organization according to these motivational variables (Bradley & Lang, 2000). The amount of initial deceleration and acceleratory activity of phasic HR reactions follows affective valence: Unpleasant stimuli produce more initial deceleration, and pleasant stimuli produce greater peak acceleration. The primary direction of HR change may vary, however, with the type of mental processing (e.g., HR has been found to be accelerative in recalling memory images and decelerative in orienting to external stimuli). The arousal dimension, in contrast, is indexed by electrodermal activity, with higher reactivity to either pleasant or unpleasant, compared with neutral, material (Hamm, Schupp, & Weike, 2003).

Polyvagal Theory

To integrate findings of cardiac vagal activation under such opposite conditions as recovery and replenishment as well as behavioral immobilization under extreme fear, several brain–behavioral models propose more than two central systems. Porges's (1995, 2007) polyvagal theory postulates three neural circuits that provide adaptive cardiovascular responses to challenges in a phylogenetically determined hierarchy, from life-threatening, to dangerous, to safe contexts, with higher (i.e., phylogenetically newer) circuits inhibiting lower (i.e., phylogenetically older) circuits. In this hierarchy of adaptive responses, the newest circuit is used first, and if it fails to provide safety, the older circuits are recruited successively.

The phylogenetically oldest component, the immobilization system, depends on the unmyelinated or vegetative vagus that originates in the dorsal motor nucleus of the vagus. This system is suggested to determine the magnitude of neurogenic bradycardia, which can be measured as the low-frequency amplitude of HRV. It is a defense system that leads to passive avoidance, freezing, behavioral shutdown, vaso–vagal syncope, and death feigning. It is associated with reduced metabolic demands and increased pain threshold; the inhibition of movement is coupled with a shift in autonomic state to support immobilization (i.e., apnea and bradycardia).

The mobilization system, phylogenetically newer and hierarchically above the immobilization system, depends on the functioning of the SNS. Activation of this system causes active avoidance, as expressed in fight–flight behaviors and cardiovascular excitation.

Still higher in the hierarchical organization and phylogenetically newer is the social communication or social engagement system that depends on the functions of the myelinated vagus, originating from the nucleus ambiguus. Its effects are reflected in the high-frequency component of HRV (RSA). This neurophysiological circuit provides an inhibitory pathway to slow HR and lower BP, which, by actively reducing sympathetic influences on the heart and dampening hypothalamic–pituitary adrenal axis activity (Porges, 2007), is said to promote the calm states necessary to express social engagement behaviors and to support health, growth, and restoration. The primary vagal regulation of the heart is viewed to function as an active "vagal brake" (Porges, 2007) that is related to behavioral and psychological processes along a continuum: At the one end are prosocial–affiliative interactions, with maintained or increased vagal breaking (causing slowed HR and decreased CO) to support social engagement behaviors and at the other end are adaptive fight–flight behaviors, with removed or reduced vagal breaking (causing accelerated HR and increased CO) to support metabolic requirements for mobilization. RSA magnitude closely parallels inter-and intraindividual variations in emotion expression, social communication, and behavioral state (but see Grossman & Taylor, 2007, for a critical discussion of polyvagal theory).

Reinforcement Sensitivity Theory

Gray's (1982; Gray & McNaughton, 2000) reinforcement sensitivity theory is similarly based on three functionally distinct yet interdependent motivational systems: a behavioral activation system (BAS), a behavioral inhibition system (BIS), and a fight–flight system (FFS). The BAS initiates behavior in response to stimuli signaling reward (approach) or relieving nonpunishment (active avoidance). Activation of the BAS generates the appetitively hopeful emotion of "anticipatory pleasure." Activity of the BAS has been associated with CVR. Whereas Fowles (1980) suggested HR as an index of BAS activation, based on findings of incentive effects on HR, cardiac–somatic coupling, and HR increase in connection with active coping in the face of threat, Beauchaine (2001) suggested PEP as a more specific index of BAS activity, reflected in beta-adrenergically mediated sympathetic influences on the heart.

The BIS inhibits behavior in response to cues for punishment (passive avoidance) or frustrative nonreward (extinction). Updates of the theory (Gray & McNaughton, 2000) capitalize on the role of the BIS in the resolution of goal conflict in general. This system generates the "watch-out-for-danger" emotion of anxiety. An association between electrodermal activity and BIS activation has been suggested, because nonspecific fluctuations increase in response to threats of physical punishment or ego threat (Beauchaine, 2001; Fowles, 1980).

The FFS was originally hypothesized to be sensitive to unconditioned aversive stimuli only (i.e., innately painful stimuli). According to the updated model, the FFS responds to all aversive stimuli, conditioned and unconditioned. This system is responsible for avoidance and escape behaviors, mediating the acute "get-me-out-of-this-place" emotion of fear. Beauchaine (2001) suggested that vagal effects on the heart reflect activity of the FFS system. Specifically, excessive vagal withdrawal (i.e., reduced RSA) occurs under negative emotional states, most notably anger, anxiety, and panic that represent excessive fight–flight responding.

Taken together, the BAS and the BIS are viewed to relate to SNS control, with the BAS controlling CVR and the BIS electrodermal activation, whereas the FFS is under PNS control. Thus, motivational predispositions, as reflected in SNS activation, are viewed to fall under BAS and BIS control, whereas regulatory functioning, as reflected in PNS activation, falls under FFS control.

Conceptual Implications: 2 + x Behavioral Systems

Recent brain–behavioral models agree that a unitary construct of activation or arousal fails to adequately capture the richness of emotional responses (Fowles, 1980), but there is no consensus on the minimal number of brain–behavioral systems. Various theories propose two opposing brain–behavioral systems (e.g., Bradley & Lang, 2000). Yet other models advance a third system with a specialized emergency function in addition to two systems coordinating motivational direction: Porges (1995, 2007) postulated an emergency system as a last resort that mediates behavioral shutdown and freezing (i.e., passive avoidance). Gray (1982; Gray & McNaughton, 2000) conceptualized the FFS as an emergency system, whereas BIS or BAS predominance decides direction of response. In both theories, the third system mediates the fear response and is associated with cardiac vagal dominance. Beyond such conceptualizations, recent research (Stemmler, Aue, & Wacker, 2007) has highlighted the possibility that there exist neurobiologically basic emotion systems, suggesting an even larger number of brain–behavioral systems (e.g., Panksepp, 1982).

Cardiovascular Response Organization in Emotion Based on Behavioral Modes

Whereas the just-discussed general brain–behavior systems have obvious advantages in helping to identify commonalities and broad dimensions of CVR in emotion, differences among patterns of CVR in emotions become particularly evident when considering specifics in the expression of emotional behavior. Specific modes of behavioral coping, related brain centers, and their temporal integration in adaptive behavior is the focus of the subsequent section. Although the defensive system will serve as an example, different behavioral modes are similarly assumed to operate in the appetitive system (e.g., Berridge & Robinson, 2003).

Basic Modes of Defensive Coping

Different defensive coping strategies, such as confrontational defense, vigilance, freezing, playing dead, or defeat, constitute highly specialized, preformed constellations of somatomotor, autonomic (including cardiovascular), and hormonal adjustments (Folkow, 2000). The brain selects the most appropriate among these reaction patterns for coping with the actual situation on the basis of continuously updated information about the environment it receives from sensory inputs. Folkow (2000) speculated that "there may exist as many [of these patterns] as there are distinctly different basic emotions as well as their combinations" (p. 112).

CVR in anger, for example, has been related to the confrontation response (Stemmler, 2009): Primarily sympathetic activation of the CVS is viewed to support persistent muscular, isometric exertion. Consequentially increased DBP and TPR counteract the decreased effective perfusion pressure in strongly contracted muscles and ensure sufficient blood supply. CVR in fear, on the other hand, has been related to a flight or vigilance response (Stemmler, 2009), engaging a protective reflex in anticipation of life-threatening blood loss: The SNS is strongly activated and the PNS strongly deactivated with increased HR and myocardial contractility. Strong alpha-adrenergically mediated vasoconstriction in the kidney, the muscles, the viscera, and the skin centralizes the distribution of blood to ensure supply to the heart, brain, and lungs. This peripheral vasoconstriction is expressed in paleness of the face and cold sweaty hands. CVR in emotion is thus viewed as organized to optimize behavioral performance of the organism.

Central Structures Matching Modes of Defensive Coping
to Environmental Demands

Expression of different modes of emotional coping within the defensive system and associated differential patterns of CVR have been found to be mediated by different regions of the midbrain periaqueductal gray (PAG; Bandler & Shipley, 1994). Specific columnar circuits of the PAG are proposed to coordinate strategies for dealing with different environmental demands that are either escapable or inescapable and in which the stressor is either of a physical or psychological nature. Moreover, the PAG is implicated in promoting recovery and healing when the stressor has passed.

Table 5.4 contrasts brain circuits mediating emotional coping responses with different types of stress and associated defensive strategies, patterns of CVR, and antinociceptive effects. The lateral PAG neuronal column mediates active coping strategies: either confrontation (rostral region) or flight (caudal region) from a source of escapable threat or pain. The hypertension elicited in active coping reflects a specific pattern according to the type of defensive behavior expressed (Keay & Bandler, 2001): In the context of the

TABLE 5.4

Brain Circuits Mediating Emotional Coping With Different Types of Stress

	Active emotional coping		Passive emotional coping
	Confrontational defense	Escape or flight	Conservation–withdrawal
Type of stressor	escapable psychological (threat)	= physical (pain)	inescapable physical (pain) or psychological (threat)
Region of PAG	lateral PAG rostral region	= caudal region	ventrolateral PAG
Defensive strategy	engagement with environment facing of stressor or threat	= turning away/running from stressor or threat	disengagement from environment quiescence or immobility ↓ somatomotor activity ↓ reactivity to environment/↓ vigilance
Autonomic response pattern	sympathoexcitation (SNS ↑) hypertension tachycardia ↓ blood flow to skeletal muscles ↓ blood flow to viscera ↑ blood flow to face	= = ↑ blood flow to skeletal muscles ↓ blood flow to viscera ↓ blood flow to face	sympathoinhibition (SNS ↓) hypotension bradycardia
Analgesia	non-opioid	=	opioid-mediated

Note. Same reaction as indicated for confrontational defense; PAG = midbrain periaqueductal gray; SNS = sympathetic nervous system. Data from Keay and Bandler (2001).

flight response, blood flow is increased to skeletal muscles but decreased to the viscera and the extracranial vasculature supplying the face. In the context of confrontational defense, blood flow is decreased to skeletal muscles and viscera but increased to the face. The ventrolateral PAG neuronal column, in contrast, mediates a more passive coping strategy (e.g., observed in response to severe hemorrhage, pain arising from deep structures, or repeated defeat in social encounters). The ventrolateral PAG might thus function to lessen the cardiovascular and emotional impact of an inescapable stressful or painful encounter and help to promote healing and later recovery.

Threat-Imminence Model

A threat-imminence model can explain the observation that behavioral tendencies and CVR in fear change as emotion intensity increases. Fanselow (1994) suggested that the defensive behavior system has three modes that are activated by different levels of threat or predator imminence. Low levels of fear are activated when entering an area that has some predatory potential and promotes preencounter defenses to reduce an animal's risk of predation. Moderate levels of fear are activated when a predator is detected in the environment and promote postencounter defenses. Extremely high levels of fear are activated when contact with the predator is occurring or inevitable and promote circa-strike defenses.

As an analog to predator imminence, Bradley and Lang (2000) proposed that stages in the "defensive cascade" are controlled by increases in judged arousal. In particular, the amplitude of the orienting (and defensive) HR response is viewed as related to an arousal continuum. At lower levels of activation, aversively motivated attending does not fundamentally differ from appetitive orienting: a brief, modest, parasympathetically driven HR deceleration that becomes larger and more sustained as stimuli are perceived to be more arousing (fear bradycardia), consistent with the hypothesis of attentional resource allocation to meaningful input. The probability of an overt defensive action increases with increasing stimulus arousal (i.e., predator imminence) occurring in the context of an increasing attentive focus and a parallel, still increasing bradycardia. Only at highest activation levels, just before action, vagal control of the heart is released, giving way to a sympathetically driven acceleration that is the classical defense response (fear tachycardia). Thus, considering the development of emotion over an arousal continuum allows structuring CVR.

Conceptual Implications: Specialized Subsystems

Recent research has started to shed light on the mechanisms by which the human brain processes social context and derives differentiated CVR. In an elegant series of studies, Wager and collaborators (Wager, Waugh, et al., 2009; Wager, van Ast, et al., 2009) demonstrated that specialized neural subsystems process social evaluative threat and mediate HR responses as well as subjective feelings of anxiety. According to their findings, two dissociable subregions of medial prefrontal cortex—dorsal and ventral—have differential roles in affective appraisal, with qualitatively different consequences for threat-induced cardiac reactivity. These results suggest pathways for the translation of social threats into both CVR and experiential responses and provide some preliminary steps toward building a model of cortical–brain stem–cardiovascular pathways in humans.

Cardiovascular Response Organization in Emotion Based on Appraisal Processes

A large number of perceptual and evaluative factors further modulates how individuals cope with environmental challenges. These are addressed by appraisal models that link emotion and CVR.

Componential Process Model

Appraisal models of emotion suggest breaking up the emotion process into molecular appraisal processes. Appraisals produce a nuanced emotional reaction and the outcome of each appraisal—rather than whole emotions—is suggested to cause direct changes in brain, body, and subjective feeling (Scherer, 1987, 2009). Scherer (2009) assigned the ANS, and with that the CVS, a regulatory support function in emotion. Instead of action tendencies as mediator between appraisal outcomes and CVR, it is assumed that there are direct connections of appraisals with cardiovascular response modalities, independent of action tendencies.

The componential patterning theory (Scherer, 1987) predicts specific cardiovascular changes under different emotions. According to this theory, the outcome of each appraisal changes the cardiovascular activation state. Changes produced by the outcome of a preceding appraisal are modified by subsequent ones. Hence, the patterning of CVR is specific to the unique evaluation "history" of the respective stimulus. To avoid constant oscillation of the organism, efferent effects occur only if a minimal degree of closure (i.e., definitiveness) of the evaluation of a specific appraisal has been achieved. Moments of closure for different appraisals are assumed to be sequentially ordered because outcomes of some appraisals constitute inputs for other appraisals. Hence, closure of the later appraisal can only be achieved after closure of the prior one has occurred. The cumulative effects of this process are expected to constitute emotion-specific profiles of CVR. Table 5.5 gives an overview of predicted effects of appraisal outcomes on CVR.

TABLE 5.5

Appraisal Outcomes, Associated Organismic Functions, and Cardiovascular Response

Appraisal outcome	Organismic functions	Cardiovascular response
Novelty and goal relevance		
Novel and goal relevant	orienting response focusing attention on arousing event	↓ HR; vasomotor changes
Intrinsic pleasantness		
Pleasant	sensitization preparing for incorporation	↓ HR
Unpleasant	defense response preparing for rejection	↑ HR
Goal conduciveness		
Conducive	relaxation (rest and recovery) trophotropic shift	↓ HR
Obstructive	activation (preparation for action) ergotropic shift	↑ adrenaline secretion, HR, SV; ↓ FT; vasoconstriction in skin; vasodilation in heart and striped muscles
Coping potential		
No or low control	organismic adjustment, withdrawal trophotropic dominance	↓ HR
High control/high power	assertion and dominance ergotropic–trophotropic balance	↑ SBP, DBP, skin temperature upper torso; ↓ HR (baroreceptor-mediated); redistribution of blood to head, chest, and hands
Control possible/low power	protection of organism, submission extreme ergotropic dominance	↑ HR, SV, SBP, FPA; ↓ DBP, skin temperature; vasoconstriction in skin; increased blood flow to striped muscles
Normative significance		
Requirements met or surpassed	relaxation, bolstering of self-esteem ergotropic shift	elements of pleasantness and high-power response
Requirements unmet	organismic activation, self-consciousness ergotropic shift	elements of the unpleasantness and low-power response, particularly blushing as an effect of peripheral blood flow to the face

Note. DBP = diastolic blood pressure; FPA = finger pulse amplitude; FT = finger temperature; HR = heart rate; SBP = systolic blood pressure; SV = stroke volume. Adapted from "The Dynamic Architecture of Emotion: Evidence for the Component Process Model," by K. R. Scherer, 2009, *Cognition and Emotion, 23,* pp. 1311–1313. Copyright 2009 by Taylor & Francis. Adapted with permission.

Motivational Intensity Theory

Research carried out within the framework of motivational intensity theory (Brehm & Self, 1989) can also be interpreted from an appraisal perspective of emotion (e.g., Kreibig, Gendolla, & Scherer, 2010). According to this model, motivation-based appraisals influence beta-adrenergically mediated CVR in the context of task performance (Wright, 1996, 1998) and subsequent evaluative feedback processing (Kreibig et al., 2010). This relation is primarily evident in measures of myocardial contractility (e.g., PEP or systolic BP, although HR and DBP also exhibit this relation under certain conditions).

Specifically, in task contexts, myocardial contractility has been demonstrated to vary proportionally with perceived control. Perceived control, in turn, is determined by the appraised character of activity that must be carried out to alter an outcome (difficulty level), the appraised effectiveness of that activity in accomplishing its purpose (instrumentality), and the appraised efficacy of the performer to do what must be done (ability; Wright, 1998). An upper limit of effort investment, and thus CVR, is determined by potential motivation that is influenced by the importance of the consequences associated with a successful outcome of the behavior, a person's current needs and goals with respect to the associated consequences, and the perceived association strength between a successful behavior outcome and the attainment of the desired consequences (Wright, 1996), as well as the degree of self-involvement (Gendolla, 2004). Unlike reinforcement sensitivity theory, this approach postulates no difference of effects on CVR depending on approach or avoidance motivation but rather that the effect depends on the intensity of motivation.

Biopsychosocial Model

The biopsychosocial model (Blascovich & Katkin, 1993; Blascovich, Mendes, Tomaka, Salomon, & Seery, 2003) links challenge versus threat appraisal in task-engaging motivated performance situations to differential patterns of CVR. If appraised personal resources are high relative to appraised demands of the performance situation, a response pattern of challenge is predicted, with increased ventricular contractility (as indexed by shortened PEP), increased CO, and decreased vascular resistance. However, if appraised demands exceed appraised personal resources, a response pattern of threat is predicted, with little or no change in CO and no change or an increase in vascular resistance. Increased HR from baseline to task performance, viewed as reflecting task engagement, is said to be common to both challenge and threat (however, see Wright & Kirby, 2003, for a substantial critique of the model and its empirical tests).

Conceptual Implications: Situation as Perceived

Because it is ultimately the individual's perception and evaluation of the situation that determines the emotional response to it, appraisal models represent a promising route of theory development. Such models bear the potential of explaining differential emotional responses, for example, between different persons within the same context or within the same person at different times. Still, the various appraisal models do not agree on the number and types of proposed appraisals. Moreover, although most appraisal models propose either a direct (e.g., Scherer, 2009) or indirect link (e.g., via action tendencies; Frijda, 1986) between appraisal outcomes and organization of CVR in emotion, little research has tested this hypothesis.

CONCLUSION

This review shows that models of CVR in emotion assume different conceptual levels on which an organizing principle may operate. Three major levels were identified: a peripheral physiological level, a brain–behavioral level, and a psychological level. On each of these levels, different models suggest different means by which cardiovascular response organization might be achieved, such as the functioning of autonomic systems or of transmitter substances on the peripheral physiological level, the functioning of behavioral systems or behavioral modes on the brain–behavioral level, and the functioning of appraisal modules on the psychological level.

As noted at the outset, models on different conceptual levels can have complementary value. For example, a basic-coping-strategies view, described in the section on the functioning of behavioral modes, can provide a complementary perspective to those models of fear and anger that address the physiological level of cardiovascular response organization, described in the section on the functioning of transmitter substances.

Clearly, the suggested classification of theories to levels depends on the relative weighing of certain aspects of each theory. It is certain that Folkow's (2000) schematic of different response modes does not solely derive from behaviors but also strongly draws on analysis of the specific structure and function of the sympatho–adreno–medullary system and also acknowledges the role of subjective evaluations. Similarly, Porges's (1995, 2007) proposal of a polyvagal theory postulates three distinct behavioral systems based on the view that there exist three distinguishable autonomic systems: an SNS as well as two separate vagal systems. Thus, as suggested here, the organization of models into level rather considers each theory in the larger context of the various models discussed.

Taken together, these models suggest different relations between emotion, motivation, and CVR. Although alternative sequences are possible, where CVR or motivation may be the first step in the chain of events, in all these models, emotion was seen as the instigator of cardiovascular change and motivational adaptation. Models on the physiological level suggest an interpretation of CVR as reflecting a modification of ANS activity in emotion for achieving an adaptive organismic state. Models on the brain–behavioral level imply that emotion modifies action readiness, as seen in CVR: The behavioral coping approach interprets CVR as reflecting action preparation in emotion, dual-system models interpret CVR in emotion as reflecting activation of brain–behavioral systems, and the behavioral-modes view interprets CVR in emotion as associated with specific situation-dependent implementations of behavioral adaptations. On the psychological level, the componential process model sees CVR as reflecting specific appraisal steps in the process of emotion generation that has motivation as a component and outcome. Motivational intensity theory can be taken as seeing CVR as reflecting the motivational input and motivational outcome of emotion. And the biopsychosocial model suggests an interpretation of CVR as indicating threat or challenge appraisals and associated means of behavioral coping.

Synthesizing these perspectives, CVR in emotion is suggested to reflect a modified motivational state as the outcome of emotion. It is important that although the correlation between emotion and observable behavior has been noted to be low, this view capitalizes on the relation between emotion and impulsive action (i.e., the uncontrolled expression of behavioral tendencies or action readiness). Thus, although emotion is viewed as being associated with cardiovascular mobilization for action, expressed behavior might still differ (Frijda, 2010). Conceptualizing emotion as an acute motive state, CVR in emotion might thus reflect acute resource mobilization under the motivational outcome state of emotion or—to borrow Frijda's (2010) words—cardiovascular responses in emotion "appear largely to result from anticipation of action requirements, action preparations, motivated abstention of action, and immobilization" (p. 576).

REFERENCES

Ax, A. F. (1953). The physiological differentiation between fear and anger in humans. *Psychosomatic Medicine, 15,* 433–442.

Bandler, R., & Shipley, M. T. (1994). Columnar organization in the midbrain periaqueductal gray: Modules for emotional expression? *Trends in Neurosciences, 17,* 379–389. doi:10.1016/0166-2236(94)90047-7

Beauchaine, T. (2001). Vagal tone, development, and Gray's motivational theory: Toward an integrated model of autonomic nervous system functioning in psychopathology. *Development and Psychopathology, 13*, 183–214. doi:10.1017/S0954579401002012

Benarroch, E. E., Daube, J. R., Flemming, K. D., & Westmoreland, B. F. (2008). *Mayo Clinic medical neurosciences: Organized by neurological systems and levels*. Florence, KY: Mayo Clinic Scientific Press.

Berntson, G. G., Cacioppo, J. T., & Quigley, K. S. (1991). Autonomic determinism: The modes of autonomic control, the doctrine of autonomic space, and the laws of autonomic constraint. *Psychological Review, 98*, 459–487. doi:10.1037/0033-295X.98.4.459

Berridge, K. C., & Robinson, T. E. (2003). Parsing reward. *Trends in Neurosciences, 26*, 507–513. doi:10.1016/S0166-2236(03)00233-9

Blascovich, J., & Katkin, E. S. (Eds.). (1993). *Cardiovascular reactivity to psychological stress and disease*. Washington, DC: American Psychological Association. doi:10.1037/10125-000

Blascovich, J., Mendes, W. B., Tomaka, J., Salomon, K., & Seery, M. (2003). The robust nature of the biopsychosocial model challenge and threat: A reply to Wright and Kirby. *Personality and Social Psychology Review, 7*, 234–243. doi:10.1207/S15327957PSPR0703_03

Bradley, M. M., & Lang, P. J. (2000). Measuring emotion: Behavior, feeling, and physiology. In R. Lane & L. Nadel (Eds.), *Cognitive neuroscience of emotion* (pp. 242–276). New York, NY: Oxford University Press.

Brehm, J. W., & Self, E. A. (1989). The intensity of motivation. *Annual Review of Psychology, 40*, 109–131. doi:10.1146/annurev.ps.40.020189.000545

Cannon, W. B. (1915). *Bodily changes in pain, hunger, fear, and rage*. New York, NY: Appleton. doi:10.1037/10013-000

Carver, C. S., & Harmon-Jones, E. (2009). Anger is an approach-related affect: Evidence and implications. *Psychological Bulletin, 135*, 183–204. doi:10.1037/a0013965

Cloninger, C. R. (1987). A systematic method for clinical depression and classification of personality variants. *Archives of General Psychiatry, 44*, 573–588.

Davidson, R. J. (1998). Affective style and affective disorders: Perspectives from affective neuroscience. *Cognition and Emotion, 12*, 307–330. doi:10.1080/026999398379628

Fanselow, M. S. (1994). Neural organization of the defensive behavior system responsible for fear. *Psychonomic Bulletin & Review, 1*, 429–438. doi:10.3758/BF03210947

Folkow, B. (2000). Perspectives on the integrative functions of the "sympatho–adrenomedullary system." *Autonomic Neuroscience: Basic and Clinical, 83*, 101–115. doi:10.1016/S1566-0702(00)00171-5

Fowles, D. C. (1980). The three arousal model: Implications of Gray's two-factor learning theory for heart rate, electrodermal activity, and psychopathy. *Psychophysiology, 17*, 87–104. doi:10.1111/j.1469-8986.1980.tb00117.x

Frijda, N. H. (1986). *The emotions*. Cambridge, England: Cambridge University Press.

Frijda, N. H. (2000). The psychologist's point of view. In M. Lewis & J. M. Haviland-Jones (Eds.), *Handbook of emotions* (pp. 59–74). New York, NY: Guilford Press.

Frijda, N. H. (2010). Impulsive action and motivation. *Biological Psychology, 84*, 570–579. doi:10.1016/j.biopsycho.2010.01.005

Funkenstein, D. H., King, S. R., & Drolette, M. (1954). The direction of anger during a laboratory stress-inducing situation. *Psychosomatic Medicine, 16*, 404–413.

Gellhorn, E. (1964). Motion and emotion: The role of proprioception in the physiology and pathology of the emotions. *Psychological Review, 71*, 457–472. doi:10.1037/h0039834

Gellhorn, E. (1970). The emotions and the ergotropic and trophotropic systems. *Psychologische Forschung, 34*, 48–66. doi:10.1007/BF00422862

Gendolla, G. H. E. (2004). The intensity of motivation when the self is involved: An application of Brehm's theory of motivation to effort-related cardiovascular response. In R. A. Wright & S. S. Greenberg (Eds.), *Motivational analyses of social behavior* (pp. 205–224). Mahwah, NJ: Erlbaum.

Gray, J. A. (1982). *The neuropsychology of anxiety*. New York, NY: Oxford University Press.

Gray, J. A., & McNaughton, N. (2000). *The neuropsychology of anxiety: An enquiry into the functions of the septo-hippocampal system*. Oxford, England: Oxford University Press.

Grossman, P., & Taylor, E. W. (2007). Toward understanding respiratory sinus arrhythmia: Relations to cardiac vagal tone, evolution, and biobehavioral functions. *Biological Psychology, 74*, 263–285. doi:10.1016/j.biopsycho.2005.11.014

Hamm, A., Schupp, H. T., & Weike, A. I. (2003). Motivational organization of emotions: Autonomic changes, cortical responses, and reflex modulation. In R. J. Davidson, K. R. Scherer, & H. H. Goldsmith (Eds.), *Handbook of affective sciences* (pp. 187–211). New York, NY: Oxford University Press.

Hess, W. R. (1957). *Functional organization of the diencephalon*. New York, NY: Grune & Stratton.

James, W. (1884). What is an emotion? *Mind, os-IX*, 188–205. doi:10.1093/mind/os-IX.34.188

Keay, K. A., & Bandler, R. (2001). Parallel circuits mediating distinct emotional coping reactions to different types of stress. *Neuroscience and Biobehavioral Reviews, 25*, 669–678. doi:10.1016/S0149-7634(01)00049-5

Kling, C. (1933). The role of the parasympathetics in emotions. *Psychological Review, 40*, 368–380. doi:10.1037/h0074922

Koizumi, K., Terui, N., Kollai, M., & Brooks, C. M. (1982). Functional significance of coactivation of vagal and sympathetic cardiac nerves. *Proceedings of the National Academy of Sciences of the United States of America, 79*, 2116–2120. doi:10.1073/pnas.79.6.2116

Kolodyazhniy, V., Kreibig, S. D., Roth, W. T., Gross, J. J., & Wilhelm, F. H. (in press). An affective computing approach to physiological emotion specificity: Towards subject-independent and stimulus-independent classification of film-induced emotions. Psychophysiology. doi:10.1111/j.1469-8986.2010.01170.x

Kreibig, S. D. (2010). Autonomic nervous system activity in emotion: A review. Biological Psychology, 84, 394–421. doi:10.1016/j.biopsycho.2010.03.010

Kreibig, S. D., Gendolla, G. H. E., & Scherer, K. R. (2010). Psychophysiological effects of emotional responding to goal attainment. Biological Psychology, 84, 474–487. doi:10.1016/j.biopsycho.2009.11.004

Obrist, P. A. (1981). Cardiovascular psychophysiology. New York, NY: Plenum Press.

Panksepp, J. (1982). Toward a general psychobiological theory of emotions. The Behavioral and Brain Sciences, 5, 407–422. doi:10.1017/S0140525X00012759

Porges, S. W. (1995). Orienting in a defensive world: Mammalian modifications of our evolutionary heritage. A Polyvagal Theory. Psychophysiology, 32, 301–318. doi:10.1111/j.1469-8986.1995.tb01213.x

Porges, S. W. (2007). The polyvagal perspective. Biological Psychology, 74, 116–143. doi:10.1016/j.biopsycho.2006.06.009

Scherer, K. R. (1987). Toward a dynamic theory of emotion: The component process model of affective states. Geneva Studies in Emotion and Communication, 1, 1–98.

Scherer, K. R. (2009). The dynamic architecture of emotion: Evidence for the component process model. Cognition and Emotion, 23, 1307–1351. doi:10.1080/02699930902928969

Schneiderman, N., & McCabe, P. M. (1989). Psychophysiologic strategies in laboratory research. In N. Schneiderman, S. M. Weiss, & P. G. Kaufman (Eds.), Handbook of research methods in cardiovascular behavioral medicine (pp. 349–364). New York, NY: Plenum Press.

Stemmler, G. (1992). The vagueness of specificity: Models of peripheral physiological emotion specificity in emotion theories and their experimental discriminability. Journal of Psychophysiology, 6, 17–28.

Stemmler, G. (2003). Methodological considerations in the psychophysiological study of emotion. In R. J. Davidson, K. R. Scherer, & H. Goldsmith (Eds.), Handbook of affective sciences (pp. 225–255). New York, NY: Oxford University Press.

Stemmler, G. (2009). Somatoviszerale aktivierung [Somatovisceral activation]. In N. Birbaumer, D. Frey, J. Kuhl, & G. Stemmler (Eds.), Psychologie der emotion, enzyklopädie der psychologie [Psychology of emotion, encyclopedia of psychology] (pp. 314–361). Göttingen, Germany: Hogrefe and Huber.

Stemmler, G., Aue, T., & Wacker, J. (2007). Anger and fear: Separable effects of emotion and motivational direction on somatovisceral responses. International Journal of Psychophysiology, 66, 141–153. doi:10.1016/j.ijpsycho.2007.03.019

Vingerhoets, A. J. (1985). The role of the parasympathetic division of the autonomic nervous system in stress and the emotions. International Journal of Psychosomatics, 32, 28–34.

Vollmer, R. R. (1996). Selective neural regulation of epinephrine and norepinephrine cells in the adrenal medulla: Cardiovascular implications. *Clinical and Experimental Hypertension, 18*, 731–751. doi:10.3109/10641969609081778

Wager, T. D., van Ast, V. A., Hughes, B. L., Davidson, M. L., Lindquist, M. A., & Ochsner, K. N. (2009). Brain mediators of cardiovascular responses to social threat: Part II. Prefrontal–subcortical pathways and relationship with anxiety. *NeuroImage, 47*, 836–851. doi:10.1016/j.neuroimage.2009.05.044

Wager, T. D., Waugh, C. E., Lindquist, M., Noll, D. C., Fredrickson, B. L., & Taylor, S. F. (2009). Brain mediators of cardiovascular responses to social threat: Part I. Reciprocal dorsal and ventral sub-regions of the medial prefrontal cortex and heart rate reactivity. *NeuroImage, 47*, 821–835. doi:10.1016/j.neuro image.2009.05.043

Wright, R. A. (1996). Brehm's theory of motivation as a model of effort and cardiovascular response. In P. M. Gollwitzer & J. A. Bargh (Eds.), *The psychology of action: Linking cognition and motivation to behavior* (pp. 424–453). New York, NY: Guilford Press.

Wright, R. A. (1998). Ability perception and cardiovascular response to behavioral challenge. In M. Kofta, G. Weary, & G. Sedek (Eds.), *Control in action: Cognitive and motivational mechanisms* (pp. 197–232). New York, NY: Plenum Press.

Wright, R. A., & Kirby, L. D. (2003). Cardiovascular correlates of challenge and threat appraisals: A critical examination of the biopsychosocial analysis. *Personality and Social Psychology Review, 7*, 216–233. doi:10.1207/S15327957PSPR0703_02

Zhou, Z., Zhu, G., Hariri, A. R., Enoch, M.-A., Scott, D., Sinha, R., . . . Goldman, D. (2008, April 24). Genetic variation in human NPY expression affects stress response and emotion. *Nature, 452*, 997–1001. doi:10.1038/nature06858

C. AFFECT AND STRESSFUL CONFLICT

6

EMOTIONAL INTENSITY THEORY AND ITS CARDIOVASCULAR IMPLICATIONS FOR EMOTIONAL STATES

ANCA M. MIRON AND JACK W. BREHM

In this chapter, we consider the implications of emotional intensity theory (Brehm, 1999; Brehm & Miron, 2006) for the study of emotion, motivation, and their cardiovascular (CV) effects. We first examine the assumptions made by this theory and then review research examining the relationship between emotional arousal and CV responses. Finally, using this theoretical framework, we make predictions with regard to the effect of obstacles to emotion on CV responses. For brevity of discussion, we focus our attention on the emotion of anger and its associated subjective, behavioral, and physiological responses.

EMOTIONAL INTENSITY THEORY

As other theorists have proposed (e.g., Duffy, 1941; Lazarus, 1991; Leeper, 1948; Oatley & Johnson-Laird, 1987), emotional intensity theory suggests that emotions have motivational properties because they furnish energy and direction for the execution of appropriate instrumental behaviors. Specifically, emotions promote fast adaptation to situational demands by helping individuals identify relevant and important events and by urging, guiding, and maintaining the behaviors necessary for dealing with these events (Brehm & Brummett, 1998; Levenson, 1999). For instance, if someone is insulted and experiences anger, all systems and resources are coordinated so that the person can deal efficiently with the situation while ignoring all other signals and events.

Because emotions are viewed as motivational states, it follows that their intensity should be affected by factors similar to those influencing the intensity of regular motivational states (Brehm, 1999). Affective systems are designed to conserve energy and mobilize resources to achieve a particular emotional goal. Events that interfere with the experience of an emotion can influence the intensity of that emotion. In the case of anger, events that interfere with feeling or expressing anger can affect its intensity.

Prior work (Brehm & Self, 1989; Brehm, Wright, Solomon, Silka, & Greenberg, 1983; Wright & Brehm, 1989) has suggested that the intensity of energization depends on goal importance and difficulty of achieving the goal. When difficulty of achieving the goal is unknown, motivational intensity is a function of goal importance. When keeping the importance of the goal constant, motivational intensity varies as a cubic function of difficulty. It is assumed that the motivational system is designed to conserve energy, and little effort will be mobilized if the goal is easy to achieve. However, the more difficult it becomes to achieve a goal, the more energy will be mobilized, up to a point where the goal becomes too difficult or impossible to achieve. In this latter case, the intensity of motivation will be completely reduced as the person will stop caring about the goal.

Similarly, if emotion indeed operates like a motivational state, its intensity should be a function not only of its instigation but also of the obstacles to experiencing or feeling the emotion. These obstacles are called *deterrents*. Thus, emotional intensity should vary as a cubic function of deterrence, just as motivational arousal varies as a cubic function of the difficulty of goal attainment. The theoretical predictions for anger, our target emotion, are displayed in Figure 6.1.

Deterrents are not restricted to factors that impede the expression of emotion, such as, in the case of anger, knowing that the insulter has power and resources to retaliate, which would diminish the angered person's urge to aggress. Deterrents can also be factors that interfere with the feeling of the emotion, such as a reason for feeling a different emotion. If someone is feeling angry and is given a reason for feeling happy, that reason can interfere with the continuation of anger. According to this paradigm (Brehm & Miron, 2006), two distinctly different emotions cannot occur at the same time (e.g., we cannot feel both angry and happy at the same moment). While we are feeling angry, we cannot simultaneously feel a second emotion because the affective system is busy dealing with the event that caused anger. Neverthe-

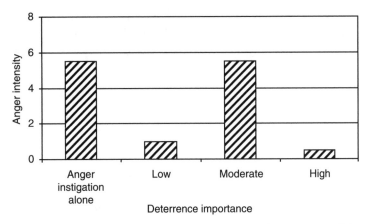

Figure 6.1. Predicted anger intensity as a cubic function of importance of deterrence to anger.

less, the reason for feeling a distinctly different emotion (happiness) while we are feeling angry affects the difficulty of maintaining anger, thereby affecting the intensity of anger in a cubic fashion.

Previous work has found strong support for the predicted cubic or non-monotonic effect of various deterrents on sadness and happiness (Brehm & Brummett, 1998; Brehm, Brummett, & Harvey, 1999; Miron, Parkinson, & Brehm, 2007; Silvia & Brehm, 2001), anger (Miron, Brummett, Ruggles, & Brehm, 2008) and on more general positive and negative affect (Brehm, Miron, & Miller, 2009). For instance, we tested whether happiness was responsive to deterrence in the form of unpleasant news about a proposed increase in graduation requirements by three, six, or nine credits (Miron et al., 2007). Across two studies, when there was a relatively insignificant reason for feeling anger (three-credit increase), happiness was reduced. As it became more difficult for participants to feel happy (six-credit increase), happiness increased. However, when the negative news became extremely important, the reason for feeling anger (nine-credit increase) overcame the reason for feeling happy, significantly reducing participants' happiness. Similarly, we found that positive affect due to truffle tasting decreased when the bad news to student participants about a potential rise in tuition was minor (i.e., students expected a 2% tuition increase), rose when participants expected a moderately large rise in tuition (8%), and decreased when participants expected a large rise in tuition (16%; Brehm et al., 2009).

As mentioned, there are at least two types of deterrence: *affective deterrence* in the form of reasons for feeling a different emotion and *instrumental deterrence* in the form of difficulty of carrying out the emotion-urged behavior. Schmitt, Miller, Branscombe, and Brehm (2008) investigated whether the difficulty of making reparations for gender inequality affected the intensity of men's guilt. Guilt increased with the difficulty of reparation and was reduced when it was very difficult to repair the inequality. Similarly, Miron and Ferguson (2009) found that the intensity of prejudiced affect was nonmonotonically affected by the manipulated difficulty of refusing to help a disliked outgroup.

APPLYING EMOTIONAL INTENSITY THEORY TO THE STUDY OF ANGER AND ITS CARDIOVASCULAR EFFECTS

According to emotional intensity theory, deterrence to anger should nonmonotonically affect anger intensity. Theoretically, if there is an important reason for feeling angry, the intensity of anger should be high when deterrence to anger is unknown (i.e., when the angered person is not aware of any salient reason for not feeling that way). A small deterrent should result in low anger and then, as the importance of deterrence increases, so should anger intensity, up to a point where deterrence becomes too great and anger is reduced. Given the energizing properties of anger (Novaco, 1975), deterrence to this emotion should also have a cubic effect on anger-associated CV activity, particularly on sympathetic nervous system (SNS) mobilization. This should be most evident in increased systolic blood pressure. Before we discuss our specific CV predictions, we first examine the existing evidence regarding the effect of deterrence on anger intensity and then review the CV processes associated with anger experience.

Previous research on reducing anger has only partially looked at the effect of deterrents on anger. Baron (1983) examined whether induction of emotional states incompatible with anger (e.g., amusement) could effectively reduce anger. According to both Baron's and our approach, people are incapable of experiencing two emotions at the same time unless a new emotion (a more important goal or a *high deterrent*) will replace the original emotion of anger. A large deterrent in the form of a cool drink, a gift, or flattery (Baron, Fortin, Frei, Hauver, & Shack, 1990) was found to reduce anger and even replace it with an incompatible emotion. However, anger intensity can be influenced not only by reasons that are more important than the event that caused anger (high deterrents) but also by reasons that are less important than the anger event (i.e., low to moderate deterrents). A low deterrent should reduce emotional intensity, whereas a moderate deterrent should maintain high intensity.

In a study by Mueller and Donnerstein (1977), participants were either angered or treated in a neutral manner by a confederate and then were subjected to one of three forms of humor (high arousing, low arousing, nonhumor). Aggression was high in the nonhumor condition. When given the opportunity to aggress against the confederate, female participants (but not males) reduced their aggression after exposure to low arousing humor, whereas maintaining aggression at a high level for highly arousing humor. These nonmonotonic effects parallel the findings obtained by Donnerstein, Donnerstein, and Evans (1975) with no, low, and high erotic stimuli. Finally, anger can be reduced by deterrents to anger-motivated behavior. Indeed, Shortell, Epstein, and Taylor (1970) found anger reduction when it was impossible for the angered person to retaliate.

We performed a more systematic test of deterrence effects on anger by instigating anger by personal insult and operationalizing deterrence as a reason for feeling happy (Miron et al., 2008). Anger and retaliation were measured after either no further treatment, a small ($1 gift certificate), a moderate ($3 gift certificate), or large irrelevant gift ($5 gift certificate) was presented. As predicted, we found that anger intensity was reduced by a small reason for feeling happy, such as a small gift, maintained at its instigated level by the medium-value gift, and somewhat reduced by the large gift. Similarly, we found that the intensity of romantic anger was a cubic function of the importance of a salient positive partner characteristic (Miron, Knepfel, & Parkinson, 2009).

Before we discuss evidence from several studies concerning the relation between emotion and CV responses, we review some of the CV measures used in these studies. *Heart rate* (HR) is the pace at which the heart pumps blood. *Systolic blood pressure* (SBP) and *diastolic blood pressure* (DBP) refer to the pressure exerted on blood vessel walls. SBP refers to the maximal pressure after a heartbeat, whereas DBP refers to the minimal pressure between two heartbeats. During physical or psychological stress, activity of the SNS increases, which can result in increased CV activity (e.g., increased cardiac contractility force, increased SBP, increased HR) to help the person adapt efficiently to the challenge (Richter, Friedrich, & Gendolla, 2008). During periods of relative safety and stability, the parasympathetic nervous system (PNS) is dominant and maintains a lower level of physiological arousal (e.g., decreased HR; Appelhans & Luecken, 2006). Nevertheless, at the beginning of a challenge period, withdrawal of the PNS can also occur, which can affect HR. Moreover, in longer stress periods, reduced SNS activity may occur together with the release of cortisol. The increase in SBP in the context of challenges or acute stress may most likely be due to stronger cardiac contractility (Obrist et al., 1974), which could also lead to increased DBP. However, especially cardiac contractility, SBP, and HR appear to be more sensitive to beta-adrenergic SNS activation than DBP (Wright, 1998). This is because contractility effects on DBP are likely to be masked by changes in peripheral vascular resistance (Berntson, Cacioppo, & Quigley, 1993).

Because changes in HR could arise from either changes in sympathetic activity or changes in parasympathetic activity or both, interpretation of HR activity as a marker of anger mobilization may be difficult (Berntson et al., 1993). Indeed, although both autonomic systems exert a constant influence on HR, PNS influence is predominant at rest and serves to maintain resting HR below the intrinsic firing rate of the sinoatrial node (the heart pacemaker that generates the heart rhythm), whereas the SNS has an excitatory influence on the firing rate of the sinoatrial node, which results in increased HR. Porges (2001) suggested that the ability of the ventral vagal complex—a set of fast-acting nervous fibers—to rapidly withdraw and reinstate an inhibitory influence on sinoatrial node activity allows for prompt engagement and disengagement of the environment without the cost of activating the slower responding SNS. Only when this withdrawal is insufficient to cope with the situational demands are other autonomic subsystems mobilized. In addition, cortical and limbic areas of the central nervous system also have important roles in the regulation of physiological and emotional processes (Thayer & Lane, 2000).

CARDIOVASCULAR BEHAVIOR AS A FUNCTION OF EMOTION INSTIGATION AND DETERRENCE

Emotions promote fast and efficient adaptation to environmental demands and challenges by enacting avoidance or approach behaviors. SNS and PNS act in concert to make this process happen. Because we assume that emotions operate like motivational states, we must also assume that emotions—particularly active emotions with clear behavioral tendencies—involve similar CV activity as do motivational states. In response to challenges, the activity of the SNS becomes dominant, producing high CV arousal to help adaptation to the challenge. Thus, the intensity of CV behavior associated with a particular emotional response should closely mimic the CV activity associated with motivational energization.

Evidence from motivation research (for a review, see Wright, 1998) has revealed that the SNS influence on the heart and vascular system increases with task difficulty. The magnitude of the CV responses such as SBP and HR is a function not only of the magnitude of the expected incentive or demand but also of the difficulty of the task performed to obtain the incentive or to cope with the demand (Eubanks, Wright, & Williams, 2002; Gendolla & Krüsken, 2002). Thus, the magnitude of the CV response is a function of both potential motivation (e.g., importance of success) and difficulty of instrumental behavior (Brehm & Self, 1989).

Ability perceptions could also affect the level of potential motivation (Ford & Brehm, 1987; Wright, 1998). If people who have low ability with regard to a particular task perceive task difficulty or challenge as possible and worthwhile to meet, they should experience more motivational energization when the challenge is low than when the challenge is moderately high. However, people with high ability regarding the task should show reduced energization when confronted with an easy challenge but more mobilization of effort when the challenge is moderately difficult. Similarly, sympathetically mediated CV responses should be greater for low-ability people than for high-ability people in an easy task condition, because they would try harder when the challenge is easy and they think they are capable of overcoming the difficulty. However, when presented with a difficult challenge, low-ability people should disengage faster and show less sympathetic responsiveness than high-ability people. If the challenge is extremely difficult, both the low and the high-ability people should disengage and show low SNS activation (Gendolla & Wright, 2005; Wright, 1998). Gendolla and Krüsken (2002) found support for these specific predictions.

On the basis of this evidence, we make three predictions with regard to the CV effects for anger, our target emotion.

Prediction 1: Anger Is Associated With Specific Cardiovascular Activity

Given that SBP and HR are more sensitive to SNS activation than DBP, we expect that these two measures will be more likely to reflect changes in anger intensity. However, stronger cardiac contractility in response to anger provocation may lead to an increase in SBP as well as to an increase in DBP. Indeed, anger has typically been found in prior research to be associated with behavior characterized by "motoric action" (Goldstein, Edelberg, Meier, & Davis, 1988). As in the case of exercise, the physiological responses associated with anger actions consist of increased cardiac output, vasoconstriction in the skin and viscera, and dilatation in the striated muscle beds (Goldstein et al., 1988). All of these are action tendencies associated with "fight" behavior, which makes significant metabolic demands on the heart (Levenson, 1992). As a result, the emotion of anger produces increases in HR and SBP as well as peripheral vascular resistance, which can also become evident in DBP (Ax, 1953; Funkenstein, King, & Drolette, 1954; Roberts & Weerts, 1982; Schachter, 1957). Similarly, when contrasting anger, happiness, and sadness with a neutral condition, only anger showed a significant increase in skin conductance and HR (Marci, Glick, Loh, & Dougerty, 2007).

Sinha, Lovallo, and Parsons (1992) confirmed that even anger imagery can produce profound effects on the CV system. Increased DBP in anger was associated with sustained levels of peripheral vascular resistance and increased cardiac output and HR, compared with changes during neutral imagery. In line with previous work (James, Yee, Harshfield, Blank, & Pickering, 1986; Martin, 1961; Roberts & Weerts, 1982; Schwartz, Weinberger, & Singer, 1981),

Sinha and Parsons (1996) found not only that HR and SBP increased significantly in response to anger imagery (as in fear and action conditions) but that DBP was also significantly increased. Schwartz et al. (1981) also found that anger differs from control conditions (relaxation and control imagery) in terms of greater increases in DBP, SBP, and HR following imagery, as well as greater increases in HR and slower recovery of SBP after exercise (which followed the imagery task). On the basis of these findings, the authors suggested that the increase in DBP in response to anger is linked to increased isometric muscle strength and vigilant sensory intake, which are necessary for preparation for a fight reaction.

Thus, anger is associated with strong activation of the SNS, and consequently is associated with increases in HR and SBP. Moreover, anger instigation tends to produce net vasoconstriction in major muscle groups, differentially elevating DBP (Schachter, 1957; Schwartz et al., 1981). Coupled activation of the SNS and PNS should thus produce a faster and more efficient reaction to the anger instigation (Berntson et al., 1993).

Several studies have found an increase in DBP but not in SBP in response to anger provocation. Bongard, Pfeiffer, al'Absi, Hodapp, and Linnenkemper (1997), for instance, found that both effortful active coping and anger provocation elevated CV activity, but anger provocation particularly affected HR and DBP. One explanation for the discrepancy in CV findings across anger studies may have to do with the person's self-perceived ability to actively cope with the source of anger. It appears that ability to cope with the anger provocation evokes beta-adrenergic stimulation, which induces increases in HR, SBP, and cardiac output. This appears to be particularly true if coping with the anger source (e.g., retaliation) is moderately difficult and requires effort on the angered person's part (Light & Obrist, 1980; Manuck, Harvey, Lechleiter, & Neal, 1978; Obrist et al., 1978; Wright, Brehm, & Bushman, 1989; Wright, 1998). Conversely, active coping has small effects on DBP and vascular resistance (Obrist et al., 1978). Indeed, field studies on anger experience (Brondolo et al., 2009) reveal that for those high in hostility, but not for those low in hostility, SBP levels were higher in traffic enforcement agents while interacting with the public (e.g., having active confrontations with angry motorists who received a summons for parking illegally) than they were during nonsocial work activities. This effect was found only for SBP, and not for HR or DBP, reflecting the agents' ability to do something about the source of anger.

However, passively coping with a task (i.e., having no control over the outcome of a situation) has been reported to induce alpha-adrenergic influences that produce increased skeletal muscle vasoconstriction and vascular resistance, with stronger effects on DBP and weaker effects on HR, SBP, and cardiac output (Obrist et al., 1978). Several investigations have indicated that anger is associated with increased vascular tonus and DBP, especially when anger cannot be expressed by direct action because of constraints inherent in the experimental situation (Bongard et al., 1997; Sinha et al., 1992). Therefore, *coping potential* (i.e., perceived ability to actively respond to provocation; Lazarus, 1991) may affect not only the intensity of anger (Brehm, 1999, p.13) but also which CV responses (i.e., SBP or DBP) would be affected.

In addition, evidence has suggested that even the type of anger instigation can have differential effects on SBP and DBP, with harassment provoking more CV reactivity (increased SBP and DBP) than frustration. In one study (Garcia-León, Reyes del Paso, Robles, & Vila, 2003), frustration had the greatest CV effects in a problem-solving task, and harassment had the greatest CV effects in a socially competitive task (a task with a relatively higher potential for active coping as the participant competed against a peer "student"). Therefore, future research on anger-related CV responses should take into account not only the availability and difficulty of coping or of goal satisfaction (Manuck et al., 1978) but also the anger induction procedures used in a particular situation.

Prediction 2: Cardiovascular Response Magnitude Is Nonmonotonically Affected by Deterrence to Anger

In this chapter, we focus on anger experience under active coping conditions—situations in which the angered person believes he or she can actively respond to provocation to meet the anger's goal. These conditions should elicit greater anger responses and larger beta-adrenergic-based CV responses than situations in which the individual cannot respond to the anger provocation. In this case, we observe differential mobilization of sympathetically mediated SBP and HR as a function of deterrence to anger. Moreover, the magnitude of anger-related SNS activity should closely resemble the cubic pattern displayed by anger, as seen in Figure 6.1. An example of deterrence to anger is difficulty of aggressing against an insulting agent. If deterrence to anger were low (e.g., it is easy to retaliate against the insulter), SNS-mediated CV response (SBP) would be low. The greater the deterrence to anger (the more difficult it is to retaliate), the higher the magnitude of sympathetically mediated response, up to a point where deterrence becomes too great and SNS responsiveness would be drastically reduced.

Hokanson and Shetler (1961) provided some evidence for this prediction. In their study, participants were insulted or not and then, depending on condition, were given an opportunity to physically aggress against the frustrator. For half of the participants, the frustrator was a student assistant (low status, easy to retaliate), and for the other half he was a visiting professor (high status, difficult to retaliate). When the frustrator had high status, SBP tended to be more elevated when the frustrated participants had an opportunity to aggress than when they did not have an opportunity to aggress (4.57 vs. 1.71 mmHg, but this difference was not significant). Thus, SBP was elevated when it was possible and moderately difficult for the participants to retaliate (in the opportunity to retaliate/high status condition).

Prediction 3: The Magnitude of Sympathetic-Nervous-System-Mediated Cardiovascular Response Is a Function of Both Anger Instigation and Deterrence Importance

On the basis of the work on motivational intensity (Gendolla & Wright, 2005), we propose that if there is a manipulation of the anger instigation (i.e., a manipulation of the potential level of anger: low vs. high) and a manipulation of deterrence to anger (anger instigation alone; low, moderate, high deterrence), the magnitude of anger-associated SNS activity should follow the interaction pattern displayed in Figure 6.2. High-anger participants should display the predicted nonmonotonic CV pattern as a function of deterrence magnitude. Low-anger individuals, however, should perceive a small deterrent to anger as having moderate deterrent power (resulting in mobilized anger and SBP) and should appraise both a moderate and a high deterrent as having high deterrent power (resulting in reduced anger and SBP).

Wright (1984) provided some initial evidence that emotions (e.g., anxiety) and their associated CV responses are affected by both the ability to accomplish the emotion's goal (avoidance) and the difficulty of achieving that goal. Ability to achieve the goal was conceptualized as a determinant of

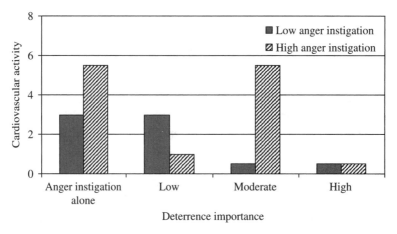

Figure 6.2. Predicted sympathetic-nervous-system-mediated cardiovascular response as a function of anger instigation and importance of deterrence to anger.

the potential level of motivation, whereas difficulty should also influence energization (Wright, 1998). Participants learned that they could avoid electric shock if they performed a preliminary task successfully, a task that consisted of either pressing one of the toggle switches (high ability) or squeezing one of the dynamometers to a level of 55 kg (low ability). Participants were also told that they could tell which instrument (A or B) they should use for performing the task by discriminating between two squares of the same color. Difficulty of discrimination was manipulated (easy, difficult, impossible).

When participants had high ability to perform the avoidance task, anxiety was a nonmonotonic function of the difficulty of the color discrimination task: Anxiety was low when it was easy, increased significantly when it was difficult, and decreased significantly when it was impossible to discern the colors. When participants had low ability, anxiety was high in the easy condition and tended to decrease in the difficult and impossible conditions (an indication that participants might have given up). The means for physiological data were generally consistent with the predictions. High-ability participants had higher HR and greater digital vasoconstriction (lower finger pulse volumes) than did low-ability participants. Moreover, high-ability/difficult discrimination participants had higher arousal levels than those in the easy and impossible discrimination cells, but only the difference between the difficult discrimination and the impossible discrimination conditions was significant.

THEORETICAL AND PRACTICAL IMPLICATIONS

The reviewed literature suggests that emotional intensity theory can be used to investigate the motivational basis of emotion-related CV activity. If SNS is mobilized to help adaptation to an event, then an obstacle to experiencing an emotion should affect SNS responses in the same way it affects emotional intensity. A trivial obstacle to emotion should reduce the SNS-mediated activity associated with that emotion (e.g., SBP), a relatively moderate obstacle should increase SNS activity, and a high obstacle should reduce sympathetic activation.

Hokanson and Shetler (1961) research provided some evidence for the effect of difficulty of retaliation on anger-associated SBP. Similarly, Wright's (1984) study uncovered preliminary evidence that both ability and difficulty of avoiding a noxious event affected anxiety feelings and related CV activity. Future research should also assess the effect of affective deterrence, in the form of reasons for feeling a different emotion, on CV activity (as shown in Figure 6.2). For example, if one has a strong reason for feeling anger, then a trivial reason for feeling happy should reduce anger-related SBP. A moderately important reason for feeling happy should result in relatively high SBP when the reason is nearly as important as the reason for feeling anger. An important reason for feeling happy should drastically reduce SBP concomitantly with reducing anger intensity. Furthermore, deterrents that are of less importance than the importance of the instigated emotion (e.g., low and moderate deterrents) should not instigate differential levels of emotion and CV activity (Brehm & Miron, 2006). This would make the measurement of the anger-related SNS activity easier in these two conditions.

If indeed deterrence has a cubic effect on CV activity, then this strategy may be more cost-efficient than other strategies that have been used to reduce unhealthy physiological activation. Because anger is accompanied by sympathetic activation, such activation may persist long after the anger provocation has ended and may even potentiate the anger (Gerin, Davidson, Christenfeld, Goyal, & Schwartz, 2006). Moreover, continued sympathetic activation maintains blood pressure elevations, which in turn have a direct effect on left ventricular and vascular hypertrophy (Diamond, 1982; Fredrikson & Matthews, 1990). Poor CV recovery may be a marker of chronic sympathetic activation and low parasympathetic tone (Gerin et al., 2006).

Various anger-reduction strategies may affect the CV consequences of anger. One strategy, distraction from anger, was found to reduce angry mood after a personally relevant anger-induction task (Rusting & Nolen-Hoeksema, 1998) and was also found to be related to faster cardiac recovery and enhanced vagal tone (Neumann, Waldstein, Sollers, Thayer, & Sorkin, 2004). Emotional stressors that lead to rumination are associated with relatively poor blood pressure recovery, whereas providing a distraction immediately after the stressor can greatly speed recovery. However, when the distractor is removed, there is a spontaneous reelevation of the blood pressure response (Glynn, Christenfeld, & Gerin, 2002). Another anger-reduction strategy—effortful anger suppression—has deleterious effects on CV health because it uniquely increases SNS activation because of efforts to suppress the emotion (Mauss & Gross, 2004).

In contrast, a deterrence-based strategy may be preferable because of its effortless nature. Indeed, our work has already revealed that a relatively small deterrent to emotion can efficiently reduce strong emotions such as anger or prejudiced affect (Miron et al., 2008; Miron et al., 2009; Miron & Ferguson, 2009). Moreover, this strategy may have more advantages than the use of distraction, emotional suppression, or the use of high deterrents in general. Future work should then benefit from a focus on small affective deterrents and their short- and long-term efficacy in reducing CV responses associated with anger, stress, or anxiety.

REFERENCES

Appelhans, B. M., & Luecken, L. J. (2006). Heart rate variability as an index of regulated emotional responding. *Review of General Psychology, 10,* 229–240. doi:10.1037/1089-2680.10.3.229

Ax, A. F. (1953). The physiological differentiation between fear and anger in humans. *Psychosomatic Medicine, 15,* 433–442.

Baron, R. A. (1983). The control of human aggression: An optimistic perspective. *Journal of Social and Clinical Psychology, 1,* 97–119. doi:10.1521/jscp.1983.1.2.97

Baron, R. A., Fortin, S. P., Frei, R. L., Hauver, L. A., & Shack, M. L. (1990). Reducing organizational conflict: The role of socially induced positive affect. *The International Journal of Conflict Management, 1,* 133–152. doi:10.1108/eb022677

Berntson, G. G., Cacioppo, J. T., & Quigley, K. S. (1993). Cardiac psychophysiology and autonomic space in humans: Empirical perspectives and conceptual implications. *Psychological Bulletin, 114,* 296–322. doi:10.1037/0033-2909.114.2.296

Bongard, S., Pfeiffer, J. S., al'Absi, M., Hodapp, V., & Linnenkemper, G. (1997). Cardiovascular responses during effortful active coping and acute experience of anger in women. *Psychophysiology, 34,* 459–466. doi:10.1111/j.1469-8986.1997.tb02390.x

Brehm, J. W. (1999). The intensity of emotion. *Personality and Social Psychology Review, 3*(1), 2–22. doi:10.1207/s15327957pspr0301_1

Brehm, J. W., & Brummett, B. H. (1998). The emotional control of behavior. In M. Kofta, G. Weary, & G. Sedek (Eds.), *Personal control in action: Cognitive and motivational mechanisms* (pp. 133–153). New York, NY: Plenum Press.

Brehm, J. W., Brummett, B. H., & Harvey, L. (1999). Paradoxical sadness. *Motivation and Emotion, 23,* 31–44. doi:10.1023/A:1021379317763

Brehm, J. W., & Miron, A. M. (2006). Can the simultaneous experience of opposing emotions really occur? *Motivation and Emotion, 30,* 13–30. doi:10.1007/s11031-006-9007-z

Brehm, J. W., Miron, A. M., & Miller, K. (2009). Affect as a motivational state. *Cognition and Emotion, 23,* 1069–1089. doi:10.1080/02699930802323642

Brehm, J. W., & Self, E. A. (1989). The intensity of motivation. *Annual Review of Psychology, 40,* 109–131. doi:10.1146/annurev.ps.40.020189.000545

Brehm, J. W., Wright, R. A., Solomon, S., Silka, L., & Greenberg, J. (1983). Perceived difficulty, energization, and the magnitude of goal valence. *Journal of Experimental Social Psychology, 19,* 21–48. doi:10.1016/0022-1031(83)90003-3

Brondolo, E., Grantham, K. I., Karlin, W., Taravella, J., Mencía-Ripley, A., Schwartz, J. E., . . . Contrada, R. J. (2009). Trait hostility and ambulatory blood pressure among traffic enforcement agents: The effects of stressful social interactions. *Journal of Occupational Health Psychology, 14,* 110–121. doi:10.1037/a0014768

Diamond, E. L. (1982). The role of anger and hostility in essential hypertension and coronary heart disease. *Psychological Bulletin, 92,* 410–433. doi:10.1037/0033-2909.92.2.410

Donnerstein, E., Donnerstein, M., & Evans, R. (1975). Erotic stimuli and aggression: Facilitation of inhibition. *Journal of Personality and Social Psychology, 32,* 237–244. doi:10.1037/0022-3514.32.2.237

Duffy, E. (1941). An explanation of "emotional" phenomena without the use of the concept "emotion." *The Journal of General Psychology, 25,* 283–293.

Eubanks, L., Wright, R. A., & Williams, B. J. (2002). Reward influence on the heart: Cardiovascular response as a function of incentive value at five levels of task demand. *Motivation and Emotion, 26,* 139–152. doi:10.1023/A:1019863318803

Ford, C. E., & Brehm, J. W. (1987). Effort expenditure following failure. In C. R. Snyder & C. E. Ford (Eds.), *Coping with negative life events: Clinical and social psychological perspectives* (pp. 51–79). New York, NY: Plenum Press.

Fredrikson, M., & Matthews, K. A. (1990). Cardiovascular responses to behavioral stress and hypertension: A meta-analytical review. *Annals of Behavioral Medicine, 12,* 30–39. doi:10.1207/s15324796abm1201_3

Funkenstein, D. H., King, S. H., & Drolette, M. (1954). The direction of anger during laboratory stress-inducing situation. *Psychosomatic Medicine, 16,* 404–413.

Garcia-León, A., Reyes del Paso, G. A., Robles, H., & Vila, J. (2003). Relative effects of harassment, frustration, and task characteristics on cardiovascular reactivity. *International Journal of Psychophysiology, 47,* 159–173. doi:10.1016/S0167-8760(02)00124-1

Gendolla, G. H. E., & Krüsken, J. (2002). Mood state, task demand, and effort-related cardiovascular response. *Cognition and Emotion, 16,* 577–603. doi:10.1080/02699930143000446

Gendolla, G. H. E., & Wright, R. A. (2005). Motivation in social settings. Studies of effort related cardiovascular arousal. In J. P. Forgas, K. Williams, & B. von Hippel (Eds.), *Social motivation* (pp. 71–90). New York, NY: Cambridge University Press.

Gerin, W., Davidson, K. W., Christenfeld, N. J. S., Goyal, T., & Schwartz, J. E. (2006). The role of angry rumination and distraction in blood pressure recovery from emotional arousal. *Psychosomatic Medicine, 68,* 64–72. doi:10.1097/01.psy.0000195747.12404.aa

Glynn, L. M., Christenfeld, N., & Gerin, W. (2002). The role of rumination in recovery from reactivity: Cardiovascular consequences of emotional states. *Psychosomatic Medicine, 64,* 714–726. doi:10.1097/01.PSY.0000031574.42041.23

Goldstein, H. S., Edelberg, R., Meier, C. F., & Davis, L. (1988). Relationship of resting blood pressure and heart rate to experienced anger and expressed anger. *Psychosomatic Medicine, 50,* 321–329.

Hokanson, J. E., & Shetler, S. (1961). Effect of overt aggression on physiological arousal. *Journal of Abnormal and Social Psychology, 63,* 446–448. doi:10.1037/h0046864

James, G. D., Yee, L. S., Harshfield, G. A., Blank, S. G., & Pickering, T. G. (1986). The influence of happiness, anger and anxiety on the blood pressure of borderline hypertensives. *Psychosomatic Medicine, 48*, 502–508.

Lazarus, R. S. (1991). *Emotion and adaption*. New York, NY: Oxford University Press.

Leeper, R. W. (1948). A motivational theory of emotion to replace "emotion as a disorganized response." *Psychological Review, 55*, 5–21. doi:10.1037/h0061922

Levenson, R. W. (1992). Autonomic nervous system differences among emotions. *Psychological Science, 3*, 23–27. doi:10.1111/j.1467-9280.1992.tb00251.x

Levenson, R. W. (1999). The intrapersonal functions of emotion. *Cognition and Emotion, 13*, 481–504. doi:10.1080/026999399379159

Light, K. C., & Obrist, P. (1980). Cardiovascular response to stress: Effects of the opportunity to avoid shock, shock experience, and performance feedback. *Psychophysiology, 17*, 243–252. doi:10.1111/j.1469-8986.1980.tb00143.x

Manuck, S. B., Harvey, A. H., Lechleiter, S. L., & Neal, K. S. (1978). Effects of coping on blood pressure responses to threat of aversive stimulation. *Psychophysiology, 15*, 544–549. doi:10.1111/j.1469-8986.1978.tb03107.x

Marci, C. D., Glick, D. M., Loh, R., & Dougerty, D. D. (2007). Autonomic and prefrontal cortex responses to autobiographic recall of emotions. *Cognitive, Affective & Behavioral Neuroscience, 7*, 243–250. doi:10.3758/CABN.7.3.243

Martin, B. (1961). The assessment of anxiety by physiological and behavioral measures. *Psychological Bulletin, 58*, 234–255. doi:10.1037/h0045492

Mauss, I. B., & Gross, J. J. (2004). Emotion suppression and cardiovascular disease: Is hiding your feelings bad for your heart? In L. R. Temoshok, A. Vingerhoets, & I. Nyklicek (Eds.), *The expression of emotion and health* (pp. 62–81). London, England: Brunner-Routledge.

Miron, A. M., Brummett, B. H., Ruggles, B., & Brehm, J. W. (2008). Deterring anger and anger-motivated behaviors. *Basic and Applied Social Psychology, 30*, 326–338. doi:10.1080/01973530802502259

Miron, A. M., & Ferguson, M. A. (2009, May). *Difficulty of refusal to help an out-group nonmonotonically affects prejudice intensity*. Paper presented at the meeting of the Midwestern Psychological Association, Chicago, IL.

Miron, A. M., Knepfel, D., & Parkinson, S. K. (2009). The surprising effect of partner flaws and qualities on romantic affect. *Motivation and Emotion, 33*, 261–276. doi:10.1007/s11031-009-9138-0

Miron, A. M., Parkinson, S. K., & Brehm, J. W. (2007). Does happiness have a motivational function? *Cognition and Emotion, 21*, 248–267. doi:10.1080/02699930600551493

Mueller, C., & Donnerstein, E. (1977). The effects of humor-induced arousal upon aggressive behavior. *Journal of Research in Personality, 11*, 73–82. doi:10.1016/0092-6566(77)90030-7

Neumann, S. A., Waldstein, S. F., Sollers, J. J., Thayer, J. F., & Sorkin, J. D. (2004). Hostility and distraction have differential influences on cardiovascular recovery from anger recall in women. *Health Psychology, 23*, 631–640. doi:10.1037/0278-6133.23.6.631

Novaco, R. W. (1975). *Anger control.* Lexington, MA: Heath.

Oatley, K., & Johnson-Laird, P. (1987). Toward a cognitive theory of emotion. *Cognition and Emotion, 1*, 29–50. doi:10.1080/02699938708408362

Obrist, P. A., Gaebelein, C. J., Teller, E. S., Langer, A. W., Grignolo, A., Light, K. C., & McCubbin, J. A. (1978). The relationship among heart rate, carotid dP/dt, and blood pressure in humans as a function of type of stress. *Psychophysiology, 15*, 102–115. doi:10.1111/j.1469-8986.1978.tb01344.x

Obrist, P. A., Lawler, J. E., Howard, J. L., Smithson, K. W., Martin, P. L., & Manning, J. (1974). Sympathetic influences on cardiac rate and contractility during acute stress in humans. *Psychophysiology, 11*, 405–427. doi:10.1111/j.1469-8986.1974.tb00566.x

Porges, S. W. (2001). The polyvagal theory: Phylogenetic substrates of a social nervous system. *International Journal of Psychophysiology, 42*, 123–146. doi:10.1016/S0167-8760(01)00162-3

Richter, M., Friedrich, A., & Gendolla, G. H. E. (2008). Task difficulty effects on cardiac activity. *Psychophysiology, 45*, 869–875. doi:10.1111/j.1469-8986.2008.00688.x

Roberts, R. J., & Weerts, T. C. (1982). Cardiovascular responding during anger and fear imagery. *Psychological Reports, 50*, 219–230.

Rusting, C. L., & Nolen-Hoeksema, S. (1998). Regulating responses to anger: Effects of rumination and distraction on angry mood. *Journal of Personality and Social Psychology, 74*, 790–803. doi:10.1037/0022-3514.74.3.790

Schachter, J. (1957). Pain, fear, and anger in hypertensives and normotensives: A psychophysiological study. *Psychosomatic Medicine, 19*, 17–29.

Schmitt, M. T., Miller, D. A., Branscombe, N. R., & Brehm, J. W. (2008). The difficulty of making reparations affects the intensity of collective guilt. *Group Processes & Intergroup Relations, 11*, 267–279. doi:10.1177/1368430208090642

Schwartz, G. E., Weinberger, D. A., & Singer, J. A. (1981). Cardiovascular differentiation of happiness, sadness, anger, and fear following imagery and exercise. *Psychosomatic Medicine, 43*, 343–364.

Shortell, J., Epstein, S., & Taylor, S. P. (1970). Instigation to aggression as a function of degree of defeat and the capacity for massive retaliation. *Journal of Personality, 38*, 313–328. doi:10.1111/j.1467-6494.1970.tb00012.x

Silvia, P. J., & Brehm, J. W. (2001). Exploring alternative deterrents to emotional intensity: Anticipated happiness, distraction, and sadness. *Cognition and Emotion, 15*, 575–592.

Sinha, R., Lovallo, W. R., & Parsons, O. A. (1992). Cardiovascular differentiation of emotions. *Psychosomatic Medicine, 54*, 422–435.

Sinha, R., & Parsons, O. A. (1996). Multivariate response patterning of fear and anger. *Cognition and Emotion, 10*, 173–198. doi:10.1080/026999396380321

Thayer, J. F., & Lane, R. D. (2000). A model of neurovisceral integration in emotion regulation and dysregulation. *Journal of Affective Disorders*, 61, 201–216. doi:10.1016/S0165-0327(00)00338-4

Wright, R. A. (1984). Motivation, anxiety, and the difficulty of avoidant control. *Journal of Personality and Social Psychology*, 46, 1376–1388. doi:10.1037/0022-3514.46.6.1376

Wright, R. A. (1998). Ability perception and cardiovascular response to behavioral challenge. In M. Kofta, G. Weary, & G. Sedek (Eds.), *Control in action: Cognitive and motivational mechanisms* (pp. 197–232). New York, NY: Plenum Press.

Wright, R. A., & Brehm, J. W. (1989). Energization and goal attractiveness. In L. A. Pervin (Ed.), *Goal concepts in personality and social psychology* (pp. 169–210). Hillsdale, NJ: Erlbaum.

Wright, R. A., Brehm, J. W., & Bushman, B. J. (1989). Cardiovascular responses to threat: Effects of the difficulty and availability of a cognitive avoidant task. *Basic and Applied Social Psychology*, 10, 161–171. doi:10.1207/s15324834basp1002_6

7

GLOOMY AND LAZY? ON THE IMPACT OF MOOD AND DEPRESSIVE SYMPTOMS ON EFFORT-RELATED CARDIOVASCULAR RESPONSE

GUIDO H. E. GENDOLLA, KERSTIN BRINKMANN,
AND NICOLAS SILVESTRINI

This chapter presents recent findings from a program of research on the systematic influence of transient mood states and depressive symptoms on resource mobilization for coping with mental challenges. The tested predictions stem from an integrative theory about the impact of mood states on behavior—the mood–behavior model (MBM; Gendolla, 2000)—under consideration of the principles of motivational intensity theory (Brehm & Self, 1989) and their integration with Obrist's (1981) active coping approach by Wright (1996).

During the past decade, most of our studies in this program of research have focused on changes in systolic blood pressure (SBP) during the induction of mood states and the subsequent performance of mental challenges. Our focus on SBP has been based on the ample evidence for its sensitive reactivity to manipulations of experienced task demand as long as success on a challenge is perceived as possible and justified (for reviews, see Wright, 1996;

The research discussed in this chapter was supported by research grants Ge 987/1-1 and Ge 987/7-1 from the Deutsche Forschungsgemeinschaft and grants 100011-108144/1 and 100014-22604/1 from the Swiss National Funds.

Wright & Kirby, 2001). Evidence for effects on diastolic blood pressure (DBP) and heart rate (HR) is existent but less consistent—which is plausible for physiological reasons. Both SBP and DBP are influenced by myocardial contractility that is potentiated by beta-adrenergic sympathetic discharge. But effects on DBP are more likely to be masked by changes in total peripheral resistance than are effects on SBP (Levick, 2003). Therefore, SBP shows similar reactivity patterns to task difficulty manipulations as measures of myocardial contractility (e.g., Richter, Friedrich, & Gendolla, 2008). HR, another frequently assessed cardiovascular parameter, is determined by both sympathetic and parasympathetic arousal and should thus only respond to effort mobilization when the sympathetic impact is stronger, which is not always the case (Berntson, Cacioppo, & Quigley, 1993; Brownley, Hurwitz, & Schneiderman, 2000; Obrist, 1981).

In this chapter, we first briefly present the theoretical reasoning about why and how moods can influence effort-related cardiovascular response. Then we present and discuss recent research that tested these predictions in experiments with manipulated mood states and in studies that investigated the impact of individual differences in depressive symptoms on effort-related responses of the cardiovascular system.

MOOD–BEHAVIOR MODEL

Moods are long-lasting affective states that are experienced without concurrent awareness of their origins (e.g., Schwarz & Clore, 1988). These characteristics of mood states have important consequences for their potential impact on behavior, which becomes clear by comparing moods with emotions: Whereas short lived, specific, object-related emotions (e.g., happy, sad, angry about . . .) provide goals (e.g., fear–security, anger–destruction) and relatively short autonomic adjustments that reflect the mobilization of resources for emotion-specific action (e.g., Kreibig, Gendolla, & Scherer, 2010; see also Chapter 5, this volume), moods are feeling states themselves without a clear motivational function. Nevertheless, the MBM posits that moods systematically influence resource mobilization in instrumental behavior by means of their informational and directive impacts.

Informational Mood Impact

Individuals can use their moods as diagnostic information for behavior-relevant appraisals such as "How difficult is the task?" or "Am I able to succeed?" Given the ample evidence that resource mobilization follows an energy conservation principle according to which individuals avoid wasting resources (Brehm & Self, 1989), the type of appraisal that is central for effort mobilization is the subjective impressions of task demand or difficulty. As for any kind of evaluative judgment (for a review, see Wyer, Clore, & Isbell, 1999), moods can influence such appraisals in a mood congruent manner—people are more optimistic and make more positive judgments in a positive than in a negative mood. Consequently, a task is experienced as more difficult in a negative mood than in a positive mood—but only as long as the diagnostic, informative value of mood for appraising demand is not called into question (Gendolla & Krüsken, 2002a). Resulting effects of mood on effort-related cardiovascular response are depicted in Figure 7.1.

When people perform a task without fixed difficulty under "do your best" instructions, mood is one type of salient information for evaluating task demand. Subjective task difficulty is thus higher in a negative mood than in a positive mood. The result is stronger effort-related cardiovascular activity in a negative mood than in a positive mood (e.g., Gendolla, Abele, & Krüsken, 2001; Gendolla & Krüsken, 2001b).

However, a negative mood does not always lead to higher effort. If people work on a task with fixed task difficulty, the MBM states that they will pragmatically use both types of information—mood and task difficulty—as demonstrated in several experiments (e.g., Gendolla & Krüsken, 2001a, 2002b). Consequently, for an easy task, effort is higher in a negative mood than in a positive mood because subjective demand and, as a result, mobilized resources are

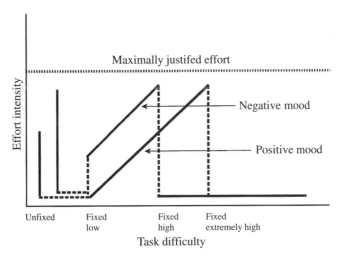

Figure 7.1. Theoretical prediction for the informational impact of mood on effort-related cardiovascular response. Adapted from "The Role of Mood States in Self-Regulation," by G. H. E. Gendolla and K. Brinkmann, 2005, *European Psychologist, 10,* p. 190. Copyright 2005 by Hogrefe and Huber. Reprinted with permission.

higher in a negative mood. But when a task is objectively difficult, effort is higher in a positive mood than in a negative mood. The reason is that here subjective demand is high but not yet too high in a positive mood, whereas it is already too high for active coping in a negative mood. Finally, when objective task difficulty is extremely high, so that active coping is obviously impossible, mood cannot provide additional diagnostic information, and mobilized resources are low because of disengagement (Gendolla & Krüsken, 2002c).

Directive Mood Impact

Besides the informational mood impact, the MBM posits that moods can have a directive impact on the instigation and direction of behavior in compliance with a hedonic motive. This directive mood impact influences the extent to which people prefer actions that are instrumental for hedonic affect-regulation (i.e., maximizing pleasure and minimizing distress). The MBM predicts that the strength of a person's hedonic motive (i.e., the momentary need for the experience of well-being) increases with mood intensity. Both intense positive and negative moods result in a high interest in activities that promise positive affect through their pleasant associations or consequences (e.g., Silvestrini & Gendolla, 2007). Referring to motivational intensity theory (Brehm & Self, 1989), opportunities for affect regulation should influence the level of justified resources (i.e., potential motivation). Up to this limit, actual effort is mobilized in proportion to the level of experienced demand.

MOOD IMPACT ON CARDIOVASCULAR RESPONSE: EMPIRICAL EVIDENCE

During the past decade, the predictions outlined so far have received ample empirical support from a series of experimental studies. The basic experimental protocol in this research consisted of (a) a habituation period to assess physiological baseline values; (b) mood inductions with video excerpts, music presentations, or autobiographical recollection tasks; and (c) a cognitive challenge—typically an attention or memory task. The dependent variable was cardiovascular reactivity—especially SBP—during the mood inductions and task performance with reference to baseline values assessed during habituation.

The following findings support the predictions of the MBM:

- Demand appraisals were higher in a negative mood and produced stronger SBP reactivity during performance than in a positive mood if task difficulty was not fixed and participants performed under "do your best" instructions (e.g., Gendolla et al., 2001; Gendolla & Krüsken, 2001b, 2002b).

- These mood effects were neutralized when the diagnostic value of mood for demand appraisals was called into question by the experimental context (Gendolla & Krüsken, 2002a).

- When participants performed tasks with fixed performance standards, they used both their mood and the performance standard to appraise demand, resulting in the anticipated crossover pattern of mood and objective task difficulty (Gendolla & Krüsken, 2001a, 2002b): For easy tasks, SBP reactivity was stronger in a negative mood than in a positive mood because subjective demand for participants in a negative mood was higher than for those in a positive mood. However, for difficult tasks, systolic reactivity was stronger in a positive mood than in a negative mood because here subjective difficulty was high but still feasible in a positive mood, whereas it was too high in a negative mood, resulting in disengagement. The effects of positive and negative moods for easy and difficult tasks resemble those of high and low ability (e.g., Wright & Dismukes, 1995) and high and low fatigue (e.g., Wright, Martin, & Bland, 2003; see Chapter 10, this volume).

- As initial support for the idea that a positive hedonic incentive justifies high effort, pleasant performance-contingent consequences of success can eliminate the motivational deficit of people who face a difficult task in a negative mood (Gendolla & Krüsken, 2002c). None of those studies had found mood effects on cardiovascular reactivity during the mood inductions.

Recent Findings on the Effect of Transient Mood States

A more recent experiment (de Burgo & Gendolla, 2009) was conducted as a more conclusive test of the MBM assumption that moods themselves are not motivational states and that they thus only have an impact on cardiovascular response when they can be used as task-relevant information for demand appraisals. After being induced into positive versus negative moods with video excerpts, participants were presented a list of letter series. In an intentional learning condition, the list presentation was clearly framed as an achievement task: Participants were explicitly instructed to correctly memorize all series within 5 min. By contrast, in an incidental learning condition, the list was merely presented and nothing was mentioned concerning memorizing or achievement measures. As in our previous studies, SBP reactivity did not differ between the mood conditions during the mood inductions, although the verbal mood manipulation checks indicated successfully manipulated positive and negative mood states. Most relevant, in the intentional learning condition, SBP reactivity was, as expected, stronger in a negative mood than in a positive mood, whereas mood had no effect in the incidental learning condition. DBP reactivity revealed a similar pattern. The results support the idea that moods have only an effect on cardiovascular response when they can be used as task-relevant information for demand appraisals.

Another recent experiment (Silvestrini & Gendolla, 2007) investigated the influence of mood on effort-related cardiovascular response in a mood regulation task. Participants were asked to regulate their feelings within 5 min to attain a hedonically positive outcome. Predictions were as follows: Based on the informational mood impact, participants in a positive mood should evaluate this task as easier than should those in a so-called neutral (i.e., less intense) mood and especially compared with those in a negative mood. However, according to the directive mood impact, both participants in a negative and a positive mood should have a higher need for well-being than should those in a neutral mood. Consequently, cardiovascular response during the mood regulation task should be higher in a negative mood (high subjective difficulty/high justified effort) than in both a neutral (relatively high difficulty/low justified effort) and a positive mood (low subjective difficulty/high justified effort).

After habituation, participants were first induced into a negative, a neutral, or a positive mood through film presentations and then performed the affect regulation task. SBP reactivity exactly described the predicted pattern and was stronger in a negative mood than in both the neutral and positive mood conditions, which did not differ from one another. In addition, changes in tonic skin conductance level resembled that pattern, which supports the idea that mood regulation is an act of difficult self-control, which is typically associated with increased electrodermal activity (e.g., Wegner, Shortt, Blake, & Page, 1990). Additional analyses of facial electromyograms during the mood induction period revealed stronger zygomaticus major reactivity in the positive mood condition than in both the neutral and negative mood cells. During the affect regulation task there was a general increase in zygomatic activity. In accordance with verbal mood manipulation checks, this indicates that the mood inductions were effective and that participants in all conditions succeeded on the affect regulation task, although those in the negative mood condition had to mobilize more resources for this outcome, as indicated by the SBP reactivity pattern.

Richter and Gendolla (2009b) considered the possibility that mood may—under certain conditions—also influence effort mobilization by its informational impact on appraisals of the instrumentality of success. Participants were induced into positive, neutral, or negative moods by an autobiographical recollection task and worked then on a memory task with unclear task difficulty. For this type of task, the difficulty of the task can be fixed; the difficulty level, however, is unknown to participants (see Chapter 4, this volume). In the administered memory task, participants were presented with letter series they had to memorize. However, they did not know how many series would appear, nor how long the task would last, nor in which time intervals the series would appear. Unlike the unfixed task difficulty tasks described earlier, participants were not asked to "do their best" but to memorize all series that would appear. Previous research has found that reward value directly determines effort intensity when task difficulty is unclear (e.g., Richter & Gendolla, 2006, 2009a).

Before task onset, participants learned that they could earn the chance of winning a monetary reward if they succeeded, and rated the probability of winning the monetary reward. Probability ratings in a positive mood were higher than those in a negative mood, suggesting that success was more worthwhile in a positive mood (high probability to get the reward) than in a negative mood (low probability of getting the reward). Corresponding to this, SBP reactivity during task performance increased from negative to positive mood. This effect was statistically mediated by participants' subjective probability ratings of winning the monetary reward for successful performance. These results demonstrate that mood can influence effort mobilization not only by taking effect on appraisals of subjective demand but also by influencing judgments of the instrumentality of success. Furthermore, the findings sustain the MBM argument that moods have no fixed effects on resource mobilization. Rather, mood impact on resource mobilization depends on the type of judgment (e.g., instrumentality vs. demand) for which they are used as information.

Effects of Depressive Symptoms

Other studies have applied the MBM reasoning to an experimental analysis of the impact of depressive symptoms on effort-related cardiovascular response. Based on the common view of depression (see Gotlib & Hammen, 2002), one could hypothesize that depression is characterized by a general motivational deficit. Our analysis, however, challenges this view, at least with respect to resource mobilization. Considering that a persistent negative mood is a core symptom of depression, we hypothesized that the impact of depressive symptoms on effort mobilization is moderated by task characteristics and mood-congruent appraisals of task demand. In general, the impact of clinical as well as subclinical depressive symptoms should resemble that of transient mood states.

Our first studies (Brinkmann & Gendolla, 2007) recruited undergraduate students with low ("nondysphoric") versus high ("dysphoric") scores on a

self-report depression scale and confronted them with tasks of unfixed difficulty ("do your best"). In one protocol, participants were presented with a list
of letter series and were asked to correctly memorize within 5 min as many
series as possible. In accordance with our hypotheses, participants who were
dysphoric showed stronger SBP reactivity at the beginning of the performance period than those who were nondysphoric. This result was replicated
in a second study using a mental concentration task. During the whole performance period, participants who were dysphoric showed stronger SBP and
HR reactivity than those who were nondysphoric. These two studies suggest
that depression is not associated with a general motivational deficit. Rather,
at least with respect to resource mobilization, a task that asks to "do one's
best" can elicit high effort in individuals who are dysphoric.

In a second pair of studies (Brinkmann & Gendolla, 2008), participants
who were dysphoric and nondysphoric performed either an easy or a difficult
version of a concentration task (Study 1) or the memory task (Study 2). In
both studies, results revealed the expected crossover interaction pattern that
had been previously observed for manipulated negative and positive moods
and fixed task difficulty: In the easy condition, participants who were dysphoric
showed stronger SBP reactivity than participants who were nondysphoric. In
the difficult task condition, however, participants who were nondysphoric
showed stronger SBP reactivity (Figure 7.2). Moreover, demand appraisals

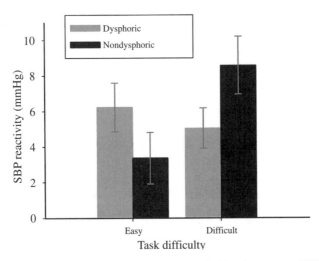

Figure 7.2. Cell means and standard errors of systolic blood pressure (SBP) reactivity
during performance on a memory task in Study 2 by Brinkmann and Gendolla (2008).
Adapted from "Does Depression Interfere With Effort Mobilization? Effects of Dysphoria and Task Difficulty on Cardiovascular Response," by K. Brinkmann and G. H. E.
Gendolla, 2008, *Journal of Personality and Social Psychology, 94,* p. 153. Copyright
2008 by the American Psychological Association. Reprinted with permission.

assessed before performance indicated that participants who were dysphoric perceived the memory task in Study 2 as more difficult. It is also notable that participants who were dysphoric and nondysphoric did not differ in cardiovascular baseline activity in any of the four studies discussed.

In summary, these findings show that depressive symptoms are not necessarily associated with a motivational deficit in effort mobilization and that task difficulty plays an important role in determining whether depression leads to enhanced or attenuated cardiovascular response: When task difficulty is unfixed or easy, individuals who are dysphoric mobilize even more effort that those who are nondysphoric.

Joint Impact of Mood, Task Difficulty, and Reward

Another line of our research focused on a differentiated analysis of the simultaneous effect of informational and directive mood impacts on effort-related cardiovascular response, as conceptualized in the MBM. These studies were built on the basic idea that actions that are instrumental for hedonic affect regulation (i.e., attaining or maintaining positive affect) justify the investment of more effort than actions without positive hedonic characteristics or outcomes. To test this, these studies simultaneously manipulated mood, task difficulty, and hedonic incentive. In terms of motivational intensity theory (Brehm & Self, 1989), positive hedonic incentive should justify relatively high resources—it makes success worthwhile. The actual intensity of mobilized effort should, however, depend on subjective task difficulty that is jointly determined by objective task difficulty and mood, as outlined earlier (e.g., Brinkmann & Gendolla, 2008; Gendolla & Krüsken, 2001a, 2002b).

Specific predictions for the joint effect of mood, task difficulty, and hedonic incentive are as follows: When success is only connected with low hedonic incentive, the amount of justified effort is low. Up to this relatively low level of maximally justified resources, effort-related cardiovascular response is determined by the informational mood impact. If a task is objectively easy, people in a negative mood tend to mobilize more effort than do people in a positive mood; if a task is objectively difficult, people in a negative mood tend to mobilize little effort, as discussed earlier. By contrast, when the hedonic incentive of success is positive, more resources are justified, because successful performance is appetitive. Those justified resources are, however, only mobilized when the level of experienced task demand necessitates this. This is the case when a negative mood is combined with a difficult task (the condition that leads to disengagement because of too high subjective demand when only low resources are justified). That is, a high hedonic incentive of success should eliminate the motivational deficit of people in a negative mood who face a difficult task.

We tested these predictions in an experiment that simultaneously manipulated mood, task difficulty, and hedonic incentive (Silvestrini & Gendolla, 2009b). After habituation and manipulation of positive versus negative moods, participants performed either an easy or a difficult memory task with either pleasant or unpleasant consequences of success. In the high hedonic incentive condition, participants were promised the presentation of a comedy video after success, whereas in the low—in fact negative—incentive condition, they expected the presentation of a distressing video after success. As depicted in Figure 7.3, SBP reactivity during task performance depicted the predicted pattern: When success provided low hedonic incentive, SBP reactivity revealed the crossover interaction pattern anticipated for the joint effect of mood and objective task difficulty. However, when the hedonic incentive of success was high, SBP reactivity of participants in the negative mood/difficult task condition increased significantly, because the positive incentive justified the high effort that was perceived as necessary here. These results suggest that it is not success per se that justifies the mobilization of high effort. Rather, positive hedonic aspects of succeeding are necessary. Corresponding results were found in an experiment in which we manipulated mood, task difficulty, and pleasantness versus unpleasantness of a task itself

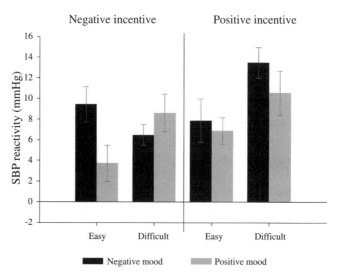

Figure 7.3. Cell means and standard errors of systolic blood pressure (SBP) reactivity during memory task performance in the experiment by Silvestrini and Gendolla (2009b). Adapted from "Mood-Regulative Hedonic Incentive Interacts with Mood and Task Difficulty to Determine Effort-Related Cardiovascular Response and Facial EMG," by N. Silvestrini and G. H. E. Gendolla, 2009, *Biological Psychology, 82,* p. 58. Copyright 2009 by Elsevier. Reprinted with permission.

(Silvestrini & Gendolla, 2009b). Task pleasantness had the same effects as positive hedonic incentive in the study discussed earlier.

Depressive Symptoms, Reward-Responsiveness, and Cardiovascular Response

The Silvestrini and Gendolla (2009b) experiment showed that hedonically positive consequences of success have a strong impact on effort-related cardiovascular response: They can motivate people who face a difficult task in a negative mood to mobilize the high effort that appears to be necessary for success. However, research on responsiveness to reward and punishment suggests that this may be different for individuals experiencing depressive symptoms: Individuals who are depressed and dysphoric do not behaviorally respond to monetary reward and punishment (e.g., Henriques & Davidson, 2000), report less behavioral approach motivation (e.g., Kasch, Rottenberg, Arnow, & Gotlib, 2002), show hypoactivation of left frontal regions associated with approach behavior (e.g., Davidson, Pizzagalli, Nitschke, & Putnam, 2002), and have altered neurotransmission and activation of cortical and subcortical reward areas (e.g., Nestler & Carlezon, 2006). On the basis of this evidence, studies by Brinkmann, Schüpbach, Ancel Joye, and Gendolla (2009) directly tested the hypothesis of a reduced responsiveness to reward and punishment in individuals who are dysphoric in terms of effort mobilization. These studies administered tasks with unclear difficulty, because this type of task permits a direct test of the effects of reward and punishment on effort mobilization (see Chapter 4, this volume). People in general mobilize more effort when reward is high than when reward is low under conditions of unclear task difficulty (Richter & Gendolla, 2006, 2009a). The reduced reward-responsiveness hypothesis suggests that this should not be the case for depressed individuals.

Participants in the first study by Brinkmann et al. (2009) performed a mental arithmetic task under one of three conditions: a reward of 10 Swiss francs for success, punishment asking for a refund of a previously received 10 Swiss francs, or no performance-contingent consequence. Results confirmed that participants with high depression scores—in contrast to those with low scores—did not respond with increased SBP reactivity to anticipated punishment. The second study replicated these results for reward. In accordance with prior studies (Richter & Gendolla, 2006, 2009a), participants who were nondysphoric showed strong increases in both SBP and myocardial contractility (reflected by a shortened pre-ejection period) if they were offered 10 Swiss francs for successful performance. In contrast, cardiovascular reactivity in participants who were dysphoric was rather low and did not differ from the neutral condition without performance-related consequences (see Figure 7.4).

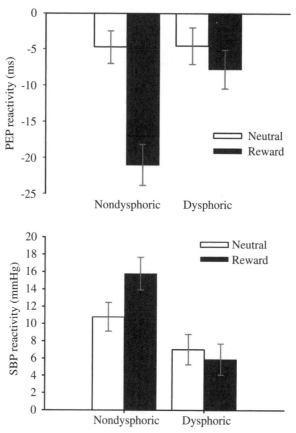

Figure 7.4. Cell means and standard errors of pre-ejection period (PEP; upper panel) and systolic blood pressure reactivity (SBP; lower panel) during performance of a mental arithmetic task in Study 2 by Brinkmann, Schüpbach, Ancel Joye, and Gendolla (2009). Adapted from "Anhedonia and Effort Mobilization in Dysphoria: Reduced Cardiovascular Response to Reward and Punishment," by K. Brinkmann, L. Schüpbach, I. Ancel Joye, and G. H. E. Gendolla, 2009, *International Journal of Psychophysiology, 74,* p. 257. Copyright 2009 by Elsevier. Reprinted with permission.

Taken together, reduced responsiveness of individuals with depression to reward and punishment is also evident in reduced effort-related cardiovascular response. More important, these studies suggest that individuals who are depressed cannot as easily be motivated to mobilize effort to cope with difficult or very difficult demands. Strategies to increase motivation and effort mobilization—such as high importance of task success or a task's incentive value itself—might not work for individuals who are depressed, though they work for people in a transitorily negative mood (e.g., Gendolla & Krüsken, 2002b; Silvestrini & Gendolla, 2009a, 2009b).

CONCLUSION

Following the first wave of research on the impact of mood states on effort-related cardiovascular response (for a review, see Gendolla & Brinkmann, 2005), the studies discussed in this chapter have brought new insights, particularly about the informational impact of mood on effort mobilization, the role of mood in affect-regulation, and the effect of depressive symptoms.

The experiment by de Burgo and Gendolla (2009) provided conclusive evidence for the assumption that moods per se are not motivational states and that moods only systematically influence resource mobilization when they can be used as information for demand appraisals. That is, moods themselves have no impact on resource mobilization—a finding that contradicts approaches that have attributed stable motivational implications to moods (e.g., Morris, 1992; Schwarz, 1990). The Richter and Gendolla (2009b) study demonstrated that mood effects on effort-related cardiovascular response are not limited to their effect on demand appraisals. When task difficulty is unclear, moods can influence effort mobilization by affecting instrumentality appraisals and thus the importance of success. This further shows that mood effects on resource mobilization heavily depend on task context.

The studies by Silvestrini and Gendolla (2009a, 2009b) showed that the effort mobilization deficit typically shown by people who face a difficult task in a negative mood (e.g., Gendolla & Krüsken, 2001b) can be eliminated if success is instrumental for hedonic affect regulation. However, regarding the effect of performance-contingent incentive in general, the studies by Brinkmann et al. (2009) suggested that such incentive effects do not apply to people experiencing depressive symptoms. Although depressive symptoms have effects on effort-related cardiovascular response that correspond to those of transient mood states when incentive is not manipulated (i.e., a merely informational impact on experienced demand; Brinkmann & Gendolla, 2007, 2008), individuals with depressive symptoms have been found to be "immune" to performance-contingent incentive. Integrating these findings suggests that depression is not associated with a general motivational deficit: Individuals with depression mobilized more effort under "do your best" instructions or for an easy task than those who were not depressed. Rather, depression seems to be related to a deficit in incentive motivation.

In this context, it is important to note that previous studies did not come to unequivocal conclusions about the enhancing or attenuating effect of depression and dysphoria on cardiovascular activity (e.g., Carroll, Phillips, Hunt, & Der, 2007; Kibler & Ma, 2004; Salomon, Clift, Karlsdóttir, & Rottenberg, 2009). According to our analysis and findings, "blunted reactivity" of depressed individuals (see Chapter 12, this volume) is explicable by disengagement due to overchallenge. This occurs when depressed individuals are confronted with difficult demands that appear to be overchallenging because of an informational impact of depressed mood on demand appraisals, as discussed earlier. This situation might also arise when only little effort is justified because of the devaluation of hedonic task consequences by people with depression. We think it is a major shortcoming of previous research that task characteristics and task difficulty of administered laboratory stressors have not been further considered. A careful and theoretically driven inspection of the behavioral challenges and contextual conditions seems necessary.

The present application of our integrative analysis is, however, not limited to negative mood and depressive symptoms. First of all, the personality construct of general negative affectivity is associated with affective, cognitive, and motivational symptoms of depression (Klein, Durbin, Shankman, & Santiago, 2002). Moreover, as a rather broad construct, negative affectivity underlies most other psychopathologies as well. Various psychosocial characteristics are similar in depression and other psychopathologies involving negative affective states (Hokanson, Rubert, Welker, Hollander, & Hedeen, 1989). The anxiety disorders are especially characterized by negative affect and show a high degree of comorbidity with depression. As our theoretical reasoning is based mainly on the influence of dispositional and transient negative mood on effort mobilization through an informational mood impact (Gendolla, 2000), one can imagine that results similar to those of depression and dysphoria may emerge for other negative affective states and traits as well. This implies that individual mood differences (clinical as well as nonclinical) play an important role in determining how people approach upcoming challenges, how vigorously they pursue their daily tasks, and at what point they disengage from effort mobilization.

REFERENCES

Berntson, G. G., Cacioppo, J. T., & Quigley, K. S. (1993). Cardiac psychophysiology and autonomic space in humans: Empirical perspectives and conceptual implications. *Psychological Bulletin, 114,* 296–322. doi:10.1037/0033-2909. 114.2.296

Brehm, J. W., & Self, E. A. (1989). The intensity of motivation. *Annual Review of Psychology, 40,* 109–131. doi:10.1146/annurev.ps.40.020189.000545

Brinkmann, K., & Gendolla, G. H. E. (2007). Dysphoria and mobilization of mental effort: Effects on cardiovascular reactivity. *Motivation and Emotion, 31,* 71–82. doi:10.1007/s11031-007-9054-0

Brinkmann, K., & Gendolla, G. H. E. (2008). Does depression interfere with effort mobilization? Effects of dysphoria and task difficulty on cardiovascular response. *Journal of Personality and Social Psychology, 94,* 146–157. doi:10.1037/0022-3514.94.1.146

Brinkmann, K., Schüpbach, L., Ancel Joye, I., & Gendolla, G. H. E. (2009). Anhedonia and effort mobilization in dysphoria: Reduced cardiovascular response to reward and punishment. *International Journal of Psychophysiology, 74*, 250–258. doi:10.1016/j.ijpsycho.2009.09.009

Brownley, K. A., Hurwitz, B. E., & Schneiderman, N. (2000). Cardiovascular psychophysiology. In J. T. Cacioppo, L. G. Tassinary, & G. G. Berntson (Eds.), *Handbook of psychophysiology* (pp. 224–264). New York, NY: Cambridge University Press.

Carroll, D., Phillips, A. C., Hunt, K., & Der, G. (2007). Symptoms of depression and cardiovascular reactions to acute psychological stress: Evidence from a population study. *Biological Psychology, 75*, 68–74. doi:10.1016/j.biopsycho.2006.12.002

Davidson, R. J., Pizzagalli, D., Nitschke, J. B., & Putnam, K. (2002). Depression: Perspectives from affective neuroscience. *Annual Review of Psychology, 53*, 545–574. doi:10.1146/annurev.psych.53.100901.135148

de Burgo, J., & Gendolla, G. H. E. (2009). Are moods motivational states? A study on effort-related cardiovascular response. *Emotion, 9*, 892–897. doi:10.1037/a0017092

Gendolla, G. H. E. (2000). On the impact of mood on behavior: An integrative theory and a review. *Review of General Psychology, 4*, 378–408. doi:10.1037/1089-2680.4.4.378

Gendolla, G. H. E., Abele, A. E., & Krüsken, J. (2001). The informational impact of mood on effort mobilization: A study of cardiovascular and electrodermal responses. *Emotion, 1*, 12–24. doi:10.1037/1528-3542.1.1.12

Gendolla, G. H. E., & Brinkmann, K. (2005). The role of mood states in self-regulation. *European Psychologist, 10*, 187–198. doi:10.1027/1016-9040.10.3.187

Gendolla, G. H. E., & Krüsken, J. (2001a). The joint impact of mood state and task difficulty on cardiovascular and electrodermal reactivity in active coping. *Psychophysiology, 38*, 548–556. doi:10.1017/S0048577201000622

Gendolla, G. H. E., & Krüsken, J. (2001b). Mood state and cardiovascular response in active coping with an affect-regulative challenge. *International Journal of Psychophysiology, 41*, 169–180. doi:10.1016/S0167-8760(01)00130-1

Gendolla, G. H. E., & Krüsken, J. (2002a). Informational mood impact on effort-related cardiovascular response: The diagnostic value of moods counts. *Emotion, 2*, 251–262. doi:10.1037/1528-3542.2.3.251

Gendolla, G. H. E., & Krüsken, J. (2002b). The joint effect of informational mood impact and performance-contingent incentive on effort-related cardiovascular response. *Journal of Personality and Social Psychology, 83*, 271–283. doi:10.1037/0022-3514.83.2.271

Gendolla, G. H. E., & Krüsken, J. (2002c). Mood, task demand, and effort-related cardiovascular response. *Cognition and Emotion, 16*, 577–603. doi:10.1080/02699930143000446

Gotlib, I. H., & Hammen, C. L. (Eds.). (2002). *Handbook of depression*. New York, NY: Guilford Press.

Henriques, J. B., & Davidson, R. J. (2000). Decreased responsiveness to reward in depression. *Cognition and Emotion, 14*, 711–724. doi:10.1080/02699930050117684

Hokanson, J. E., Rubert, M. P., Welker, R. A., Hollander, G. R., & Hedeen, C. (1989). Interpersonal concomitants and antecedents of depression among college students. *Journal of Abnormal Psychology, 98*, 209–217. doi:10.1037/0021-843X.98.3.209

Kasch, K. L., Rottenberg, J., Arnow, B. A., & Gotlib, I. H. (2002). Behavioral activation and inhibition systems and the severity and course of depression. *Journal of Abnormal Psychology, 111*, 589–597. doi:10.1037/0021-843X.111.4.589

Kibler, J. L., & Ma, M. (2004). Depressive symptoms and cardiovascular reactivity to laboratory behavioral stress. *International Journal of Behavioral Medicine, 11*, 81–87. doi:10.1207/s15327558ijbm1102_3

Klein, D. N., Durbin, C. E., Shankman, S. A., & Santiago, N. J. (2002). Depression and personality. In I. H. Gotlib & C. L. Hammen (Eds.), *Handbook of depression* (pp. 115–140). New York, NY: Guilford Press.

Kreibig, S. D., Gendolla, G. H. E., & Scherer, K. R. (2010). Psychophysiological effects of emotional responding to goal attainment. *Biological Psychology, 84*, 474–487. doi:10.1016/j.biopsycho.2009.11.004

Levick, J. R. (2003). *Introduction to cardiovascular physiology* (4th ed.). New York, NY: Oxford University Press.

Morris, W. N. (1992). A functional analysis of the role of mood in affective system. *Review of personality and social psychology. Emotion, 13*, 256–293.

Nestler, E. J., & Carlezon, W. A. (2006). The mesolimbic dopamine reward circuit in depression. *Biological Psychiatry, 59*, 1151–1159. doi:10.1016/j.biopsych.2005.09.018

Obrist, P. A. (1981). *Cardiovascular psychophysiology: A perspective*. New York, NY: Plenum Press.

Richter, M., Friedrich, A., & Gendolla, G. H. E. (2008). Task difficulty effects on cardiac activity. *Psychophysiology, 45*, 869–875. doi:10.1111/j.1469-8986.2008.00688.x

Richter, M., & Gendolla, G. H. E. (2006). Incentive effects on cardiovascular reactivity in active coping with unclear difficulty. *International Journal of Psychophysiology, 61*, 216–225. doi:10.1016/j.ijpsycho.2005.10.003

Richter, M., & Gendolla, G. H. E. (2009a). The heart contracts to reward: Monetary incentives and pre-ejection period. *Psychophysiology, 46*, 451–457. doi:10.1111/j.1469-8986.2009.00795.x

Richter, M., & Gendolla, G. H. E. (2009b). Mood impact on cardiovascular reactivity when task difficulty is unclear. *Motivation and Emotion, 33*, 239–248. doi:10.1007/s11031-009-9134-4

Salomon, K., Clift, A., Karlsdóttir, M., & Rottenberg, J. (2009). Major depressive disorder is associated with attenuated cardiovascular reactivity and impaired recovery among those free of cardiovascular disease. *Health Psychology, 28,* 157–165. doi:10.1037/a0013001

Schwarz, N. (1990). Feelings as information: Information and motivational functions of affective states. In E. T. Higgins & R. M. Sorrentino (Eds.), *Motivation and cognition: Foundations of social behavior* (Vol. 2, pp. 527–561). New York, NY: Guilford Press.

Schwarz, N., & Clore, G. L. (1988). How do I feel about it? The informative function of affective states. In K. Fiedler & J. P. Forgas (Eds.), *Affect, cognition, and social behavior* (pp. 44–62). Göttingen, Germany: Hogrefe.

Silvestrini, N., & Gendolla, G. H. E. (2007). Mood state effects on autonomic activity in mood regulation. *Psychophysiology, 44,* 650–659. doi:10.1111/j.1469-8986.2007.00532.x

Silvestrini, N., & Gendolla, G. H. E. (2009a). The joint effect of mood, task valence, and task difficulty on effort-related cardiovascular response and facial EMG. *International Journal of Psychophysiology, 73,* 226–234. doi:10.1016/j.ijpsycho.2009.03.004

Silvestrini, N., & Gendolla, G. H. E. (2009b). Mood-regulative hedonic incentive interacts with mood and task difficulty to determine effort-related cardiovascular response and facial EMG. *Biological Psychology, 82,* 54–63. doi:10.1016/j.biopsycho.2009.05.005

Wegner, D. M., Shortt, J. W., Blake, A. W., & Page, M. S. (1990). The suppression of exciting thoughts. *Journal of Personality and Social Psychology, 58,* 409–418. doi:10.1037/0022-3514.58.3.409

Wright, R. A. (1996). Brehm's theory of motivation as a model of effort and cardiovascular response. In P. M. Gollwitzer & J. A. Bargh (Eds.), *The psychology of action: Linking cognition and motivation to behavior* (pp. 424–453). New York, NY: Guilford Press.

Wright, R. A., & Dismukes, A. (1995). Cardiovascular effects of experimentally induced efficacy (ability) appraisals at low and high levels of avoidant task demand. *Psychophysiology, 32,* 172–176. doi:10.1111/j.1469-8986.1995.tb03309.x

Wright, R. A., & Kirby, L. D. (2001). Effort determination of cardiovascular response: An integrative analysis with applications in social psychology. *Advances in Experimental Social Psychology, 33,* 255–307. doi:10.1016/S0065-2601(01)80007-1

Wright, R. A., Martin, R. E., & Bland, J. L. (2003). Energy resource depletion, task difficulty, and cardiovascular response to a mental arithmetic challenge. *Psychophysiology, 40,* 98–105. doi:10.1111/1469-8986.00010

Wyer, R. S., Clore, G. L., & Isbell, L. M. (1999). Affect and information processing. *Advances in Experimental Social Psychology, 31,* 1–77. doi:10.1016/S0065-2601(08)60271-3

8

CARDIOVASCULAR REACTIVITY TO STRESS: THE ROLE OF MOTIVATIONAL CONFLICT

JUSTIN E. STANLEY AND RICHARD J. CONTRADA

The cardiovascular system has long been used as a window into the motivational, personality, and stress processes thought to promote heart disease. Cardiovascular indices enjoy this popularity because they are accessible to fairly inexpensive instruments and because the cardiovascular system is highly responsive to neurobiological influences underlying psychological phenomena. At a more basic level, the premise of this work is that associations between cardiovascular and behavioral processes have significant implications for adaptation.

As this volume demonstrates, the cardiovascular psychophysiology of motivational and stress-related states potentially involved in cardiovascular disease is an active and productive research area. Stress, motivational intensity, personality dispositions, and mood states appear to be associated with health-damaging cardiovascular adjustments. Central and autonomic nervous system underpinnings of those adjustments are being characterized, and much has been learned about social–contextual and situational variables that instigate and regulate these processes.

Preparation of this chapter was supported by a Rutgers Academic Excellence Award and a grant from the Charles and Johanna Busch Foundation.

However, less systematic attention has been given to cardiovascular consequences of conflicted motivation, mixed social motives, and emotional ambivalence. Such phenomena have, of course, received considerable attention in various areas of psychology. But, in most cases, these literatures have remained isolated from one another, and implications for cardiovascular function have not been thoroughly addressed. This may be a significant oversight. Instances of conflicted, mixed, and ambivalent motivations may be common, owing both to operating features of the human mind and to the structure and patterning of human life. And they may play a special role in producing health-damaging perturbations of the cardiovascular system.

This chapter provides an overview of research linking motivational conflict, mixtures, and ambivalence to cardiovascular reactivity. We use the term *motivational conflict* to refer to a variety of psychological constructs that have as a shared feature conflicted or opposing inclinations, orientations, or environmental presses. We use the term *cardiovascular reactivity* (CVR) to refer to environmentally induced, psychologically mediated alterations in neuroendocrine and autonomic nervous system activity that culminate in heart and blood vessel responses such as changes in myocardial performance and vascular tone, most commonly measured as elevations in blood pressure and heart rate over resting, baseline activity.

We begin with a brief discussion of the philosophical and psychoanalytic roots of research on motivational conflict and of highly influential analyses of motivational conflict based on learning theory. We then turn to circumscribed, middle-level theoretical models and empirical studies examining cardiovascular function in relation to general psychological processes whereby situational factors promote motivational conflict, personality constructs that entail individual differences in motivational conflict, and person–situation interaction models. We conclude with a set of considerations that may guide future research on motivational conflict.

PHILOSOPHICAL AND PSYCHOANALYTIC ROOTS

Motivational conflict has featured prominently in Western philosophy. Plato's tripartite model of the soul outlines discrete motivational entities— the appetite, reason, and the will—and allocates to them differing shares in the control of behavior. Plato's view anticipated Freud's well-known division of the psyche into id, ego, and superego; less appreciated is the evaluative space allotted in Plato's configuration for irresolvable conflicts that create states of motivational vacillation (Plass, 1978). Aristotle was attentive to this issue, having distinguished between single-minded decision making, or *virtue*, and emotionally ambivalent decision-making, or *continence* (Watson, 1977).

These and other accounts of the ambivalence inherent in the self formed a backdrop to the earliest psychological theories of the human mind. Freud described a motivational field of intrapsychic drives that operate simultaneously and independently from one another. Their coactivation and conflict are experienced obliquely, in the form of anxiety, depression, and the somatizing disorders generated by repressive defenses (Freud, 1957). Freud's studies of somatic reactions to conflict inspired research on psychophysical symptoms, including that of Alexander (1950) on psychosomatic disorders caused by psychological conflict.

LEARNING THEORY ANALYSES

Lewin's (1935) field analysis of motivational conflict influenced early research on stimulus–response dimensions of goal conflict, most notably the work of Miller. Miller's (1944) well-known paradigm involves a rat's approach to a surface where it had been both shocked and rewarded with food in the past. The nearer the rat approaches, the stronger grows the tendency to retreat, defining an *avoidance gradient*. The farther the rat goes, the stronger grows the tendency to approach the food, defining an *approach gradient*. Miller formulated several spatial, temporal, and analytic principles of motivational conflict. He and Dollard, a psychoanalyst, sought to elucidate the relationship between inhibited goal responses and neurotic symptoms, work that fed into a broader current of psychodynamic thinking about motivational conflict (Dollard & Miller, 1950).

Gray expanded on earlier models by providing physiological evidence for separable appetitive and aversive motivational systems (Gray, 1982). In a typical study, a rat moved down a runaway where it had previously encountered motivationally significant stimuli. The rat would be inhibited in its approach if the location was associated with previous punishment or frustrative nonreward. Anxiolytic drugs counteracted this inhibition but did not impede active behavioral avoidance of unconditioned aversive stimuli. Findings such as these led Gray to propose reinforcement sensitivity theory, positing distinct motivational systems: fight–flight system (FFS), behavioral activation system (BAS), and behavioral inhibition system (BIS).

It was originally posited that the FFS generates responses to unconditioned aversive stimuli; the BAS to unconditioned and conditioned appetitive stimuli; and the BIS to conditioned aversive stimuli (Gray, 1982). Later, Gray and McNaughton (2000) introduced further distinctions between the BIS and FFS (reconceptualized as a fight–flight–freeze system, or FFFS), incorporating differences between fear and anxiety and emphasizing the role that defensive direction plays in their differential elicitation. When an organism retreats from threat, this is active avoidance, a fear (FFFS) response. When an organism approaches a fear-inducing threat, the conflict elicits anxiety, a BIS response, as well as fear and frustration. The BIS inhibits prepotent behavioral tendencies and elicits risk assessment behaviors, increasing cognitively biasing fear and frustration effects, such as rumination and obsession. McNaughton and Corr (2004) observed that autonomic arousal increases additively in conflict, relative to the strength of competing approach and avoidance tendencies.

Gray's (1982) model provided a conceptual framework for much human and animal research on motivational conflict. Increases in systolic blood pressure have been observed in animals facing approach–avoidance conflicts (Lawler, Barker, Hubbard, & Schaub, 1980), as have differential heart rate (HR) reactivity and neuroendocrine responses in humans confronting appetitive and aversive challenges (Lovallo, Pincomb, & Brackett, 1990). Fowles (1980) extended Gray's model to integrate BIS activity with personality. He obtained strong evidence for the hypothesis that impulsive behaviors are correlated with weakened BIS responsivity, as indexed by poor skin-conductance conditioning to cues of threatened punishment and frustrative nonreward. Extensions of Fowles's model include Damasio, Tranel, and Damasio's (1990) studies of executive functioning and impulse control in brain-injured patients; Gross and Thompson's (2007) work on emotional suppression (discussed later); and Carver, Sutton, and Scheier's (2000) integration of physiological and emotional factors in motivation.

PROCESS-FOCUSED APPROACHES: PSYCHOLOGICAL MEDIATION OF MOTIVATIONAL CONFLICT

Typically, CVR is conceptualized as a physiological response to psychological stress. In his highly influential theory, Lazarus argued that stress is initiated by *appraisal*, a cognitive–evaluative process in which the person assesses possible danger or benefit to his or her physical or psychological well-being (*primary appraisal*) and evaluates available means of managing that danger and its impact (*secondary appraisal*; e.g., Lazarus & Folkman, 1984). In *threat*, there is a perception of potential damage; in *harm* or *loss*, damage has already been sustained; and in *challenge*, there are elements of both threat and possible gain.

In a different view of appraisal, Blascovich's (2008) *biopsychosocial model* (BPSM) focuses on evaluations a person makes of situational demands and resources. Threat occurs when resources are evaluated as not adequate to meet situational demands, and challenge when resources are evaluated as outweighing demands. A key premise of the BPSM is that threat and challenge induce contrasting psychophysiological patterns. Threat is associated with moderate cardiac reactivity and an increase or no change in peripheral vascular resistance. By contrast, challenge is associated with high cardiac reactivity and a decline in peripheral vascular resistance. Although it might be surmised that threat and challenge map onto avoidance motivation and approach motivation respectively, Blascovich (2008) and others (e.g., Tomaka & Palacios-Esquivel, 1997) have discussed several reasons why this may not be the case. One is that an individual's goal hierarchy may be such that attaining a super-ordinate goal for which overall available resources appear adequate (challenge) may require confronting subordinate goal situations in which they do not (threat). Another involves patterns of change in demands and resources that may induce coactivation of behavioral approach and avoidance. Tomaka and Palacios-Esquivel (1997) obtained partial support for these hypotheses.

As in the work of Lewin (1935) and Miller (1944), Cacioppo and colleagues (Cacioppo & Berntson, 1999; Cacioppo, Gardner, & Berntson, 1999) emphasized in the *evaluative space model* (ESM) the existence of separate subsystems for appetitive (positive) and aversive (negative) processing of stimuli. In *reciprocal activation*, a stimulus simultaneously increases positivity and decreases negativity (or vice versa). By themselves, instances of reciprocal activation appear to fit one-dimensional, bipolar conceptions of affective space. However, the ESM also posits a *coactivation* mode involving simultaneous increases (or decreases) in appetitive and aversive processes, giving rise to states of conflict. Cacioppo and Berntson (1999) characterized states of coactivation as unpleasant and unstable but also as promotive of exploration in novel, seemingly hospitable situations, while creating vigilance and preparation for rapid retreat should danger arise. Depending on environmental demands and constraints, coactivated positivity and negativity may transition to reciprocal activation, fitting a bipolar, unidimensional model as the organism chooses between approach and avoidance (Cacioppo et al., 1999; Finan, Zautra, & Wershba, 2010).

The ESM provides an explicit basis for expecting that individuals may often confront situations that evoke feelings of ambivalence. Van Harreveld, van der Pligt, and de Liver (2009) developed a model to account for affective and physiological reactivity to ambivalence. It focuses on predecisional ambivalence, whose unpleasantness is increased by the accessibility and salience of positive and negative components of the decision, as well as by the need to make a dichotomous choice. The arousal caused by predecisional ambivalence is mediated by uncertainty about possible consequences and the anticipated negative affects engendered by an incorrect choice. Strategies used to reduce ambivalence include procrastination, denial of responsibility, and effortful information processing. If cognitive resources are lacking, "low road" information processing (biased, heuristic) will be favored over the more cognitively taxing route of unbiased, and more elaborate, information processing (van Harreveld et al., 2009).

Appraisal and other stimulus evaluation processes typically promote behavioral response selection, whether or not they produce ambivalence. In stress theory, the term *coping* refers to cognitive and behavioral responses aimed at dealing with situations that give rise to a stress appraisal and at managing their impact (Lazarus & Folkman, 1984). Coping may be directed at altering the initiating situation (*problem-focused coping*) or at ameliorating its impact on the person (*emotion-focused coping*). The vigor and intensity of coping efforts have been linked to the form and magnitude of physiologic responses to stress. This proposition can be traced to Walter Cannon's (1915/1929) emergency/fight-or-flight mechanism and runs through Glass's (1977) controllability model of Type A behavior and sympathetic–adrenomedullary activity, and Obrist's (1981) work on active coping and beta-sympathetic cardiovascular influences.

As discussed more fully later, motivational conflict may occur when coping and other behavioral tendencies are constrained by circumstances. In some cases, these situational factors activate emotion regulation. Gross and Thompson (2007) discussed five emotion regulation processes—situation selection, situation modification, attentional deployment, cognitive change, and response modulation—and provided an overview of their impact. Perhaps one of the clearest findings concerns response modulation, which occurs late in the emotion episode and refers to influences on physiologic, experiential, or behavioral response tendencies. Conscious inhibition of the behavioral expression of emotion appears to increase sympathetic nervous system (SNS) stimulation of the cardiovascular system (Demaree et al., 2006).

PERSON-FOCUSED APPROACHES: MOTIVATIONAL CONFLICT IN PERSONALITY

Many personality dispositions involve opposing tendencies of various kinds. The sampling we provide next emphasizes those that explicitly incorporate motivational conflict and appear to have physiological correlates. However, we begin with a discussion of the Type A coronary-prone behavior pattern. Although motivational conflict is not a defining feature of Type A behavior, there are elements of Type A that can be conceptualized in such terms. More important, research on Type A behavior has had an enormous impact on the study of CVR, including work involving derivatives of the Type A construct that explicitly entail motivational conflict.

Type A Behavior Pattern and Related Constructs

Type A behavior consists of achievement-striving, competitiveness, impatience, anger and hostility, and vigorous vocal and motor mannerisms

(Friedman & Rosenman, 1974). The relative absence of these characteristics is referred to as *Type B*. Glass (1977) conceptualized Type A behavior as a style of coping with potentially uncontrollable stressors. Initial reports implicated Type A behavior as an independent risk factor for coronary heart disease (CHD) when measured using a structured interview. It was hypothesized that Type A behavior confers coronary risk through its association with sympathetic–adrenomedullary system activity and concomitant elevations in circulating catecholamine levels, hemodynamic activity, and other physiologic changes. Recently, interest in Type A has waned in light of inconsistencies in findings involving disease endpoints, in favor of a focus on its anger and hostility components.

McClelland's (1979) work on inhibited power motivation reflects a motivational perspective on Type A. Working from a previous formulation of power motivation, McClelland proposed that inhibiting the power motive increases cardiovascular risk. He measured the inhibited power motive by having participants write a story on assigned themes. He found that hypertensive subjects, as compared with nonhypertensives, tended to inject elements of power into their stories and to more frequently use negating words and phrases, which prior research had shown to be a useful index of activity inhibition. Subsequent research (McClelland, Floor, Davidson, & Saron, 1980; McClelland & Jemmott, 1980) examined inhibited power motivation in relation to cardiovascular and immune system functioning.

As noted previously, research on specific aspects of the global Type A pattern has identified anger and hostility as its chief risk-enhancing elements (Williams, Smith, Gunn, & Uchino, 2010). Anger and hostility do not inherently involve conflict. However, interest in anger and hostility revived hypotheses associated with the psychosomatic tradition that involve individual differences in the manner and degree to which anger-related impulses are expressed. Such personality constructs often have been conceptualized in terms of intrapsychic conflicts involving anger, hostility, and their expression. Several have been studied in relation to CVR as well as to CHD endpoints. As discussed later in this chapter, anger and hostility also play into interpersonal conflict.

One example of a conflicted, anger-related personality construct is *defensive hostility* (Jamner, Shapiro, Goldstein, & Hug, 1991). It combines *trait hostility*, defined as cynicism, anger, and aggressiveness, measured by the Cook-Medley Hostility Scale (Cook & Medley, 1954), with defensiveness, or a tendency to avoid, deny, or minimize threat and negative emotions, measured by the Marlowe-Crowne Social Desirability Scale (MCSDS; Crowne & Marlowe, 1960). Defensive hostility has been linked to ambulatory cardiovascular activity (Jamner et al., 1991), CVR to a laboratory stressor (Helmers & Krantz, 1996; Jorgensen, Abdul-Karim, Kahan, & Frankowski, 1995), stress-induced myocardial ischemia (Helmers et al., 1995), and coronary artery disease (Jorgensen et al., 2001). Jorgensen et al. (2001) and Jorgensen and Thibodeau (2006) conceptualized defensive hostility in terms of approach–avoidance conflict involving coactivation of a desire for social approval and vigilance for potentially hostile acts of others.

Related constructs focus on anger as opposed to the broader, more attitudinal, hostility concept. The Type A structured interview has been used to assess *anger-in*, a coping style entailing a tendency to minimize outward expression of anger (e.g., Dembroski, MacDougall, Williams, Haney, & Blumenthal, 1985). Other work has used Spielberger's (1988) State–Trait Anger Expression Inventory, which has *anger-in*, *anger-out*, and *anger-control* subscales. These constructs have been studied in relation to CVR (for a review, see Schum, Jorgensen, Verhaeghen, Sauro, & Thibodeau, 2003) and to sustained blood pressure elevations (Jorgensen, Johnson, Kolodziej, & Schreer, 1996). However, they have not always been conceptualized in terms of motivational conflict or within other explicit psychological frameworks. Recently, Jorgensen and Kolodziej (2007) described a model that incorporates low anger expression, guilt associated with aggressive impulses, and defensive strivings to avoid social disapproval.

Repressive Coping and Its Variants

In parallel with the anger and hostility constructs discussed previously, *repressive coping* involves a threat-avoidant orientation with reference to anxiety or to negative emotions more broadly defined. Weinberger, Schwartz, and Davidson (1979) introduced repressive coping, assessed as a combination of low trait anxiety as measured by the Taylor (1953) Manifest Anxiety Scale (MAS), and high defensiveness as measured by the MCSDS (Crowne & Marlowe, 1960). Remaining score patterns were taken to identify truly low anxious (low MAS, low MCSDS), high anxious (high MAS, low MCSDS), and defensively high anxious individuals (high MAS, high MCSDS). Numerous psychophysiological studies of repressive coping have been conducted (Krohne, 1996). Although there are inconsistencies, repressive coping appears related to a response pattern in which cardiovascular responses to laboratory stressors are high relative to negative affect ratings (e.g., Newton & Contrada, 1992; Weinberger et al., 1979).

The *Type D behavior pattern* (Denollet, Pedersen, Vrints, & Conraads, 2006) involves negative affectivity, a general tendency to experience negative emotions, and social inhibition, a tendency to inhibit self-expression in social interactions. Although the evidence base is not yet extensive, there are findings to suggest that Type D is associated with CHD risk (Denollet, Martens, Nyklicek, Conraads, & de Gelder, 2008; Denollet et al., 2006). There is also evidence to suggest that Type D behavior may be associated with cardio-vascular responses to laboratory stressors (Denollet et al., 2006).

Attachment Style

Attachment research has long emphasized the role of conflicting motivations in affiliative relationships. Disruptions of normative attachment patterns are variously defined as *insecure attachment styles* or *insecure attachment states of mind*. These patterns can be differentiated through experimental instruments such as the Strange Situation procedure and the Adult Attachment Interview (AAI; Ainsworth, Blehar, Waters, & Wall, 1978; Main & Goldwyn, 1994). They include anxious or resistant styles, characterized by conflicted, over-involved behavior and emotional expressivity, and avoidant styles, characterized by dismissive behavior toward caregivers. Insecure attachment styles have negative consequences for emotion regulation and psychosocial development (Belsky & Rovine, 1987). Research on long-term effects of infant attachment experiences indicates that internal working models persist into adulthood, structuring adult relationships through expectancies of security and rejection (Hamilton, 2000).

The Gray/Fowles model has been applied in studies of insecure adult attachment patterns, most notably by Dozier and Kobak (1992). They conceived of adult attachment states according to two coactive dimensions: primary secure/anxious states and secondary deactivating/hyperactivating strategies. The secondary strategies correspond to the categorization of attachment styles in the Strange Situation studies (Ainsworth et al., 1978). The deactivating strategy, characteristic of the avoidant personality, involves giving vague, incoherent, and "circling" answers in response to attachment-relevant questions in the AAI, indicative of underlying response conflict (Main & Goldwyn, 1994). Dozier and Kobak (1992) posited that use of deactivating strategies during the AAI should be associated with increased CVR, especially in response to questions related to perceptions of insecurity and abandonment. This hypothesis was supported, leading to the suggestion that, in both infants and adults, autonomic activity can reflect effortful engagement in self-distraction in response to attachment-related conflict. Roisman (2007) extended Dozier and Kobak's studies to establish differential effects on cardiovascular functioning of deactivating and hyperactivating strategies. The use of deactivating strategies in attachment-relevant contexts provokes increases in electrodermal activity, in accord with Fowles's model (Roisman, 2007). Subsequent studies of attachment avoidance have suggested a prominent role for cardiovascular measures. A review of adult attachment studies point to potentially chronic, health-damaging alterations in stress psychophysiology, including higher diastolic blood pressure and lower vagal tone (Maunder & Hunter, 2008).

Goal Conflict

Goal conflict occurs when "a goal that a person wishes to accomplish interferes with the attainment of at least one other goal that the individual simultaneously wishes to accomplish" (Emmons & Kaiser, 1996, p. 531). Goal conflict constructs emphasizing approach–avoidance dynamics include those found in the work of Elliot and Sheldon (1998). Avoidance-oriented achievement goals, in this framework, focus on the avoidance of negative outcomes and states, evoking the avoidance behaviors characterized in Gray and McNaughton's (2000) framework. Elliot and Sheldon found that self-reports of avoidance-oriented goal strivings can be reliably correlated with negative affect and somatic symptomatology.

Another approach to goal conflict involves *personal strivings*, defined by Emmons (1986) as goal-directed trends underlying individuals' behavioral choices. Emmons and King (1988) linked personal strivings conflict to ratings of stress, poor subjective well-being, and physical and psychiatric symptoms. Ewart and Jorgensen (2004) and Dixon, Dixon, and Spinner (1991) found that self-reports and behavioral observations reflecting personal strivings—the desire to influence others' behavior, and the tension between work and interpersonal commitments, respectively—were correlated cardiovascular measures, including elevated blood pressure and HR.

MOTIVATIONAL CONFLICT IN PERSON–SITUATION INTERACTIONS

Motivational conflict may arise when psychological attributes that are not inherently conflict-related interact with features of certain kinds of situations. This notion falls within a person–situation interactionism that emerged from the debate about personality traits that was initiated by Mischel (1968). The interplay between persons and situations has been conceptualized in more complex ways, as in reciprocal determinism (Bandura, 1986) and person–situation transactionism (Williams et al., 2010). Research within these traditions has identified physiological responses to processes of interplay between person and situations, often including potentially disease-promoting cardiovascular activity. Indeed, assignment of constructs to an earlier section of this chapter, Person-Focused Approaches: Motivational Conflict in Personality, was somewhat arbitrary, as they are generally conceptualized as influencing behavioral and physiological activity only when activated by certain environmental events and conditions. However, this section focuses on cases of person–situation interplay that explicitly involve conflict.

Person–Environment Fit

Theory concerning *person–environment fit* (PEF; Caplan & Harrison, 1993) conceptualizes both persons and environments (typically, work environments) using corresponding dimensions (Quick, Nelson, Quick, & Orman, 2001). The focus is on describing, understanding, and improving actual or perceived PEF as a way of promoting psychological and physical health. Relative lack of PEF can be seen as instances of conflict between factors such as job goals or demands, on the one hand, and a person's abilities or experiences, on the other. Perhaps most relevant to this chapter is the effort–reward imbalance model (Siegrist, 1996), which has shown some utility in predicting cardiovascular disease endpoints. In addition, a PEF framework has been used to identify situations in which Type A individuals are likely to show elevated cardiovascular activity (e.g., Chesney et al., 1981). However, for the most part, PEF theory has focused on strain, burnout, and physical and psychological well-being, rather than on measures reflecting stress-related cardiovascular activity (for a recent review, see Pandey, Quick, Rossi, Nelson, & Martin, 2010).

Situational Constraints on Emotion Regulation

In the individual difference constructs discussed earlier, the source of conflict regarding emotional expression was either unspecified or stemmed from an intrapersonal disposition. However, conflict about emotional expression often may arise from interactions between personal dispositions and environmental factors. In this regard, Engebretson, Matthews, and Scheier (1989) reported a laboratory study that provided some support for a *matching hypothesis* in which cardiovascular activity is enhanced when the individual's preferred mode of coping with anger is incongruent with situational affordances and constraints. Their perspective may inform earlier accounts of poorer health outcomes, discussed earlier, that appear to reflect lack of fit between person and environment. Psychophysiological extensions of this research have been pursued by Burns (1995) and Bongard and al'Absi (2003).

Psychophysiology of Social Relationships

Interpersonal conflict can be viewed as a special case of motivational conflict in which incompatible motives are embodied within different, interacting individuals. Many forms of interpersonal conflict have been studied, including that within dyads, families, and other groups, and that between individuals falling within different social categories. Marital relationships have been of particular interest, in part because of the chronic nature and potential health impact of marital stressors (McGonagle, Kessler, & Schilling, 1992).

Marital conflict is reliably associated with elevations in HR, blood pressure (e.g., Mayne, O'Leary, McCrady, Contrada, & Labouvie, 1997), and other potentially health-damaging physiological responses (Kiecolt-Glaser, Gouin, & Hantsoo, 2010).

Gottman's engagement/withdrawal model conceptualizes marital conflict in terms of spouses' differential reactivity to stress and tolerance of negative affect (Gottman & Levenson, 1988). In the prototypical scenario, the wife tries to engage in discussions of relationship problems, and the husband withdraws, provoking further unsuccessful attempts to engage. Research suggests that the experience of heightened SNS activation is uncomfortable for withdrawing husbands and that withdrawal is a defensive reaction (Gottman & Levenson, 1988). Subsequent work in this area has de-emphasized differences in stress tolerance that were attributed solely to gender, placing greater emphasis on emotion regulation dynamics, including variations in individuals' levels of arousal and tolerance of ambivalence-induced distress (Verhofstadt, Buysse, De Clercq, & Goodwin, 2005), and it has extended physiological measures to include parasympathetic tone and inflammatory activity (Maunder, Lancee, Nolan, Hunter, & Tannenbaum, 2006; Gouin et al., 2009).

MOTIVATIONAL CONFLICT AND CARDIOVASCULAR REACTIVITY: TOWARD A THEORETICAL FRAMEWORK

This brief overview of research on motivational conflict and CVR has identified a number of considerations that may be useful for framing future work on this topic. A schematic depiction of selected elements of such a synthesis is displayed in Figure 8.1. One suggestion is that it would be useful to elaborate further the perceptual processes that mediate situational generation of motivational conflict. For example, the Lazarus and Folkman (1984) conception of a challenge appraisal raises the question as to whether adding the possibility of a positive outcome to a situation of simple threat of a negative (vs. benign) outcome would further increase cardiovascular activity. A related question is whether a situation that is challenging in the Lazarus-Folkman sense (i.e., because behavioral performance may simultaneously avoid negative outcomes and achieve desired ones) produces the same pattern of cardiovascular adjustments that has been associated with the somewhat different form of challenge, highlighted by the BPSM of Blascovich (2008), in which resources outweigh demands.

Additional issues are raised by attempts to delineate the temporal junctures at which motivational conflict is produced by perceptual processes and undergoes regulation by other factors. There are probably several points of interest as stimulus selection and interpretation unfold. Ambivalent stimulus

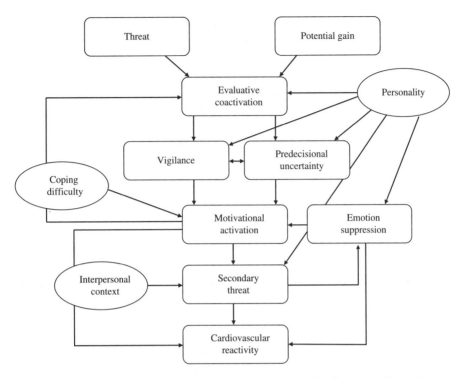

Figure 8.1. Motivationally significant situations often contain elements of both threat and potential gain. Appraisal of such situations leads to coactivation of positive and negative evaluation (ambivalence). Vigilance is heightened for the detection of changes in threat level, and, where a dichotomous choice is required, predecisional uncertainty will develop. Motivational activation ensues to an intensity determined by factors that include the strength of positive and negative evaluation components and the difficulty of relevant instrumental acts. The social context and/or conflicted personality attributes may promote activation of a secondary threat process, the source of which is a negative appraisal of the consequences of emotional experience and expression. Secondary threat may lead to emotion suppression, a self-regulation function that amplifies motivational activation and perhaps increases cardiovascular reactivity (CVR) more directly as well. Degree of motivational activation and higher order processes that regulate motivation are among the factors that influence the magnitude and duration of sympathetically mediated CVR.

evaluations may arise at early stages of processing, but cardiovascular adjustments take longer to become mobilized. This is in part a consequence of the time required for descending pathways to activate peripheral autonomic and neuroendocrine mechanisms (Obrist, 1981). But it is also likely a reflection of processing time needed to evaluate contextual information, including that pertaining to behavioral options, their likelihood of success, and relevant situational constraints. Among the more important influences at later processing stages are perceptions that favor preparation for and initiation of moderately effortful coping activity (Obrist, 1981) that call for suppression of emotional experience or expression (Gross & Thompson, 2007) or initiate other forms of controlled regulation of motivational activation (Carver, Johnson, & Joormann, 2008) and that promote vigilance for further inputs that would require a change in initial behavioral inclinations (Cacioppo et al., 1999).

Another set of questions concern the manner in which processes of motivational conflict, operating at the psychological level, combine to determine the magnitude and patterning of CVR. One suggestion is that the intensity or arousal potential of two opposing motivational processes summate to produce greater CVR than would be associated with either process when activated separately (McNaughton & Corr, 2004). On the other hand, van Harreveld et al. (2009) argued that it is cognitive uncertainty regarding negative outcomes that explains physiological responses in situations of motivational conflict, at least when dichotomous decision making is required. Betensky and Contrada (2010) discussed alternative explanations for findings indicating that contrasting cognitive and motivational factors (i.e., depressed mood and trait aggression) may combine synergistically to produce heightened CVR to emotional provocation.

Further integration of process- and person-focused approaches also would seem warranted. It is reasonable to suppose that relevant personality attributes predispose to motivational conflict through their effects on stimulus selection, evaluation, and interpretation and response selection, preparation, and implementation. This may reflect processes in which personality factors promote activation of conflicting primary and secondary goals in response to certain situations. For example, it has been suggested that individuals characterized by the repressive coping style possess a desire to maintain their efforts in coping with the situation and to appear stoical in the face of emotional perturbation (Newton & Contrada, 1992). As a consequence, motivationally significant situations pose dual threats: a primary threat, occasioned, for example, by a difficult performance requirement and the secondary threat of experiencing and being seen to express negative emotion. Heightened CVR may arise as a consequence of the combined effects of these two threat appraisals, possibly because they result in coactivation of conflicting motivational mechanisms (e.g., active avoidance and behavioral inhibition). A dual-threat formulation may provide a useful way to conceptualize several personality factors that involve defensiveness or inhibition (e.g., inhibited power motivation, defensive hostility, anger-expression traits, Type D behavior).

The foregoing considerations may facilitate research on ambivalence in marriages and other personal relationships (Holt-Lunstad, Uchino, Smith, & Hicks, 2007; Uchino & Garvey, 1997). Conflicting motives may be coactivated as a consequence of insecure attachment models and associated emotional regulation strategies. In the "engage-and-withdraw" pattern (Gottman

& Levenson, 1988), for example, what evokes the perception of threat, and subsequent withdrawal, may be anticipatory negative emotional arousal experienced during a conversation that is threatening because it touches on attachment-related topics. An avoidant response resembling repressive coping, involving the secondary threat of emotional upset, may then be activated (Maunder et al., 2006; Verhofstadt et al., 2005). Thus, motivational conflict may be both cause and consequence of heightened CVR. Active avoidance is seldom possible in such situations; ambivalence-related CVR may be maintained by the repeated recurrence of perceptions of the simultaneous need to engage with such a friend and of the inhibition of avoidance motives (Holt-Lunstad, Uchino, Smith, Olson-Cerny, & Nealey-Moore, 2003).

CONCLUSION

Stress-promoting events and conditions are multifaceted; they often carry the potential for opportunity, as well as danger, and even the simplest cases will often afford more than one course of response. No less complex are the motivational and emotional systems that are activated in the individual facing these situations, and for good reason, because our evolutionary success reflects a considerable capacity for flexibility. Even as the individual undergoes preparation for a first, best behavioral solution to adverse conditions, other possible responses may be evaluated, contemplated, and incipiently executed. This capacity for ambivalence—the breathing room between evaluation and action that elaborates and enriches our motivational–affective life—is an achievement of no little consequence in the evolution of cognitive agents and is likely associated with the development of neural architecture subserving emotional and motivational regulation (e.g., Carver et al., 2000; Gray, 1982; Gray & McNaughton, 2000; Gross & Thompson, 2007). As a manifestation of our decision-making abilities, ambivalence may have adaptive value, but it also may carry a cost because of its physiological impact.

The primary evolved function of the cardiovascular system is not to express a person's inner psychological world or social relationships. However, the heart and blood vessels are responsive to a number of processes that are activated in motivationally charged situations. Myocardial and vascular changes therefore accompany cognition, emotion, and behavioral preparation in moments of adaptive significance. Our affectively laden evaluations are not often bipolar in nature, and when they are, they rarely remain so for long. Our lives are simultaneously enriched and endangered by our capacity to be ambivalent: to plan, perseverate, inhibit, and ruminate. Greater understanding of conflicted, mixed, and ambivalent motivations may add to the already impressive body of knowledge that has been acquired regarding the role of motivation and stress in cardiovascular function and disease.

"There are two wills in us, because neither by itself is the whole will" (Augustine, 1961, p. 172).

REFERENCES

Ainsworth, M., Blehar, M., Waters, E., & Wall, S. (1978). *Patterns of attachment: A psychological study of the Strange Situation.* Hillsdale, NJ: Erlbaum.

Alexander, F. (1950). *Psychosomatic medicine: Its principles and applications.* New York, NY: Norton.

Augustine. (1961). *Confessions* (R. S. Pine-Coffin, Trans.). New York, NY: Penguin.

Bandura, A. (1986). *Social foundations of thought and action: A social cognitive theory.* Englewood Cliffs, NJ: Prentice Hall.

Belsky, J., & Rovine, M. (1987). Temperament and attachment security in the Strange Situation: An empirical rapprochement. *Child Development, 58,* 787–795. doi:10.2307/1130215

Betensky, J. D., & Contrada, R. J. (2010). Depressive symptoms, trait aggression, and cardiovascular reactivity to a laboratory stressor. *Annals of Behavioral Medicine, 39,* 184–191. doi:10.1007/s12160-010-9176-6

Blascovich, J. (2008). Challenge, threat, and health. In J. Shah & W. Gardner (Eds.), *Handbook of motivation science* (pp. 481–493). New York, NY: Guilford Press.

Bongard, S., & al'Absi, M. (2003). Domain-specific anger expression assessment and blood pressure during rest and acute stress. *Personality and Individual Differences, 34,* 1383–1402. doi:10.1016/S0191-8869(02)00106-X

Burns, J. W. (1995). Interactive effects of traits, states, and gender on cardiovascular reactivity during different situations. *Journal of Behavioral Medicine, 18,* 279–303. doi:10.1007/BF01857874

Cacioppo, J. T., & Berntson, G. G. (1999). The affect system: Architecture and operating characteristics. *Current Directions in Psychological Science, 8,* 133–137. doi:10.1111/1467-8721.00031

Cacioppo, J. T., Gardner, W. L., & Berntson, G. G. (1999). The affect system has parallel and integrative processing components: Form follows function. *Journal of Personality and Social Psychology, 76,* 839–855. doi:10.1037/0022-3514.76.5.839

Cannon, W. B. (1929). *Bodily changes in pain, hunger, fear, and rage.* Boston, MA: Branford. (Original work published 1915)

Caplan, R. D., & Harrison, R. V. (1993). Person–environment fit theory: Some history, recent developments, and future directions. *Journal of Social Issues, 49,* 253–276. doi:10.1111/j.1540-4560.1993.tb01192.x

Carver, C. S., Johnson, S. L., & Joormann, J. (2008). Serotonergic function, two-mode models of self-regulation, and vulnerability to depression: What depression has in common with impulsive aggression. *Psychological Bulletin, 134*, 912–943. doi:10.1037/a0013740

Carver, C. S., Sutton, S. K., & Scheier, M. F. (2000). Action, emotion, and personality: Emerging conceptual integration. *Personality and Social Psychology Bulletin, 26*, 741–751. doi:10.1177/0146167200268008

Chesney, M. A., Sevelius, G., Black, G. W., Ward, M. M., Swan, G. E., & Rosenman, R. H. (1981). Work environment, Type A behavior, and coronary heart disease risk factors. *Journal of Occupational Medicine, 23*, 551–555.

Cook, W. W., & Medley, D. M. (1954). Proposed hostility and Pharisaic-virtue scales for the MMPI. *Journal of Applied Psychology, 38*, 414–418. doi:10.1037/h0060667

Crowne, D. P., & Marlowe, D. (1960). A new scale of social desirability independent of psychopathology. *Journal of Consulting Psychology, 24*, 349–354. doi:10.1037/h0047358

Damasio, A. R., Tranel, D., & Damasio, H. (1990). Individuals with sociopathic behavior caused by frontal damage fail to respond autonomically to social stimuli. *Behavioural Brain Research, 41*, 81–94. doi:10.1016/0166-4328(90)90144-4

Demaree, H. A., Schmeichel, B. J., Robinson, J. L., Pu, J., Everhart, D. E., & Berntson, G. G. (2006). Up- and down-regulating facial disgust: Affective, vagal, sympathetic, and respiratory consequences. *Biological Psychology, 71*, 90–99. doi:10.1016/j.biopsycho.2005.02.006

Dembroski, T. M., MacDougall, J. M., Williams, R. B., Haney, T. L., & Blumenthal, J. A. (1985). Components of Type A, hostility, and anger-in: Relationship to angiographic findings. *Psychosomatic Medicine, 47*, 219–233.

Denollet, J., Martens, E., Nyklicek, I., Conraads, V., & de Gelder, B. (2008). Clinical events in coronary patients who report low distress: Adverse effect of repressive coping. *Health Psychology, 27*, 302–308. doi:10.1037/0278-6133.27.3.302

Denollet, J., Pedersen, S., Vrints, C., & Conraads, V. (2006). Usefulness of type D personality in predicting five-year cardiac events above and beyond concurrent symptoms of stress in patients with coronary heart disease. *The American Journal of Cardiology, 97*, 970–973. doi:10.1016/j.amjcard.2005.10.035

Dixon, J. P., Dixon, J., & Spinner, J. (1991). Tensions between career and interpersonal commitments as a risk factor for cardiovascular disease among women. *Women & Health, 17*, 33–57. doi:10.1300/J013v17n03_03

Dollard, J. & Miller, N. (1950). *Personality and psychotherapy: An analysis in terms of learning, thinking, and culture*. New York, NY: McGraw-Hill.

Dozier, M., & Kobak, R. R. (1992). Psychophysiology in attachment interviews: Converging evidence for deactivating strategies. *Child Development, 63*, 1473–1480. doi:10.2307/1131569

Elliot, A. J., & Sheldon, K. (1998). Avoidance personal goals and the personality–illness relationship. *Journal of Personality and Social Psychology, 75*, 1282–1299. doi:10.1037/0022-3514.75.5.1282

Emmons, R. A. (1986). Personal strivings: An approach to personality and subjective well-being. *Journal of Personality and Social Psychology, 51*, 1058–1068. doi:10.1037/0022-3514.51.5.1058

Emmons, R. A., & Kaiser, H. A. (1996). Goal orientation and emotional well-being: Linking goals and affect through the self. In L. L. Martin & A. Tesser (Eds.), *Striving and feeling: Interactions among goals, affect, and self-regulation* (pp. 79–98). Mahwah, NJ: Erlbaum.

Emmons, R. A., & King, L. A. (1988). Conflict among personal strivings: Immediate and long-term implications for psychological and physical well-being. *Journal of Personality and Social Psychology, 54*, 1040–1048. doi:10.1037/0022-3514.54.6.1040

Engebretson, T. O., Matthews, K. A., & Scheier, M. F. (1989). Relations between anger expression and cardiovascular reactivity: Reconciling inconsistent findings through a matching hypothesis. *Journal of Personality and Social Psychology, 57*, 513–521. doi:10.1037/0022-3514.57.3.513

Ewart, C. K., & Jorgensen, R. S. (2004). Agonistic interpersonal striving: Social–cognitive mechanism of cardiovascular risk in youth? *Health Psychology, 23*, 75–85. doi:10.1037/0278-6133.23.1.75

Finan, P. H., Zautra, A. L., & Wershba, R. (2010). The dynamics of emotion in adaptation to stress. In R. Contrada & A. Baum (Eds.), *Handbook of stress science: Biology, psychology, and health* (pp. 209–220). New York, NY: Springer.

Fowles, D. C. (1980). The three arousal model: Implications of Gray's two-factor learning theory for heart rate, electrodermal activity, and psychopathy. *Psychophysiology, 17*, 87–104. doi:10.1111/j.1469-8986.1980.tb00117.x

Freud, S. (1957). The unconscious. In J. Strachey (Ed. & Trans.), *The standard edition of the complete psychological works of Sigmund Freud* (Vol. 14, pp. 159–215). London, England: Hogarth Press. (Original work published 1915)

Friedman, M., & Rosenman, R. H. (1974). *Type A behavior and your heart*. New York, NY: Fawcett.

Glass, D. C. (1977). *Behavior patterns, stress, and coronary disease*. Hillsdale, NJ: Erlbaum.

Gottman, J. M., & Levenson, R. W. (1988). The social psychophysiology of marriage. In P. Noller & M. A. Fitzpatrick (Eds.), *Perspectives on marital interactions* (pp. 182–200). Clevedon, England: Multilingual Matters.

Gouin, J.-P., Glaser, R., Loving, T., Malarkey, W., Stowell, J., & Houts, C. (2009). Attachment avoidance predicts inflammatory responses to marital conflict. *Brain, Behavior, and Immunity, 23*, 898–904. doi:10.1016/j.bbi.2008.09.016

Gray, J. A. (1982). *The neuropsychology of anxiety: An enquiry into the functions of the septo-hippocampal system*. Oxford, England: Oxford University Press.

Gray, J. A., & McNaughton, N. (2000). *The neuropsychology of anxiety* (2nd ed.). Oxford, England: Oxford University Press.

Gross, J. J., & Thompson, R. A. (2007). Emotion regulation: Conceptual foundations. In J. J. Gross (Ed.), *Handbook of emotion regulation* (pp. 3–24). New York, NY: Guilford Press.

Hamilton, C. E. (2000). Continuity and discontinuity of attachment from infancy to adolescence. *Child Development, 71,* 690–694. doi:10.1111/1467-8624.00177

Helmers, K. F., & Krantz, D. S. (1996). Defensive hostility, gender, and cardiovascular levels and responses to stress. *Annals of Behavioral Medicine, 18,* 246–254. doi:10.1007/BF02895286

Helmers, K. F., Krantz, D. S., Merz, C. N. B., Klein, J., Kop, W. J., Gottdiener, J. S., & Rozanski, A. (1995). Defensive hostility: Relationship to multiple markers of cardiac ischemia in patients with coronary disease. *Health Psychology, 14,* 202–209. doi:10.1037/0278-6133.14.3.202

Holt-Lunstad, J., Uchino, B., Smith, T., & Hicks, A. (2007). On the importance of relationship quality: The impact of ambivalence in friendships on cardiovascular functioning. *Annals of Behavioral Medicine, 33,* 278–290. doi:10.1007/BF02879910

Holt-Lunstad, J., Uchino, B. N., Smith, T. W., Olson-Cerny, C., & Nealey-Moore, J. B. (2003). Social relationships and ambulatory blood pressure: Structural and qualitative predictors of cardiovascular function during everyday social interactions. *Health Psychology, 22,* 388–397. doi:10.1037/0278-6133.22.4.388

Jamner, L. D., Shapiro, D., Goldstein, I. B., & Hug, R. (1991). Ambulatory blood pressure and heart rate in paramedics: Effects of cynical hostility and defensiveness. *Psychosomatic Medicine, 53,* 393–406.

Jorgensen, R. S., Abdul-Karim, K., Kahan, T. A., & Frankowski, J. J. (1995). Defensiveness, cynical hostility, and cardiovascular reactivity: A moderator analysis. *Psychotherapy and Psychosomatics, 64,* 156–161. doi:10.1159/000289006

Jorgensen, R. S., Frankowski, J. J., Lantinga, L. J., Phadke, K., Sprafkin, R. P., & Abdul-Karim, K. W. (2001). Defensive hostility and coronary heart disease: A preliminary investigation of male veterans. *Psychosomatic Medicine, 63,* 463–469.

Jorgensen, R. S., Johnson, B. T., Kolodziej, M. E., & Schreer, G. E. (1996). Elevated blood pressure and personality: A meta-analytic review. *Psychological Bulletin, 120,* 293–320. doi:10.1037/0033-2909.120.2.293

Jorgensen, R. S., & Kolodziej, M. E. (2007). Suppressed anger, evaluative threat, and cardiovascular reactivity: A tripartite profile approach. *International Journal of Psychophysiology, 66,* 102–108. doi:10.1016/j.ijpsycho.2007.03.015

Jorgensen, R. S., & Thibodeau, R. (2006) Defensive hostility and cardiovascular disease: Theoretical and empirical bases for an interpersonal approach–avoidance conflict perspective. In E. Molinari, A. Compare, & G. Parati (Eds.), *Clinical psychology and heart disease* (pp. 217–32). New York, NY: Springer.

Kiecolt-Glaser, J. K., Gouin, J. P., & Hantsoo, L. (2010). Close relationships, inflammation, and health. *Neuroscience and Biobehavioral Reviews, 35,* 33–38. doi:10.1016/j.neubiorev.2009.09.003

Krohne, H. W. (1996). Individual differences in coping. In M. Zeidner & N. S. Endler (Eds.), *Handbook of coping: Theory, research, applications* (pp. 381–409). New York, NY: Wiley.

Lawler, J. E., Barker, G. F., Hubbard, J. W., & Schaub, R. G. (1980). Pathophysiological changes associated with stress-induced hypertension in the borderline hypertensive rat. *Clinical Science, 9,* 307–310.

Lazarus, R. S., & Folkman, S. (1984). *Stress, appraisal, and coping*. New York, NY: Springer.

Lewin, K. (1935). *A dynamic theory of personality*. New York, NY: McGraw-Hill.

Lovallo, W. R., Pincomb, G. A., & Brackett, D. J. (1990). Heart rate reactivity as a predictor of neuroendocrine responses to aversive and appetitive challenges. *Psychosomatic Medicine, 52*, 17–26.

Main, M., & Goldwyn, R. (1994). *Adult attachment rating and classification system*. Unpublished manuscript, Department of Psychology, University of California at Berkeley.

Maunder, R. G., & Hunter, J. J. (2008). Attachment relationships as determinants of physical health. *Journal of the American Academy of Psychoanalysis and Dynamic Psychiatry, 36*, 11–32. doi:10.1521/jaap.2008.36.1.11

Maunder, R. G., Lancee, W., Nolan, R., Hunter, J., & Tannenbaum, D. (2006). The relationship of attachment insecurity to subjective stress and autonomic function during standardized acute stress in healthy adults. *Journal of Psychosomatic Research, 60*, 283–290. doi:10.1016/j.jpsychores.2005.08.013

Mayne, T. J., O'Leary, A., McCrady, B., Contrada, R., & Labouvie, E. (1997). The differential effects of acute marital distress on emotional, physiological, and immune functions in maritally distressed men and women. *Psychology & Health, 12*, 277–288. doi:10.1080/08870449708407405

McClelland, D. C. (1979). Inhibited power motivation and high blood pressure in men. *Journal of Abnormal Psychology, 88*, 182–190. doi:10.1037/0021-843X.88.2.182

McClelland, D. C., Floor, E., Davidson, R., & Saron, C. (1980). Stressed power motivation, sympathetic activation, immune function, and illness. *Journal of Human Stress, 6*, 11–19.

McClelland, D. C., & Jemmott, J. B. (1980). Power motivation, stress and physical illness. *Journal of Human Stress, 6*, 6–15.

McGonagle, K. A., Kessler, R. C., & Schilling, E. A. (1992). The frequency and determinants of marital disagreements in a community sample. *Journal of Social and Personal Relationships, 9*, 507–524. doi:10.1177/0265407592094003

McNaughton, N., & Corr, P. (2004). A two-dimensional neuropsychology of defense: Fear/anxiety and defensive distance. *Neuroscience and Biobehavioral Reviews, 28*, 285–305. doi:10.1016/j.neubiorev.2004.03.005

Miller, N. (1944). Experimental studies of conflict. In J. Hunt (Ed.), *Personality and the behavioral disorders* (Vol. 1, pp. 431–465). New York, NY: Ronald Press.

Mischel, W. (1968). *Personality and assessment*. New York, NY: Wiley.

Newton, T. L., & Contrada, R. J. (1992). Verbal–autonomic response dissociation in repressive coping: The influence of social context. *Journal of Personality and Social Psychology, 62*, 159–167. doi:10.1037/0022-3514.62.1.159

Obrist, P. A. (1981). *Cardiovascular psychophysiology*. New York, NY: Plenum Press.

Pandey, A., Quick, J., Rossi, A. M., Nelson, D. L., & Martin, W. (2010). Stress and the workplace: Ten years of science. In R. Contrada & A. Baum (Eds.), *Hand-*

book of stress science: Biology, psychology, and health (pp. 137–150). New York, NY: Springer.

Plass, P. (1978). Anxiety, repression, and morality: Plato and Freud. *Psychoanalytic Review, 65*, 533–556.

Quick, J. C., Nelson, D. L., Quick, J. D., & Orman, D. K. (2001). An isomorphic theory of stress: The dynamics of person–environment fit. *Stress and Health, 17*, 147–157. doi:10.1002/smi.893

Roisman, G. I. (2007). The psychophysiology of adult attachment relationships: Autonomic reactivity in marital and premarital interactions. *Developmental Psychology, 43*, 39–53. doi:10.1037/0012-1649.43.1.39

Schum, J. L., Jorgensen, R. S., Verhaeghen, P., Sauro, M., & Thibodeau, R. (2003). Trait anger, anger expression, and ambulatory blood pressure: A meta-analytic review. *Journal of Behavioral Medicine, 26*, 395–415. doi:10.1023/A:1025767900757

Siegrist, J. (1996). Adverse health effects of high-effort/low-reward conditions. *Journal of Occupational Health Psychology, 1*, 27–41. doi:10.1037/1076-8998.1.1.27

Spielberger, C. D. (1988). *State–Trait Anger Expression Inventory (STAXI): Research edition*. Odessa, FL: Psychological Assessment Resources.

Taylor, J. A. (1953). A personality scale of manifest anxiety. *Journal of Abnormal and Social Psychology, 48*, 285–290. doi:10.1037/h0056264

Tomaka, J., & Palacios-Esquivel, R. L. (1997). Motivational systems and stress-related cardiovascular reactivity. *Motivation and Emotion, 21*, 275–296. doi:10.1023/A:1024414005745

Uchino, B. N., & Garvey, T. G. (1997). The availability of social support reduces cardiovascular reactivity to acute psychological stress. *Journal of Behavioral Medicine, 20*, 15–27. doi:10.1023/A:1025583012283

van Harreveld, F., van der Pligt, J., & de Liver, Y. (2009). The agony of ambivalence and ways to resolve it: Introducing the MAID model. *Personality and Social Psychology Review, 13*, 45–61. doi:10.1177/108868308324518

Verhofstadt, L., Buysse, A., De Clercq, A., & Goodwin, R. (2005). Emotional arousal and negative affect in marital conflict: The influence of gender, conflict structure, and demand-withdrawal. *European Journal of Social Psychology, 35*, 449–467. doi:10.1002/ejsp.262

Watson, G. (1977). Skepticism about weakness of will. *The Philosophical Review, 86*, 316–339. doi:10.2307/2183785

Weinberger, D. A., Schwartz, G. E., & Davidson, R. J. (1979). Low-anxious, high-anxious, and repressive coping styles: Psychometric patterns and behavioral and physiological responses to stress. *Journal of Abnormal Psychology, 88*, 369–380. doi:10.1037/0021-843X.88.4.369

Williams, P., Smith, T. W., Gunn, H. E., & Uchino, B. N. (2010). Personality and stress: Individual differences in exposure, reactivity, recovery, and restoration. In R. Contrada & A. Baum (Eds.), *Handbook of stress science: Biology, psychology, and health* (pp. 231–246). New York, NY: Springer.

D. FATIGUE

9

PAUSE AND PLAN: SELF-REGULATION AND THE HEART

SUZANNE C. SEGERSTROM, JAIME K. HARDY, DANIEL R. EVANS, AND NATALIE F. WINTERS

Self-regulation, or the ability to modulate one's thoughts, actions and emotions, is necessary for achieving one's goals and functioning well. Poor self-regulation can lead to ineffective problem solving, passive coping techniques, difficulties altering one's mood, and difficulties in overriding impulses (Vohs & Baumeister, 2004). Evidence of self-regulatory failure can be seen in many of the problems plaguing society, such as obesity, aggression, and drug and alcohol abuse. The process of self-regulation may be conscious and deliberate or unconscious and automatic. Likewise, the substrates of self-regulation may be accessible or inaccessible to consciousness. Although individuals have some insight into their typical self-regulatory capacity, they are often unaware of phasic decrements in their ability to meet self-regulatory demands (Baumeister, Bratslavsky, Muraven, & Tice, 1998; Vohs & Baumeister, 2004). Therefore, self-regulation is a more expansive concept than self-control, which typically connotes only conscious control over the self. Furthermore, self-regulation can encompass both psychosocial and physiological systems; indeed, one aim of this chapter is to demonstrate how psychological and cardiac regulation are related.

In the present chapter, we address how parasympathetic control over the heart is related to self-regulatory strength and the self-regulatory process. The ability to self-regulate has both tonic and phasic elements. Personality traits such as conscientiousness capture some of the between-person variance in ability to self-regulate; people who score high on these personality traits also better regulate their thoughts, emotions, and behaviors (e.g., Tangney, Baumeister, & Boone, 2004). Self-regulatory ability also fluctuates within people. Self-regulation appears to draw on a discrete energy source that can be fatigued after use, analogous to the way a muscle can fatigue after exercise. Preliminary acts of self-regulation negatively affect performance at a subsequent, unrelated self-regulatory task. For example, participants who had to force themselves to eat radishes over chocolate gave up sooner on an unsolvable problem than those who had not been forced to self-regulate. Similarly, those who had to suppress emotion while viewing a film performed worse at a subsequent anagram task than those in the control condition (Baumeister et al., 1998). Baumeister and colleagues (1998) termed this phenomenon *depletion*. However, here we use the term *self-regulatory fatigue* to reflect the fact that people can be motivated to override this effect (e.g., Muraven & Slessareva, 2003), which is possible with fatigue but not depletion.

The phenomenon of self-regulatory fatigue cuts across a number of domains, including but not limited to suppressing emotion, redirecting attention, executive cognitive functioning, making choices, resisting temptation, and inhibiting aggression. Tasks as diverse as suppressing emotions, suppressing thoughts, exaggerating facial emotion, and resisting eating tempting food led to decreases in tasks that were equally diverse, including physical endurance, ice cream intake in dieters, working memory span, and aggressive responding to a provocation (DeWall, Baumeister, Stillman, & Gailliot, 2007; Muraven, Tice, & Baumeister, 1998; Schmeichel, 2007; Vohs & Heatherton, 2000). It is notable that many studies demonstrating self-regulatory fatigue compared the effects of self-regulatory effort with those of another effortful activity that did not involve self-regulation, such as mental arithmetic, listing thoughts, information processing, and memory maintenance (Baumeister et al., 1998; Muraven et al., 1998; Schmeichel, 2007; Schmeichel, Vohs, & Baumeister, 2003). In these studies, effort did not result in self-regulatory fatigue unless it was specifically self-regulatory effort involving, for example, controlling, inhibiting, suppressing, or overriding. Therefore, self-regulatory effort appears to be a special case of psychological effort with unique effects on subsequent behavior; next we show that self-regulation may also have unique effects on physiology.

SELF-REGULATION AND CARDIAC REGULATION: CENTRAL MECHANISMS

What do self-regulatory strength and fatigue have to do with the heart? Areas of the brain thought to be responsible for regulating thoughts, emotions, and behavior appear to overlap significantly with those parts of the brain that regulate the rhythms of the heart. Benarroch (1993) theorized that there was a set of functionally reciprocal neural structures, dubbed the *central autonomic network* (CAN), that integrate autonomic, neuroendocrine, and behavioral responses with emotion, attention, and executive functions. The CAN includes areas of the prefrontal and cingulate cortices, amygdala, hypothalamus, periaquaductal gray, solitary tract nucleus, nucleus ambiguus, dorsal motor nucleus, and medulla; the cortical areas are responsible for higher order autonomic control that exert their effects on heart rhythm through the parasympathetic output of the vagus nerve (Benarroch, 1993; Berntson et al., 1997). Other researchers have identified a functionally and anatomically similar system to the CAN (Damasio, 1998; Devinsky, Morrell, & Vogt, 1995; Masterman & Cummings, 1997), leading some to argue for their functional equivalence (Thayer, 2007; Thayer & Lane, 2009).

One measure of parasympathetic control of the heart is *heart rate variability* (HRV), the oscillation in intervals between successive heartbeats. Although there are multiple methods for calculating HRV, there is general agreement that time domain measures, such as the root mean squared successive differences (rMSSD) between interbeat intervals (IBI), the standard deviation of the interval between heartbeats (SDNN), and spectral analysis of HRV in the high frequency range (.15–.40 Hz; HF power), reflect predominantly parasympathetic vagal control of the heart (Berntson et al., 1997; Task Force of the European Society of Cardiology and the North American Society of Pacing and Electrophysiology, 1996). Another measure of HRV is the *peak-to-valley* method, which calculates the average differences between maximum and minimum IBI within a respiratory cycle and reflects predominantly parasympathetic influences. The ratio of low frequency (.04–.15 Hz; LF) to HF power is thought to reflect a combination of sympathetic and parasympathetic influences on the heart (Task Force of the European Society of Cardiology and the North American Society of Pacing and Electrophysiology, 1996).

The prefrontal cortex is a particularly relevant component of the CAN for self-regulation. Self-regulatory tasks such as emotion regulation, delay discounting, and sustained thought suppression correlate with activity in the prefrontal cortex (Lieberman et al., 2007; Mitchell et al., 2007; Shamosh et al., 2008). In the self-regulatory fatigue paradigm, such fatigue negatively and selectively affects performance on tasks that are complex or "executive," but not on other effortful cognitive tasks (Schmeichel et al., 2003). In naturalistic settings, better executive cognitive function, thought to localize largely in the prefrontal cortex, correlates with better cognitive control, as reflected in mind-wandering, worry, and rumination (Crowe, Matthews, & Walkenhorst, 2007; Davis & Nolen-Hoeksema, 2000; Kane et al., 2007; von Hippel, Vasey, Gonda, & Stern, 2008).

Research using animal models implicates the prefrontal cortex in the control of cardiac chronotropy (Oppenheimer & Cechetto, 1990; Ter Horst & Postema, 1997; Verberne & Owens, 1998). In humans, regional cerebral blood flow (rCBF) in the prefrontal cortex tends to correlate positively with HRV and negatively with heart rate (HR), as HRV and HR are typically inversely related (Critchley, Corfield, Chandler, Mathias, & Dolan, 2000; Gianaros, Van der Veen, & Jennings, 2004; Lane et al., 2009; Lane, Reiman, Ahern, & Thayer, 2001). It is important to note that some studies with small sample sizes have failed to find a relationship between rCBF to prefrontal cortical structures and HR response to effortful mental arithmetic tasks (Shapiro et al., 2000; Soufer et al., 1998). However, taken as a whole, research using rCBF supports the positive relationship between HRV and activation of the prefrontal cortex.

Studies employing other methodologies also tend to support the relationship between self-regulation-induced activation of cortical structures and cardiac responses. For example, pharmacological deactivation of the prefrontal cortex leads to a corresponding decrease in HRV in patients with epilepsy (Ahern et al., 2001). Other studies using separate but parallel sessions to record cardiac and brain activity (through functional magnetic resonance imaging) in response to an isotonic handgrip exercise task in one experiment and the Stroop task in another have revealed increased activity in the prefrontal cortex and anterior cingulate cortex that correlated with HRV (HF power; Matthews, Paulus, Simmons, Nelesen, & Dimsdale, 2004; Wong, Masse, Kimmerly, Menon, & Shoemaker, 2007). In summary, converging evidence from differing methodologies generally supports the positive relationship between activation of the prefrontal cortex and parasympathetically mediated HRV.

CARDIAC PREDICTORS AND CORRELATES OF SELF-REGULATORY STRENGTH AND FATIGUE: PAUSE AND PLAN

The correlation between the central structures that subserve self-regulation and those that exert cardiac control leads to two predictions, one having to do with phasic self-regulatory exercise and one having to do with tonic self-regulatory strength. First, when people are actively self-regulating, HRV should be higher than when they are acting without self-regulating, potentially because of activation of shared central structures. Second, people with higher resting HRV should have better capacity for self-regulation, reflecting the tonic strength of central inhibitory structures. These hypotheses have been the subject of studies from our laboratory.

The first study (Segerstrom & Solberg Nes, 2007) compared the effects of a task that was high in self-regulatory demand and low in stress (i.e., negative subjective experience) with a task that was high in stress and low in self-regulation. Undergraduate students ($N = 168$) were randomly assigned to high or low self-regulation or high or low stress. In the self-regulation conditions, the instructions involved either eating warm chocolate cookies while resisting carrots presented on the same tray (low self-regulation) or eating the carrots while resisting the cookies (high self-regulation). In the stress conditions, the instructions involved either reading patriotic texts as quickly as possible while being criticized (high stress) or relaxing (low stress).

The conditions were compared with regard to their effects on affect, HR and HRV (rMSSD), tonic skin conductance level (SCL), and performance on a subsequent self-regulatory task. The effects of self-regulatory effort differed from those of stress on almost all dimensions. Eating carrots resulted in shorter persistence at a subsequent anagram task than eating cookies, indicating self-regulatory fatigue, whereas there were no differences in persistence after stress versus relaxation. There were no differences between the self-regulation conditions in mood, whereas there were pronounced differences in mood between the stress conditions, with stress being associated with more affective arousal than relaxation. Psychologically, therefore, the consequences of engaging in self-regulation were quite different from those of engaging in a stressful activity that did not involve self-regulation.

It is not surprising, then, that there were also different physiological consequences. Between the self-regulation conditions, high self-regulation was associated with lower HR and higher HRV than low self-regulation, but there were no differences in SCL. Between the stress conditions, stress was associated with higher HR and SCL and lower HRV. These results have important implications. First, "flexing" the self-regulatory "muscle" is accompanied by a decrease in HR. Second, this is a very different process from confronting stress, both psychologically and physiologically. Although both high-demand tasks (resisting temptation and pressured reading) involved effort, the quality of that effort differed. Whereas many stressful or effortful tasks involve action or preparation for action (i.e., fight or flight), self-regulation often involves not acting, or, when action occurs, it involves overriding the prepotent response (i.e., "pause and plan"). These qualitative differences are reflected in different physiological responses.

In the second study (Fantini, 2005), undergraduate students ($N = 82$) were randomly assigned to a high self-regulation task or a low self-regulation task. These tasks were both cognitive, although one involved inhibition and the other rote memorization (Muraven & Slessareva, 2003). The high self-regulation task involved asking students to think about anything they wanted except a white bear for 5 min; this instruction typically results in paradoxical intrusions of white bears that then must be inhibited. The low self-regulation task involved memorizing a list of 20 words for 5 min.

As in the first study, there were few differences between the tasks in subjective experience, except that attentive affect (e.g., interest) was higher in the low self-regulation condition. Also as in the first study, HR was significantly lower when participants were engaging in the self-regulatory task (white bear) than the rote task (memorization). Figure 9.1 shows a significant interaction between time and condition in which HR increased during the memory task, but not during the thought suppression task. This effect was obtained despite the fact that the thought suppression task was rated slightly but significantly more difficult, demanding, and stressful than the memory task ($M = 2.65$ vs. 2.26 on a 5-point scale).

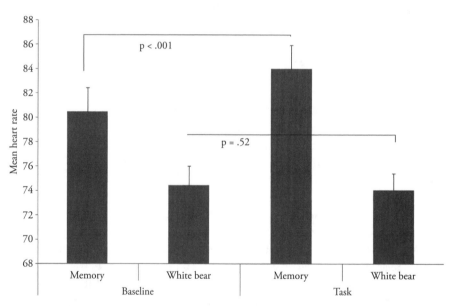

Figure 9.1. Heart rate at baseline and during the memorization and white bear suppression tasks (Fantini, 2005). Heart rate significantly increased during the low self-regulation memory but not high self-regulation white bear task. Data from Fantini (2005).

The mechanism involved, however, is unclear because there were no effects of the manipulation on either the parasympathetic measure of HRV (rMSSD) or the sympathetic measure of SCL. In this study, stress and self-regulation were co-occurring. The white bear and memory tasks were both appraised as difficult and demanding relative to the food tasks (cf. M = 1.69 for eating carrots and 1.20 for eating cookies, on the same 5-point scale; Segerstrom & Solberg Nes, 2007), both tasks resulted in significant increases in SCL, and both tasks were associated with poorer subsequent performance on a test task (described later) than a no-task control group. Although the slower HR during self-regulation replicated our previous finding, when self-regulation co-occurs with stress, physiological correlates may not be as clear as when tasks are more "pure" in their self-regulatory demand with regard to stress. One possibility is that tasks that are both stressful and require self-regulation result in complex patterns of coactivation of the sympathetic and parasympathetic nervous systems (Berntson, Cacioppo, & Quigley, 1993).

With regard to relationships between tonic HRV and self-regulatory capacity, both of these studies supported a relationship between high resting HRV and better ability to self-regulate. In the first study (Segerstrom & Solberg Nes, 2007), there was a significant correlation between HRV at baseline and persistence at the anagram task that was independent of prior self-regulatory effort ($r = .23$). Figure 9.2 illustrates this relationship. Predicted persistence increased by over 50% from the lowest to highest baseline HRV. In the

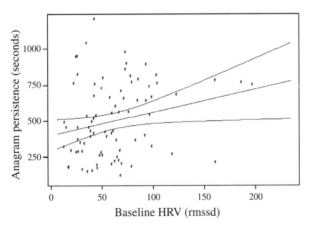

Figure 9.2. Baseline heart rate variability (HRV) and anagram persistence. The regression line is shown with its 95% confidence interval. rmssd = root mean squared successive differences in the interbeat interval. Adapted from "Heart Rate Variability Indexes Self-Regulatory Strength, Effort, and Fatigue," by S. C. Segerstrom and L. Solberg Nes, 2007, *Psychological Science, 18*, p. 279. Copyright 2007 by Wiley-Blackwell. Adapted with permission.

second study, the test task was the random number generation task, in which participants are required to generate a string of numbers at 800 ms intervals in time with a metronome, with the goal of avoiding nonrandom patterns (Miyake, Friedman, Emerson, Witzki, & Howerter, 2000). Self-regulatory strength was not associated with the latter goal, but it was associated with ability to keep up with the metronome. Despite a ceiling effect, there was a correlation between baseline HRV and number of responses generated during the 3-min task period ($r = .19$) that was of about the same magnitude as the correlation between HRV and anagram persistence.

Other studies replicated this correlation and also suggested when and how this relationship may be strained. The first (Solberg Nes, Carlson, Crofford, de Leeuw, & Segerstrom, 2010) randomly assigned 50 chronic pain patients and 50 control participants to high and low self-regulation conditions, after which they underwent an anagram test task. As in the undergraduate students, there was a positive correlation between baseline HRV and anagram persistence ($r = .29$). However, this relationship was moderated both by pain group and self-regulation condition. Among controls, higher HRV was strongly related to longer persistence, particularly in the low self-regulation condition. However, higher HRV was only weakly related to persistence in the chronic pain patients. Chronic pain likely created a priori self-regulatory fatigue (cf. Solberg Nes, Roach, & Segerstrom, 2009), and so the strength implied by higher HRV might have been expended on managing pain rather than persisting at the anagram task. Therefore, although strength in the face of sequential self-regulatory demands appears to be well predicted by baseline HRV, simultaneous self-regulatory demands may be less well predicted.

The effects of simultaneous self-regulatory demands were further illuminated by an experimental study of pain persistence (Evans, Eisenlohr-Moul, Button, Baer, & Segerstrom, 2010). In this study, 63 undergraduate students were randomly assigned to either control attention to a painful stimulus in a mindful way (i.e., by observing and accepting the sensation) or to use whatever coping strategy worked best for them. The stimulus was a cold pressor task, in which participants submerged one hand in very cold water; pain persistence was the duration they kept their hands in the water. As in the other studies, there was a positive correlation between baseline HRV and self-regulatory performance—in this case, pain persistence ($r = .29$). However, this relationship was moderated by condition: When participants also had to control their attention and be mindful, there was a small correlation between HRV and persistence ($r = .16$); when they coped according to their preferences, a large correlation was obtained ($r = .63$).

Although higher baseline HRV typically predicts improved persistence on a subsequent self-regulatory task following an initially fatiguing activity, few studies have directly examined the outcomes of simultaneous self-regulatory demands or the role of baseline HRV in predicting such outcomes. Both studies reviewed earlier (Evans et al., 2010; Solberg Nes et al., 2010) suggest that combining the self-regulatory demand of pain—chronic in one and acute in the other—with another, co-occurring self-regulatory task tends to neutralize the expected salutary effect of higher baseline HRV. One way to make sense of this uncoupling of baseline HRV from persistence during simultaneous self-regulatory demands is to distinguish between self-regulatory endurance and self-regulatory strength. Extending the muscle metaphor of self-regulation, simultaneous regulatory tasks may require strength, the maximum possible force generated, whereas sequential tasks may require endurance, the ability to sustain exertion over time. The weakening of the relationship between baseline HRV and persistence during simultaneous regulatory tasks in these two studies lead us to believe that baseline HRV may represent a measure of the capacity for regulatory endurance rather than strength.

CONVERGING EVIDENCE

There is converging evidence for both phasic and tonic relationships between HRV and self-regulation, although more exists for the latter than the former. One study specifically compared HRV during high versus low self-regulatory effort. In that study, participants who engaged in emotion regulation had higher HRV (HF power at .15–.50 Hz) during the task than those who did not control their emotion (Butler, Wilhelm, & Gross, 2006). Although they did not set out to measure self-regulation per se, Luft, Takase, and Darby (2009) compared HRV in the time (SDNN and rMSSD) and spectral (LF/HF ratio) domains during a series of cognitive tasks and found that HRV was higher during executive working memory tasks than in simple attention and reaction time tasks.

A different phasic effect that may relate to self-regulatory effort has to do with the disengagement of the parasympathetic "brake." According to polyvagal theory, during demand, the parasympathetic vagal brake is released, resulting in a decrease in HRV and increase in sympathetic drive to allow a greater response (Porges, 2007). It has been hypothesized that withdrawal of vagal control during a challenge represents greater flexibility and adaptability, and larger decreases in HRV during a challenging task have correlated with more adaptive coping behaviors. Children who had greater HRV (HF power at .15–.50 Hz) reactivity while watching a sad film had more adaptive emotion regulation responses and fewer depressive symptoms (Gentzler, Santucci, Kovacs, & Fox, 2009). Phasic down-regulation of HRV (HF power at .12–.40 Hz) during an attention regulation task was not seen in those high in social anxiety compared with those low in anxiety, suggesting that tonic cognitive and emotional dysregulation associated with social anxiety is associated with poor vagal reactivity (Movius & Allen, 2005). It should be noted that the ability to disengage the vagal brake during challenging tasks may be different from the ability to engage the vagal brake during self-regulatory tasks. Again, the quality of the task in terms of its stressfulness versus its self-regulatory demand appears to be important to the cardiac changes that accompany the task. Finally, the ability to release the vagal brake is likely dependent on the degree to which the brake is applied, and so the relationship between HRV reactivity and ability to self-regulate (e.g., as reflected in tonic emotion regulation) is consistent with relationships between higher tonic HRV and better self-regulation.

The converging evidence regarding tonic HRV includes studies of both cognitive and emotional regulation. HRV has been linked with cognitive performance, particularly on executive cognitive tasks. Those with high HRV (rMSSD) at baseline performed better on a working memory test and continuous performance test, with better response times and greater accuracy than those with low HRV (Hansen, Johnsen, & Thayer, 2003). When resting HRV (rMSSD) was manipulated through physical detraining, there was a decrease in cognitive function performance in conjunction with decreased resting HRV compared with those who continued their exercise regimen (Hansen, Johnsen, Sollers, Stenvik, & Thayer, 2004). Among elite athletes, higher resting HRV (HF power) predicted fewer anticipation errors on a series of computerized cognitive tasks, suggesting a greater ability to control and inhibit impulsive responding (Luft et al., 2009). However, in an epidemiological study (UK Whitehall II), no correlation was found between cognitive function (using batteries assessing short term verbal, memory, reasoning, vocabulary and semantic fluency) and HRV (rMSSD and HF power) in a group of middle-aged men and women (Britton et al., 2008).

HRV has also been associated with emotional regulation, particularly inhibition of emotional expression. Higher HRV (HF power) predicted better suppression of negative affect while watching a film (Demaree, Pu, Robinson, Schmeichel, & Everhart, 2006). However, this effect was not limited to down-regulation: Those with low resting HRV (HF power) had more difficulty exaggerating their emotional responses (Demaree, Robinson, Everhart, & Schmeichel, 2004). It is important to note that the subjective experience of negative or positive affect did not significantly differ between groups in these experiments. Finally, participants with higher resting HRV (HF power) spontaneously exhibited less facial expression while watching a negative film, even though self-reported emotional distress was similar across conditions. Consistent with a self-regulatory fatigue effect, those who controlled their facial expressions most had the poorest performance on a subsequent working memory task (Pu, Schmeichel, & Demaree, 2009).

The results of this latter study indicate that higher resting HRV can predict more self-regulation even when people are not directed to self-regulate. Insofar as undirected emotion regulation may be unconscious or automatic, HRV may be relevant to such processes as well as to conscious self-control. Further supporting this possibility, resting HRV (HF power) correlated with cognitive accessibility of intelligence words after experimentally manipulated failure at a purported intelligence test (but not after success). The inhibition of intrusive thoughts about failure is often an adaptive self-regulatory task, and higher accessibility of words related to failure suggests less inhibitory control (Geisler & Kubiak, 2009). These results indicate that the inverse relationship between resting HRV and worry and rumination in naturalistic settings may be in part a function of the efficiency of nonconscious inhibitory processes.

In other laboratory studies, young adults with higher resting HRV (rMSSD and HF power) had more differentiated startle eye-blink responses across positive and negative images (Ruiz-Padial, Sollers, Vila, & Thayer, 2003). Young men with higher resting HRV (peak-to-valley) had faster emotional recovery from anger-inducing situations (Diamond & Hicks, 2005). More rejection-sensitive men and women had higher hostility and poorer emotional control during an experimental partner conflict task, but only if they were also low in resting HRV (HF power; Gyurak & Ayduk, 2008). Outside of the laboratory, resting HRV (MSSD) correlated positively with questionnaire measures of self-regulatory success such as emotional control, inhibition of impulses, and frustration tolerance in children, adolescents, and young adults (MSSD, Allen, Matthews, & Kenyon, 2000; HF power, Fabes & Eisenberg, 1997) and with thought control in middle-aged alcoholics (MSSD; Ingjaldsson, Laberg, & Thayer, 2003).

There is, therefore, abundant evidence linking high resting HRV to measures of self-regulation. The phasic evidence is more complex, but higher HR and lower HRV during stressful tasks may reflect the ability to disengage the vagal brake, whereas lower HRV and higher HRV during self-regulatory tasks may reflect the further engagement of the brake.

PAUSE AND PLAN: THE PHYSIOLOGICAL PROFILE OF SELF-REGULATION

Our studies of the cardiovascular correlates of self-regulation and self-regulatory fatigue converge with other studies that find that higher HRV, a measure of parasympathetic control of the heart, is a predictor and a correlate of self-regulatory strength and effort, respectively. This profile differs markedly from that resulting from stress. During fight or flight, the cardiovascular system anticipates the physical demands associated with fighting or fleeing by increasing HR and blood pressure and initiating vascular changes that shunt blood away from the viscera and toward the large muscles (Lovallo & Thomas, 2000). During self-regulation, however, there is more evidence that the cardiovascular system becomes quiescent, with HR being slower than when self-regulatory demand is low.

One possibility is that cardiac changes are an epiphenomenon of self-regulation, whereby activity in the CAN that is directed at controlling mental or behavioral processes also slows the heart as a byproduct. Another, intriguing possibility is that self-regulation has a functional physiological profile, pause and plan, that involves slowing activity in the periphery. The proposition of a functional relationship between peripheral activity, both autonomic and somatic, and the cognitive or behavioral demands of the environment is not new. Beatrice and John Lacey first proposed such a relationship almost 50 years ago, as did their student Paul Obrist later (for a review, see Öhman, Hamm, & Hugdahl, 2000). Although they differed in some particulars, they all proposed that in cases in which the environment demanded perception but not action, HR decreased. For the Laceys, slower HR resulted in increased "cortical sensitivity" and efficient cognitive processing. For Obrist, HR was thought to reflect the degree of somatic metabolic demand: HR was lower when the organism prepared for reflection and attention and higher when the organism prepared for action and effort. In both cases, however, HR changes were thought to reflect "physiological adjustments promoting optimal transactions with the environment" (Öhman et al., 2000, p. 554).

More recent data have advanced the possibility that reductions in metabolic activity in the periphery and concomitant reduction in glucose use may help promote a high-glucose state, which appears to foster better self-regulation. Experimental evidence suggests that administering glucose before self-regulatory or executive tasks improves self-regulatory capacity (Donohoe & Benton, 1999; Gailliot et al., 2007; Gailliot, Peruche, Plant, & Baumeister, 2008; Scholey, Sunram-Lee, Greer, Elliott, & Kennedy, 2009). Therefore, the physiological state associated with higher blood glucose appears to promote higher capacity for self-regulation, perhaps because of the higher blood glucose itself but more probably indirectly through changes in other neurohormonal factors.

Finally, systems other than the heart may also be inhibited. There is some evidence that the immune system may also be slowed when self-regulatory demand is high (Segerstrom, 2007). As suggested by early models, somatic activity may also be inhibited. The behavioral response of freezing seen in many mammals may also be related to human pause and plan insofar as freezing is associated with "situations involving potential or poorly understood threat characteristics" that require further assessment before action should be taken (Blanchard & Blanchard, 1989, p. 80). Freezing is also associated with slower HR, suggesting that both motor and autonomic responses are inhibited.

The pause and plan profile is new relative to fight or flight and therefore not as well understood. However, as new investigations more carefully parse the demands of their tasks, this profile should emerge more clearly. And, as with fight or flight, the effects of pause and plan on systems other than the heart will surely emerge as well (cf. Segerstrom, 2007).

REFERENCES

Ahern, G. L., Sollers, J. L., Lane, R. D., Labiner, D. M., Herring, A. M., Weinand, M. E., . . . Thayer, J. F. (2001). Heart rate and heart rate variability changes in the intracarotid sodium amobarbitol test. *Epilepsia, 42*, 912–921. doi:10.1046/j.1528-1157.2001.042007912.x

Allen, M. T., Matthews, K. A., & Kenyon, K. L. (2000). The relationships of resting baroreflex sensitivity, heart rate variability and measures of impulse control in children and adolescents. *International Journal of Psychophysiology, 37*, 185–194. doi:10.1016/S0167-8760(00)00089-1

Baumeister, R. F., Bratslavsky, E., Muraven, M., & Tice, D. M. (1998). Ego depletion: Is the active self a limited resource? *Journal of Personality and Social Psychology, 74*, 1252–1265. doi:10.1037/0022-3514.74.5.1252

Benarroch, E. E. (1993). The central autonomic network: Functional organization, dysfunction, and perspective. *Mayo Clinic Proceedings, 68*, 988–1001.

Berntson, G. G., Bigger, J. T., Eckberg, D. L., Grossman, P., Kaufmann, P. G., Malik, M., . . . van der Molen, M. W. (1997). Heart rate variability: Origins, methods, and interpretive caveats. *Psychophysiology, 34*, 623–648. doi:10.1111/j.1469-8986.1997.tb02140.x

Berntson, G. G., Cacioppo, J. T., & Quigley, K. S. (1993). Cardiac psychophysiology and autonomic space in humans: Empirical perspectives and conceptual implications. *Psychological Bulletin, 114*, 296–322. doi:10.1037/0033-2909.114.2.296

Blanchard, R. J., & Blanchard, D. C. (1989). Antipredator defensive behaviors in a visible burrow system. *Journal of Comparative Psychology, 103*, 70–82. doi:10.1037/0735-7036.103.1.70

Britton, A., Singh-Manoux, A., Hnatkova, K., Malik, M., Marmot, M. G., & Shipley, M. (2008). The association between heart rate variability and cognitive impairment in middle-aged men and women: The Whitehall II Cohort Study. *Neuroepidemiology, 31*, 115–121. doi:10.1159/000148257

Butler, E. A., Wilhelm, F. H., & Gross, J. J. (2006). Respiratory sinus arrhythmia, emotion, and emotion regulation during social interaction. *Psychophysiology, 43*, 612–622. doi:10.1111/j.1469-8986.2006.00467.x

Critchley, H. D., Corfield, D. R., Chandler, M. P., Mathias, C. J., & Dolan, R. J. (2000). Cerebral correlates of autonomic cardiovascular arousal: A functional neuroimaging investigation of in humans. *The Journal of Physiology, 523,* 259–270. doi:10.1111/j.1469-7793.2000.t01-1-00259.x

Crowe, S. F., Matthews, C., & Walkenhorst, E. (2007). Relationship between worry, anxiety, and thought suppression and the components of working memory in a non-clinical sample. *Australian Psychologist, 42,* 170–177. doi:10.1080/00050060601089462

Damasio, A. R. (1998). Emotion in the perspective of an integrated nervous system. *Brain Research Reviews, 26,* 83–86. doi:10.1016/S0165-0173(97)00064-7

Davis, R. N., & Nolen-Hoeksema, S. (2000). Cognitive inflexibility among ruminators and nonruminators. *Cognitive Therapy and Research, 24,* 699–711. doi:10.1023/A:1005591412406

Demaree, H., Pu, J., Robinson, J., Schmeichel, B., & Everhart, E. (2006). Predicting facial valence to negative stimuli from resting RSA: Not a function of active emotion regulation. *Cognition and Emotion, 20,* 161–176. doi:10.1080/02699930500260427

Demaree, H. A., Robinson, J. L., Everhart, D. E., & Schmeichel, B. J. (2004). Resting RSA is associated with natural and self-regulated responses to negative emotional stimuli. *Brain and Cognition, 56,* 14–23. doi:10.1016/j.bandc.2004.05.001

Devinsky, O., Morrell, M. J., & Vogt, B. A. (1995). Contributions of anterior cingulate cortex to behavior. *Brain, 118,* 279–306.

DeWall, C. N., Baumeister, R. F., Stillman, T. F., & Gailliot, M. T. (2007). Violence restrained: Effects of self-regulation and its depletion on aggression. *Journal of Experimental Social Psychology, 43,* 62–76. doi:10.1016/j.jesp.2005.12.005

Diamond, L. M., & Hicks, A. M. (2005). Attachment style, current relationship security, and negative emotions: The mediating role of physiological regulation. *Journal of Social and Personal Relationships, 22,* 499–518. doi:10.1177/0265407505054520

Donohoe, R. T., & Benton, D. (1999). Cognitive functioning is susceptible to the level of blood glucose. *Psychopharmacology, 145,* 378–385. doi:10.1007/s002130051071

Evans, D. R., Eisenlohr-Moul, T., Button, D., Baer, R. A., & Segerstrom, S. C. (2010). *Novel mindful coping reduces pain tolerance associated with high heart rate variability.* Manuscript submitted for publication.

Fabes, R. A., & Eisenberg, N. (1997). Regulatory control and adults' stress-related responses to daily life events. *Journal of Personality and Social Psychology, 73,* 1107–1117. doi:10.1037/0022-3514.73.5.1107

Fantini, N. (2005). *Exploring ego depletion, heart rate, and motivation: Is the heart a good index?* (Unpublished undergraduate honors thesis). University of Kentucky.

Gailliot, M. T., Baumeister, R. F., DeWall, C. N., Maner, J. K., Plant, E. A., Tice, D. M., . . . Schmeichel, B. J. (2007). Self-control relies on glucose as a limited energy source: Willpower is more than a metaphor. *Journal of Personality and Social Psychology, 92,* 325–336. doi:10.1037/0022-3514.92.2.325

Gailliot, M. T., Peruche, B. M., Plant, E. A., & Baumeister, R. F. (2008). Stereotypes and prejudice in the blood: Sucrose drinks reduce prejudice and stereotype. *Journal of Experimental Social Psychology, 45*, 288–290. doi:10.1016/j.jesp.2008.09.003

Geisler, F. C. M., & Kubiak, T. (2009). Heart rate variability predicts self-control in goal pursuit. *European Journal of Personality, 23*, 623–633. doi:10.1002/per.727

Gentzler, A. L., Santucci, A. K., Kovacs, M., & Fox, N. A. (2009). Respiratory sinus arrhythmia reactivity predicts emotion regulation and depressive symptoms in at-risk and control children. *Biological Psychology, 82*, 156–163. doi:10.1016/j.biopsycho.2009.07.002

Gianaros, P. J., Van der Veen, F. M., & Jennings, J. R. (2004). Regional cerebral blood flow correlates with heart period and high frequency heart period variability during working memory tasks: Implications for the cortical and subcortical regulation cardiac autonomic activity. *Psychophysiology, 41*, 521–530. doi:10.1111/1469-8986.2004.00179.x

Gyurak, A., & Ayduk, O. (2008). Resting respiratory sinus arrhythmia buffers against rejection sensitivity via emotion control. *Emotion, 8*, 458–467. doi:10.1037/1528-3542.8.4.458

Hansen, A. L., Johnsen, B. H., Sollers, J. J., Stenvik, K., & Thayer, J. F. (2004). Heart rate variability and its relation to prefrontal cognitive function: The effects of training and detraining. *European Journal of Applied Physiology, 93*, 263–272. doi:10.1007/s00421-004-1208-0

Hansen, A. L., Johnsen, B. H., & Thayer, J. F. (2003). Vagal influence on working memory and attention. *International Journal of Psychophysiology, 48*, 263–274. doi:10.1016/S0167-8760(03)00073-4

Ingjaldsson, J. T., Laberg, J. C., & Thayer, J. F. (2003). Reduced heart rate variability in chronic alcohol abuse: Relationship with negative mood, chronic thought suppression, and compulsive drinking. *Biological Psychiatry, 54*, 1427–1436. doi:10.1016/S0006-3223(02)01926-1

Kane, M. J., Brown, L. H., McVay, J. C., Silvia, P. J., Myin-Germeys, I., & Kwapil, T. R. (2007). For whom the mind wanders and when: An experience-sampling study of working memory and executive control in daily life. *Psychological Science, 18*, 614–621. doi:10.1111/j.1467-9280.2007.01948.x

Lane, R. D., McCrae, K., Reiman, E. M., Chen, K., Ahern, G. L., & Thayer, G. F. (2009). Neural correlates of heart rate variability during emotion. *NeuroImage, 44*, 213–222. doi:10.1016/j.neuroimage.2008.07.056

Lane, R. D., Reiman, E. M., Ahern, E. L., & Thayer, J. F. (2001). Activity in medial prefrontal cortex correlates with vagal component of heart rate variability during emotion. *Brain and Cognition, 47*, 97–100.

Lieberman, M. D., Eisenberger, N. I., Crockett, M. J., Tom, S. M., Pfeifer, J. H., & Way, B. M. (2007). Putting feelings into words: Affect labeling disrupts amygdala activity to affective stimuli. *Psychological Science, 18*, 421–428. doi:10.1111/j.1467-9280.2007.01916.x

Lovallo, W. R., & Thomas, T. L. (2000). Stress hormones in psychophysiological research: Emotional, behavioral, and cognitive implications. In J. T. Cacioppo, L. G. Tassinary, & G. G. Berntson (Eds.), *Handbook of psychophysiology* (2nd ed., pp. 342–367). Cambridge, England: Cambridge University Press.

Luft, C. D., Takase, E., & Darby, D. (2009). Heart rate variability and cognitive function: Effects of physical effort. *Biological Psychology, 82*, 186–191. doi:10.1016/j.biopsycho.2009.07.007

Masterman, D. L., & Cummings, J. L. (1997). Frontal-subcortical circuits: The anatomic basis of executive, social, and motivated behaviors. *Journal of Psychopharmacology (Oxford, England), 11*, 107–114. doi:10.1177/026988119701100203

Matthews, S. C., Paulus, M. P., Simmons, A. N., Nelesen, R. A., & Dimsdale, J. E. (2004). Functional subdivisions within anterior cingulate cortex and their relationship to autonomic nervous system function. *NeuroImage, 22*, 1151–1156. doi:10.1016/j.neuroimage.2004.03.005

Mitchell, J. P., Heatherton, T. F., Kelley, W. M., Wyland, C. L., Wegner, D. M., & Macrae, C. N. (2007). Separating sustained from transient aspects of cognitive control during thought suppression. *Psychological Science, 18*, 292–297. doi:10.1111/j.1467-9280.2007.01891.x

Miyake, A., Friedman, N. P., Emerson, M. J., Witzki, A. H., & Howerter, A. (2000). The unity and diversity of executive functions and their contributions to complex "frontal lobe" tasks: A latent variable analysis. *Cognitive Psychology, 41*, 49–100.

Movius, H. L., & Allen, J. J. B. (2005). Cardiac vagal tone, defensiveness, and motivational style. *Biological Psychology, 68*, 147–162. doi:10.1016/j.biopsycho.2004.03.019

Muraven, M., & Slessareva, E. (2003). Mechanisms of self-control failure: Motivation and limited resources. *Personality and Social Psychology Bulletin, 29*, 894–906. doi:10.1177/0146167203029007008

Muraven, M., Tice, D. M., & Baumeister, R. F. (1998). Self-control as a limited resource: Regulatory depletion patterns. *Journal of Personality and Social Psychology, 74*, 774–789. doi:10.1037/0022-3514.74.3.774

Öhman, A., Hamm, A., & Hugdahl, K. (2000). Cognition and the autonomic nervous system: Orienting, anticipation, and conditioning. In J. T. Cacioppo, L. G. Tassinary, & G. G. Berntson (Eds.), *Handbook of psychophysiology* (2nd ed., pp. 533–575). Cambridge, England: Cambridge University Press.

Oppenheimer, S. M., & Cechetto, D. F. (1990). Cardiac chronotropic organization of the rat insular cortex. *Brain Research, 533*, 66–72. doi:10.1016/0006-8993(90)91796-J

Porges, S. W. (2007). The polyvagal perspective. *Biological Psychology, 74*, 116–143. doi:10.1016/j.biopsycho.2006.06.009

Pu, J., Schmeichel, B. J., & Demaree, H. A. (2009). Cardiac vagal control predicts spontaneous regulation of negative emotional expression and subsequent cognitive performance. *Biological Psychology, 82*, 186–195.

Ruiz-Padial, E., Sollers, J. J., Vila, J., & Thayer, J. F. (2003). The rhythm of the heart in the blink of an eye: Emotion-modulated startle magnitude covaries with heart rate variability. *Psychophysiology, 40*, 306–313. doi:10.1111/1469-8986.00032

Schmeichel, B. J. (2007). Attention control, memory updating, and emotion regulation temporarily reduce the capacity for executive control. *Journal of Experimental Psychology, 136*, 241–255.

Schmeichel, B. J., Vohs, K. D., & Baumeister, R. F. (2003). Intellectual performance and ego depletion: Role of the self in logical reasoning and other information processing. *Journal of Personality and Social Psychology, 85*, 33–46. doi:10.1037/0022-3514.85.1.33

Scholey, A. B., Sunram-Lee, S. E., Greer, J., Elliott, J., & Kennedy, D. O. (2009). Glucose administration prior to a divided attention task improves tracking performance but not word recognition: Evidence against differential memory enhancement? *Psychopharmacology, 202*, 549–558. doi:10.1007/s00213-008-1387-1

Segerstrom, S. C. (2007). Stress, energy, and immunity: An ecological view. *Current Directions in Psychological Science, 16*, 326–330. doi:10.1111/j.1467-8721.2007.00522.x

Segerstrom, S. C., & Solberg Nes, L. (2007). Heart rate variability indexes self-regulatory strength, effort, and fatigue. *Psychological Science, 18*, 275–281. doi:10.1111/j.1467-9280.2007.01888.x

Shamosh, N. A., DeYoung, C. G., Green, A. E., Reis, D. L., Johnson, M. R., Conway, A. R. A., . . . Gray, J. R. (2008). Individual differences in delay discounting: Relation to intelligence, working memory, and anterior prefrontal cortex. *Psychological Science, 19*, 904–911. doi:10.1111/j.1467-9280.2008.02175.x

Shapiro, P. A., Sloan, R. P., Bagiella, E., Kuhl, J. P., Anjilvel, S., & Mann, J. J. (2000). Cerebral activation, hostility, and cardiovascular control during mental stress. *Journal of Psychosomatic Research, 48*, 485–491. doi:10.1016/S0022-3999(00)00100-8

Solberg Nes, L., Carlson, C. R., Crofford, L. J., de Leeuw, R., & Segerstrom, S. C. (2010). Self-regulatory deficits in fibromyalgia and temporomandibular disorders. *Pain, 151*, 37–44. doi:10.1016/j.pain.2010.05.009

Solberg Nes, L., Roach, A. R., & Segerstrom, S. C. (2009). Executive function, self-regulation, and chronic pain: A review. *Annals of Behavioral Medicine, 37*, 173–183. doi:10.1007/s12160-009-9096-5

Soufer, R., Bremner, J. D., Arrighi, J. A., Cohen, I., Zaret, B. L., Burg, M. M., & Goldman-Rakic, P. (1998). Cerebral cortical hyperactivation in response to mental stress in patients with coronary artery disease. *Proceedings of the National Academy of Sciences of the United States of America, 95*, 6454–6459. doi:10.1073/pnas.95.11.6454

Tangney, J. P., Baumeister, R. F., & Boone, A. L. (2004). High self-control predicts good adjustment, less pathology, better grades, and interpersonal success. *Journal of Personality, 72*, 271–324. doi:10.1111/j.0022-3506.2004.00263.x

Task Force of the European Society of Cardiology and the North American Society of Pacing and Electrophysiology. (1996). Heart rate variability: Standards of measurement, physiological interpretation, and clinical use. *European Heart Journal, 17*, 354–381.

Ter Horst, G. J., & Postema, F. (1997). Forebrain parasympathetic control of heart activity: Retrograde transneuronal viral labeling in rat. *The American Journal of Physiology, 273*, 2926–2930.

Thayer, J. F. (2007). What the heart says to the brain (and vice-versa) and why we should listen. *Psychological Topics, 16*, 241–250.

Thayer, J. F., & Lane, R. D. (2009). Claude Bernard and the heart-brain connection: Further elaboration of a model of neurovisceral integration. *Neuroscience and Biobehavioral Reviews, 33*, 81–88. doi:10.1016/j.neubiorev.2008.08.004

Verberne, A. J., & Owens, N. C. (1998). Cortical modulation of the cardiovascular system. *Progress in Neurobiology, 54*, 149–168. doi:10.1016/S0301-0082(97)00056-7

Vohs, K. D., & Baumeister, R. F. (2004). Understanding self-regulation. In R. F. Baumeister & K. D. Vohs (Eds.), *Handbook of self-regulation* (pp. 1–12). New York, NY: Guilford Press.

Vohs, K. D., & Heatherton, T. (2000). Self-regulatory failure: A resource-depletion approach. *Psychological Science, 11*, 249–254. doi:10.1111/1467-9280.00250

von Hippel, W., Vasey, M. W., Gonda, T., & Stern, T. (2008). Executive function deficits, rumination, and late-onset depressive symptoms in older adults. *Cognitive Therapy and Research, 32*, 474–487. doi:10.1007/s10608-006-9034-9

Wong, S. W., Masse, N., Kimmerly, D. S., Menon, R. S., & Shoemaker, J. K. (2007). Ventral medial prefrontal cortex and cardiovagal control in conscious humans. *NeuroImage, 35*, 698–708. doi:10.1016/j.neuroimage.2006.12.027

10

MULTIFACETED EFFECTS OF FATIGUE ON EFFORT AND ASSOCIATED CARDIOVASCULAR RESPONSES

REX A. WRIGHT AND CHRISTOPHER C. STEWART

In this chapter, we discuss a recent component of a broader research program that has been ongoing in our laboratory for many years. The broader research program has been concerned with the determinants and cardiovascular (CV) consequences of effort in people confronted with performance challenges (e.g., Wright & Kirby, 2001). The recent component concerns the role that fatigue might play in determining effort and associated CV responses to performance challenge. In considering the role of fatigue, we define *fatigue* as resource depletion within a performance system and *effort* as task engagement, that is, the investment of energy toward some purpose (Higgins, 2006; Kahneman, 1973). We also draw on an analysis advanced earlier pertaining to the role that ability (i.e., performance capacity; Bandura, 1982, 1986) should play in determining effort and associated CV responses (Wright, 1998).

Our fatigue research assumes that ability inversely corresponds to fatigue, that is, that ability falls as fatigue rises and vice versa. An implication is that fatigue effects on effort and associated CV responses should correspond in at least some respects with those of ability. The ability analysis mentioned previously and research related to it suggest that ability effects on effort and associated CV responses are multifaceted, with improved ability enhancing the responses under some performance conditions, reducing them under other performance conditions, and having no impact on them under still other performance conditions. This means that insofar as fatigue effects parallel those of ability, they should be multifaceted as well.

In the sections that follow, we first describe the ability analysis and some studies that bear out its validity. We then draw linkages to the question of how fatigue should influence effort and associated CV responses and provide a flavor of evidence that we and others have obtained that is relevant to them. We conclude by considering theoretical and practical issues of note.

ABILITY, EFFORT, AND CARDIOVASCULAR RESPONSE

The ability analysis that underlies our fatigue research begins with a proposition proffered by Paul Obrist (e.g., Obrist, 1981), who spent much of his career exploring the possibility that CV responses often attributed to motives (e.g., those to take in vs. reject the environment or to flee vs. attack) and emotions (e.g., anxiety, empathy) might be better understood in behavioral terms. Obrist noted that the chief biological function of the CV system is to sustain action. Accordingly, he reasoned that the system should not be directly responsive to factors that vary independent of behavior. To be clear, Obrist did not deny that motives and emotions could affect CV responses. Rather, he suggested that they should do so only secondarily, by altering immediately intended or ongoing activity.

Obrist's early research established associations between somatic–motor activity and heart rate (HR) that were mediated by activation in the parasympathetic branch of the autonomic nervous system (e.g., Obrist, Webb, & Sutterer, 1969). This work was noteworthy in part because it provided an alternative account of research findings related to an intake versus rejection motive analysis developed by Obrist's postdoctoral advisor, John Lacey (B. Lacey & J. Lacey, 1980). Later work led Obrist to the idea of central relevance here. It indicated that people manifest CV adjustments that cannot be explained somatically when they are provided the chance to attain or avoid an outcome by meeting some performance standard. Obrist found that study participants evinced stronger CV responses under conditions that, intuitively, would seem conducive to effortful active coping. Further, the responses that they evinced appeared largely, if not exclusively, due to sympathetic nervous system stimulation. Thus, Obrist concluded that sympathetic nervous system (more specifically, beta-adrenergic) influence on the heart and vasculature varies with effort, with greater effort yielding stronger sympathetic responses. In time, this came to be known as his *active coping hypothesis*.

A Framework for Predicting Effort: Brehm's Motivation Intensity Theory

With Obrist's active coping hypothesis in place as a working given, the ability analysis continued by applying a theory of motivation intensity by Jack Brehm (Brehm & Self, 1989) and an ability extension from it to make effort and associated CV response predictions more refined than those that could be made intuitively. A key assumption of motivation intensity theory is that effort is a valued resource that performers expend only when expenditure yields a return (i.e., a benefit) that exceeds the value of the effort expended. A further assumption is that when performers expend effort, they do so only to the degree that it is needed. Together, these call into question the common notion that effort varies as a function of success importance, with people trying more when much is at stake and trying less when little is at stake. They suggest, instead, that effort should be determined by what can, will, and must be done to meet a performance challenge. So long as success is viewed as possible and worthwhile (i.e., worth the required effort), then effort should correspond to the perceived difficulty of the challenge. That is, performers should invest more effort the more difficult the challenge appears to be. However, if success is viewed as impossible or excessively difficult given the benefit that it will accrue, then effort should be low. Thus, as depicted in the upper panel of Figure 10.1, effort should bear a nonmonotonic relation to difficulty, first rising and then falling abruptly, with the fall occurring where demand exceeds what performers can or will do.

In the context of Brehm's theory, the proximal determinant of effort should be performers' difficulty appraisals with respect to the challenge at hand. Theoretically, these should be determined in part by features of the challenge (the degree of objective demand). However, they also should be determined by the ability (performance capacity) of the performer. To illustrate, a dockworker with no mathematical training would be expected to struggle more with (appraise as more difficult) an arithmetic challenge than would a skilled mathematician. Similarly, an elderly person with mild Alzheimer's dementia would be expected to struggle more with a memory challenge than would a typical college freshman. Speaking generally, one would expect difficulty appraisals to be inversely proportional to ability, which means that ability should play a separate (though conceptually related) role from challenge character in determining relevant effort and associated CV responses.

The separate role that ability should play can be illustrated figuratively in two ways. One is by (a) depicting objective challenge difficulty along the

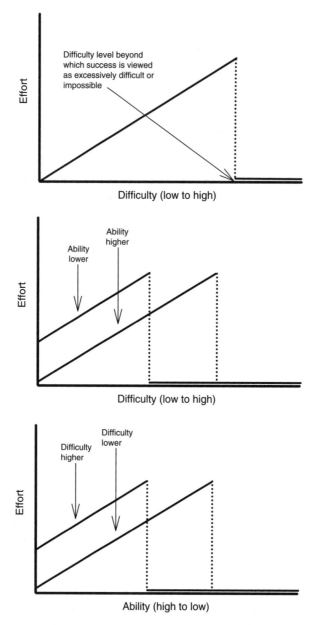

Figure 10.1. Upper panel: Relation between effort and difficulty. Middle panel: Relation between effort and objective difficulty for performers with lower and higher ability. Lower panel: Relation between effort and ability for performers confronted with challenges that, objectively, are more and less difficult.

x axis of the graph in the upper panel of Figure 10.1 and (b) drawing separate effort functions for performers with low and high ability, assuming that those with less ability will have to deploy greater effort to meet a challenge at any given difficulty level. By way of analogy, low-ability performers should have to deploy greater effort for the same reason that consumers who possess a devalued currency have to spend more monetary units to make a purchase. Specifically, their effort is "worth" less (i.e., is less likely to yield a performance increment) than the effort of high-ability performers (e.g., Heider, 1958; Kukla, 1972; cf. Bandura, 1982). As seen in the middle panel of Figure 10.1, such a depiction highlights several points:

- Effort and associated CV responses should be stronger for low- than for high-ability performers so long as the low-ability group perceives success as both possible and worthwhile.
- Low-ability performers should withhold effort and display reduced CV responses at a lower difficulty level than should high-ability performers, creating a window of difficulty levels within which effort and associated CV responses are weaker for these performers.
- Effort and associated CV responses should be weak for both ability groups under conditions where success calls for more than high-ability performers can or will do.

The second way that one can illustrate the separate role of ability is by depicting ability along the *x* axis of the upper panel graph (high to low) and drawing functions to reflect effort under low and high (objective) difficulty conditions. As seen in the lower panel of Figure 10.1, this depiction highlights the added theoretical point that if ability is low enough, effort and associated CV responses should be weak even if, objectively, a challenge is easy to meet.

A point implicit in both these depictions is that ability effects on effort and associated CV responses should be moderated by success importance, that is, the magnitude of the benefit that is contingent on good performance (what is at stake). When performers view success as possible, their decision of whether or not to try should depend on their assessment of whether the benefit of success will outweigh its cost (value of effort expended). If they believe that benefit is greater, they should try in proportion to difficulty and evince corresponding CV responses. However, if they believe that cost is greater, they should withhold effort and experience little CV arousal. Thus, so long as the two ability groups view success as possible, their points of disengagement along the objective difficulty continuum should be determined by importance, with lower importance appraisals yielding earlier drop points.

Summary

The ability analysis begins with the assumption that sympathetically mediated CV responses vary with effort. It then applies motivation intensity theory and an extension from it to make effort and CV response predictions. The theory and extension imply that effort and associated CV responses for low- and high-ability people should first rise with challenge difficulty and then fall sharply, with the falls occurring where success is viewed as excessively difficult or impossible. They also imply that (a) effort and associated CV responses should be greater for low-ability performers so long as the low-ability group views success as possible and worthwhile and (b) a reverse effort and CV response pattern (i.e., reflecting stronger responses for high-ability performers) should be found where a challenge calls for more than low-ability performers—but not high-ability performers—can or will do. Where a challenge calls for more than both low- and high-ability groups can or will do, both groups should exert low effort and experience little sympathetic CV arousal. So long as the groups view success as possible, their point of disengagement along an objective difficulty continuum should depend on success importance, that is, how much is at stake.

EVIDENCE RELEVANT TO THE ABILITY ANALYSIS

Evidence relevant to the preceding ability analysis has been reviewed elsewhere (e.g., Wright, 1998) and therefore need not be discussed in detail here. For present purposes, it is sufficient to note that the most compelling support comes from studies that examined CV responses associated with measured or manipulated ability factors under difficulty and importance conditions that should, in theory, be conducive to different ability effects. An example is a study by Wright and Dill (1993) that used a performance feedback procedure to lead half of its participants to believe that they had low ability with respect to a scanning task and half to believe that they had high ability with respect to the task. Later, the participants were presented a related scanning challenge and told they could earn a prize by meeting an objectively high or low performance standard. As expected, systolic blood pressure (SBP) responses assessed just before and during the scanning period were in a crossover interactional pattern, reflecting relatively greater responsiveness for low-ability participants when the standard was low but the reverse of that when the standard was high. The crossover effect was expected for SBP responses because those responses are partially determined by the forcefulness of heart contraction, an outcome that is believed to be determined chiefly (if not solely) by sympathetic nervous system arousal (e.g., see Chapter 2, this volume; Obrist, 1981). Analysis of the diastolic blood pressure (DBP) data revealed an interaction pattern as well, with corresponding means.

A further example is a study by Gendolla and Krüsken (2001) that altered ability perception through a manipulation of mood. The investigators reasoned that performers in an unfavorable mood should tend to have lower ability appraisals than performers in a favorable mood. As a consequence, those in an unfavorable mood should evince effort and associated CV responses comparable with those of the low-ability groups described earlier, whereas those in a favorable mood should evince effort and associated CV responses comparable with those of the high-ability groups described earlier (see Chapter 7, this volume). Unfavorable and favorable moods were induced by the presentation of sad or happy music, respectively. After mood induction, participants were presented an easy or difficult version of a letter-cancellation task and had CV measures taken during the work period. Once again, SBP responses were in a crossover interactional pattern. When the challenge was easy, an unfavorable mood enhanced the responses; when it was difficult, an unfavorable mood retarded them. Like the Wright and Dill (1993) study, this study produced a similar response pattern for DBP.

Among the most illuminating of the available ability studies are additional mood experiments from the Gendolla laboratory (Gendolla & Krüsken, 2002). The experiments are especially illuminating because they crossed mood not only with challenge difficulty but also with a performance contingency manipulation that can reasonably be assumed to have affected success importance. The experiments were highly similar procedurally; thus, it is necessary here to describe only the first. Participants initially went through a mood induction procedure that involved watching a sad (unfavorable mood) or funny (favorable mood) film presentation. They then were presented with an easy or difficult memory task with instructions that a relaxation period would either (a) necessarily follow the performance period (success importance modest) or (b) follow only if they did well (success importance high).

The central prediction was that the ability (mood) factor would exert its usual interactional influence on effort and associated CV responses when importance was moderate but have a main effect influence on these responses when importance was high. More specifically, when importance was modest, an unfavorable mood was expected to enhance the responses if difficulty was low but retard them if difficulty was high. By contrast, when importance was high, an unfavorable mood was expected to enhance the responses at both difficulty levels. The reason for the latter expectation was that high importance participants in an unfavorable mood were expected to view success as worthwhile even when difficulty was high. Analysis of SBP responses measured during performance yielded the relevant Mood × Difficulty × Contingency interaction, with means fitting the anticipated pattern.

In summary, the strongest support for the ability analysis comes from studies that examined CV responses associated with ability factors under difficulty and importance conditions that should be conducive to different ability effects. Studies have repeatedly documented the interactional relation between ability and difficulty. They also have documented the suggestion that success importance should determine ability influence at different levels of objective difficulty so long as performers believe that they are capable of meeting the challenge at hand.

LINKAGES TO FATIGUE

Readers will recall the assumption mentioned at the outset of this chapter regarding the impact of fatigue on ability—that ability inversely corresponds to fatigue. In light of this, linkages between the ability analysis and the question of fatigue influence on effort and associated CV responses become obvious. The broad implication is that fatigue effects should match those of ability in at least some respects, with responses of fatigued performers corresponding to those of low-ability performers and responses of nonfatigued (rested) performers corresponding to those of high-ability performers. Specific implications are (a) fatigued performers should exert more effort and evince stronger sympathetic CV responses than nonfatigued performers so long as they view success as possible and worthwhile; (b) fatigued performers should withhold effort and evince reduced sympathetic CV responses at a lower objective difficulty level than should nonfatigued performers, creating a window of difficulty levels within which effort and associated CV responses are weaker for fatigued performers; (c) effort and associated CV responses should be weak irrespective of fatigue where success calls for more than nonfatigued performers can or will do; and (d) so long as success is possible, success importance should determine the difficulty level at which fatigued and nonfatigued people withhold effort and, as a result, show reduced CV responsiveness.

Speaking summarily, one could say that fatigue influence on effort and associated CV responses should be determined by the difficulty of a challenge in combination with the importance of meeting it. When fatigue leaves unaltered a belief that success is possible and worthwhile, it should augment effort and CV responsiveness. That is, it should lead performers to exert compensatory effort and experience heightened arousal as a result. By contrast, when fatigue causes success to appear impossible or excessively difficult, it should retard effort and CV responsiveness. That is, it should lead performers to withhold effort and experience minimal arousal as a result. Finally, when fatigue leaves unaltered a belief that success is impossible or excessively difficult, it should have no impact on effort and CV responsiveness. That is, it should leave unchanged performers' inclination to exert low effort and experience low arousal.

FATIGUE EVIDENCE

Evidence relevant to the aforementioned fatigue implications is diverse and still emerging, with the most compelling coming from recent studies that were conducted with this fatigue perspective in mind. The recent studies can be organized into three groups: (a) ones that manipulated muscular fatigue, (b) ones that manipulated mental fatigue, and (c) ones that examined CV correlates of naturally occurring fatigue. In this section, we describe studies of each type, conveying a flavor of the empirical support that is available.

Manipulated Muscular Fatigue

The earliest of the recent fatigue studies was an experiment that involved a muscular challenge (Wright & Penacerrada, 2002). The purposes were to examine (a) the implication that CV responsiveness should be proportional to fatigue where a performance challenge can and will be met and (b) the idea that muscular fatigue effects should tend to be challenge-specific, that is, confined to challenges that involve the depleted system. Participants first performed left- or right-handedly a set of easy (low fatigue) or difficult (high fatigue) hand dynamometer grips. Specifically, the low fatigue participants made a series of 12 grips at 5-s intervals with the goal of merely moving the dynamometer needle on each grip. The high-fatigue participants made the same grips at the same pace but with the goal of moving the needle to its highest point on each grip. Once the initial grip period was completed, the participants made and held with their right hand a modest grip while CV measures were taken. As expected, SBP responses were stronger under high-fatigue conditions among participants who gripped first with their right hand, but unrelated to fatigue among participants who gripped first with their left hand.

Findings from this study have been conceptually replicated and extended in multiple subsequent studies. An example of a study that replicated the handgrip fatigue effect is an experiment by Marcora, Bosio, and de Morree (2008, Experiment 1). The experiment induced leg fatigue through a drop-jump procedure that required participants to jump 100 times at 20-s intervals from a 40-centimeter platform. Later, the participants cycled at a fixed load level with strong encouragement to persist while CV responses were measured.

Results indicated stronger HR responses and marginally stronger ($p < .10$) mean arterial blood pressure (MAP) responses in the fatigued condition relative to a control condition in which no fatigue was induced.

An obvious inconsistency between the results of the immediately preceding study and the results of the handgrip study pertains to the CV outcomes that were affected by fatigue. Whereas the handgrip study produced a fatigue effect for SBP, the preceding study produced a fatigue effect for HR. The inconsistency can be interpreted in terms of two considerations. First, heavy exercise is expected to generate powerful vasodilation in large muscle groups, an event that could reduce or eliminate entirely the impact of increased heart contraction force on blood pressure (e.g., Obrist, 1981). Second, whereas HR is believed to be under parasympathetic nervous system control at low levels of muscular engagement, it is believed to be under sympathetic nervous system control when muscular engagement is high. Thus, during heavy exercise, HR could sometimes correspond more closely to effort than blood pressure.

An example of a study that both replicated and extended findings from the early hand grip study is a recent experiment that involved an obesity simulation protocol (Hogan, Shim, Duncan, Faunce, & Wright, 2010). It examined not only the implication that fatigue should augment effort and associated CV responses so long as it leaves unaltered a belief that success is possible and worthwhile but also the implication that fatigue should retard those responses that cause success to appear impossible or excessively difficult. Participants first walked on a flat treadmill for 10 min while wearing a vest fitted with 5 or 25 pounds of weight. Shortly thereafter, they mounted a recumbent stationary bicycle and were asked to pedal for 10 min with the chance to earn a modest incentive if they maintained a low (40 rpm) or high (60 rpm) cycling pace, that is, met a low or high cycling performance standard.

Investigators assumed that heavy vest participants would fatigue more than light vest participants while walking. Thus, they predicted that the heavy vest participants would evince stronger effort and associated CV responses during cycling when the standard was low (40 rpm), but weaker effort and associated CV responses during cycling when the standard was high (60 rpm). Voluntary terminations after the 6th cycling minute clouded interpretation of later cycling data. However, up to minute 6, HR and SBP results were supportive, with analyses yielding expected Weight (fatigue) × Standard interactions ($ps \leq .007$). Whereas HR and SBP responses tended to be stronger in the heavy vest condition when the standard was low (HR Ms in beats per min = 36.75 [heavy vest] and 29.44 [light vest]; SBP Ms in millimeters of mercury = 19.63 [heavy vest] and 11.38 [light vest]), they were weaker in that condition when the standard was high (HR Ms in beats per min = 33.54 [heavy vest] and 49.33 [light vest]; SBP Ms in millimeters of mercury = 12.22 [heavy vest] and 28.33 [light vest]).

Manipulated Mental Fatigue

The first study that manipulated mental fatigue (Wright, Martin, & Bland, 2003) also examined the twin implications discussed previously, that fatigue should (a) augment effort and associated CV responses when it leaves unaltered a belief that success is possible and worthwhile but (b) retard those responses when it causes success to appear impossible or excessively difficult. It did so assuming that mental systems can become resource depleted in the same fashion that muscular systems can (Muraven & Baumeister, 2000) and that mental fatigue influence on effort compares with muscular fatigue influence on effort.

The investigators created low and high levels of mental fatigue by requiring participants initially to perform for 5 min an easy or difficult counting task. More specifically, they required participants to either count forward from zero in increments of one at 5-s intervals (fatigue low) or count backwards from 375 in increments of three at the same pace (fatigue high). After the counting period, the investigators presented participants mental arithmetic problems with instructions that they could earn a prize if they attained a low (30th percentile) or high (80th percentile) performance standard. As expected, analysis of CV data collected during the arithmetic work period indicated a Fatigue × Difficulty interaction for SBP. Whereas high-fatigue participants tended to have stronger responses when the standard was low, they had weaker responses when the standard was high. Analysis of the DBP and MAP data revealed the same interactions with means in similar patterns.

Like findings from the earliest study that manipulated muscular fatigue, findings from this study have been replicated and extended. Several of the subsequent studies aimed not only to reproduce the original mental fatigue effects but also to evaluate the extent to which mental fatigue effects are challenge specific, that is, limited to challenges relevant to the activity that induced the fatigue. An example is an experiment that (a) induced different levels of fatigue by requiring participants to perform an easy (fatigue low) or difficult (fatigue high) counting task at the beginning of the experimental session and then (b) presented the participants with either an arithmetic challenge (fatigue relevance high) or a letter scanning challenge (fatigue relevance low) with instructions that they would avoid a noise if they attained a modest (50th percentile) performance standard (Wright et al., 2007, Experiment 1). Analysis of the CV data collected during the second work period indicated stronger DBP and MAP responses for high-fatigue participants regardless of the character of the challenge presented. SBP responses corresponded with DBP and MAP responses, although the fatigue effect in that case was not reliable.

A follow-up employed a similar procedure but included a high (90th percentile) performance standard instead of a modest one and provided participants the chance to win a prize instead of the chance to avoid noise

(Wright et al., 2007, Experiment 2). Investigators raised the standard to evaluate the suggestion that the relation observed initially between fatigue and CV response should reverse if objective difficulty is increased to a particular level. They made use of an appetitive incentive to diversify the protocol and document the generalizability of the findings. Once again, analysis of CV data from the second work period provided no evidence of challenge specificity. However, it did reveal near-reliable ($p = .07$) fatigue effects for SBP and MAP, reflecting the anticipated weaker responses among high-fatigue participants.

A replication outside the group designed to examine the challenge specificity issue used a different procedure for manipulating fatigue and crossed its fatigue manipulation with a manipulation of success importance (Stewart, Wright, Hui, & Simmons, 2009). In this case, participants performed initially an easy (fatigue low) or difficult (fatigue high) version of a letter-cancellation task (see Gendolla & Krüsken, 2001). The difficult version presented arrays of d and p letters paired with one, two, three, four, or no apostrophes. Participants were to circle at 3-s intervals d letters linked to two, and only two, apostrophes. The easy version did the same, except that it allowed participants to circle d letters without the two-apostrophe restriction.

Shortly after fatigue induction, participants were presented a set of single-digit multiplication problems with instructions that they would earn a strong (51/52—importance high) or weak (1/52—importance low) chance of winning a prize if they attained a moderate (50th percentile) performance standard. The central prediction was that fatigue would potentiate effort and associated CV responses during the second period when the chance of winning (and thus importance) was high but not when the chance of winning (and thus importance) was low. Potentiation was not expected under low chance (importance) conditions because available benefit under those conditions was not expected to be great enough to justify the added effort requirement associated with fatigue. SBP responses assessed were supportive. Whereas they were proportional to fatigue for high chance participants, they were low regardless of fatigue for low chance participants. Analyses revealed the same interactional pattern for DBP and MAP.

Although the preceding study was not designed to address the challenge specificity issue, it might be noted that it did so indirectly because it varied the character of the tasks used in its fatigue induction (first) and fatigue influence (second) work periods. Its fatigue induction (scanning) task included no quantitative element, and in its difficult version required considerable inhibitory control, that is, restraint against the impulse to circle tempting, but incorrect, d letters. By contrast, its fatigue influence (multiplication) task was quantitative and involved minimal restraint. Despite these task differences, clear fatigue effects were present during multiplication, suggesting that fatigue influence was general, not challenge specific.

Naturally Occurring Fatigue

The final group of recent fatigue studies includes studies that examined CV correlates of naturally occurring fatigue. These studies examined natural fatigue chiefly to document the real world validity of findings from studies involving experimental fatigue manipulations. As is illustrated in the examples to follow, results have been more variable than those from the studies that included fatigue manipulations but are still interpretable in the present theoretical terms.

The first study (Nolte, Wright, Turner, & Contrada, 2008) did not have fatigue as its central focus but provided compelling fatigue indications nonetheless. For reasons unrelated to present concerns, it presented participants an easy (two trigram) or moderately difficult (six trigram) memory challenge with instructions that they could earn a small (8%) chance to win a spiral notebook if they were successful. At the beginning of the session, participants had completed a questionnaire that included items from the energy and tiredness (sleepiness) subscales of the Thayer (1989) Activation–Deactivation Affect Adjective Checklist (ADACL). Further, CV measures were taken during the memorization period. Thus, the protocol allowed investigation of relations between natural fatigue appraisals and CV responses.

Fatigue was operationalized in terms of an index created by combining the (reversed) Energy and Tiredness subscale scores. Its influence was examined using regression analyses that included fatigue and task difficulty as predictors. Findings indicated an interactional response pattern for SBP consistent with the fatigue implications outlined earlier, if one assumes that success importance was low, which seems reasonable, given the trivial benefit available. Where difficulty was low, responses rose with fatigue to a point and then dropped. They dropped, presumably, because the easy task called for more than the highly fatigued participants were willing to do. When difficulty was high, responses were pronounced when fatigue was low, but fell with fatigue from that point. They fell, presumably, because the difficult task called for more than the moderately and highly fatigued participants were willing to do. Response patterns for DBP and MAP were similar, although more variable statistically.

A second study (Schmidt, Richter, Gendolla, & Van der Linden, 2010) was conceived with fatigue in mind. It made CV assessments during a 5-min period in which participants were asked to memorize four quadrams (strings of four random letters), a task described as easy. Later, the participants completed various questionnaire measures, including a standard measure of chronic insomnia (Insomnia Severity Index; Morin, 1993), a standard measure of fatigue (Multidimensional Fatigue Questionnaire; Gentile, Delacroizière, Favre, Sambuc, & San Marco, 2003), and "in-house" measures designed to assess sleep quality the night before and feelings of fatigue on waking. Investigators reasoned that chronically poor sleep should yield fatigue and compensatory effort so long as success is viewed as possible and worthwhile. Consequently, they predicted a positive correspondence between insomnia severity index scores and effort-related CV responses during the task period. Analysis of the CV data revealed the expected correspondences for SBP and MAP, with responses rising across groups identified as having no insomnia, subthreshold insomnia, and clinical insomnia. However, it showed no other fatigue effects, that is, no other correlations between measures of fatigue and CV response.

A third study (Stewart, Wright, Hui, Simmons, & Contrada, 2011) involved reexamination of data from the fatigue induction period of the Stewart et al. (2009) experiment. As noted earlier, this experiment induced fatigue by having participants perform an easy (fatigue low) or difficult (fatigue high) version of a letter-cancellation task. Fatigue assessments were made at baseline by administration of the Energy and Tiredness (sleepiness) subscales of Thayer's ADACL. Thus, the experiment provided a second chance to examine natural-fatigue and CV-response relations under easy and moderately difficult task conditions. It is notable that natural fatigue influence was not examined during the second (multiplication) period on the assumption that effects of natural fatigue would be masked after the fatigue intervention.

Initial analysis revealed that the Energy and Tiredness subscale scores were less well correlated than they were in the comparable Nolte et al. (2008) study. Further, they were differentially related to CV response outcomes. Consequently, the subscales were not combined but examined separately as predictors, in concert with the task difficulty factor. Analyses that operationalized fatigue in terms of energy scores indicated another interactional response pattern for SBP. However, the interaction in this case was somewhat different in character from the one observed by Nolte et al. Specifically, where difficulty was low, responses rose steadily with fatigue (linear trend $p = .009$), something that would be expected if effort requirements were viewed as warranted by even the most fatigued participants. Where difficulty was high, responses (a) were weakly pronounced when fatigue was low, (b) continued rising with fatigue to a point, and then (c) fell to a low level (quadratic trend $p = .001$). This is a pattern that would be expected if effort requirements were viewed as warranted by the mildly and moderately fatigued participants but not by the highly fatigued participants.

The interactional response pattern for SBP is strikingly illustrated by change score means computed for participants with low, moderate, and high fatigue (i.e., reversed energy) scores, defining low and high scores as those falling 1 standard deviation below and above the mean of all fatigue scores, respectively, and defining moderate scores as those falling between. In the easy condition, mean SBP response values for those with low, moderate, and high scores were 3.84, 6.05, and 12.32, respectively. In the difficult condition, values for the same groups were 4.53, 12.49, and 4.78, respectively. As in the Nolte et al. (2008) study, analyses on the DBP and MAP data indicated similar response patterns but yielded less consistent statistical effects. Analyses that operationalized fatigue in terms of tiredness produced no effects.

Differences between the SBP results in this study and those in the Nolte et al. (2008) study could reflect higher success importance appraisals among this study's participants. In theory, higher importance appraisals would have led participants to persist in the face of higher fatigue. However, the differences also could indicate that fatigue was simply lower overall in this study or (perhaps relatedly) that the study's tasks were viewed as less challenging. Lower fatigue would imply that there was less to persist against at low, moderate, and high fatigue levels. Lower difficulty appraisals would imply that, phenomenologically, less was being called for at each difficulty level. Both effects would increase the chance that participants at any given fatigue level would strive to meet the challenge with which they were confronted (Figure 10.1). Evidence comes from analyses that compared energy scores and task difficulty ratings between the studies. Results indicated study main effects for both measures ($ps < .001$). Consistent with the fatigue and difficulty suggestions described earlier, energy scores were higher (higher energy = lower fatigue) and difficulty ratings were lower in the present case.

Irregularities among findings from the preceding three and other natural fatigue studies are easy to identify and not fully understood. Consider, for example, the irregularity in findings for tiredness moving from the Nolte et al. (2008) study to the Stewart et al. (2011) study. However, in reflecting, readers might wish to focus less on puzzlements and more on compatibilities. Although the findings are not perfectly consistent, they fit together in notable respects. They also fit with findings from studies that have included fatigue manipulations and, to our knowledge, include no components that compellingly contradict the present fatigue view. Thus, fair conclusions are that the findings (a) can be understood in the present fatigue analysis terms and (b) provide some evidence that spontaneous fatigue yields effects comparable with those yielded by fatigue induced in a laboratory context.

Summary

To summarize, three types of recent studies have provided the most compelling evidence relevant to the fatigue implications identified earlier. These include studies that have manipulated muscular fatigue, studies that have manipulated mental fatigue, and studies that have examined CV correlates of naturally occurring fatigue. The muscular fatigue studies have documented the suggestions that fatigue should (a) augment effort and associated CV responses when it leaves unaltered a belief that success is possible and worthwhile but (b) retard those responses when it causes success to appear impossible or excessively difficult. The mental fatigue studies have documented these implications as well and, in addition, confirmed the moderating influence of success importance. The natural fatigue studies have yielded more variable findings but ones that can be understood in the present theoretical terms and constitute evidence that the implied fatigue effects occur in real-world settings.

CONCLUSION

We have discussed a component of our broader research program concerned with fatigue influence on effort and associated CV responses. The guiding analysis suggests that fatigue should have different effects depending on the difficulty of the challenge and the importance of meeting it. When fatigue leaves unaltered a belief that success is possible and worthwhile, it should augment effort and CV responsiveness. By contrast, when fatigue causes success to appear impossible or excessively difficult, it should retard effort and CV responsiveness. Finally, when fatigue leaves unaltered a belief that success is impossible or excessively difficult, it should have no impact on effort and CV responsiveness. Data that we and others have collected provide—we think—persuasive support.

Attentive readers might notice relevancies between the present fatigue analysis and the ego depletion analysis proposed by Baumeister (e.g., Muraven & Baumeister, 2000). Relevancies are there and worth noting. However, the analyses are not redundant. In its original form at least, the Baumeister analysis was concerned with depletion within a particular performance system, specifically, that involved in self-control. By contrast, the present analysis is broadly concerned with depletion in performance systems. In addition, the Baumeister analysis is concerned with resource depletion influence on performance, whereas the present analysis is concerned with resource depletion influence on effort and associated CV responses. The present analysis has implications for performance insofar as effort affects that outcome (Harkins, 2006). Indeed, it has potential for improving ego depletion predictions because it highlights conditions under which compensatory striving should occur and sometimes allow depleted individuals to maintain control. But the analysis was not developed with performance as a focus. In our view, these two analyses are complementary rather than competitive.

Attentive readers also might see connections between the present analysis and the biopsychosocial analysis of CV response proposed by Blascovich (e.g., Blascovich & Tomaka, 1996). On the face of it, there would appear to be connections because both analyses concern CV adjustments under conditions where performance resources bear different relations to demand. However, close inspection reveals marked differences in the two lines of thought. One crucial difference pertains to the analyses' conception of demand. Whereas the present analysis equates demand with difficulty, the Blascovich analysis construes demand as an amalgam of required effort, uncertainty, and danger appraisals. Another difference pertains to the mechanism hypothesized to mediate CV adjustment. Whereas the present analysis focuses on effort, the Blascovich analysis focuses on appraisals of challenge and threat. We believe that our analysis accounts better for the findings discussed here, as well as other relevant findings. But we are open to being proven wrong and would welcome a comprehensive literature review that compared the predictive validity of the competing perspectives.

Although fatigue research inspired by the present fatigue analysis has progressed well, it has not answered all questions. One point of ambiguity relates to the question of whether fatigue effects on effort and associated CV responses are challenge specific, that is, confined to challenges highly relevant to the activity that induced the fatigue. The early muscle fatigue study from our laboratory provided evidence to this effect, but a battery of mental fatigue studies did not. A possible indication is that there is specificity within muscular, but not mental processing, realms. However, additional research is required to draw confident conclusions in this regard.

A second point of ambiguity concerns our assumption that ability appraisals fall as fatigue rises. This has been evaluated but not confirmed (e.g., Wright et al., 2003). The lack of confirmation could reflect the influence of uninteresting methodological factors. However, it also could be telling with respect to reality. One alternative possibility is that fatigue affects ability appraisals implicitly, leading to higher difficulty assessments without a dispositional insight. Another possibility is that fatigue does not affect ability appraisals but rather affects difficulty assessments directly. Once again, additional work will be required to understand this.

Still another point of ambiguity concerns the possible impact of fatigue on perceptions of success importance. Our working assumption has been that importance appraisals vary independently of fatigue. However, mechanisms could exist that would entangle the outcomes. For example, fatigue could sometimes lead to a blue mood, which could sometimes lead to lower outcome expectancies (i.e., expectancies of goal attainment, given success) and, thus, lower importance appraisals (Richter & Gendolla, 2009). Yet again, more research will be required.

We are confident that ambiguities such as these will be resolved in time, and we are comfortable considering practical implications without having all puzzle pieces in place. Among the most important implications are ones pertaining to health. Many readers will be aware of linkages established between persistently elevated CV responses and negative health outcomes, including hypertension, coronary artery disease, and dementia (de la Torre, 2002; see also Chapters 11 and 14, this volume; cf, Chapter 12, this volume). In light of these, a straightforward suggestion is that fatigue could be variously toxic in some life circumstances. Specifically, it could be variously toxic when it leads to chronic compensatory striving. Our analysis provides a road map for identifying both situational and personal factors that should moderate such striving. Thus, the analysis could eventually be of value for identifying people whose health might be at risk and possibly also for developing interventions designed to combat fatigue toxicity where it is indicated.

REFERENCES

Bandura, A. (1982). Self-efficacy mechanism in human agency. *American Psychologist, 37*, 122–147. doi:10.1037/0003-066X.37.2.122

Bandura, A. (1986). *Social foundations of thought and action: A social cognitive theory.* Englewood Cliffs, NJ: Prentice Hall.

Blascovich, J., & Tomaka, J. (1996). The biopsychosocial model of arousal regulation. In M. P. Zanna (Ed.), *Advances in experimental social psychology* (Vol. 28, pp. 1–51). New York, NY: Academic Press.

Brehm, J. W., & Self, E. (1989). The intensity of motivation. In M. R. Rozenweig & L. W. Porter (Eds.), *Annual review of psychology* (pp. 109–131). Palo Alto, CA: Annual Reviews.

de la Torre, J. C. (2002). Alzheimer disease as a vascular disorder: Nosological evidence. *Stroke, 33*, 1152–1162. doi:10.1161/01.STR.0000014421.15948.67

Gendolla, G. H. E., & Krüsken, J. (2001). The joint impact of mood state and task difficulty on cardiovascular and electrodermal reactivity in active coping. *Psychophysiology, 38*, 548–556. doi:10.1017/S0048577201000622

Gendolla, G. H. E., & Krüsken, J. (2002). The joint effect of informational mood impact and performance-contingent incentive on effort-related cardiovascular response. *Journal of Personality and Social Psychology, 83*, 271–283. doi:10.1037/0022-3514.83.2.271

Gentile, S., Delacroizière, J. C., Favre, F., Sambuc, R., & San Marco, J. L. (2003). Validation of the French Multidimensional Fatigue Inventory (MFI 20). *European Journal of Cancer Care, 12*, 58–64. doi:10.1046/j.1365-2354.2003.00295.x

Harkins, S. G. (2006). Mere effort as the mediator of the evaluation–performance relationship. *Journal of Personality and Social Psychology, 91*, 436–455. doi:10.1037/0022-3514.91.3.436

Heider, F. (1958). *The psychology of interpersonal relations.* New York, NY: Wiley. doi:10.1037/10628-000

Higgins, E. T. (2006). Value from hedonic experience *and* engagement. *Psychological Review, 113*, 439–460. doi:10.1037/0033-295X.113.3.439

Hogan, B. K., Shim, J. J., Duncan, J., Faunce, C., & Wright, R. A. (2010, May). *Interactional influence of fatigue and difficulty on cardiovascular response: An obesity simulation utilizing an aerobic exercise challenge.* Poster session presented at the meeting of the Society for the Study of Motivation, Boston, MA.

Kahneman, D. (1973). *Attention and effort.* Englewood Cliffs, NJ: Prentice Hall.

Kukla, A. (1972). Foundations of an attributional theory of performance. *Psychological Review, 79*, 454–470. doi:10.1037/h0033494

Lacey, B. C., & Lacey, J. I. (1980). Cognitive modulation in time dependent primary bradycardia. *Psychophysiology, 17*, 209–221. doi:10.1111/j.1469-8986.1980.tb00137.x

Marcora, S. M., Bosio, A., & de Morree, H. M. (2008). Locomotor muscle fatigue increases cardiorespiratory responses and reduces performance during intense cycling exercise independent of metabolic stress. *American Journal of Physiology: Regulatory, Integrative and Comparative Physiology, 294*, R874–R883. doi:10.1152/ajpregu.00678.2007

Morin, C. M. (1993). *Insomnia: Psychological assessment and management.* New York, NY: Guilford Press.

Muraven, M., & Baumeister, R. F. (2000). Self-regulation and the depletion of limited resources: Does self-control resemble a muscle? *Psychological Bulletin, 126*, 247–259. doi:10.1037/0033-2909.126.2.247

Nolte, R. N., Wright, R. A., Turner, C., & Contrada, R. J. (2008). Reported fatigue, difficulty, and cardiovascular response to a memory challenge. *International Journal of Psychophysiology, 69*, 1–8. doi:10.1016/j.ijpsycho.2008.02.004

Obrist, P. A. (1981). *Cardiovascular psychophysiology: A perspective.* New York, NY: Plenum Press.

Obrist, P. A., Webb, R. A., & Sutterer, J. R. (1969). Heart rate and somatic changes during aversive conditioning and a simple reaction time task. *Psychophysiology, 5*, 696–723. doi:10.1111/j.1469-8986.1969.tb02872.x

Richter, M., & Gendolla, G. H. E. (2009). Mood impact on cardiovascular reactivity when task difficulty is unclear. *Motivation and Emotion, 33*, 239–248. doi:10.1007/s11031-009-9134-4

Schmidt, R. E., Richter, M., Gendolla, G. H. E., & Van der Linden, M. (2010). Young poor sleepers mobilize extra effort in an easy memory task: Evidence from cardiovascular measures. *Journal of Sleep Research, 19*, 487–495. doi:10.1111/j.1365-2869.2010.00834.x

Stewart, C. C., Wright, R. A., Hui, S. A., & Simmons, A. (2009). Outcome expectancy as a moderator of mental fatigue influence on cardiovascular response. *Psychophysiology, 46*, 1141–1149. doi:10.1111/j.1469-8986.2009.00862.x

Stewart, C. C., Wright, R. A., Hui, S. A., Simmons, A., & Contrada, R. J. (2011). *The association between energy level and blood pressure response to a visual scanning task varies across low and moderate levels of difficulty.* Manuscript in preparation.

Thayer, R. E. (1989). *The biopsychology of mood and arousal*. New York, NY: Oxford University Press.

Wright, R. A. (1998). Ability perception and cardiovascular response to behavioral challenge. In M. Kofta, G. Weary, & G. Sedek (Eds.), *Control in action: Cognitive and motivational mechanisms* (pp. 197–232). New York, NY: Plenum Press.

Wright, R. A., & Dill, J. C. (1993). Blood pressure reactivity and incentive appraisals as a function of perceived ability and objective task demand. *Psychophysiology, 30*, 152–160. doi:10.1111/j.1469-8986.1993.tb01728.x

Wright, R. A., Junious, T. R., Neal, C., Avello, A., Graham, C., Herrmann, L., . . . Walton, N. (2007). Mental fatigue influence on effort-related cardiovascular response: Difficulty effects and extension across cognitive performance domains. *Motivation and Emotion, 31*, 219–231. doi:10.1007/s11031-007-9066-9

Wright, R. A., & Kirby, L. D. (2001). Effort determination of cardiovascular response: An integrative analysis with applications in social psychology. In M. Zanna (Ed.), *Advances in experimental social psychology* (Vol. 33, pp. 255–307). San Diego, CA: Academic Press.

Wright, R. A., Martin, R. E., & Bland, J. L. (2003). Energy resource depletion, task difficulty, and cardiovascular response to a mental arithmetic challenge. *Psychophysiology, 40*, 98–105. doi:10.1111/1469-8986.00010

Wright, R. A., & Penacerrada, D. (2002). Energy resource depletion, ability perception, and cardiovascular response to behavioral challenge. *Psychophysiology, 39*, 182–187. doi:10.1111/1469-8986.3920182

II

APPLICATIONS

A. HEALTH AND CARDIOVASCULAR RESPONSE

11

CARDIOVASCULAR REACTIVITY AND HEALTH

STEPHAN BONGARD, MUSTAFA AL'ABSI,
AND WILLIAM R. LOVALLO

It has been long suspected that persons displaying exaggerated physiological responses to emotional or stressful situations are at greater risk of developing acute and chronic diseases, particularly in the cardiovascular system. Research has demonstrated that individuals differ in the pattern and magnitude of cardiovascular responses to stress. Also, situational conditions differ in their potential to evoke cardiovascular responses.

In this chapter, we discuss some evidence for the assumption that cardiovascular stress responses are either an indicator of or maybe even a cause for cardiovascular disease development. We review empirical evidence from animal, epidemiological, experimental, and clinical research, and we describe the physiological pathways that seem to mediate the association between cardiovascular reactivity and disease. Special emphasis is given to motivational constructs such as *mental effort* or *perceived task difficulty*, which modulate the activity of the hypothalamic–pituitary–adrenocortical (HPA) axis and cardiovascular reactivity and its responses to acute stressors. The influence of the sympatho–adrenomedullary and endogenous opioid systems is described as well. Emotional moderators of the stress response (e.g., anger) and their link to cardiovascular pathology are also discussed. We close this chapter with a brief description of a model that integrates findings from research on cardiovascular reactivity and health and that might provide guidance for future research in this area.

DEFINITION OF REACTIVITY

Cardiovascular reactivity has been defined as a tendency to produce relatively large or small responses to a psychological or physical stressor (Krantz & Manuck, 1984; Lovallo, 2005a, 2005b). This definition is based on the assumption that chronically enhanced reactivity may cause pathological changes leading to increased risk of cardiovascular disease. Relevant to the focus of this book, it is also important to identify the role of motivational factors contributing to individual differences in reactivity. However, linking cardiovascular reactivity to disease assumes that reactivity is stable across time and across situations. Here, measures of cardiovascular reactivity may be reliable in the short term (weeks and months) when appropriate assessment procedures are used (Kamarck & Lovallo, 2003). The generalizability of reactivity from the lab to the field has also been investigated, though the findings are inconsistent (Kamarck & Lovallo, 2003). For a discussion of problems, such as content and construct validity of cardiovascular reactivity, the interested reader might refer to the Kamarck and Lovallo (2003) paper.

Not all heart rate and blood pressure elevations can be considered to be potentially harmful for someone's health. Cardiovascular responses to physical exercise, for example, are usually considered beneficial. However, cardiovascular responses that exceed metabolic demands may be harmful or signal the presence of preclinical disease. In addition, emotional reactions that may have had an evolutionary advantage are seen by some as being harmful in modern societies. For example, the experience of anger is associated with strong cardiovascular activation originally intended to prepare the organism for fight or flight (Plutchik, 1994), a response that is often maladaptive in today's civilized societies. Therefore, cardiovascular responses that exceed metabolic or other adaptive demands can be considered maladaptive and potentially harmful (Turner, Carroll, Hanson, & Sims, 1988).

REACTIVITY AND CARDIOVASCULAR HEALTH

The concept of reactivity is of particular significance in biobehavioral models of cardiovascular diseases such as essential hypertension, coronary heart disease, or stroke. There is no direct proof of a causal relationship between heightened cardiovascular reactivity and cardiovascular disease. Support for this assumption comes from different lines of evidence described in the following paragraphs.

Evidence From Lab Studies on Clinical Groups

Studies of patients with and without coronary heart disease show that individuals with an impaired cardiovascular system produce significantly greater diastolic blood pressure responses to mentally challenging tasks (e.g., Corse, Manuck, Cantwell, Giordani, & Matthews, 1982). This effect is independent of whether the person is aware of his or her disease status (Steptoe, Melville, & Ross, 1984). One might argue that heightened cardiovascular reactivity in patients is a symptom of disease rather than a causal factor. Therefore, studies comparing cardiovascular stress responses of healthy persons at high risk of disease are a stronger proof of the reactivity hypothesis because they strengthen the interpretation that psychophysiological dysfunction precedes disease onset.

Studies on High-Risk Populations

Individuals with a family history of essential hypertension have a higher risk of developing this disease themselves (Pierce, Grim, & King, 2005). Although such persons may show only modestly elevated resting blood pressure, their responses to laboratory stressors are often exaggerated (al'Absi, Lovallo, McKey, & Pincomb, 1994; al'Absi et al., 1998; Fredrikson & Matthews, 1990). In addition, persons at risk of hypertension show exaggerated responses that are not confined to the cardiovascular system. We have found that when at rest in a novel experimental environment, individuals with borderline hypertension show enhanced adrenocortical activation relative to low-risk controls (al'Absi & Lovallo, 1993), they have stronger cardiovascular and neuroendocrine responses during work on mental arithmetic and psychomotor stress (al'Absi, Everson, & Lovallo, 1995; al'Absi et al., 1994), and these tendencies are exaggerated in the presence of psychostimulants, such as caffeine (al'Absi, Everson, et al., 1995; al'Absi, Lovallo, Pincomb, Sung, & Wilson, 1995). We have obtained similar results in individuals who are normotensive and who have a positive parental history. Other investigators have confirmed a heightened adrenocortical activity in persons at high risk of hypertension (Räikkönen, Hautanen, & Keltikangas-Jarvinen, 1996; Watt et al., 1992). This work suggests that hypertension risk is associated with increased activation of the autonomic nervous system (Julius & Nesbitt, 1996) and the cardiovascular control centers of the hypothalamus and medulla (Lovallo & Wilson, 1992) paralleled by enhanced responses of the HPA (al'Absi & Wittmers, 2003). In turn, the enhanced

HPA response to novelty implicates increased reactivity of prefrontal and limbic system areas.

This discussion is complementary to other methods of assessing the state of the field. For meta-analytical reviews of family history of hypertension, see also Fredrikson and Matthews (1990); Manuck, Kamarck, Kasprowicz, and Waldstein (1993); and Pierce et al. (2005). Though such studies make it more likely that enhanced and/or prolonged cardiovascular reactivity precedes cardiovascular diseases, they cannot rule out that both cardiovascular reactivity and cardiovascular diseases are affected by preclinical conditions or an unknown third factor. A proof of a causal relationship between heightened cardiovascular reactivity and cardiovascular diseases can only be demonstrated in experimental designs, and, for ethical reasons, such designs are only possible in animals.

Experimental Animal Studies

In studies with monkeys it has been demonstrated that extreme behavioral stress results in chronic blood pressure elevations (Harris & Brady, 1977). For example, repeated and relatively long-lasting periods in a shock–avoidance paradigm led to a steady monthly increase of blood pressure levels in adolescent rhesus monkeys (Forsyth, 1969). Similarly, repeated threat and rank order competitions in groups of cynomolgus monkeys caused greater atherosclerosis in the coronary artery in those animals that demonstrated heightened heart rate responses to the stressors (Kaplan, Manuck, Clarkson, Lusso, & Taub, 1982; Manuck, Kaplan, & Clarkson, 1983). Thus, these kinds of animal studies teach us that long-lasting and repeated cardiovascular challenges can lead to chronic elevations of an individual's blood pressure and to alterations in the vascular tissue, which have high clinical significance. These experimental studies, of course, cannot be conducted with humans. Here the best research designs for discovering possible causal relationships between cardiovascular reactivity and disease are longitudinal studies.

Longitudinal Studies

In humans, some longitudinal studies have attempted to predict future resting blood pressures by documenting cardiovascular reactivity to laboratory stressors at study entry. Heightened resting blood pressure is a well-established risk factor for essential hypertension and coronary heart disease (Burt et al., 1995). For example, Everson, Kaplan, Goldberg, and Salonen (1996) examined blood pressure reactivity in anticipation of an exercise stress test in men who were normotensive. Exaggerated blood pressure reactivity in anticipation of a bicycle exercise challenge predicted hypertension status after 4 years.

Although 4 years is a rather short period, Wood, Sheldon, Elveback, and Schirger (1984) predicted essential hypertension status over a period of 45 years using blood pressure responses to a cold pressor test as the predictor.

Relative to coronary heart disease, Keys and colleagues (1971) examined blood pressure responses to the cold pressor test in healthy men and predicted the development of coronary heart disease over 20 years. Persons with elevated diastolic blood pressure responses to the cold pressor test were 2.4 times more likely to experience a myocardial infarction or to die than those who showed weaker responses to the stressor.

In a thorough review of longitudinal studies relating cardiovascular reactivity to preclinical and clinical states, Treiber and others (2003) concluded that despite inconsistencies in the literature, a small and growing body of evidence now links cardiovascular reactivity to measures of subclinical and clinical cardiovascular diseases.

INTERNAL AND EXTERNAL FACTORS INFLUENCING REACTIVITY

Given the association between cardiovascular reactivity and disease and mortality risk, it seems worthwhile to establish factors that influence or moderate cardiovascular reactivity. We can roughly differentiate between internal factors, such as personality traits, and external factors, such as type of task. In the following paragraphs, we discuss prominent exponents for each of these factors, namely, anger and anger expression as examples of personality influences and active coping as task factor.

Anger as an Internal Factor Influencing Reactivity

Trait anger has been linked to both cardiovascular reactivity and disease risk. Anger is considered to be a basic emotion associated with a particular cardiovascular response pattern (Stemmler, 2004). For example, in a laboratory study in which effort-related active coping with a mental challenge and anger provocation by harassment of female volunteers were manipulated independently, we found anger-related increases in systolic and diastolic blood pressure for about 10 mmHg and an increase in heart rate for 12 beats per min (Bongard, Pfeiffer, al'Absi, Hodapp, & Linnenkemper, 1997). Only anger-associated heart rate and diastolic blood pressure responses were additive to those elicited by the effort manipulation.

Research has also indicated that anger expression may be involved in influencing cardiovascular diseases. For example, outward anger expression has been related to greater blood pressure and heart rate reactivity during the performance of acute behavioral challenges (Siegman, 1993; Suchday & Larkin, 2001), and it is associated with increased risk of hypertension (Everson, Goldberg, Kaplan, Julkunen, & Salonen, 1998). We have demonstrated that taking situational and domain-specific considerations into account results in more consistent associations between anger and cardiovascular stress measures. Open anger expression, especially in the work domain, showed better associations with elevated blood pressure than open anger expression in the home domain (Bongard & al'Absi, 2003, 2005). A review by Strike and Steptoe (2005) reported evidence demonstrating that acute states of anger can trigger myocardial infarction and sudden cardiac death in susceptible individuals.

Large longitudinal studies indicate a link between anger disposition and increased risk of cardiovascular diseases. For example, a study with a large sample of African Americans demonstrated an association of anger experience with increased risk of coronary heart disease (Williams et al., 2000). Studies have also found that anger was associated with a 2- to 3-fold increase in the risk of developing other cardiovascular diseases, including angina pectoris, myocardial infarction, or sudden cardiac death (Kawachi, Sparrow, Spiro, Vokonas, & Weiss, 1996). Finally, a meta-analysis of studies assessing ambulatory blood pressure showed that the experience of anger was positively associated with blood pressure (Schum, Jorgensen, Verhaeghen, Sauro, & Thibodeau, 2003).

These studies and reviews indicate that anger trait and anger expression style may moderate the impact of stress on the cardiovascular system, depending on the expression style and the situational demands. These emotional traits may also predict increased proneness for cardiovascular diseases and accelerated progression in coronary heart disease, essential hypertension, and stroke.

Task Factors Influencing Reactivity

A central aspect of the elicitation of cardiovascular responses is the responder's motivational state. It has been repeatedly demonstrated that the degree of effort to exert control during a laboratory task can increase the size of cardiovascular responses and that administration of tasks that are very easy or too difficult can result in lowered coping efforts and smaller responses (Bongard, Hodapp, Frisch, & Lennartz, 1994; Obrist et al., 1978; Steptoe, 1983). In a dual task paradigm, we were able to demonstrate that individuals allocate more cognitive resources and mental effort to a task when they can cope with it actively than when they have to cope with it passively (Bongard, 1995). In this study, task performance data correlated positively with indicators of sympathetic activation of the cardiovascular system (heart rate, pulse transit time, systolic but not diastolic blood pressure). Wright (1996) concluded that effort mobilization in active coping situations is reflected in beta-adrenergic sympathetic activation of the organism.

More important than the task configuration is an individual's subjective appraisal of the task characteristics and the appraisal of his or her capacities to cope with the task's demands (Lazarus & Folkman, 1984; Lovallo, 2005a). When people are made to believe that they have control of a task's outcome even though they factually do not, they expend more effort on the task and show exaggerated cardiovascular responses (Hodapp, Bongard, & Heiligtag, 1992; Manuck, Harvey, Lechleiter, & Neal, 1978).

Gendolla (2000) incorporated the active coping and mental effort concepts into his mood–behavior model (MBM). The MBM suggests that moods—unlike emotions—are not motivational states but that they nevertheless affect situation appraisals when people are to perform a task and are about to decide how much effort they will invest. In a positive mood, demand appraisals will be more optimistic and people will spend less effort to cope with a challenge, whereas in a negative mood they experience higher difficulty and consequently invest more effort but disengage earlier. On the basis of the MBM, Gendolla, Abele, and Krüsken (2001) demonstrated that a negative mood leads to higher demand appraisals and consequently higher effort mobilization operationalized as systolic blood pressure responses compared with positive mood when performing an attention-demanding task.

MECHANISMS LINKING REACTIVITY AND CARDIOVASCULAR DISEASES

Next we present system-specific discussions about the systems that mediate any possible links between reactivity and diseases, including cardiovascular diseases.

Hypothalamic–Pituitary–Adrenocortical Axis

The HPA includes the hypothalamic paraventricular nucleus, the pituitary, and the adrenal cortex. The release of corticotropin-releasing factor (CRF) by the hypothalamus stimulates synthesis of adrenocorticotropic hormone (ACTH) by the pituitary, which in turn increases production of cortisol by the adrenal gland. The HPA acts to maintain normal homeostatic functions during most conditions, and it rapidly responds to both physiological demands and psychological stressors. The cortisol response to psychological stressors, such as public speaking, is evidence of inputs to the hypothalamus from the amygdala and prefrontal cortex (Iversen, Kupfermann, & Kandel, 2000).

Animal studies support a relationship between HPA reactivity to stress and subsequent cardiovascular disease. Spontaneously hypertensive rats (Hashimoto et al., 1989) have shown proportional relationships between exaggerated corticosterone secretion along with blood pressure dysregulation (Hashimoto et al., 1989), and plasma corticosterone levels were positively related to blood pressure elevation following ether stress (Hashimoto et al., 1989). However, adrenalectomy produces a vasodilatation effect and abolishes pressor response to catecholamines, an effect that is reversed by administration of glucocorticoids (Walker & Williams, 1992).

The relationship between HPA activity and hypertension development in spontaneously hypertensive rats may bear relevance to human studies. For example, early cross-sectional investigations showed increased urinary excretion of cortisol metabolites in patients with hypertension (Soro, Ingram, Tonolo, Glorioso, & Fraser, 1995), whereas other studies did not show such abnormalities (Vermeulen, Verdonck, Van der Straeten, & Daneels, 1967). Research in spontaneously hypertensive rats and recent research in patients with hypertension has focused on sensitivity to cortisol at the receptor level (Bamberger, Schulte, & Chrousos, 1996) and cortisol half-life and metabolic activity (Walker, Best, Shackleton, Padfield, & Edwards, 1996). This research demonstrates a potential involvement of cortisol in hypertension development through multiple mechanisms that extend beyond systemic cortisol concentration abnormalities (Walker et al., 1996).

Both cortisol and ACTH increase blood pressure in normotensives (Williamson, Kelly, & Whitworth, 1996), and both are associated with expansion of plasma volume and increase in plasma atrial natriuretic hormone concentrations. Furthermore, results from studies conducted with healthy subjects have indicated that cortisol administration at doses between 80 and 200 mg/day increases blood pressure (Williamson et al., 1996). This blood pressure increase is associated with but not dependent on sodium retention and volume expansion (Kelly, Mangos, Williamson, & Whitworth, 1998).

Sympatho–Adrenomedullary System

The sympathetic nervous system, one of two autonomic system branches, controls the activity of multiple systems involved in regulating and executing the fight–flight response. Relative to cardiovascular functions, the sympathetic system regulates cardiac and vascular activity. During periods of stress, sympathetic outflow will directly stimulate cardiac contractility and rate. In addition, increased sympathetic activation increases contractile activity of the blood vessels and contributes to blood pressure rises. When this system is active, catecholamines are released from the adrenal medulla into the circulation system and also from nerve terminals on innervated organs.

The release of epinephrine during periods of stress increases the rate and contractility of cardiac contractions. Centrally, norepinephrine is released by the locus coeruleus. The noradrenergic pathway then participates in orchestrating both the peripheral and central response to acute stress. This system also interacts with other systems involved in regulating the stress response, including the HPA axis, the serotonergic system, and the opioid system (Aston-Jones, Ennis, Pieribone, Nickell, & Shipley, 1986; Chrousos & Gold, 1992). The extensive animal literature provides direct evidence of the specific links of the central noradrenergic pathway with the corticotropic system and the dopaminergic system, and the involvement of these interactions in various normal pathological conditions have been treated by several laboratories (Dallman, 1993; Rivier & Vale, 1983; Van de Kar & Blair, 1999).

Endogenous Opioid System

Another system involved in regulating the cardiovascular and neuro-endocrine responses to stress is the endogenous opioid system. For example, accumulated evidence suggests that this system directly modulates HPA activity (Burnett, Scott, Weaver, Medbak, & Dinan, 1999). Studies demonstrating the role of this system have used the opioid blockade protocol. Here removing the opioidergic inhibitory inputs to the hypothalamic neurons specialized in releasing CRF using opioid receptor blockade medications increases ACTH and cortisol (Delitala, Trainer, Oliva, Fanciulli, & Grossman, 1994; Wand & Schumann, 1998). Research has shown that individuals with hypertension and those at increased risk of the disorder exhibit greater endogenous opiate activity (Fontana et al., 1994). We found differences in sensitivity to endogenous blockade among individuals at high and low risk of hypertension (al'Absi, France, Harju, France, & Wittmers, 2006). Studies by McCubbin (1993; McCubbin, Surwit, Williams, Nemeroff, & McNeilly, 1989) have suggested that exaggerated cardiovascular reactivity and increased HPA axis activation frequently seen in individuals prone to hypertension may reflect a diminished opioidergic inhibitory feedback to hypothalamic areas involved in regulating the sympathetic and endocrine response to stress (McCubbin et al., 1989).

Other Factors

Other systems including the serotonergic pathway may also be involved in mediating stress reactivity. It is also likely that stress reactivity may be manifested behaviorally in terms of engaging in behaviors that increase risk factors for cardiovascular diseases, such as smoking, poor diet, and physical inactivity. Reactivity may also increase the propensity for other harmful behaviors, including a greater likelihood of seeking out substances such as tobacco and alcohol (Brady & Sonne, 1999; Whalen, Jamner, Henker, & Delfino, 2001).

INTEGRATION OF FACTORS INFLUENCING CARDIOVASCULAR REACTIVITY

Evidence that enhanced reactivity is a risk factor for cardiovascular disease is increasing. To integrate the material we have presented, we refer to a model of the psychophysiological response–disease relationship that may be useful in accounting for sources of increased reactivity and in understanding connections to cardiovascular disease. This model has been described in detail elsewhere (Lovallo, 2005a; Lovallo & Gerin, 2003), but the following are its main features.

The goal of formulating this model was to provide a way of dividing the central nervous system and periphery into levels that could be accessed through appropriate study designs and data interpretation. The motivation was the belief that research on reactivity and disease risk could progress faster and more mechanistically if it were possible to consider reactivity differences at a systems level. The bulk of previous work on reactivity and disease has been conducted at an association level. A measure of interest—say heart rate response—is usually examined in relation to current level of disease risk or in light of future disease development. Although this is useful for establishing an association between response magnitude and disease, there may be at least three levels of organization in the brain and peripheral tissues where persons may come to have large or small reactions to stress. Figure 11.1 summarizes these levels.

Level I makes reference to higher level brain systems that formulate our reactions to external events as a result of interactions between the prefrontal cortex and limbic system. Level II refers to lower level brain systems that receive inputs from Level I systems and from responses to the peripheral tissues through the autonomic nervous system and endocrine system. Level III refers to the peripheral tissues that react to these Level II outputs. The internal mechanisms affecting each level and the interactions between levels are given more extensive treatment elsewhere and the reader is referred to these sources (Lovallo, 2005a; Lovallo & Gerin, 2003).

The key issue for consideration here is that if a single measure of reactivity is the focus of study, this measure may have large or small reactions to a given stressor because of psychological processes or prior experience (Level I) that would affect how the individual may appraise an event (Lazarus & Folkman, 1984) and form emotional responses to it (Gianaros et al., 2008; Iversen, Iversen, & Saper, 2000; Rolls, 2000). These processes form the basis of psychological stress responses that may have much to do with a person's

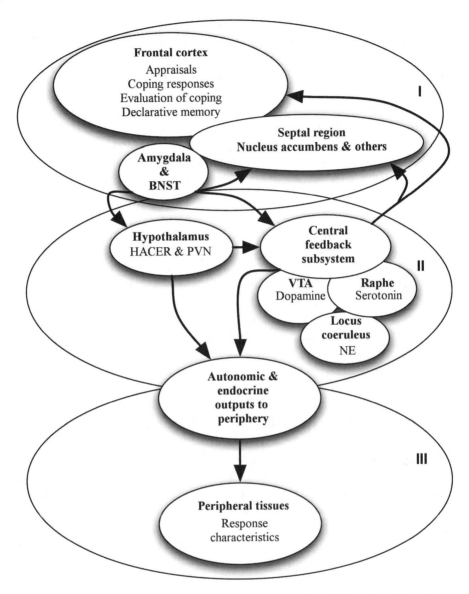

Figure 11.1. Levels of organization in the brain and peripheral tissues where persons may experience reactions to stress. BNST = bed nucleus of the stria terminalis; HACER = hypothalamic area controlling emotional responses; NE = norepinephrine; PVN = paraventricular nucleus; VTA = ventral tegmental area. Adapted from "Cardiovascular Reactivity: Mechanisms and Pathways to Cardiovascular Disease," by W. R. Lovallo, 2005, *International Journal of Psychophysiology, 58,* pp. 122. Copyright 2005 by Elsevier. Adapted with permission.

personality, temperament, or how these are shaped by past life events. Clearly, exaggerated responses at this level would have a disparate impact on Level II, with consequences for the size of the peripheral response measured in the laboratory. However, there is evidence that descending Level I activity that is the same for two persons may still result in different peripheral responses because of the reactive nature and homeostatic set points regulated in the hypothalamus and brainstem (Iversen, Iversen, et al., 2000). We have shown that individuals with prehypertension may produce large cortisol responses to exposure to a novel laboratory environment than do low-risk persons, despite reporting similar perceptions and sense of activation (al'Absi & Lovallo, 1993). Others have shown that hypertensive patients may have a higher density of hypothalamic receptors for corticotrophin releasing factor, a primary determinant of stress endocrine output (Goncharuk, Van Heerikhuize, Swaab, & Buijs, 2002). Maintaining a distinction between Level I and Level II processes therefore helps us recognize that two persons may differ in reactivity because of psychological factors (or prefrontal–limbic interactions), whereas others may generate larger descending activation due to the hypothalamus and brainstem. Finally, even if Levels I and II produce similar levels of output, a person may have larger responses than another because of purely peripheral systems differences operating at Level III. Examples of such peripheral differences are the hypertrophy of blood vessel walls known to occur during hypertension development (Folkow, 1990) or dysregulation of autonomic reactivity in persons with diabetes or during normal aging (Charkoudian & Rabbitts, 2009; Verrotti, Loiacono, Mohn, & Chiarelli, 2009). The ultimate value of this attempt at a mechanistic approach to reactivity and disease is that it helps to divide the system into meaningful levels that may help in connecting the source of individual differences to the measure of reactivity in question and the disease under study. Treating all persons alike may obscure true relationships by including persons with different sources of reactivity elevations as part of the same group.

A final note is that another chapter speculates on potential implications of small responses to stress and expresses the hypothesis that these may also have implications for thoughts about cardiovascular disease etiology (see Chapter 12, this volume). Two points are important to note in this context. First, if large reactions to stress signal that the system is not functioning at an optimal homeostatic level, then small responses should signal the same thing because both would signal deviations from normal homeostatic function (Lovallo, 2011). Second, the three-level model described here is equally useful for considering sources of low reactivity as high reactivity. Our discussion of reduced reactivity does not contradict the general analysis presented here but instead expresses a hypothesis that complements present thinking about stress reactivity and disease.

REFERENCES

al'Absi, M., Everson, S. A., & Lovallo, W. R. (1995). Hypertension risk factors and cardiovascular reactivity to mental stress in men. *International Journal of Psychophysiology, 20,* 155–160. doi:10.1016/0167-8760(95)00029-1

al'Absi, M., France, C., Harju, A., France, J., & Wittmers, L. (2006). Adrenocortical and nociceptive responses to opioid blockade in hypertension-prone men and women. *Psychosomatic Medicine, 68,* 292–298. doi:10.1097/01.psy.0000203240.64965.bd

al'Absi, M., & Lovallo, W. R. (1993). Cortisol concentrations in serum of borderline hypertensive men exposed to a novel experimental setting. *Psychoneuroendocrinology, 18,* 355–363. doi:10.1016/0306-4530(93)90011-9

al'Absi, M., Lovallo, W. R., McKey, B., & Pincomb, G. (1994). Borderline hypertensives produce exaggerated adrenocortical responses to mental stress. *Psychosomatic Medicine, 56,* 245–250.

al'Absi, M., Lovallo, W. R., McKey, B., Sung, B. H., Whitsett, T. L., & Wilson, M. F. (1998). Hypothalamic–pituitary–adrenocortical responses to psychological stress and caffeine in men at high and low risk for hypertension. *Psychosomatic Medicine, 60,* 521–527.

al'Absi, M., Lovallo, W. R., Pincomb, G. P., Sung, B. H., & Wilson, M. F. (1995). Adrenocortical effects of caffeine at rest and during mental stress in borderline hypertensive men. *International Journal of Behavioral Medicine, 2,* 275.

al'Absi, M., & Wittmers, L. E., Jr. (2003). Enhanced adrenocortical responses to stress in hypertension-prone men and women. *Annals of Behavioral Medicine, 25,* 25–33. doi:10.1207/S15324796ABM2501_04

Aston-Jones, G., Ennis, M., Pieribone, V. A., Nickell, W. T., & Shipley, M. T. (1986, November 7). The brain nucleus locus coeruleus: Restricted afferent control of a broad efferent network. *Science, 234,* 734–737. doi:10.1126/science.3775363

Bamberger, C. M., Schulte, H. M., & Chrousos, G. P. (1996). Molecular determinants of glucocorticoid receptor function and tissue sensitivity to glucocorticoids. *Endocrine Reviews, 17,* 245–261.

Bongard, S. (1995). Mental effort during active and passive coping: A dual-task analysis. *Psychophysiology, 32,* 242–248.

Bongard, S., & al'Absi, M. (2003). Domain-specific anger expression assessment and blood pressure during rest and acute stress. *Personality and Individual Differences, 34,* 1383–1402. doi:10.1016/S0191-8869(02)00106-X

Bongard, S., & al'Absi, M. (2005). Domain-specific anger expression and blood pressure in an occupational setting. *Journal of Psychosomatic Research, 58,* 43–49. doi:10.1016/j.jpsychores.2004.04.370

Bongard, S., Hodapp, V., Frisch, M., & Lennartz, K. (1994). Effects of active and passive coping on task-performance and cardiovascular reactivity. *Journal of Psychophysiology, 8,* 219–230.

Bongard, S., Pfeiffer, J. S., al'Absi, M., Hodapp, V., & Linnenkemper, G. (1997). Cardiovascular responses during active coping and acute experience of anger in women. *Psychophysiology, 34,* 459–466. doi:10.1111/j.1469-8986.1997.tb02390.x

Brady, K. T., & Sonne, S. C. (1999). The role of stress in alcohol use, alcoholism treatment, and relapse. *Alcohol Research & Health, 23,* 263–271.

Burnett, F. E., Scott, L. V., Weaver, M. G., Medbak, S. H., & Dinan, T. G. (1999). The effect of naloxone on adrenocorticotropin and cortisol release: Evidence for a reduced response in depression. *Journal of Affective Disorders, 53,* 263–268. doi:10.1016/S0165-0327(98)00127-X

Burt, V. L., Whelton, P., Roccella, E. J., Brown, C., Cutler, J. A., Higgins, M., . . . Labarthe, D. (1995). Prevalence of hypertension in the US adult population: Results from the Third National Health and Nutrition Examination Survey, 1988–1991. *Hypertension, 25,* 305–313.

Charkoudian, N., & Rabbitts, J. A. (2009). Sympathetic neural mechanisms in human cardiovascular health and disease. *Mayo Clinic Proceedings, 84,* 822–830. doi:10.4065/84.9.822

Chrousos, G. P., & Gold, P. W. (1992). The concepts of stress and stress system disorders. Overview of physical and behavioral homeostasis. *JAMA, 267,* 1244–1252. doi:10.1001/jama.267.9.1244

Corse, C. D., Manuck, S. B., Cantwell, J. D., Giordani, B., & Matthews, K. A. (1982). Coronary-prone behavior pattern and cardiovascular response in persons with and without coronary heart disease. *Psychosomatic Medicine, 44,* 449–459.

Dallman, M. F. (1993). Stress update: Adaptation of the hypothalamic–pituitary–adrenal axis to chronic stress. *Trends in Endocrinology and Metabolism, 4,* 62–69. doi:10.1016/S1043-2760(05)80017-7

Delitala, G., Trainer, P. J., Oliva, O., Fanciulli, G., & Grossman, A. B. (1994). Opioid peptide and alpha-adrenoceptor pathways in the regulation of the pituitary–adrenal axis in man. *Journal of Endocrinology, 141,* 163–168. doi:10.1677/joe.0.1410163

Everson, S. A., Goldberg, D. E., Kaplan, G. A., Julkunen, J., & Salonen, J. T. (1998). Anger expression and incident hypertension. *Psychosomatic Medicine, 60,* 730–735.

Everson, S. A., Kaplan, G. A., Goldberg, D. E., & Salonen, J. T. (1996). Anticipatory blood pressure response to exercise predicts future high blood pressure in middle-aged men. *Hypertension, 27,* 1059–1064.

Folkow, B. (1990). "Structural factor" in primary and secondary hypertension. *Hypertension, 16,* 89–101.

Fontana, F., Bernardi, P., Merlo, P. E., Boschi, S., De Iasio, R., Capelli, M., . . . Spampinato, S. (1994). Endogenous opioid system and atrial natriuretic factor in normotensive offspring of hypertensive parents at rest and during exercise test. *Journal of Hypertension, 12,* 1285–1290. doi:10.1097/00004872-199411000-00011

Forsyth, R. P. (1969). Blood pressure responses to long-term avoidance schedules in the restrained rhesus monkey. *Psychosomatic Medicine, 31,* 300–309.

Fredrikson, M., & Matthews, K. A. (1990). Cardiovascular responses to behavioural stress and hypertension: A meta-analytic review. *Annals of Behavioral Medicine, 12*, 30–39. doi:10.1207/s15324796abm1201_3

Gendolla, G. H. E. (2000). On the impact of mood on behavior: An integrative theory and a review. *Review of General Psychology, 4*, 378–408. doi:10.1037/1089-2680.4.4.378

Gendolla, G. H. E., Abele, A. E., & Krüsken, J. (2001). The informational impact of mood on effort mobilization: A study of cardiovascular and electrodermal responses. *Emotion, 1*, 12–24. doi:10.1037/1528-3542.1.1.12

Gianaros, P. J., Sheu, L. K., Matthews, K. A., Jennings, J. R., Manuck, S. B., & Hariri, A. R. (2008). Individual differences in stressor-evoked blood pressure reactivity vary with activation, volume, and functional connectivity of the amygdala. *The Journal of Neuroscience, 28*, 990–999. doi:10.1523/JNEUROSCI.3606-07.2008

Goncharuk, V. D., Van Heerikhuize, J., Swaab, D. F., & Buijs, R. M. (2002). Paraventricular nucleus of the human hypothalamus in primary hypertension: Activation of corticotropin-releasing hormone neurons. *The Journal of Comparative Neurology, 443*, 321–331. doi:10.1002/cne.10124

Harris, A. H., & Brady, J. V. (1977). Long-term studies of cardiovascular control in primates. In G. E. Schwartz & J. Beatty (Eds.), *Biofeedback: Theory and research* (pp. 243–264). New York, NY: Academic Press.

Hashimoto, K., Makino, S., Hirasawa, R., Takao, T., Sugawara, M., Murakami, K., . . . Ota, Z. (1989). Abnormalities in the hypothalamo–pituitary–adrenal axis in spontaneously hypertensive rats during development of hypertension. *Endocrinology, 125*, 1161–1167. doi:10.1210/endo-125-3-1161

Hodapp, V., Bongard, S., & Heiligtag, U. (1992). Active coping, expression of anger, and cardiovascular reactivity. *Personality and Individual Differences, 13*, 1069–1076. doi:10.1016/0191-8869(92)90022-H

Iversen, S., Iversen, L., & Saper, C. B. (2000). The autonomic nervous system and the hypothalamus. In E. R. Kandel, J. H. Schwartz, & T. M. Jessell (Eds.), *Principles of neural science* (4th ed., pp. 960–981). New York, NY: McGraw-Hill.

Iversen, S., Kupfermann, I., & Kandel, E. R. (2000). Emotional states and feelings. In E. R. Kandel, J. H. Schwartz, & T. M. Jessell (Eds.), *Principles of neural science* (4th ed., pp. 982–997). New York, NY: McGraw-Hill.

Julius, S., & Nesbitt, S. (1996). Sympathetic overactivity in hypertension. A moving target. *American Journal of Hypertension, 9*, 113S–120S. doi:10.1016/0895-7061(96)00287-7

Kamarck, T. W., & Lovallo, W. R. (2003). Cardiovascular reactivity to psychological challenge: Conceptual and measurement considerations. *Psychosomatic Medicine, 65*, 9–21. doi:10.1097/01.PSY.0000030390.34416.3E

Kaplan, J. R., Manuck, S. B., Clarkson, T. B., Lusso, F. M., & Taub, D. M. (1982). Social status, environment, and atheriosclerosis in cynomolgus monkeys. *Arteriosclerosis, 2*, 359–368.

Kawachi, I., Sparrow, D., Spiro, A., III, Vokonas, P., & Weiss, S. T. (1996). A prospective study of anger and coronary heart disease: The Normative Aging Study. *Circulation, 94,* 2090–2095.

Kelly, J. J., Mangos, G., Williamson, P. M., & Whitworth, J. A. (1998). Cortisol and hypertension. *Clinical and Experimental Pharmacology & Physiology, 25*(S1), S51–S56. doi:10.1111/j.1440-1681.1998.tb02301.x

Keys, A., Taylor, H. L., Blackburn, H., Brozek, J., Anderson, J. T., & Simonson, E. (1971). Mortality and coronary heart disease among men studied for 23 years. *Archives of Internal Medicine, 128,* 201–214. doi:10.1001/archinte.128.2.201

Krantz, D. S., & Manuck, S. B. (1984). Acute psychophysiologic reactivity and risk of cardiovascular disease: A review and methodologic critique. *Psychological Bulletin, 96,* 435–464. doi:10.1037/0033-2909.96.3.435

Lazarus, R. S., & Folkman, S. (1984). *Stress, appraisal and coping.* New York, NY: Springer.

Lovallo, W. R. (2005a). Cardiovascular reactivity: Mechanisms and pathways to cardiovascular disease. *International Journal of Psychophysiology, 58,* 119–132. doi:10.1016/j.ijpsycho.2004.11.007

Lovallo, W. R. (2005b). *Stress & health: Biological and psychological interactions* (2nd ed.). Thousand Oaks, CA: Sage.

Lovallo, W. R. (2011). Do low levels of stress reactivity signal poor states of health? *Biological Psychology, 86,* 121–128. doi:10.1016/j.biopsycho.2010.01.006

Lovallo, W. R., & Gerin, W. (2003). Psychophysiological reactivity: Mechanisms and pathways to cardiovascular disease. *Psychosomatic Medicine, 65,* 36–45. doi:10.1097/01.PSY.0000033128.44101.C1

Lovallo, W. R., & Wilson, M. F. (1992). A biobehavioral model of hypertension development. In J. R. Turner, A. Sherwood, & K. C. Light (Eds.), *Individual differences in cardiovascular response to stress* (pp. 265–280). New York, NY: Plenum Press.

Manuck, S. B., Harvey, A. H., Lechleiter, S. L., & Neal, K. S. (1978). Effects of coping on blood pressure responses to threat of aversive stimulation. *Psychophysiology, 15,* 544–549. doi:10.1111/j.1469-8986.1978.tb03107.x

Manuck, S. B., Kamarck, T. W., Kasprowicz, A. S., & Waldstein, S. R. (1993). Stability and patterning of behaviorally evoked cardiovascular reactivity. In J. Blascovitch & S. E. Katkin (Eds.), *Cardiovascular reactivity to psychological stress and disease* (pp. 111–134). Washington, DC: American Psychological Association. doi:10.1037/10125-005

Manuck, S. B., Kaplan, J. R., & Clarkson, T. B. (1983). Behaviorally induced heart rate reactivity and atherosclerosis in cynomolgus monkeys. *Psychosomatic Medicine, 45,* 95–108.

McCubbin, J. A. (1993). Stress induced endogenous opioids: Behavioral and circulatory interactions. *Biological Psychology, 35,* 91–122. doi:10.1016/0301-0511(93)90008-V

McCubbin, J. A., Surwit, R. S., Williams, R. B., Nemeroff, C. B., & McNeilly, M. (1989). Altered pituitary hormone response to naloxone in hypertension development. *Hypertension, 14,* 636–644.

Obrist, P. A., Gaebelein, C. J., Teller, E. S., Langer, A. W., Grignolo, A., Light, K. C., & McCubbin, J. A. (1978). The relationship among heart rate, carotid dP/dt, and blood pressure in humans as a function of type of stress. *Psychophysiology, 15,* 102–115. doi:10.1111/j.1469-8986.1978.tb01344.x

Pierce, T. W., Grim, R. D., & King, J. S. (2005). Cardiovascular reactivity and family history of hypertension: A meta-analysis. *Psychophysiology, 42,* 125–131. doi:10.1111/j.0048-5772.2005.267.x

Plutchik, R. (1994). *The psychology and biology of emotion.* New York, NY: Harper.

Räikkönen, K., Hautanen, A., & Keltikangas-Jarvinen, L. (1996). Feelings of exhaustion, emotional distress, and pituitary and adrenocortical hormones in borderline hypertension. *Journal of Hypertension, 14,* 713–718. doi:10.1097/00004872-199606000-00006

Rivier, C., & Vale, W. (1983, September 22). Modulation of stress-induced ACTH release by corticotropin-releasing factor, catecholamines and vasopressin. *Nature, 305,* 325–327. doi:10.1038/305325a0

Rolls, E. T. (2000). Précis of the brain and emotion. *Behavioral and Brain Sciences, 23,* 177–191. doi:10.1017/S0140525X00002429

Schum, J. L., Jorgensen, R. S., Verhaeghen, P., Sauro, M., & Thibodeau, R. (2003). Trait anger, anger expression, and ambulatory blood pressure: A meta-analytic review. *Journal of Behavioral Medicine, 26,* 395–415. doi:10.1023/A:1025767900757

Siegman, A. W. (1993). Cardiovascular consequences of expressing, experiencing, and repressing anger. *Journal of Behavioral Medicine, 16,* 539–569. doi:10.1007/BF00844719

Soro, A., Ingram, M. C., Tonolo, G., Glorioso, N., & Fraser, R. (1995). Evidence of coexisting changes in 11 beta-hydroxysteroid dehydrogenase and 5 beta-reductase activity in subjects with untreated essential hypertension. *Hypertension, 25,* 67–70.

Stemmler, G. (2004). Physiological processes during emotion. In P. Philippot & R. S. Feldman (Eds.), *The regulation of emotion* (pp. 33–70). Mahwah, NJ: Erlbaum.

Steptoe, A. (1983). Stress, helplessness and control: The implications of laboratory studies. *Journal of Psychosomatic Research, 27,* 361–367. doi:10.1016/0022-3999(83)90067-3

Steptoe, A., Melville, D., & Ross, A. (1984). Behavioral response demands, cardiovascular reactivity and essential hypertension. *Psychosomatic Medicine, 46,* 33–48.

Strike, P. C., & Steptoe, A. (2005). Behavioral and emotional triggers of acute coronary syndromes: A systematic review and critique. *Psychosomatic Medicine, 67,* 179–186. doi:10.1097/01.psy.0000155663.93160.d2

Suchday, S., & Larkin, K. T. (2001). Biobehavioral responses to interpersonal conflict during anger expression among anger-in and anger-out men. *Annals of Behavioral Medicine, 23,* 282–290. doi:10.1207/S15324796ABM2304_7

Treiber, F. A., Kamarck, T., Schneiderman, N., Sheffield, D., Kapuku, G., & Taylor, T. (2003). Cardiovascular reactivity and development of preclinical and clinical disease states. *Psychosomatic Medicine, 65,* 46–62.

Turner, J. R., Carroll, D., Hanson, J., & Sims, J. (1988). A comparison of additional heart rates during active psychological challenge calculated from upper body and lower body dynamic exercise. *Psychophysiology, 25,* 209–216. doi:10.1111/j.1469-8986.1988.tb00990.x

Van de Kar, L. D., & Blair, M. L. (1999). Forebrain pathways mediating stress-induced hormone secretion. *Frontiers in Neuroendocrinology, 20,* 1–48. doi:10.1006/frne.1998.0172

Vermeulen, A., Verdonck, G., Van der Straeten, M., & Daneels, R. (1967). Evaluation of the efficiency of 11-beta-hydroxylation of 11- deoxycortisol in human subjects. *The Journal of Clinical Endocrinology and Metabolism, 27,* 365–370. doi:10.1210/jcem-27-3-365

Verrotti, A., Loiacono, G., Mohn, A., & Chiarelli, F. (2009). New insights in diabetic autonomic neuropathy in children and adolescents. *European Journal of Endocrinology, 161,* 811–818. doi:10.1530/EJE-09-0710

Walker, B. R., Best, R., Shackleton, C. H., Padfield, P. L., & Edwards, C. R. (1996). Increased vasoconstrictor sensitivity to glucocorticoids in essential hypertension. *Hypertension, 27,* 190–196.

Walker, B. R., & Williams, B. C. (1992). Cortocosteroids and vascular tone: Mapping the messenger maze. *Clinical Science, 82,* 597–605.

Wand, G. S., & Schumann, H. (1998). Relationship between plasma adrenocorticotropin, hypothalamic opioid tone, and plasma leptin. *The Journal of Clinical Endocrinology and Metabolism, 83,* 2138–2142. doi:10.1210/jc.83.6.2138

Watt, G. C., Harrap, S. B., Foy, C. J., Holton, D. W., Edwards, H. V., Davidson, H. R., . . . Fraser, R. (1992). Abnormalities of glucocorticoid metabolism and the renin-angiotensin system: A four-corners approach to the identification of genetic determinants of blood pressure. *Journal of Hypertension, 10,* 473–482. doi:10.1097/00004872-199205000-00011

Whalen, C. K., Jamner, L. D., Henker, B., & Delfino, R. J. (2001). Smoking and moods in adolescents with depressive and aggressive dispositions: Evidence from surveys and electronic diaries. *Health Psychology, 20,* 99–111. doi:10.1037/0278-6133.20.2.99

Williams, J. E., Paton, C. C., Siegler, I. C., Eigenbrodt, M. L., Nieto, F. J., & Tyroler, H. A. (2000). Anger proneness predicts coronary heart disease risk: Prospective analysis from the atherosclerosis risk in communities (ARIC) study. *Circulation, 101,* 2034–2039.

Williamson, P. M., Kelly, J. J., & Whitworth, J. A. (1996). Dose-response relationships and mineralocorticoid activity in cortisol-induced hypertension in humans. *Journal of Hypertension, 14*(Suppl.), S37–S41.

Wood, D. L., Sheldon, D. S., Elveback, L. R., & Schirger, A. (1984). Cold pressor test as a predictor of hypertension. *Hypertension, 6,* 301–306.

Wright, R. A. (1996). Brehm's theory of motivation as a model of effort and cardiovascular response. In P. M. Gollwitzer & J. A. Bargh (Eds.), *The psychology of action: Linking cognition and motivation to behavior* (pp. 424–453). New York, NY: Guilford Press.

12

THE BEHAVIORAL AND HEALTH COROLLARIES OF BLUNTED PHYSIOLOGICAL REACTIONS TO ACUTE PSYCHOLOGICAL STRESS: REVISING THE REACTIVITY HYPOTHESIS

DOUGLAS CARROLL, ANNA C. PHILLIPS, AND WILLIAM R. LOVALLO

The *reactivity hypothesis* contends that large-magnitude cardiovascular reactions to acute psychological stress play a role in the development of cardiovascular pathology. It is certainly the case that the cardiovascular adjustments, particularly cardiac output, observed during acute psychological stress differ from those that occur during physical exertion in that the latter are closely coupled with the metabolic demands of motor behavior, whereas the former are properly regarded as metabolically exaggerated (Carroll, Phillips, & Balanos, 2009). Thus, it is easy to see why, in contrast to the biologically appropriate and health-enhancing adjustments during physical activity, large-magnitude cardiovascular reactions to psychological stress might be considered pathophysiological. More direct evidence in support of the reactivity hypothesis comes from a number of large scale cross-sectional and prospective observational studies that attest to positive associations between the magnitude of cardiovascular reactions to acute psychological stress tasks and future blood pressure status (Carroll, Ring, Hunt, Ford, & Macintyre, 2003; Carroll, Smith, Sheffield, Shipley, & Marmot, 1995; Carroll et al., 2001; Markovitz, Raczynski, Wallace, Chettur, & Chesney, 1998; Matthews, Woodall, & Allen, 1993; Newman, McGarvey, & Steele, 1999), markers of systemic atherosclerosis (Barnett, Spence, Manuck, & Jennings, 1997; Everson et al., 1997; Lynch, Everson, Kaplan, Salonen, & Salonen, 1998; Matthews et al., 1998), and left ventricular mass and/or hypertrophy of the heart (Georgiades, Lemne, de Faire, Lindvall, & Fredrikson, 1997; Kapuku et al., 1999; Murdison et al., 1998). However, in our understandable enthusiasm to characterize the circumstances and motivational antecedents of excessive reactivity and its consequences for health, we have largely neglected the other end of the continuum: low reactivity. The implicit assumption is that low physiological reactivity in the face of acute psychological challenge is the more adaptive response, with no negative consequences for health or behavior, that is, low reactivity is benign or even protective.

The aim of this chapter is to challenge this presumption and to suggest that low or blunted reactivity may be anything but an adaptive response and, indeed, may be a factor in poor health and motivational dysregulation, by which we mean the malfunctioning of the physiological systems that support motivated behavior. Although at this stage empirical evidence is limited, there is an emerging picture that blunted reactivity is associated with a range of adverse behavioral and health outcomes.

ACUTE STRESS AND IMMUNE FUNCTION

Although the cardiovascular system remains a major focus for scientists interested in the interaction of behavioral and biological processes, in recent years increasing attention has been directed at immune function. There is now a developing consensus that chronic psychological stress down-regulates immune function. For example, bereavement, relatively poor marital relations, and caregiving for a spouse with dementia or a child with a developmental disability are all associated with a poorer antibody response to a range of medical vaccinations (Gallagher, Phillips, Drayson, & Carroll, 2009a; Gallagher, Phillips, Drayson, & Carroll, 2009b; Glaser, Sheridan, Malarkey, MacCallum, & Kiecolt-Glaser, 2000; Kiecolt-Glaser, Glaser, Gravenstein, Malarkey, & Sheridan, 1996; Phillips, Carroll, Burns, et al., 2006; Vedhara et al., 1999). A poorer antibody response signifies compromised host defenses.

In contrast, the effects of acute behavioral stress on immune function would appear to be immune enhancing. The *acute stress-induced immuno-enhancement hypothesis* proposes that acute stress up-regulates various aspects of immunity and that this has functional implications for host defense (Edwards et al., 2007). Secretory immunoglobulin A is regarded as the major antibody in immune defense at mucosal surfaces; whereas chronic stress is associated with its down-regulation (Phillips, Carroll, Evans, et al., 2006), acute psychological stress has been repeatedly shown to elicit increases in secretory immunoglobulin A secretion rate (Bosch & Carroll, 2007). Further, acute stress is also associated with increases in the number of circulating lymphocytes, most notably those, such as natural killer cells and particular subtypes of cytotoxic T-cell, that are better at killing pathogens (Bosch, Berntson, Cacioppo, & Marucha, 2005). These and other changes suggest that exposure to acute stress, and by implication large-magnitude stress reactions, might actually enhance the immune system's ability to respond to antigen challenge.

More direct functional evidence comes from vaccination studies. In rodents, several acute stress exposures have been shown to enhance the immune response to nonmedical vaccination challenges (Dhabhar, 2003; Millán et al., 1996; Silberman, Wald, & Genaro, 2003). A recent human study from the Birmingham group exposed participants to a mental arithmetic stress task immediately prior to vaccination. Women exposed to the acute stress had higher peak antibody responses to the A/Panama influenza strain than did women in a no stress control condition (Edwards et al., 2006). In addition, acute stress exposure prior to vaccination was also associated with an enhanced antibody response to meningococcal A in men (Edwards et al., 2008).

However, what about individual differences in reactivity to acute stress? The acute stress-induced immuno-enhancement hypothesis would imply that it would be the most reactive that would reap the greatest immunological dividend. We now have provisional evidence that this might be the case. Those who showed the greatest cortisol reactions to an acute stress task were more likely to mount a better antibody response to the A/Panama strain of the influenza vaccination (Phillips, Carroll, Burns, & Drayson, 2005). Further, greater blood pressure reactions toward the end of an acute stress task were characteristic of individuals who mounted a better antibody response to the A/Panama and B/Shangdong influenza strains (Phillips, Carroll, Burns, & Drayson, 2009). Clearly, these preliminary results require replication. Thus, whereas high reactivity contributes to and exacerbates inflammatory cardiovascular disease, low reactivity may compromise immunity and our ability to fight infectious disease.

BLUNTED REACTIVITY AND SELF-REPORTED HEALTH

If reactivity has wider implications for health than originally envisaged, it is perhaps surprising that little attention has been paid to whether reactivity is associated with self-reported health. The results of prospective epidemiological studies testify that poor self-reported health predicts various adverse health outcomes including increased mortality, independently of traditional risk factors and medical status (Idler & Benyamini, 1997). If self-reported health is affected by cardiovascular morbidity and its precursory processes, it might be expected to be negatively related to reactivity. However, self-reported health is likely to be a function of numerous factors and to depend on the integrity of multiple biological systems. It is unlikely that it is determined simply by the subjective impact of occult or manifest cardiovascular disease. A system that would appear to be critical in this context is the immune system. Indeed, it has been proposed that what we experience as illness, sickness, and pain is, at least in part, determined by feedback from the immune system to the central nervous system (Maier & Watkins, 1998). If immune activity is a critical factor in subjective health, then the direction of the association between cardiovascular reactivity and self-reported health may be other than that we postulated earlier.

We were able to examine this issue both cross-sectionally and prospectively in the West of Scotland Twenty-07 Study (Phillips, Der, & Carroll, 2009). Participants were all from the Glasgow area and had been followed up at regular intervals since the initial baseline survey in 1987. At the third follow-up in 1995–1996, cardiovascular reactions to a time-pressured psychological stress task, the paced auditory serial arithmetic test, were measured (Carroll et al., 2003), following numerous other assessments of factors such as self-reported health, depressive symptomatology, body mass index, waist and hip circumference, smoking and other unhealthy behaviors, resting blood pressure, and medication status. Reactivity data were available for over 1,600 participants, 36% of whom were 24-year-olds, 38% were 44-year-olds, and 26% were 63-year-olds. There was a roughly even split between sexes and manual and nonmanual socioeconomic groups. With the exception of reactivity, these assessments were repeated at the fourth follow-up, 5 years later in 2000–2001, at which point data were available for nearly 1,300 participants. It is important to note that reactivity in this sample was positively associated with future resting blood pressure levels 5 years later and with the upward drift of blood pressure between the third and fourth follow-ups (Carroll et al., 2003).

Returning to the matter of cardiovascular reactivity and self-reported health, in cross-sectional analyses, those with excellent or good self-reported health exhibited larger cardiovascular reactions than those with fair or poor subjective health. In prospective analyses, participants who had larger, not smaller, cardiovascular reactions to stress were more likely to report excellent or good health 5 years later, taking into account their reported health status at the earlier assessment and adjusting for a range of possible confounders. We were recently made aware of data from a study of 725 Dutch men and women ages 55 to 60 years; those with large cardiovascular reactions to acute stress reported better health than those with small reactions, and the same held true for cortisol reactivity (de Rooij & Roseboom, 2010). Thus, it would seem that blunted reactivity may be related to poor self-reported health and may presage a relative deterioration in subjective health over time.

DEPRESSION AND BLUNTED REACTIVITY

Another possible corollary of reactivity is depression and high levels of depressive symptomatology. Depression has been linked prospectively to mortality in general and death from cardiovascular disease in particular (Hemingway & Marmot, 1999; Wulsin, Vaillant, & Wells, 1999). Depression has also been related to physiological adaptations that suggest altered autonomic function. For example, enhancement of cardiac sympathetic activity relative to vagal tone has been reported in those with depression and subclinical depressive symptoms (Carney et al., 1988; Light, Kothandapani, & Allen, 1998). Thus, the speculation that such autonomic dysregulation in depression may also be manifest as exaggerated cardiovascular reactions to stress is appealing. A meta-analysis of 11 relevant studies found small to moderate effect sizes indicative of a positive association between depressive symptomatology and cardiovascular reactions to acute psychological stress (Kibler & Ma, 2004). Unfortunately, none of the aggregate effects were statistically significant. The studies included in the meta-analysis generally tested small samples, and few of them adjusted for potential confounding variables such as demographic factors and medication status.

More recently, we reported on a cross-sectional analysis of the West of Scotland data comparing depression and the magnitude of cardiovascular reactions with acute psychological stress (Carroll, Phillips, Hunt, & Der, 2007). Depression was measured using the Hospital Anxiety and Depression Scale (Zigmond & Snaith, 1983) and the data analyzed both as continuous symptom scores and as a binary variable, using scores ≥ 8 to signify possible pathology. Higher depressive symptom scores and possible depression were associated with lower, not higher, cardiovascular reactivity. The association was still evident following adjustment for sociodemographic, anthropometric, task performance, and medication status variables. A contemporary study of 100 patients with coronary artery disease found a similar direction of relationship between symptoms of depression and cardiovascular reactivity to a public speaking stressor (York et al., 2007). Again, the relationship survived control for a reasonably comprehensive collection of covariates. We also examined the prospective association between cardiovascular reactions to acute stress and symptoms of depression in the West of Scotland Study. Cardiovascular reactions to acute psychological stress were negatively associated with subsequent depressive symptomatology; the lower the reactivity, the higher the depression scores 5 years later. This negative relationship withstood adjustment for symptom scores at the earlier time point, as well as for sociodemographic factors and medication status.

What might be the peripheral mechanisms underlying the link between cardiovascular reactivity and symptoms of depression? One possibility is altered sympathetic nervous system function. However, the prevailing wisdom is that depression and symptoms of depression are associated with increased, not decreased, sympathetic nervous system activity, as indexed by a shift to enhanced cardiac sympathetic activity relative to vagal tone (Carney et al., 1988), increased plasma noradrenaline concentrations (Rudorfer, Ross, Linnoila, Sherer, & Potter, 1985), and increased 24-hr urinary noradrenaline excretion (Hughes, Watkins, Blumenthal, Kuhn, & Sherwood, 2004) in individuals with depression or depressive symptomatology. However, this tells us only about the tonic state. It does not indicate how the system responds to challenge. More pertinent to reactivity is the status and responsiveness of beta-adrenergic receptors. There is some evidence that individuals with depression or depressive symptomatology show decreased beta-adrenergic receptor responsiveness (Mazzola-Pomietto, Azorin, Tramoni, & Jeanningros, 1994; Yu, Kang, Ziegler, Mills, & Dimsdale, 2008). What we might tentatively speculate is that blunted beta-adrenergic receptor responsiveness, as indexed by low cardiovascular reactivity to acute stress, may be a risk marker for developing high levels of depressive symptomatology.

OBESITY AND BLUNTED REACTIVITY

We also examined the relationships between cardiovascular reactivity and obesity and adiposity in the West of Scotland data (Carroll, Phillips, & Der, 2008). Both cross-sectional and prospective analyses were conducted. Contrary to expectations based on the indicative rather than definitive outcomes of the few previous small-scale studies, we found clear evidence that low cardiac reactivity was associated with a greater body mass index, more abdominal adiposity and greater likelihood of being obese. When the sample was trichotomized into lean (body mass index < 25 kg/m^2), overweight (> 25 but < 30 kg/m^2), and obese (> 30 kg/m^2), there was an orderly but negative dose–response relationship with cardiac reactivity. In addition, in prospective analyses low cardiac reactivity was associated with an increased risk of being obese 5 years later, even taking into account obesity status at the earlier time point. These outcomes withstood adjustment for sociodemographic factors, stress task performance, smoking, and medication status.

There is some other evidence that whereas obese persons have elevated sympathetic tone in the resting state, their sympathetic nervous system may be less responsive to stimulation. For example, after ingestion of a meal, there is a postprandial sympathetic nervous system response as reflected by higher plasma norepinephrine concentrations and an increased low- to high-frequency ratio in the heart rate variability spectrum (Tentolouris et al., 2003; Welle, Lilavivat, & Campbell, 1981). However, this effect has been observed to be much smaller in obese as opposed to lean individuals (Tentolouris et al., 2003). Further, changes in heart rate and muscle sympathetic nerve stimulation after the infusion of antihypertensive and antihypotensive drugs were found to be significantly smaller in the obese than the nonobese (Grassi et al., 1995). In summary, the finding that it is low cardiac reactivity that characterizes obesity would appear to be credible. Indeed, low reactivity, possibly by reflecting generally blunted sympathetic nervous system response to acute challenge, may even be a risk marker for developing obesity.

MIGHT BLUNTED REACTIVITY BE A MARKER FOR MOTIVATIONAL DYSREGULATION?

Whereas the cardiovascular health consequences of excessive cardiovascular reactivity constitute a coherent whole, it is difficult to see what unites these apparently diverse corollaries of blunted reactivity. Leaving aside self-reported health, as its determinants have yet to be subjected to concerted study, depression and obesity are both characterized, to an extent, by behavioral expressions of disordered motivation. Here we tentatively explore the possibility that blunted reactivity may be a marker of such motivational dysregulation. Later in this chapter, we review the evidence that common addictions are also associated with blunted reactivity. In such instances, the case that blunted reactivity reflects motivational dysregulation is almost certainly easier to make. For the moment, though, let us focus our attention on obesity and depression.

Family and twin studies indicate a genetic predisposition toward obesity. In a study of over 500 Danish adopted children, weight was found to be associated with the weight of their biological but not their adoptive parents (Stunkard et al., 1986). Further, in a study of over 90 identical twin pairs, either reared together or apart, genetic factors were observed to account for around 70% of the variation in weight (Stunkard, Harris, Pedersen, & McClearn, 1990). In humans, the precise gene candidates have proved elusive, as have the upstream processes that are being influenced by genetics. However, one postulated candidate process is a dysfunctional biological response to food. The striatum (see Figure 12.1) plays a role in consumatory food reward, and obese individuals are characterized by fewer striatal dopamine receptors. Dopamine antagonists increase appetite and promote weight gain, whereas dopamine agonists promote weight loss (de Leon, Diaz, Josiassen, Cooper, & Simpson, 2007; Leddy et al., 2004). Recently, in both a cross-sectional and a prospective imaging study it was observed that the response of the striatum to food (chocolate milkshake) intake was negatively associated with body mass index and that the association was particularly

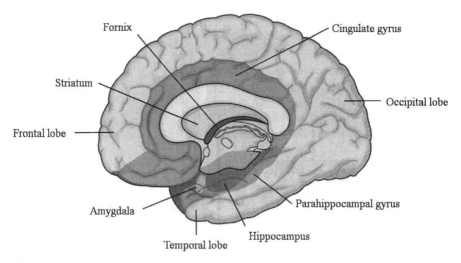

Figure 12.1. Diagram of the brain.

strong in those individuals who possessed the A1 allele of the *Taq1A* gene (Stice, Spoor, Bohon, & Small, 2008). The authors postulated that this striatal hyporeponsiveness to food might elicit compensatory overeating.

Among the motivational deficits that characterize depression is diminished emotional responsiveness to pleasant stimuli and reward. For example, in a recent study, depressed patients and controls were exposed to a number of anticipatory conditions, including anticipation of reward (money) and anticipation of punishment (cold pressor). Depressed patients exhibited blunted emotional reactions to anticipated reward relative to controls but did not differ from controls in their emotional responsiveness to anticipated punishment (McFarland & Klein, 2009). Again, the striatum, which has a central role in processing reward, would appear to be implicated. In an imaging study, there was less activation of the striatum to positive, but not negative, stimuli in depressed patients relative to healthy controls (Epstein et al., 2006). Although highly speculative, it is possible that blunted cardiovascular reactions to psychological challenge in the obese and those with high levels of depressive symptomatology are a peripheral analogue of this hyporesponsiveness of the central reward system.

STRESS REACTIVITY AND ADDICTION

Whereas it may seem intuitive that excessive physiological reactions to psychological stress might have relevance for the onset or progression of cardiovascular disease and not beyond the bounds of reason that low reactivity might have consequences for other health outcomes, it is perhaps less immediately obvious that stress reactivity might relate to addictive behavior (Lovallo, 2006, 2007). However, if our speculations on motivational dysregulation have any merit, then blunted reactivity might conceivably signal risk of addiction. We have argued elsewhere that our characteristic physiological response tendencies may have origins at three levels in our system (Lovallo, 2005). At the highest level of the central nervous system, our cognitions and emotions, and their corresponding patterns of brain activity, may result in either excessively large or small physiological output responses depending on some combination of genetic make-up and prior experience. At a lower level we include the hypothalamus and brainstem: the brain's output systems that form the physiological and behavioral responses to the higher centers that underpin our thoughts and emotions. Finally, at the peripheral level are the body's motor responses that result in cardiovascular reactions, endocrine responses, and also overt behaviors.

Here we comment only on the highest level of the system, because of its special relevance for emotions and behaviors. The brain structures in question, their anatomical interconnections, and their patterns of response to motivating circumstances are currently the subject of much research, and these have been described in some detail (Damasio et al., 2000). To review briefly, these structures involve the extended amygdala system (including the striatum), the prefrontal cortex, and feedback from the body to these areas. The extended amygdala is now understood to be the core structure in forming emotional responses to danger as well as things we may wish to obtain (Rolls, 2000). Persons in whom the amygdala has been damaged or lost through disease are emotionally unresponsive and have a tendency to fail to avoid danger (Adolphs et al., 2005; Buchanan, Etzel, Adolphs, & Tranel, 2006). Similarly, persons who have intact amygdalae but who have lost their connections to the prefrontal cortex are similarly unable to form normal behavioral and physiological responses to appetitive or aversive circumstances (Bechara, Damasio, & Damasio, 2003). Still other evidence implicates two prefrontal areas as being critically involved in this process of appraising events and the forming of responses to coping with these events: the dorsolateral prefrontal cortex, an area shown to be critical for the operation of working memory (Ungerleider, 1995), and the anterior cingulate gyrus and related sections of the cortex that bring together information concerning the approach–avoidance value of events with formulations of response strategies (Barch et al., 2001; Blair et al., 2006).

The other crucial piece of the apparatus is the anterior portion of the insular cortex, the part of the brain that receives feedback from our internal organs and literally helps us to know how we feel about what is going on and allows us to make decisions based on those feelings (Critchley, Wiens,

Rotshtein, Ohman, & Dolan, 2004; Damasio, 1994). Persons with existing damage to the insular cortex similarly have difficulty making decisions, and persons with recently acquired insular damage may show sudden changes in habits and preferences, including abruptly quitting smoking (Naqvi, Rudrauf, Damasio, & Bechara, 2007). These neural circuits that converge at the striatum and ventromedial prefrontal cortex shape the motivation of our behavior, and these appear to be the same ones that underlie the process of addiction. Koob (2003) described extensive alteration of neurochemical communication among these structures and among these areas as experimental animals are exposed to increasing amounts of self-administered drugs of abuse, and recent work shows actual reconfiguration of neural connectivity in these areas following alcohol exposure (Xie et al., 2009).

In short, these structures and their patterns of interaction will affect not only physiology but also feelings and behaviors. If one is willing to accept this perspective, then it becomes highly plausible that physiological reactivity might not only signal risk of ill health but also may serve as a window into less obvious conditions, such as the addictions. Although we strongly suspect that brain areas associated with differences between individuals in physiological reactivity to stress are the same ones involved in a range of other disorders, addictions among them, this contention needs strong confirmation through the use of neuroimaging. Research is beginning to emerge on physiological response tendencies in light of resting patterns and reactivity-related activity of the limbic system and prefrontal cortex (Gianaros et al., 2008). In similar fashion, research comparing resting and reactive patterns of brain activity in persons at risk of addiction is needed (Acheson, Robinson, Glahn, & Lovallo, 2009; Glahn, Lovallo, & Fox, 2007).

SMOKING, ALCOHOLISM, AND BLUNTED REACTIVITY

At a peripheral level, evidence is emerging that low or blunted cardiovascular and cortisol reactivity is characteristic of those with substance dependencies and may indeed be a general marker for risk of addiction (Lovallo, 2006). Let us consider smoking; the act of smoking per se is associated with increases in cardiovascular activity and cortisol (Kirschbaum, Wust, & Strasburger, 1992; Pomerleau, Fertig, Seyler, & Jaffe, 1983). However, habitual smokers have been found to show diminished salivary and plasma cortisol (al'Absi, Wittmers, Erickson, Hatsukami, & Crouse, 2003; Kirschbaum, Scherer, & Strasburger, 1994; Rohleder & Kirschbaum, 2006) and cardiovascular (Girdler, Jamner, Jarvik, Soles, & Shapiro, 1997; Phillips, Der, Hunt, & Carroll, 2009; Roy, Steptoe, & Kirschbaum, 1994) reactions to a range of acute psychological stress tasks. It is unlikely that these effects reflect temporary abstinence during stress testing and its effects on stress task engagement (Roy et al., 1994). Blunted cardiovascular reactivity has been observed in female smokers regardless of whether they were wearing a nicotine replacement patch or not (Girdler et al., 1997). In addition, cardiovascular reactivity has been compared among nonsmokers, smokers who abstained from smoking, and smokers who continued to smoke at their usual rate. Smokers, irrespective of their assigned condition, showed blunted cardiovascular and cortisol reactions to acute stress (al'Absi et al., 2003). Given that cardiovascular and cortisol stress reactivity are strongly correlated (Cacioppo, 1994; Lovallo, Pincomb, Brackett, & Wilson, 1990), it is perhaps unsurprising that attenuated reactivity in one system is paralleled by the diminished reactions of the other. Further, this cardiovascular and cortisol hyporesponsiveness has been found to predict relapse among smokers who have recently quit smoking (al'Absi, 2006; al'Absi, Hatsukami, & Davis, 2005). Thus, low reactivity not only characterizes those addicted to smoking but also may be a risk marker of some prognostic significance (Lovallo, 2006, 2007).

Those addicted to alcohol have also been found to exhibit blunted cardiovascular and cortisol stress reactivity (Lovallo, Dickensheets, Myers, Thomas, & Nixon, 2000; Panknin, Dickensheets, Nixon, & Lovallo, 2002). In addition, relatively low reactivity would appear to be a characteristic of nonalcoholics with a family history of alcoholism. In the Oklahoma Family Health Patterns Project, young adults with a positive family history, particularly those with low sociability scores, showed lower cortisol and cardiac reactions to psychological stress than did those with a negative family history of alcoholism and high sociability scores (Sorocco, Lovallo, Vincent, & Collins, 2006). Other studies of the offspring of parents addicted to alcohol or drugs provide further evidence: Boys with a positive family history who showed a blunted cortisol response to stress were more likely to experiment subsequently with cigarettes and marijuana (Moss, Vanyukov, Yao, & Kirillova, 1999). The data suggest that low reactivity may not only be a characteristic of those with a dependency but may also actually predate the addiction and signal risk of future addiction. Accordingly, in blunted reactivity we may have a marker of motivational dysregulation linked to inherited risk of a wide range of addictions (Lovallo, 2006).

CONCLUSION

The prevailing evidence testifies that large-magnitude cardiovascular reactions to acute psychological stress place individuals at risk of the upward drift of resting blood pressure and hypertension as well as atherosclerosis and increased left ventricular mass. However, it is low, not high, reactivity that appears to be associated with depression, predicts the development of obesity, and is implicated in poor self-reported health. Further, acute stress exposure, although an issue for inflammatory disease, would appear to enhance other aspects of immunity in a way that may benefit our ability to ward off infection. Finally, research has also indicated that blunted cardiovascular and cortisol reactivity is characteristic of individuals with an alcohol or tobacco dependence and, indeed, may predict risk of addiction and the likelihood of relapse following abstinence. It would appear that, depending on the outcomes in question, departures from the norm in either direction may pose problems, suggesting that in both instances the system is operating in a biased state, whether at the level of the higher central nervous system, at the level of the hypothalamus and brainstem, or at the level of the periphery. One of the challenges is to understand the neural substrates of both hypo- and hyperreactivity to acute stress.

The data conform to an inverted-U model where high and low reactivity can be considered maladaptive depending on the outcome in question. The inverted U has a substantial pedigree in psychophysiology. Originally characterized as the Yerkes-Dodson law, the inverted U proposed to describe the relationship between motivation and performance on one hand and physiological arousal on the other, such that there is an optimal midpoint in the arousal continuum where performance is best served (Yerkes & Dodson, 1908). Accordingly, we may simply be putting a few new clothes on a much loved but rather old doll. It is important to appreciate at this stage, however, that a model that conceives of continuous positive associations between reactivity and some outcomes and continuous negative associations between reactivity and other outcomes can also fit the results. We depict these two models in Figures 12.2 and 12.3. Time will tell which best serves any revision of the

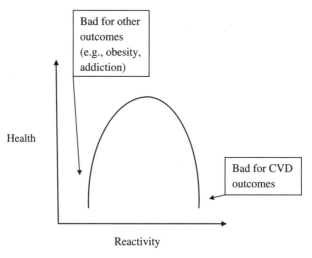

Figure 12.2. An inverted-U relationship between reactivity and outcome.

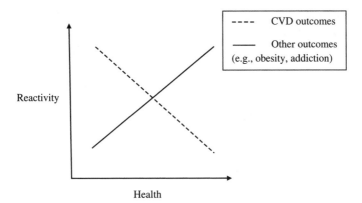

Figure 12.3. Two orthogonal linear relationships between reactivity and outcome.

reactivity hypothesis. Although we strongly suspect that the brain areas associated with physiological reactivity differences between individuals are the same ones involved in a range of other disorders, including addictions, this contention needs strong confirmation through the use of neuroimaging and prospective studies. Nevertheless, at this stage it would appear that blunted, as well as excessive, reactivity may be a maladaptive response.

REFERENCES

Acheson, A., Robinson, J. L., Glahn, D. C., & Lovallo, W. R. (2009). Differential activation of the anterior cingulate cortex and caudate nucleus in persons with a family history of alcoholism during a gambling simulation: Studies from the Oklahoma Family Health Patterns Project. *Drug and Alcohol Dependence, 100,* 17–23. doi:10.1016/j.drugalcdep.2008.08.019

Adolphs, R., Gosselin, F., Buchanan, T. W., Tranel, D., Schyns, P., & Damasio, A. R. (2005, January 6). A mechanism for impaired fear recognition after amygdala damage. *Nature, 433,* 68–72. doi:10.1038/nature03086

al'Absi, M. (2006). Hypothalamic–pituitary–adrenocortical responses to psychological stress and risk for smoking relapse. *International Journal of Psychophysiology, 59,* 218–227. doi:10.1016/j.ijpsycho.2005.10.010

al'Absi, M., Hatsukami, D., & Davis, G. L. (2005). Attenuated adrenocorticotropic responses to psychological stress are associated with early smoking relapse. *Psychopharmacology, 181,* 107–117. doi:10.1007/s00213-005-2225-3

al'Absi, M., Wittmers, L. E., Erickson, J., Hatsukami, D., & Crouse, B. (2003). Attenuated adrenocortical and blood pressure responses to psychological stress in ad libitum and abstinent smokers. *Pharmacology, Biochemistry, and Behavior, 74,* 401–410. doi:10.1016/S0091-3057(02)01011-0

Barch, D. M., Braver, T. S., Akbudak, E., Conturo, T., Ollinger, J., & Snyder, A. (2001). Anterior cingulate cortex and response conflict: Effects of response modality and processing domain. *Cerebral Cortex, 11*, 837–848. doi:10.1093/cercor/11.9.837

Barnett, P. A., Spence, J. D., Manuck, S. B., & Jennings, J. R. (1997). Psychological stress and the progression of carotid artery disease. *Journal of Hypertension, 15*, 49–55. doi:10.1097/00004872-199715010-00004

Bechara, A., Damasio, H., & Damasio, A. R. (2003). Role of the amygdala in decision making. *Annals of the New York Academy of Sciences, 985*, 356–369. doi:10.1111/j.1749-6632.2003.tb07094.x

Blair, K., Marsh, A. A., Morton, J., Vythilingam, M., Jones, M., Mondillo, K., . . . Blair, J. R. (2006). Choosing the lesser of two evils, the better of two goods: Specifying the roles of ventromedial prefrontal cortex and dorsal anterior cingulate in object choice. *The Journal of Neuroscience, 26*, 11379–11386. doi:10.1523/JNEUROSCI.1640-06.2006

Bosch, J. A., Berntson, G. G., Cacioppo, J. T., & Marucha, P. T. (2005). Differential mobilization of functionally distinct natural killer subsets during acute psychologic stress. *Psychosomatic Medicine, 67*, 366–375. doi:10.1097/01.psy.0000160469.00312.8e

Bosch, J. A., & Carroll, D. (2007). Stress and mucosal secretory immunity. In G. Fink (Ed.), *Encyclopedia of stress* (2nd ed., pp. 768–774). Oxford, England: Academic Press. doi:10.1016/B978-012373947-6.00264-6

Buchanan, T. W., Etzel, J. A., Adolphs, R., & Tranel, D. (2006). The influence of autonomic arousal and semantic relatedness on memory for emotional words. *International Journal of Psychophysiology, 61*, 26–33. doi:10.1016/j.ijpsycho.2005.10.022

Cacioppo, J. T. (1994). Social neuroscience: Autonomic, neuroendocrine, and immune responses to stress. *Psychophysiology, 31*, 113–128. doi:10.1111/j.1469-8986.1994.tb01032.x

Carney, R. M., Rich, M. W., teVelde, A., Saini, J., Clark, K., & Freedland, K. E. (1988). The relationship between heart rate, heart rate variability and depression in patients with coronary artery disease. *Journal of Psychosomatic Research, 32*, 159–164. doi:10.1016/0022-3999(88)90050-5

Carroll, D., Phillips, A. C., & Balanos, G. M. (2009). Metabolically exaggerated cardiac reactions to acute psychological stress revisited. *Psychophysiology, 46*, 270–275. doi:10.1111/j.1469-8986.2008.00762.x

Carroll, D., Phillips, A. C., & Der, G. (2008). Body mass index, abdominal adiposity, obesity and cardiovascular reactions to psychological stress in a large community sample. *Psychosomatic Medicine, 70*, 653–660. doi:10.1097/PSY.0b013e31817b9382

Carroll, D., Phillips, A. C., Hunt, K., & Der, G. (2007). Symptoms of depression and cardiovascular reactions to acute psychological stress: Evidence from a population study. *Biological Psychology, 75*, 68–74. doi:10.1016/j.biopsycho.2006.12.002

Carroll, D., Ring, C., Hunt, K., Ford, G., & Macintyre, S. (2003). Blood pressure reactions to stress and the prediction of future blood pressure: Effects of sex, age, and socioeconomic position. *Psychosomatic Medicine, 65,* 1058–1064. doi:10.1097/01.PSY.0000097330.58739.26

Carroll, D., Smith, G. D., Sheffield, D., Shipley, M. J., & Marmot, M. G. (1995). Pressor reactions to psychological stress and prediction of future blood pressure: Data from the Whitehall II Study. *British Medical Journal, 310,* 771–776.

Carroll, D., Smith, G. D., Shipley, M. J., Steptoe, A., Brunner, E. J., & Marmot, M. G. (2001). Blood pressure reactions to acute psychological stress and future blood pressure status: A 10-year follow-up of men in the Whitehall II study. *Psychosomatic Medicine, 63,* 737–743.

Critchley, H. D., Wiens, S., Rotshtein, P., Ohman, A., & Dolan, R. J. (2004). Neural systems supporting interoceptive awareness. *Nature Neuroscience, 7,* 189–195. doi:10.1038/nn1176

Damasio, A. R. (1994). *Descartes' error: Emotion, reason, and the human brain.* New York, NY: Putnam.

Damasio, A. R., Grabowski, T. J., Bechara, A., Damasio, H., Ponto, L. L., Parvizi, J., & Hichwa, R. D. (2000). Subcortical and cortical brain activity during the feeling of self-generated emotions. *Nature Neuroscience, 3,* 1049–1056. doi:10.1038/79871

de Leon, J., Diaz, F. J., Josiassen, R. C., Cooper, T. B., & Simpson, G. M. (2007). Weight gain during a double-blind multidosage clozapine study. *Journal of Clinical Psychopharmacology, 27,* 22–27. doi:10.1097/JCP.0b013e31802e513a

de Rooij, S. R. & Roseboom, T. J. (2010). Further evidence for an association between self-reported health and cardiovascular as well as cortisol reactions to acute psychological stress. *Psychophysiology, 47,* 1172–1175. doi:10.1111/j.1469-8986.2010.01023.x

Dhabhar, F. S. (2003). Stress, leukocyte trafficking, and the augmentation of skin immune function. *Annals of the New York Academy of Sciences, 992,* 205–217. doi:10.1111/j.1749-6632.2003.tb03151.x

Edwards, K. M., Burns, V. E., Adkins, A. E., Carroll, D., Drayson, M., & Ring, C. (2008). Meningococcal A vaccination response is enhanced by acute stress in men. *Psychosomatic Medicine, 70,* 147–151. doi:10.1097/PSY.0b013e318164232e

Edwards, K. M., Burns, V. E., Allen, L. M., McPhee, J. S., Bosch, J. A., Carroll, D., . . . Ring, C. (2007). Eccentric exercise as an adjuvant to influenza vaccination in humans. *Brain, Behavior, and Immunity, 21,* 209–217. doi:10.1016/j.bbi.2006.04.158

Edwards, K. M., Burns, V. E., Reynolds, T., Carroll, D., Drayson, M., & Ring, C. (2006). Acute stress exposure prior to influenza vaccination enhances antibody response in women. *Brain, Behavior, and Immunity, 20,* 159–168. doi:10.1016/j.bbi.2005.07.001

Epstein, J., Pan, H., Kocsis, J. H., Yang, Y., Butler, T., Chusid, J., . . . Silbersweig, D. A. (2006). Lack of ventral striatal response to positive stimuli in depressed versus normal subjects. *The American Journal of Psychiatry, 163*, 1784–1790. doi:10.1176/appi.ajp.163.10.1784

Everson, S. A., Lynch, J. W., Chesney, M. A., Kaplan, G. A., Goldberg, D. E., Shade, S. B., . . . Salonen, J. T. (1997). Interaction of workplace demands and cardiovascular reactivity in progression of carotid atherosclerosis: population based study. *British Medical Journal, 314*, 553–558.

Gallagher, S., Phillips, A. C., Drayson, M., & Carroll, D. (2009a). Caregiving for a child with intellectual disabilities is associated with a poor antibody response to influenza vaccination. *Psychosomatic Medicine, 71*, 341–344. doi:10.1097/PSY.0b013e31819d1910

Gallagher, S., Phillips, A. C., Drayson, M., & Carroll, D. (2009b). Parental caregivers of children with developmental disabilities mount a poor antibody response to pneumococcal vaccination. *Brain, Behavior, and Immunity, 23*, 338–346. doi:10.1016/j.bbi.2008.05.006

Georgiades, A., Lemne, C., de Faire, U., Lindvall, K., & Fredrikson, M. (1997). Stress-induced blood pressure measurements predict left ventricular mass over three years among borderline hypertensive men. *European Journal of Clinical Investigation, 27*, 733–739. doi:10.1046/j.1365-2362.1997.1800729.x

Gianaros, P. J., Sheu, L. K., Matthews, K. A., Jennings, J. R., Manuck, S. B., & Hariri, A. R. (2008). Individual differences in stressor-evoked blood pressure reactivity vary with activation, volume, and functional connectivity of the amygdala. *The Journal of Neuroscience, 28*, 990–999. doi:10.1523/JNEUROSCI.3606-07.2008

Girdler, S. S., Jamner, L. D., Jarvik, M., Soles, J. R., & Shapiro, D. (1997). Smoking status and nicotine administration differentially modify hemodynamic stress reactivity in men and women. *Psychosomatic Medicine, 59*, 294–306.

Glahn, D. C., Lovallo, W. R., & Fox, P. T. (2007). Reduced amygdala activation in young adults at high risk of alcoholism: Studies from the Oklahoma Family Health Patterns Project. *Biological Psychiatry, 61*, 1306–1309. doi:10.1016/j.biopsych.2006.09.041

Glaser, R., Sheridan, J., Malarkey, W. B., MacCallum, R. C., & Kiecolt-Glaser, J. K. (2000). Chronic stress modulates the immune response to a pneumococcal pneumonia vaccine. *Psychosomatic Medicine, 62*, 804–807.

Grassi, G., Seravalle, G., Cattaneo, B. M., Bolla, G. B., Lanfranchi, A., Colombo, M., . . . Mancia, G. (1995). Sympathetic activation in obese normotensive subjects. *Hypertension, 25*, 560–563.

Hemingway, H., & Marmot, M. (1999). Evidence based cardiology: Psychosocial factors in the aetiology and prognosis of coronary heart disease. Systematic review of prospective cohort studies. *British Medical Journal, 318*, 1460–1467.

Hughes, J. W., Watkins, L., Blumenthal, J. A., Kuhn, C., & Sherwood, A. (2004). Depression and anxiety symptoms are related to increased 24-hour urinary norepinephrine excretion among healthy middle-aged women. *Journal of Psychosomatic Research, 57,* 353–358.

Idler, E. L., & Benyamini, Y. (1997). Self-rated health and mortality: A review of twenty-seven community studies. *Journal of Health and Social Behavior, 38,* 21–37. doi:10.2307/2955359

Kapuku, G. K., Treiber, F. A., Davis, H. C., Harshfield, G. A., Cook, B. B., & Mensah, G. A. (1999). Hemodynamic function at rest, during acute stress, and in the field: Predictors of cardiac structure and function 2 years later in youth. *Hypertension, 34,* 1026–1031.

Kibler, J. L., & Ma, M. (2004). Depressive symptoms and cardiovascular reactivity to laboratory behavioral stress. *International Journal of Behavioral Medicine, 11,* 81–87. doi:10.1207/s15327558ijbm1102_3

Kiecolt-Glaser, J. K., Glaser, R., Gravenstein, S., Malarkey, W. B., & Sheridan, J. (1996). Chronic stress alters the immune response to influenza virus vaccine in older adults. *Proceedings of the National Academy of Sciences of the United States of America, 93,* 3043–3047. doi:10.1073/pnas.93.7.3043

Kirschbaum, C., Scherer, G., & Strasburger, C. J. (1994). Pituitary and adrenal hormone responses to pharmacological, physical, and psychological stimulation in habitual smokers and nonsmokers. *The Journal of Clinical Investigation, 72,* 804–810.

Kirschbaum, C., Wust, S., & Strasburger, C. J. (1992). "Normal" cigarette smoking increases free cortisol in habitual smokers. *Life Sciences, 50,* 435–442. doi:10.1016/0024-3205(92)90378-3

Koob, G. F. (2003). Alcoholism: Allostasis and beyond. *Alcoholism: Clinical and Experimental Research, 27,* 232–243. doi:10.1097/01.ALC.0000057122.36127.C2

Leddy, J. J., Epstein, L. H., Jaroni, J. L., Roemmich, J. N., Paluch, R. A., Goldfield, G. S., & Lerman, C. (2004). Influence of methylphenidate on eating in obese men. *Obesity Research, 12,* 224–232. doi:10.1038/oby.2004.29

Light, K. C., Kothandapani, R. V., & Allen, M. T. (1998). Enhanced cardiovascular and catecholamine responses in women with depressive symptoms. *International Journal of Psychophysiology, 28,* 157–166. doi:10.1016/S0167-8760(97)00093-7

Lovallo, W. R. (2005). *Stress and health: Biological and psychological interactions* (2nd ed.). Thousand Oaks, CA: Sage.

Lovallo, W. R. (2006). Cortisol secretion patterns in addiction and addiction risk. *International Journal of Psychophysiology, 59,* 195–202. doi:10.1016/j.ijpsycho.2005.10.007

Lovallo, W. R. (2007). Individual differences in response to stress and risk for addiction. In M. al'Absi (Ed.), *Stress and addiction: Biological and psychological mechanisms* (pp. 227–248). Burlington, MA: Academic Press. doi:10.1016/B978-012370632-4/50014-0

Lovallo, W. R., Dickensheets, S. L., Myers, D. A., Thomas, T. L., & Nixon, S. J. (2000). Blunted stress cortisol response in abstinent alcoholic and polysubstanceabusing men. *Alcoholism: Clinical and Experimental Research, 24,* 651–658. doi:10.1111/j.1530-0277.2000.tb02036.x

Lovallo, W. R., Pincomb, G. A., Brackett, D. J., & Wilson, M. F. (1990). Heart rate reactivity as a predictor of neuroendocrine responses to aversive and appetitive challenges. *Psychosomatic Medicine, 52,* 17–26.

Lynch, J. W., Everson, S. A., Kaplan, G. A., Salonen, R., & Salonen, J. T. (1998). Does low socioeconomic status potentiate the effects of heightened cardiovascular responses to stress on the progression of carotid atherosclerosis? *American Journal of Public Health, 88,* 389–394. doi:10.2105/AJPH.88.3.389

Maier, S. F., & Watkins, L. R. (1998). Cytokines for psychologists: Implications of bidirectional immune-to-brain communication for understanding behaviour, mood, and cognition. *Psychological Review, 105,* 83–107. doi:10.1037/0033-295X.105.1.83

Markovitz, J. H., Raczynski, J. M., Wallace, D., Chettur, V., & Chesney, M. A. (1998). Cardiovascular reactivity to video game predicts subsequent blood pressure increases in young men: The CARDIA study. *Psychosomatic Medicine, 60,* 186–191.

Matthews, K. A., Owens, J. F., Kuller, L. H., Sutton-Tyrrell, K., Lassila, H. C., & Wolfson, S. K. (1998). Stress-induced pulse pressure change predicts women's carotid atherosclerosis. *Stroke, 29,* 1525–1530.

Matthews, K. A., Woodall, K. L., & Allen, M. T. (1993). Cardiovascular reactivity to stress predicts future blood pressure status. *Hypertension, 22,* 479–485.

Mazzola-Pomietto, P., Azorin, J. M., Tramoni, V., & Jeanningros, R. (1994). Relation between lymphocyte beta-adrenergic responsivity and the severity of depressive disorders. *Biological Psychiatry, 35,* 920–925. doi:10.1016/0006-3223(94)91238-6

McFarland, B. R., & Klein, D. N. (2009). Emotional reactivity in depression: Diminished responsiveness to anticipated reward but not to anticipated punishment or to nonreward or avoidance. *Depression and Anxiety, 26,* 117–122. doi:10.1002/da.20513

Millán, S., González-Quijano, M. I., Giordano, M., Soto, L., Martin, A. I., & López-Calderón, A. (1996). Short and long restraint differentially affect humoral and cellular immune functions. *Life Sciences, 59,* 1431–1442. doi:10.1016/0024-3205(96)00471-7

Moss, H. B., Vanyukov, M., Yao, J. K., & Kirillova, G. P. (1999). Salivary cortisol responses in prepubertal boys: The effects of parental substance abuse and association with drug use behavior during adolescence. *Biological Psychiatry, 45,* 1293–1299. doi:10.1016/S0006-3223(98)00216-9

Murdison, K. A., Treiber, F. A., Mensah, G., Davis, H., Thompson, W., & Strong, W. B. (1998). Prediction of left ventricular mass in youth with family histories of essential hypertension. *American Journal of the Medical Sciences, 315,* 118–123. doi:10.1097/00000441-199802000-00008

Naqvi, N. H., Rudrauf, D., Damasio, H., & Bechara, A. (2007, January 26). Damage to the insula disrupts addiction to cigarette smoking. *Science, 315*, 531–534. doi:10.1126/science.1135926

Newman, J. D., McGarvey, S. T., & Steele, M. S. (1999). Longitudinal association of cardiovascular reactivity and blood pressure in Samoan adolescents. *Psychosomatic Medicine, 61*, 243–249.

Panknin, T. L., Dickensheets, S. L., Nixon, S. J., & Lovallo, W. R. (2002). Attenuated heart rate responses to public speaking in individuals with alcohol dependence. *Alcoholism: Clinical and Experimental Research, 26*, 841–847.

Phillips, A. C., Carroll, D., Burns, V. E., & Drayson, M. (2005). Neuroticism, cortisol reactivity, and antibody response to vaccination. *Psychophysiology, 42*, 232–238. doi:10.1111/j.1469-8986.2005.00281.x

Phillips, A. C., Carroll, D., Burns, V. E., & Drayson, M. T. (2009). Cardiovascular activity and the antibody response to vaccination. *Journal of Psychosomatic Research, 67*, 37–43. doi:10.1016/j.jpsychores.2008.12.002

Phillips, A. C., Carroll, D., Burns, V. E., Ring, C., Macleod, J., & Drayson, M. (2006). Bereavement and marriage are associated with antibody response to influenza vaccination in the elderly. *Brain, Behavior, and Immunity, 20*, 279–289. doi:10.1016/j.bbi.2005.08.003

Phillips, A. C., Carroll, D., Evans, P., Bosch, J. A., Clow, A., Hucklebridge, F., & Der, G. (2006). Stressful life events are associated with low secretion rates of immunoglobulin A in saliva in the middle aged and elderly. *Brain, Behavior, and Immunity, 20*, 191–197. doi:10.1016/j.bbi.2005.06.006

Phillips, A. C., Der, G., & Carroll, D. (2009). Self-reported health and cardiovascular reactions to psychological stress in a large community sample: Cross-sectional and prospective associations. *Psychophysiology, 46*, 1020–1027.

Phillips, A. C., Der, G., Hunt, K., & Carroll, D. (2009). Haemodynamic reactions to acute psychological stress and smoking status in a large community sample. *International Journal of Psychophysiology, 73*, 273–278. doi:10.1016/j.ijpsycho.2009.04.005

Pomerleau, O. F., Fertig, J. B., Seyler, L. E., & Jaffe, J. (1983). Neuroendocrine reactivity to nicotine in smokers. *Psychopharmacology, 81*, 61–67. doi:10.1007/BF00439275

Rohleder, N., & Kirschbaum, C. (2006). The hypothalamic–pituitary–adrenal (HPA) axis in habitual smokers. *International Journal of Psychophysiology, 59*, 236–243. doi:10.1016/j.ijpsycho.2005.10.012

Rolls, E. T. (2000). Neurophysiology and functions of the primate amygdala, and the neural basis of emotion. In J. P. Aggleton (Ed.), *The amygdala: A functional analysis* (pp. 447–478). Oxford, England: Oxford University Press.

Roy, M. P., Steptoe, A., & Kirschbaum, C. (1994). Association between smoking status and cardiovascular and cortisol stress responsivity in healthy young men. *International Journal of Behavioral Medicine, 1*, 264–283. doi:10.1207/s15327558ijbm0103_6

Rudorfer, M. V., Ross, R. J., Linnoila, M., Sherer, M. A., & Potter, W. Z. (1985). Exaggerated orthostatic responsivity of plasma norepinephrine in depression. *Archives of General Psychiatry, 42,* 1186–1192.

Silberman, D. M., Wald, M. R., & Genaro, A. M. (2003). Acute and chronic stress exert opposing effects on antibody responses associated with changes in stress hormone regulation of T-lymphocyte reactivity. *Journal of Neuroimmunology, 144,* 53–60. doi:10.1016/j.jneuroim.2003.08.031

Sorocco, K. H., Lovallo, W. R., Vincent, A. S., & Collins, F. L. (2006). Blunted hypothalamic–pituitary–adrenocortical axis responsivity to stress in persons with a family history of alcoholism. *International Journal of Psychophysiology, 59,* 210–217. doi:10.1016/j.ijpsycho.2005.10.009

Stice, E., Spoor, S., Bohon, C., & Small, D. M. (2008, October 17). Relation between obesity and blunted striatal response to food is moderated by *TaqIA* A1 allele. *Science, 322,* 449–452. doi:10.1126/science.1161550

Stunkard, A. J., Harris, J. R., Pedersen, N. L., & McClearn, G. E. (1990). The body-mass index of twins who have been reared apart. *The New England Journal of Medicine, 322,* 1483–1487. doi:10.1056/NEJM199005243222102

Stunkard, A. J., Sorensen, T. I., Hanis, C., Teasdale, T. W., Chakraborty, R., Schull, W. J., . . . Schulsinger, F. (1986). An adoption study of human obesity. *The New England Journal of Medicine, 314,* 193–198. doi:10.1056/NEJM198601233140401

Tentolouris, N., Tsigos, C., Perea, D., Koukou, E., Kyriaki, D., Kitsou, E., . . . Katsilambros, N. (2003). Differential effects of high-fat and high-carbohydrate isoenergetic meals on cardiac autonomic nervous system activity in lean and obese women. *Metabolism: Clinical and Experimental, 52,* 1426–1432. doi:10.1016/S0026-0495(03)00322-6

Ungerleider, L. G. (1995, November 3). Functional brain imaging studies of cortical mechanisms for memory. *Science, 270,* 769–775. doi:10.1126/science.270.5237.769

Vedhara, K., Cox, N. K., Wilcock, G. K., Perks, P., Hunt, M., Anderson, S., . . . Shanks, N. M. (1999). Chronic stress in elderly carers of dementia patients and antibody response to influenza vaccination. *The Lancet, 353,* 627–631. doi:10.1016/S0140-6736(98)06098-X

Welle, S., Lilavivat, U., & Campbell, R. G. (1981). Thermic effect of feeding in man: Increased plasma norepinephrine levels following glucose but not protein or fat consumption. *Metabolism: Clinical and Experimental, 30,* 953–958. doi:10.1016/0026-0495(81)90092-5

Wulsin, L. R., Vaillant, G. E., & Wells, V. E. (1999). A systematic review of the mortality of depression. *Psychosomatic Medicine, 61,* 6–17.

Xie, G. Q., Wang, S. J., Li, J., Cui, S. Z., Zhou, R., Chen, L., & Yuan, X. R. (2009). Ethanol attenuates the HFS-induced, ERK-mediated LTP in a dose-dependent manner in rat striatum. *Alcoholism: Clinical and Experimental Research, 33,* 121–128. doi:10.1111/j.1530-0277.2008.00818.x

Yerkes, R. M., & Dodson, J. D. (1908). The relation of strength of stimulus to rapidity of habit-hyphen formation. *The Journal of Comparative Neurology and Psychology, 18,* 459–482. doi:10.1002/cne.920180503

York, K. M., Hassan, M., Li, Q., Li, H., Fillingim, R. B., & Sheps, D. S. (2007). Coronary artery disease and depression: Patients with more depressive symptoms have lower cardiovascular reactivity during laboratory-induced mental stress. *Psychosomatic Medicine, 69,* 521–528. doi:10.1097/PSY.0b013e3180cc2601

Yu, B. H., Kang, E. H., Ziegler, M. G., Mills, P. J., & Dimsdale, J. E. (2008). Mood states, sympathetic activity, and in vivo beta-adrenergic receptor function in a normal population. *Depression and Anxiety, 25,* 559–564. doi:10.1002/da.20338

Zigmond, A. S., & Snaith, R. P. (1983). The Hospital Anxiety and Depression Scale. *Acta Psychiatrica Scandinavica, 67,* 361–370. doi:10.1111/j.1600-0447.1983.tb09716.x

B. SOCIAL STRIVING AND SEX (GENDER) INFLUENCE

13

AGONISTIC STRIVING, EMOTION REGULATION, AND HYPERTENSION RISK

CRAIG K. EWART

Troubled social relationships characterized by hostility and anger increase the risk of a variety of health problems, including cardiovascular disease. Risk is greatest in those chronically exposed to interpersonal conflict (Ewart, Taylor, Kraemer, & Agras, 1991; Kiecolt-Glaser & Newton, 2001). This chapter offers a motivational analysis of self-regulatory mechanisms that foster frequent conflict but can be altered by behavioral intervention (Ewart, 1994; Ewart, Elder, Sliwinski, Smyth, & Jorgensen, in press; Ewart, Taylor, Kraemer, & Agras, 1984). A motivational analysis focuses on self-goals and regulatory strategies that increase stress exposure.

In most health research, interpersonal constructs such as hostility, anger, and dominance are characterized as stable traits or dispositions; that is, as behavioral types, trends, or averages that vary from one person to another. These averages may be informative when associated with individual differences in illness risk. But the traits or types do not reveal the mechanisms that create them; behavioral averages in themselves do not explain why the averages

The preparation of this chapter was supported by grant R01-HL084333 from the National Heart, Lung, and Blood Institute, awarded to Craig K.Ewart, and by the Center for Health and Behavior, Syracuse University.

exist (Cervone, 2004). Nor do the type or trait frameworks that have dominated research in health psychology suggest how to devise such explanations. Constructs such as Type A behavior, hostility, and dominance have been operationalized as collections of assorted behavioral responses, beliefs, appraisals, affects, and attitudes that correlate modestly with each other and also with a health outcome of interest. Typically missing is an integrative conception of an underlying causal mechanism or process to explain why the various elements occur together and to clarify how they are organized and how they work together to foster stress.

The present social–motivational account addresses this need. Derived from social action theory, this view proposes that chronic interpersonal stress arises through everyday encounters that involve trying to influence, persuade, manage, or control other people (Ewart, 2009). Such striving tends to foster behaviors that are directly or indirectly aggressive, provoke negative reactions, spark coercive exchanges, trigger angry emotions, and induce cardiovascular changes that eventually damage health (Ewart, 1991). Social action theory holds that personal goals drive and sustain this transactional process by shaping interpersonal appraisals and behaviors during social encounters (Ewart et al., in press). Striving to influence or impress others may increase vigilance to possible challenges, thus priming emotions of anger, anxiety, or contempt (Baumeister, Bushman, & Campbell, 2000). But self-goals also may protect against stress when they foster self-improvement strivings (Diener, Suh, Lucas, & Smith, 1999).

MEASURING IMPLICIT GOALS

The social action model of stress and cardiovascular risk was developed in Project Heart, a series of community-based studies conducted in Baltimore, Maryland, in the mid-1980s (and subsequently extended to the city of Syracuse, in upper New York) that investigated how chronic exposure to social and psychological stressors affects the development of hypertension from adolescence into young adulthood in high-risk urban African American and Caucasian populations (e.g., Ewart, 1994, 2004; Ewart & Jorgensen, 2004; Ewart & Kolodner, 1991, 1993, 1994). Goals, and the self-regulatory capabilities that facilitate them, have been a primary focus of this research, which uses a narrative assessment technique administered during the Social Competence Interview (SCI) to identify self-goals and emotion regulation capabilities that increase or lower participants' stress exposure in everyday settings (Ewart, Jorgensen, Suchday, Chen, & Matthews, 2002; Ewart & Kolodner, 1991).

In much health research, phenomena such as personal goals and emotion regulation styles are measured with personality questionnaires. But self-report methods may not be ideal ways to measure the goals that motivate people's actions in stressful encounters. Goals that guide social encounters often are components of implicit, "embodied" action schemas (Niedenthal, 2007) that are not a focus of direct self-conscious attention or appraisal. This makes implicit action goals difficult to recall and articulate. Quick shifts of affect and emotional expression and suppression during stressful exchanges also can be difficult to accurately self-monitor and report. The semistructured, 10-min SCI protocol was developed to permit rapid assessment of implicit goals, strategies, and expressive styles through an evocative story completion task.

The interviewer helps the participant to quickly identify, describe, and reexperience a problem situation that causes recurring personal stress. The participant then is asked to pretend that he or she is a movie director making a documentary film about a person like the participant who confronts a similar problem. The interviewer invites the participant to invent a desirable but realistic ending for the film and to develop a plot narrative that connects the initial problem situation to the desired ending. This plot is used to characterize the participant's goal or striving in circumstances that often give rise to stress; the film ending indicates the goal and the narrative reveals the specific instrumental means and self-regulatory strategies that the participant thinks would resolve the problem in a desirable way. A participant's ability to describe stressful situations in vivid detail, and to express the emotions they arouse, indicates the goal's importance in everyday life and suggests the likelihood that a given striving will foster recurring stress during normal activities. Ratings of SCI responses by interviewers and independent observers allow us to ask whether certain types of goals increase one's exposure to stressors that endanger health and whether such exposure is modulated by the ability to regulate negative affect (Ewart et al., 2002; Ewart & Kolodner, 1994).

MOTIVATIONAL PROFILES OF PSYCHOLOGICAL STRESS

An extensive review of goal theories and taxonomies generated a coding scheme with behavioral descriptions of participants' strivings on dimensions that could be coded with high levels of interrater agreement (Ewart et al., 2002). Goal theorists often distinguish between inner-focused goals aimed at altering the self and outer-focused goals aimed at altering one's external surroundings (Ford, 1992). This separation has interesting parallels in stress research: Focusing attention externally versus inwardly alters the awareness and processing of aversive stimuli (Lambie & Marcel, 2002); attending to internal pain stimuli as opposed to external social challenges alters patterns of cardiovascular responding (Ewart, Jorgensen, Schroder, Suchday, & Sherwood, 2004; Obrist, 1981). The conceptual framework used to analyze stress-related goals in the Project Heart studies therefore included the distinction between an inward goal focus on changing the self and an outward goal focus on changing the environment.

Initial research with the SCI supported the importance of this distinction by revealing that young people's goals in stressful situations typically fall into one of two broad categories. One class of goals includes trying to influence, manage, or dominate other people: Aims typical of this category involve trying to defend oneself against attacks; to win support, sympathy, or affection; to make new friends; to find allies; or to become more intimate with someone. Participants' "stress film" narratives often describe attempts to get someone to be nicer or to make others stop doing something hurtful or to change another person's attitude or to get them to behave differently. We use the term *agonistic* to describe this category of goals, which involves striving to assert one's will over another, a struggle connoted by the Greek word *agon*.

The other major class of self-goals is characterized by an opposing motivational stance: Instead of striving to control others, one struggles to direct, improve, or control the self. Aims that typify this category include striving to attain a personally valued standard of performance, a desired experience, or a personal quality. Stress film narratives often describe struggles to juggle competing goals, manage time pressures and deadlines, perform well on tests or work assignments, please important others, change one's personality, or modify a vexing habit. We use the term *transcendent* to describe this category of goals, which are characterized by a struggle to rise above or move beyond one's present condition by mastering, directing, or regulating the self. We hypothesized that striving to alter one's social environment, as opposed to oneself, would be associated with higher blood pressure (BP) and greater risk of cardiovascular disease (CVD; Christenfeld, Glynn, Kulik, & Gerin, 1998; Wright, Dill, Green, & Anderson, 1998).

Prominent theories of emotion and psychological stress have postulated a link between heightened emotional arousal and threats to important goals (Lazarus, 1991). Conceptions of goal embodiment indicate that an action goal is not an abstract idea but includes the perceptions, bodily sensations, motor tendencies, and affective states that one often experiences when pursing that aim. Our coding scheme therefore included an assessment of participants' expressed emotions as they recounted a distressing experience during the SCI. Ratings of emotionally expressive, vigorous speech were used to index goal importance and engagement. We hypothesized that a high level of expressed emotion would magnify the correlation between agonistic striving to influence others, cardiovascular arousal, and attendant hypertension risk (Ewart & Kolodner, 1994).

Analyses of goal orientation and expressiveness rating data within this conceptual framework in large multiethnic samples of low-income urban youth disclosed, first, that agonistic (externally focused) and transcendent (internally focused) strivings represented dichotomous, mutually exclusive categories rather than a continuous dimension of striving ranging from inward to outward focus. Second, the agonistic versus transcendent direction of goal focus combined with the level of emotional expressiveness to form three emergent goal-expression configurations or profiles. Data from the first Project Heart study (Ewart, 1994) suggested that one large group of participants exhibited a profile characterized by high emotional expressiveness, a strongly agonistic goal focus, and low transcendence focus, whereas a second large group exhibited a profile characterized by high emotional expressiveness, low agonistic focus, and a strongly transcendent goal focus.

Examination of the data with scatterplot and cluster analysis methods suggested three qualitatively distinct group profiles. One pattern represented a distinctive *agonistic striving* (AS) profile—energetically seeking to influence or control others—and a second pattern represented a distinctive *transcendence striving* (TS) profile—energetically seeking to alter or control the self. A third group profile was characterized by low emotional expressiveness and a relative lack of goal focus. Individuals with this third pattern appeared more guarded and were less self-disclosing; they seemed stressed and unhappy, yet had difficulty describing stressful situations in detail and devising a coherent coping narrative. We labeled this pattern *avoidant*, or *dissipated*, to reflect our impression that these individuals' inability to envision attractive goals and strategies seemed to weaken or "dissipate" their motivation and ability to act. Hence, we labeled this profile *dissipated striving* (DS).

CARDIOVASCULAR CONSEQUENCES

Might the three motivational stress profiles affect health? Social action theory suggests that an agonistic goal focus is more likely to expose one to recurring interpersonal conflict and evoke angry emotions than is a transcendent goal focus. Attempts to influence others, even if not openly aggressive, involve trying to control the course of an interpersonal encounter, an aim that is known to increase heart rate and BP (Brown & Smith, 1992; Ewart et al., 1991). Striving to influence another person tends to pit one's own expectations, needs, and desires against those of the other, making it easy to provoke an unwanted reaction. It can be difficult to predict or control the other person's responses. A substantial body of experimental research in humans and animals has shown that the magnitude of stress responses evoked by aversive stimuli generally is inversely related to an organism's ability to predict or control the threat (Bandura, 1997). An agonistic goal focus readily renders one vigilant in uncertain social encounters and warily primed to react quickly—a behavioral state often associated with a cardiovascular response pattern characterized by increased systemic vasoconstriction and total peripheral resistance. This is the pattern of responses elicited by the SCI (Ewart et al., 2004).

This predominantly vascular response pattern has long been regarded as one of a group of stress-related mechanisms that are associated with, and may contribute to, increased hypertension risk (Henry & Stephens, 1977; Schwartz et al., 2003). Studies of watchful vigilance during interpersonal exchanges have encouraged the hypothesis that hostility and mistrust may increase cardiovascular risk by fostering vigilant attention to social threats, resulting in increased vasoconstriction that is reflected in elevated total peripheral resistance (TPR; Ewart et al., 2004; Smith, Ruiz, & Uchino, 2000). Rises in vasoconstriction and TPR, if frequent and prolonged, may foster hypertrophy of resistance vessel walls (Gibbons, 1998), contributing to vascular remodeling that facilitates the emergence of sustained hypertension, endothelial dysfunction, and the development of arterial plaques that contribute to coronary heart disease and stroke (Milgard & Lind, 1998). In this way, recurring agonistic struggles may foster vascular changes that interact with neurohormonal regulatory mechanisms to create a complex pathophysiology of risk (Schwartz et al., 2003). But individuals whose stressful experiences result largely from pursuing self-development goals (transcendence striving) should be less likely to generate chronically stressful interpersonal environments that promote vascular remodeling by frequently inducing and sustaining hypervigilant states.

This is not to argue that transcendence strivings are not stressful. On the contrary, goals such as struggling to meet a deadline or to achieve a personal performance ideal can induce intense anxiety. Yet such strivings aim at self-states or behaviors that often are easier to predict and control than are outcomes of struggles to control other people. Persons with a transcendent self-improvement focus might be expected to experience vigilant, hyperaroused states largely at times or in settings that they could anticipate in advance (e.g., deadlines, performance evaluations) and for which they may be able to generate effective coping strategies. Therefore, persons with a transcendent self-focus, as distinguished from an agonistic other-focus, should appear less vigilant or wary around others, enjoy more supportive relationships, and exhibit lower levels of cardiovascular arousal during their everyday social interactions.

TESTING THE SOCIAL–MOTIVATIONAL MODEL

To evaluate this possibility, we tested the hypothesis that the AS stress profile is associated with greater hypertension risk as indexed by elevated levels of ambulatory BP during normal daily activities, especially social interactions, whereas the contrasting TS profile is associated with lower BP (Ewart & Jorgensen, 2004). Assessment of SCI narratives and ambulatory BP in 187 African American and Caucasian youth supported these predictions. Cluster analyses of SCI ratings revealed that the sample contained the three predicted motivational subgroups, with profiles that closely fit the AS, TS, and DS patterns. The three stress profiles were observed with similar frequencies across categories of gender and race. Planned comparisons contrasting the AS and TS profile groups' mean levels of ambulatory BP during daily activities supported our predictions. Analyses that controlled for body mass index (BMI), race, and gender revealed that persons with the AS and the TS profiles exhibited similar increases in BP during the SCI stress protocol. But their diastolic BP (DBP) levels during normal daily activities differed greatly. In persons with the AS profile, DBP during social interactions rose to significantly higher levels than it did in persons with the TS profile; the mean difference between the AS and TS groups was 4.6 mmHg, which was equal to about two thirds of the standard deviation (SD) of resting DBP. Further planned comparisons disclosed that the AS and TS profile group differences were evident even when calculated as the mean level of DBP recorded during all waking activities, suggesting that the AS profile is associated with a significantly higher risk of developing hypertension in early adulthood. During nighttime sleep, both motivational groups exhibited similar levels of DBP. The ambulatory DBP of the DS profile group, for which no predictions had been made, was like that of the TS group.

The finding that profile group differences were reflected largely in the levels of DBP is consistent with the fact that DBP is highly sensitive to TPR changes related to vasoconstriction, as well as with evidence that a pronounced rise in DBP, relative to systolic BP (SBP), is associated with threat appraisals (e.g., Blascovich, Spencer, Quinn, & Steele, 2001) and is the hemodynamic signature of the SCI, where it reflects a sharp rise in TPR and only modest changes in cardiac output (Ewart et al., 2004). The finding that the BP levels of the profile groups did not differ significantly during nighttime sleep is consistent with the hypothesis that the higher DBP of AS participants reflects social control motives, as well as with evidence that the slowly developing pathologies that produce sustained hypertension are not reflected in elevated levels of resting BP until late in the third or the fourth decade of life (Treiber et al., 2003).

SOCIAL–EMOTIONAL COMPETENCE: A PROTECTIVE FACTOR?

These findings supported the view that the AS, TS, and DS profiles may represent qualitatively different motivational categories and might have interesting connections with emerging research literatures (Chida & Hamer, 2008) that link stress-related illness to chronic overarousal involving hostility and anger (relevant to AS) to chronic underarousal related to fatigue, dysphoria, and depression (relevant, perhaps, to DS) and to the possibility that stressful experiences might facilitate personal growth and foster emotional resilience (relevant to TS). Social action theory suggests, however, that these mechanisms involve more than AS goals, because individuals who seek to influence others and are highly skilled in doing so, or who are able to regulate their stressful emotions, may experience less interpersonal conflict and arousal than those would-be controllers who lack social–emotional competence. Thus, social–emotional competence may moderate the degree to which AS goals foster recurring conflict, anger arousal, and their adverse cardiovascular consequences (Ewart & Jorgensen, 2004).

We therefore conducted a new study to determine whether the impact of AS on BP in daily life is moderated by self-regulatory competence—specifically, by the ability to regulate the angry emotions that often have been linked to CVD risk (Jorgensen, Johnson, Kolodziej, & Schreer, 1996; Smith, 1992). Research on the acquisition of social skills and self-regulatory competence suggests that the ability to regulate angry affect plays an important role in moderating stress exposure and impact (Eisenberg, Fabes, Guthrie, & Reiser, 2000); an earlier Project Heart study found that styles of emotional expression moderated the association between measures of trait negative affect and ambulatory BP (Ewart & Kolodner, 1994). But a tendency to generate frequent interpersonal conflict may make it difficult to develop effective social and self-regulatory skills (Granic & Patterson, 2006). And angry outbursts can serve agonistic goals; learning to control others with anger may preclude learning to regulate hostile affect. Thus, frequent interpersonal conflict could erode self-regulatory skills or impede their development. Given growing evidence that hypertension begins early in life (Elkasabany, Urbina, Daniels, & Berenson, 1998), early difficulties in regulating angry affect could set the stage for later health problems.

The new research, conducted in Syracuse, New York, involved a suite of three successive studies, in the same participant sample, to test the hypotheses that the AS profile is more likely to induce recurring interpersonal stress and anger than is the TS profile and that hypertension risk is greatest in persons with an AS goal focus who also exhibit poor anger regulation skills. Study 1 tested the hypotheses that the AS, TS, and DS motivational profiles would be replicated in a new population of low-income urban youth in a different city and region of the United States and that persons with the AS profile display social behaviors and emotional responses that increase their exposure to recurring interpersonal stress, anger arousal, and threat-induced vasoconstriction or TPR, as reflected in higher DBP. Study 2 tested the hypothesis that the ability to regulate and recover from anger is diminished in persons with the AS profile. And Study 3 tested the hypotheses that the AS profile is associated with more frequent and intense anger during normal daily activities and that agonistic control motives and anger regulation skills interact to moderate prevailing levels of ambulatory DBP, especially during interpersonal encounters. In addition to testing hypothesized (a priori) AS and TS profile group differences, we also performed post hoc exploratory comparisons with the DS profile group to obtain more information about this pattern.

DOES AGONISTIC STRIVING INCREASE STRESS EXPOSURE?

Participants were 264 African American and Caucasian students who attended a large public high school that drew students from low- to middle-income neighborhoods of Syracuse. The sample was 55% female, 42% African American and 40% Caucasian, with the other 18% reporting a variety of racial and multiracial identities. As in all previous Project Heart studies, the assessment protocols were administered in a field laboratory situated in the school in a room dedicated to the study. Participants' goal-directed strivings, emotional expressiveness, social competence, and social impact were rated by SCI interviewers and also by trained observers using SCI audio recordings (for details, see Ewart, Ditmar, Suchday, & Sonnega, 2007; Ewart et al., in press; Ewart et al., 2002). Social competence was indexed by scales rating the "appropriateness" and "effectiveness" of problem solutions suggested by participants' film narratives. Social impact was rated on four scales representing combinations of affiliation and dominance derived from the interpersonal circumplex model of Kiesler et al. (Kiesler, 1983); the impact dimensions included Critical-Aggressive (sarcastic, unkind, hostile), Guarded Oppositional (distrustful, oppositional, defiant), Responsible-Generous (sympathetic, helpful, generous), and Modest-Trusting (dependent, clinging, passive).

As in the previous research, participants' scores on the agonistic, transcendence, and expressiveness indices were subjected to cluster analyses, which indicated that the sample contained three distinctly different clusters whose means closely matched the three motivational profiles identified earlier in the Baltimore sample (Ewart & Jorgensen, 2004). Of the 264 participants, 95% exhibited motivational profiles that matched either the AS, TS, or DS pattern. The percentages of participants in each profile group (cluster) were nearly identical (Ewart et al., in press). The composition of the profile groups did not differ with respect to gender, race, BMI, or resting BP. The three motivational profiles thus appear to occur widely, across differences of region, race, and gender and are unrelated to body size and casual BP.

Planned profile group comparisons contrasting the AS and TS groups tested the hypothesis that the AS profile is associated with social behaviors that increase exposure to recurring interpersonal stress and angry arousal. Results supported this prediction. Problem solutions of AS participants were rated as less Appropriate and less Effective than the problem solutions proposed by those with the TS profile. The AS profile group also had a more negative and less positive social impact; their demeanor during the SCI was rated as more Critical-Aggressive, less Responsible-Generous, and less Modest-Trusting than that of the TS profile group. Thus, the former may have greater difficulty resolving problems that cause them recurring stress and may be more likely to provoke unwanted reactions from others that trigger anger.

Analyses of cardiovascular responses (reactivity) to the SCI showed that, as in previous research (e.g., Ewart & Jorgensen, 2004; Ewart et al., 2004; Maisto, Ewart, Connors, Funderburk, & Krenek, 2009), the SCI evoked large surges in DBP, which rose by an average 1.8 SDs above the resting pre-SCI baseline level. As in the Baltimore sample (Ewart & Jorgensen, 2004), the SCI affected the cardiovascular responses of persons with the TS profile as strongly as it did persons with the AS profile; group differences in DBP reactivity were not statistically significant. The experience of recalling and reliving a recurring personal stressor during the SCI had a similarly powerful impact in both the AS and the TS profile groups.

Although we had no hypotheses about the DS profile, post hoc comparisons with the AS and TS profile groups shed some light on this pattern. The Appropriateness and Effectiveness of problem solutions offered by DS participants were rated lower than those of the TS group, and similar to those of the AS group. The social impact of persons with the DS profile was rated as the most Guarded-Oppositional, and the least Responsible-Generous of the three groups. The DS group's BP reactivity to the SCI did not differ from that of the other two groups.

The results generally support the hypothesis that the AS profile is likely to be more stress inducing than the TS profile. Although the SCI elicited equally large BP changes in all three profile groups, it is possible that persons with the AS profile experience stress more often because they regulate angry emotions less effectively and thus evoke more frequent or more sustained surges of BP. We therefore performed a second study to test this possibility.

DOES AGONISTIC STRIVING IMPAIR ANGER REGULATION AND RECOVERY?

A second study tested the hypothesis that AS and the recurring interpersonal stress it generates impair the ability to regulate and recover from angry emotions. Specifically, when aroused, persons with the AS profile (a) exhibit fewer attempts to regulate their anger and (b) have difficulty recovering from angry emotions. All participants were asked to perform a standard anger-recall task that made it possible to compare the profile groups on anger regulation, or how they managed their angry feelings during a recent real-life incident. To assess their ability to recover from angry emotions, we devised a new assessment technique, guided by the idea that affect regulation in stressful situations is achieved by shifting one's attention away from distressing thoughts or stimuli and attending selectively to positive thoughts and external cues (Gross, 2001).

People often are advised to regulate unpleasant emotions by reframing the situation or by reconstruing threatening events as "challenges" that offer opportunities for personal growth (transcendence). Such advice invokes attention-shifting mechanisms that let one modulate emotional states. But in the midst of a heated exchange, it often is impossible to modulate anger by stopping to think of something else or to privately reappraise or reformulate the problem. Resolving the conflict often entails quickly refocusing both parties' attention on a goal or concern that they share; one transcends the dispute by deftly focusing on a shared higher level objective or mutually agreeable topic of conversation that removes the source of antagonism. But this calls for the ability to quickly summon positive self-thoughts, memories, hopes, and expectations that may enhance mutual understanding and to communicate them in a nonhostile way. To test participants' ability to quickly access positive self-thoughts when angered, we developed a new attention-shifting task, the *anger transcendence challenge* (ATC; Ewart, 2005). Participants first recall and relive a recent situation when they became very angry. Then they are asked to quickly switch to a completely different task, an affiliative self-disclosure exercise that asks them to generate friendly affect in an imaginary interpersonal encounter. The recovery hypothesis posits that persons with the AS profile will exhibit less positive or friendly affect when performing the affiliative self-disclosure task following anger recall than will persons with the TS profile.

The sample included 213 (85%) of the participants who took part in the previous study, and the present study was conducted 2.5 months later in the same field laboratory. The anger recall (AR) task involved reexperiencing a recent incident when "you became so angry you thought you were going to 'lose it'" (i.e., lose self-control). The ATC task involved recalling an important personal memory that "you might share with a new friend" (i.e., to enhance intimacy) and then describing one's life and friendships "one year from now." BP was recorded at 1-min intervals throughout a 6-min recovery period.

Anger regulation behaviors and recovery skills were assessed from interview audio recordings by trained observers who followed a detailed coding manual (Ewart, 2005). Indices of anger regulation were derived by rating behaviors described in participants' accounts of their actions during and following the incident, as well as their demeanor when recounting it in the interview. Coders rated five aspects of anger regulation on dimensions drawn from the literature on anger and CVD risk (e.g., Siegman & Smith, 1994): "anger intensity," "aggressive behavior," "hostile reaction" (e.g., continuing resentment), "anger suppression," and "constructive problem solving." Participants' ability to recover from anger was coded separately by a different team of trained observers and was indexed as the amount of friendly affect that the participant expressed during the ATC task (personal memory and future projection). Friendly Affect was defined by three items: Friendly Demeanor, Positive Affective Content, and Positive Non-Verbal Emotional Tone.

Planned contrasts comparing the AS and the TS profile groups' behavior during their recent anger episodes revealed that, as predicted, those with the AS profile exhibited less effort to regulate anger than individuals with the TS profile, as indexed by observer ratings of Anger Intensity, Aggression, and continuing Hostile Reaction, and by less use of Constructive Problem-Solving in their anger narratives. The one regulatory activity exhibited with higher frequency by the AS group was Anger Suppression, reflecting perhaps an attempt to keep a hostile exchange from escalating dangerously out of control.

The prediction that reliving a recent anger experience would cause persons with the AS profile to exhibit higher levels of DBP reactivity was supported. Planned group contrasts controlling for BMI, gender, and race disclosed that DBP levels increased more during AR in the AS profile group than the TS profile group. Group differences in SBP and heart rate (HR) reactivity were not statistically significant.

The hypothesis that persons with the AS profile would exhibit greater difficulty recovering from anger was tested by comparing the AS and TS profile groups on the indices of Friendly Affect expressed during the ATC task. Contrary to our prediction, the group differences in Friendly Affect were not statistically significant. Corresponding comparisons contrasting changes in BP and HR recovery curves during the ATC task and post-task baseline revealed no significant differences between the AS and TS groups. Together, the Friendly Affect and cardiovascular recovery data indicated that persons with the AS profile did not have greater difficulty recovering from anger than did persons with the TS profile.

Post hoc Scheffe-adjusted exploratory group comparisons contrasting the DS profile group with the AS group indicated that, during the AR task, persons with the DS profile exhibited lower levels of anger arousal (Anger Intensity, Aggression, Hostile Reaction, Anger Suppression) but displayed similar (low) levels of Constructive Problem-Solving. Comparisons with the TS group indicated that persons with the DS profile exhibited lower levels of Anger Intensity and Constructive Problem-Solving. The DS profile group expressed less Friendly Affect during ATC than did individuals with the other profiles, suggesting that the DS profile may be associated with difficulty in generating positive emotions.

The results of Study 2 thus supported the hypothesis that the AS profile is associated with more overt, aggressive, and unregulated anger and with greater vascular resistance (DBP reactivity) during anger recall but not with an inability to recover from anger. Yet it is possible that an AS focus causes people to become intensely angry much more often and that those individuals with the AS profile who also have difficulty generating positive affect following anger have the highest levels of DBP.

DO AGONISTIC STRIVING AND ANGER REGULATION TOGETHER MODULATE BLOOD PRESSURE?

This possibility was tested in Study 3 (Ewart et al., in press), which sought to replicate the earlier finding in Baltimore that persons with the AS profile exhibit elevated mean levels of DBP during normal daily activities, especially during social interactions (Ewart & Jorgensen, 2004), and to determine whether this might reflect a tendency to become angry more often or more intensely. The research also tested the moderation (interaction) hypothesis that persons with the AS profile who lack the ability to generate Friendly Affect during the ATC exhibit the highest levels of DBP. Participants included 167 (78%) of those who had participated in Study 2. Immediately after completing the ATC task protocol described previously, participants wore an ambulatory blood pressure monitor for 2 consecutive days and nights; the monitor recorded BP at 30-min intervals throughout the day at and at 60-min intervals during sleep, while participants recorded their waking activities and emotions on an electronic diary each time the monitor recorded BP.

Planned group contrasts tested the predictions that persons with the AS profile would experience angry emotions more frequently and more intensely during the course of their daily activities than persons with the TS profile. Results revealed that the AS and TS profile groups experienced feelings of anger with similar average frequency and intensity over the 48-hr monitoring period. Thus, our prediction that the AS profile fosters more frequent or intense anger was not supported.

Support was found, however, for the predictions that persons with the AS profile exhibit higher mean levels of DBP (and SBP) during normal social interactions than do persons with the TS profile and that those who have difficulty generating Friendly Affect following anger recall (ATC task) have the highest BP levels. Planned group contrasts controlling for BMI, gender, and race found that Profile Group and the Profile Group × Friendly Affect interaction term each accounted for unique variance in BP outcomes (the Friendly Affect main effect was not significant). Planned comparisons between the AS and TS groups revealed that the mean DBP level of the AS group during social interactions exceeded that of the TS group by 4.5 mmHg, or two thirds of the SD of resting DBP, which was virtually the same AS–TS group DBP difference observed in the Baltimore sample (Ewart & Jorgensen, 2004). As in Baltimore, the profile group differences in DBP were evident during all waking activities but not during sleep.

Tests of the hypothesized Profile Group × Friendly Affect interaction effect on DBP, which regressed Friendly Affect on DBP separately in each Profile Group, revealed that low friendly affect predicted higher DBP only in the AS group. Thus, the combination of an AS focus and poor anger recovery skills (low Friendly Affect during the ATC task) is associated with significantly higher mean levels of DBP when interacting with others.

Post hoc comparisons with the DS group showed that persons with this profile experienced anger with the same frequency and intensity as did the other profile groups. The mean DBP of the DS group during social interactions was 3.2 mmHg lower than the corresponding DBP of the AS group; the magnitude of this difference was identical to that observed in the Baltimore sample (Ewart & Jorgensen, 2004). Thus, the important finding that the AS profile is associated with significantly higher BP during social encounters was replicated in a new multiethnic sample. The magnitudes of the large group differences in BP, and related higher levels of CVD risk, in the Baltimore and Syracuse populations were nearly identical.

CONCLUSION

Analyses of stress narratives produced by a broad spectrum of youth from low- to middle-income neighborhoods of two very different American cities reveal that the vast majority display either an AS motivational profile that induces recurring stress by striving to control others, a TS profile that induces recurring stress by striving to control the self, or a DS profile characterized by the lack of an apparent goal focus. Comparable percentages of individuals exhibit each profile, which occur with equal frequency across categories of race and gender and are unrelated to body size or to resting levels of BP or HR. Although AS and TS profiles are highly stressful, the AS profile appears to be much more harmful; persons with the AS profile are more likely to provoke negative reactions from others and to devise less competent strategies for coping with recurring stressors. When angered, they become intensely aroused and overtly aggressive. They readily express (and suppress) their angry feelings, make little use of constructive problem solving approaches, and experience lingering hostile resentment. Contrary to expectations, however, results of the anger regulation task did not indicate that persons with the AS profile have greater difficulty regulating angry emotions when they wish to.

The AS and TS groups exhibited comparably large BP responses (reactivity) when reliving a personal stressor during the SCI, yet the AS group displayed larger BP responses to interpersonal conflict. Their DBP rose to higher levels when they recalled an anger-provoking incident, a finding that suggests greater susceptibility to socially induced vasoconstriction.

Implications for Cardiovascular Disease Risk

In both the Baltimore and the Syracuse studies, the AS profile was associated with significantly higher cardiovascular risk, as indexed by elevated DBP during social interactions and while awake more generally. After controlling for BMI, gender, and race, the magnitude of the absolute difference between the mean DBP of persons with the AS profile and persons with the TS profile during social interactions (4.6 mmHg in Baltimore and 4.5 mmHg in Syracuse; Ewart & Jorgensen, 2004) equaled about two thirds of the SD of resting DBP in both samples. Given that social interactions were reported on about half of the occasions when ambulatory BP was recorded during waking hours, it appears that persons with the AS profile who also have difficulty recovering from anger may be at especially high long-term CVD risk (Elkasabany et al., 1998). Similar comparisons with the DS group showed that the mean DBP of persons in the AS group exceeded the latter by exactly 3.2 mmHg (one-half SD of resting DBP) in both samples. This close replication of the three motivational profile groups, with large group BP differences of virtually identical magnitudes in two widely separated populations, is noteworthy indeed.

Implications for Understanding the Dissipated Striving Profile

Because we had no a priori hypotheses about the DS profile, we conducted exploratory (Scheffe-adjusted) post hoc group comparisons to gain insight into this pattern. This group was rated as less socially competent than the TS group and appeared more wary and "guarded" than the others. They exhibited the lowest level of anger arousal during the AR task, yet, like the AS group, made less use of Constructive Problem Solving when angered. Compared with AS and TS groups, they generated significantly less Friendly Affect during the ATC task and generally appeared unhappy, withdrawn, and perhaps vulnerable to social isolation, which is associated with a variety of health risks (Hawkley & Cacioppo, 2007). This profile merits further study.

Implications for Understanding the Role of Anger

Anger and hostility long have been a focus of theorizing about the connections between psychosocial processes and illness (Jorgensen et al., 1996; Siegman & Smith, 1994). Persons with the AS profile, as predicted, exhibited higher levels of anger intensity and less anger regulation during the anger recall task, along with higher levels of DBP. Yet they did not have difficulty recovering from anger by generating friendly affect. Instead, it turned out that one's motivational focus, specifically, the difference between having an AS versus a TS profile, was much more important in predicting differences in cardiovascular risk than were differences in anger. Persons with the AS profile did not report feeling angry more often or more intensely during the day than did peers with the TS profile. Above all, their self-rated anger did not correlate with their DBP levels. Instead, it was the AS profile, and not anger, that predicted much higher ambulatory DBP, especially during social interactions.

Indeed, present findings suggest the possibility that the often-reported connections between anger or hostility and indices of cardiovascular risk may reflect the fact that both anger and increased risk are joint outcomes of striving to influence, manage, or control other people; angry affect and elevated BP may be coeffects of agonistic striving. Anger often may be a control tactic serving agonistic goals. It seems likely, moreover, that agonistic struggles to influence, control, or dominate others may generate patterns of social interaction that are capable of evoking large rises in BP even when they do not arouse angry emotions.

Implications for Preventing Stress-Related Illness

A social–motivational analysis of agonistic and transcendent striving systematizes a wide and varied body of research literature in the field of psychological stress and illness risk. The concept of agonistic striving offers an integrative conception of causal mechanisms to explain how the assorted appraisals, attitudes, beliefs, behaviors, and emotions so often referenced in traits such as hostility, anger, or dominance arise and how they cohere and interact to affect health. Self-goals motivate, organize, and guide perceptions, appraisals, emotions, actions, and physiological responses to explain how they form an ordered sequence of events and together generate a coherent pattern and profile. Self-regulatory capabilities help moderate the relationships between self-goals, actions, and outcomes.

This integrative motivational analysis of "profiles in striving" has important implications for interventions to promote cardiovascular health by reducing psychological stress. Present evidence suggests, first, that agonistic goals should be identified, evaluated, and possibly modified and, second, that an important subgroup of individuals with an agonistic goal focus also may benefit from supplementary training in emotion regulation (e.g., attention control, meditation, communication, relaxation) techniques. At the same time, present data also imply that emotion regulation training alone is not likely to lower stress responses unless agonistic goals are identified and altered.

Finally, findings from the Project Heart studies have consistently demonstrated that the SCI yields practical information about stress-generating mechanisms that is not accessible to the self-report measures and standard personality scales widely used in health research (Ewart, Elder, & Smyth, 2011; Schoolman, Elder, Parekh, & Ewart, 2010). We recently reported that participants' ratings of personal strivings expressed in their SCI narratives, using rating scales identical to those used by interviewers and independent coders, correlated modestly with interviewer and coder ratings (Schoolman et al., 2010). Yet it was only the SCI interviewer and coder ratings—not the participants' self-ratings—that predicted ambulatory BP in the natural environment. Emotionally evocative stress narratives thus afford a unique window into implicit motives that significantly affect BP and increase hypertension risk by shaping social encounters in everyday settings.

REFERENCES

Bandura, A. (1997). *Self-efficacy: The exercise of control*. New York, NY: Freeman.

Baumeister, R. F., Bushman, B. J., & Campbell, W. K. (2000). Self-esteem, narcissism, and aggression: Does violence result from low self-esteem or from threatened egotism? *Current Directions in Psychological Science, 9*, 26–29. doi:10.1111/1467-8721.00053

Blascovich, J., Spencer, S. J., Quinn, D., & Steele, C. (2001). African Americans and high blood pressure: The role of stereotype threat. *Psychological Science, 12*, 225–229. doi:10.1111/1467-9280.00340

Brown, P. C., & Smith, T. W. (1992). Social influence, marriage, and the heart: Cardiovascular consequences of interpersonal control in husbands and wives. *Health Psychology, 11*, 88–96. doi:10.1037/0278-6133.11.2.88

Cervone, D. (2004). The architecture of personality. *Psychological Review, 111*, 183–204. doi:10.1037/0033-295X.111.1.183

Chida, Y., & Hamer, M. (2008). Chronic psychosocial factors and acute physiological responses to laboratory-induced stress in healthy populations: A quantitative review of 30 years of investigations. *Psychological Bulletin, 134*, 829–885. doi:10.1037/a0013342

Christenfeld, N., Glynn, L. M., Kulik, J. A., & Gerin, W. (1998). The social construction of cardiovascular reactivity. *Annals of Behavioral Medicine, 20*, 317–325. doi:10.1007/BF02886381

Diener, E., Suh, E. M., Lucas, R. E., & Smith, H. L. (1999). Subjective well-being: Three decades of progress. *Psychological Bulletin, 125*, 276–302. doi:10.1037/0033-2909.125.2.276

Eisenberg, N., Fabes, R. A., Guthrie, I. K., & Reiser, M. (2000). Dispositional emotionality and regulation: Their role in predicting quality of social functioning. *Journal of Personality and Social Psychology, 78*, 136–157. doi:10.1037/0022-3514.78.1.136

Elkasabany, A. M., Urbina, E. M., Daniels, S. R., & Berenson, G. S. (1998). Prediction of adult hypertension by K4 and K5 diastolic blood pressure in children: The Bogalusa Heart Study. *The Journal of Pediatrics, 132*, 687–692. doi:10.1016/S0022-3476(98)70361-0

Ewart, C. K. (1991). Familial transmission of essential hypertension: Genes, environments, and chronic anger. *Annals of Behavioral Medicine, 13*, 40–47.

Ewart, C. K. (1994). Nonshared environments and heart disease risk: Concepts and data for a model of coronary-prone behavior. In E. Hetherington, D. Reiss, & R. Plomin (Eds.), *The separate social worlds of siblings* (pp. 175–204). Hillsdale, NJ: Erlbaum.

Ewart, C. K. (2004). Social environments, agonistic stress, and elevated blood pressure in urban youth. In R. Portman, J. Sorof, & J. Ingelfinger (Eds.), *Pediatric hypertension* (pp. 335–350). Totowa, NJ: Humana Press.

Ewart, C. K. (2005). *Manual for the Anger Transcendence Challenge*. Unpublished manuscript, Department of Psychology, Syracuse University, NY.

Ewart, C. K. (2009). Changing our unhealthy ways: Emerging perspectives from social action theory. In R. DiClemente, R. Crosby, & M. Kegler (Eds.), *Emerging theories in health promotion practice and research* (2nd ed., pp. 359–391). New York, NY: Jossey-Bass.

Ewart, C. K., Ditmar, M. M., Suchday, S., & Sonnega, J. R. (2007). *Manual for the Social Competence Interview*. Unpublished manuscript, Department of Psychology, Syracuse University, NY.

Ewart, C. K., Elder, G. J., Sliwinski, M., Smyth, J. M., & Jorgensen, R. S. (in press). Do agonistic motives matter more than anger? Three studies of cardiovascular risk in adolescents. *Health Psychology*.

Ewart, C. K., Elder, G. J., & Smyth, J. M. (2011). *How implicit motives and everyday self-regulatory capabilities shape cardiovascular risk in youth*. Manuscript submitted for publication.

Ewart, C. K., & Jorgensen, R. S. (2004). Agonistic interpersonal striving: Social–cognitive mechanism of cardiovascular risk in youth? *Health Psychology, 23*, 75–85. doi:10.1037/0278-6133.23.1.75

Ewart, C. K., Jorgensen, R. S., Schroder, K. E., Suchday, S., & Sherwood, A. (2004). Vigilance to a persisting personal threat: Unmasking cardiovascular consequences in adolescents with the Social Competence Interview. *Psychophysiology, 41*, 799–804. doi:10.1111/j.1469-8986.2004.00199.x

Ewart, C. K., Jorgensen, R. S., Suchday, S., Chen, E., & Matthews, K. A. (2002). Measuring stress resilience and coping in vulnerable youth: The Social Competence Interview. *Psychological Assessment, 14,* 339–352. doi:10.1037/1040-3590.14.3.339

Ewart, C. K., & Kolodner, K. B. (1991). Social Competence Interview for assessing physiological reactivity in adolescents. *Psychosomatic Medicine, 53,* 289–304.

Ewart, C. K., & Kolodner, K. B. (1993). Predicting ambulatory blood pressure during school: Effectiveness of social and nonsocial reactivity tasks in black and white adolescents. *Psychophysiology, 30,* 30–38. doi:10.1111/j.1469-8986.1993.tb03202.x

Ewart, C. K., & Kolodner, K. B. (1994). Negative affect, gender, and expressive style predict ambulatory blood pressure in adolescents. *Journal of Personality and Social Psychology, 66,* 596–605. doi:10.1037/0022-3514.66.3.596

Ewart, C. K., Taylor, C. B., Kraemer, H. C., & Agras, W. S. (1984). Reducing blood pressure reactivity during interpersonal conflict: Effects of marital communication training. *Behavior Therapy, 15,* 473–484. doi:10.1016/S0005-7894(84)80050-7

Ewart, C. K., Taylor, C. B., Kraemer, H. C., & Agras, W. S. (1991). High blood pressure and marital discord: Not being nasty matters more than being nice. *Health Psychology, 10,* 155–163. doi:10.1037/0278-6133.10.3.155

Ford, M. E. (1992). *Motivating humans: Goals, emotions, and personal agency beliefs.* Newbury Park, CA: Sage.

Gibbons, G. H. (1998). Pathobiology of hypertension. In E. J. Topol (Ed.), *Comprehensive cardiovascular medicine* (pp. 2907–2918). Philadelphia, PA: Lippincott-Raven.

Granic, I., & Patterson, G. R. (2006). Toward a comprehensive model of antisocial development: A dynamic systems approach. *Psychological Review, 113,* 101–131. doi:10.1037/0033-295X.113.1.101

Gross, J. J. (2001). Emotion regulation in adulthood: Timing is everything. *Current Directions in Psychological Science, 10,* 214–219. doi:10.1111/1467-8721.00152

Hawkley, L. C., & Cacioppo, J. T. (2007). Aging and loneliness: Downhill quickly? *Current Directions in Psychological Science, 16,* 187–191. doi:10.1111/j.1467-8721.2007.00501.x

Henry, J. P., & Stephens, P. M. (1977). *Stress, health, and the social environment: A sociobiologic approach to medicine.* New York, NY: Springer-Verlag.

Jorgensen, R. S., Johnson, B. J., Kolodziej, M. E., & Schreer, G. E. (1996). Elevated blood pressure and personality: A meta-analytic review. *Psychological Bulletin, 120,* 293–320. doi:10.1037/0033-2909.120.2.293

Kiecolt-Glaser, J. K., & Newton, T. L. (2001). Marriage and health: His and hers. *Psychological Bulletin, 127,* 472–503. doi:10.1037/0033-2909.127.4.472

Kiesler, D. J. (1983). The 1982 Interpersonal Circle: A taxonomy for complementarity in human transactions. *Psychological Review, 90,* 185–214. doi:10.1037/0033-295X.90.3.185

Lambie, J. A., & Marcel, A. J. (2002). Consciousness and the varieties of emotion experience: A theoretical framework. *Psychological Bulletin, 109,* 219–259.

Lazarus, R. S. (1991). Progress on a cognitive–motivational–relational theory of emotion. *American Psychologist, 46,* 819–834. doi:10.1037/0003-066X.46.8.819

Maisto, S. A., Ewart, C. K., Connors, G. J., Funderburk, J. S., & Krenek, M. (2009). Use of the Social Competence Interview and the Anger Transcendence Challenge in individuals with alcohol use disorder. *Journal of Behavioral Medicine, 32,* 285–293. doi:10.1007/s10865-009-9201-z

Millgard, J., & Lind, L. (1998). Acute hypertension impairs endothelium-dependent vasodilation. *Clinical Science, 94,* 601–607.

Niedenthal, P. M. (2007, May 18). Embodying emotion. *Science, 316,* 1002–1005. doi:10.1126/science.1136930

Obrist, P. A. (1981). *Cardiovascular psychophysiology: A perspective.* New York, NY: Plenum Press.

Schoolman, J. H., Elder, G. J., Parekh, M., & Ewart, C. K. (2010, March). *Control motives, social competence, and blood pressure in natural settings: A multi-informant analysis.* Poster session presented at the meeting of the American Psychosomatic Society, Portland, OR.

Schwartz, A. R., Gerin, W., Davidson, K. W., Pickering, T. G., Brosschot, J. F., Thayer, J. F., . . . Linden, W. (2003). Toward a causal model of cardiovascular responses to stress and the development of cardiovascular disease. *Psychosomatic Medicine, 65,* 22–35. doi:10.1097/01.PSY.0000046075.79922.61

Siegman, A. W., & Smith, T. W. (Eds.). (1994). *Anger, hostility, and the heart.* Hillsdale, NJ: Erlbaum.

Smith, T. W. (1992). Hostility and health: Current status of a psychosomatic hypothesis. *Health Psychology, 11,* 139–150. doi:10.1037/0278-6133.11.3.139

Smith, T. W., Ruiz, J. M., & Uchino, B. N. (2000). Vigilance, active coping, and cardiovascular reactivity during social interaction in young men. *Health Psychology, 19,* 382–392. doi:10.1037/0278-6133.19.4.382

Treiber, F. A., Kamarck, T. W., Schneiderman, N., Sheffield, D., Kapuku, G., & Taylor, T. (2003). Cardiovascular reactivity and development of preclinical and clinical disease states. *Psychosomatic Medicine, 65,* 46–62.

Wright, R. A., Dill, J. C., Green, R. G., & Anderson, C. A. (1998). Social evaluation influence on cardiovascular response to a fixed behavioral challenge: Effects across a range of difficulty levels. *Annals of Behavioral Medicine, 20,* 277–285. doi:10.1007/BF02886377

14

INTERPERSONAL MOTIVES AND CARDIOVASCULAR RESPONSE: MECHANISMS LINKING DOMINANCE AND SOCIAL STATUS WITH CARDIOVASCULAR DISEASE

TIMOTHY W. SMITH, JENNY M. CUNDIFF, AND BERT N. UCHINO

Cardiovascular reactivity (CVR) plays a central role in models of cardio-vascular disease (CVD). These models contain two distinct conceptualizations (Smith & Gerin, 1998) of increases in heart rate (HR), blood pressure, and related parameters in response to stressors as influences on atherosclerosis, hypertension, and related conditions (e.g., coronary heart disease, stroke). In the first, CVR is an individual difference; persons with characteristically greater responses to stressors and/or delayed poststressor recovery are hypothesized to be at increased risk of CVD. Considerable evidence supports this general view (Chida & Steptoe, 2010; see also Chapter 11, this volume). In the second, CVR represents a mediating mechanism linking personality traits (e.g., hostility) and interpersonal processes (e.g., marital conflict; social isolation) with CVD.

Many of these risk factors and, as a result, many widely studied psycho-social influences on CVR, fall along the affiliation or communion dimension of social life (Smith & Cundiff, 2010). Social support, for example reduces risk of CVD (Uchino, 2004) and reflects the availability of warm and caring rela-tionships. Conflict in close relationships and personality traits such as anger increase risk (Chida & Steptoe, 2009; DeVogli, Chandola, & Marmot, 2007) and represent the opposite, hostile, or quarrelsome pole of this dimension (Smith, Traupman, Uchino & Berg, 2010). However, other psychosocial risk factors (e.g., trait dominance, low socioeconomic status) are aligned with a second dimension of social life—control or agency—ranging from the experience or expression of status, power, interpersonal influence, and dominance to submissiveness, deference, subordination, low rank, and passivity in social relations (Newton, 2009; Smith et al., 2008).

In this chapter, we discuss this vertical dimension as an influence on CVR. In doing so, we highlight important social determinants of CVR, specifically, motivation and effort to achieve and maintain status, motivation and effort to exert influence or control over others and exposure to expressions of influence, control, and status by others. This literature has suggested that psychosocial risk factors related to control and agency might influence the development of CVD through the mechanism of CVR.

THE INTERPERSONAL CIRCUMPLEX AND PSYCHOSOCIAL RISK OF CARDIOVASCULAR DISEASE

These two dimensions of interpersonal phenomena—affiliation (i.e., warmth vs. hostility) and control (i.e., dominance vs. submissiveness)—define the *interpersonal circumplex* (IPC; Kiesler, 1983), depicted in Figure 14.1. The IPC can be used to describe moment-to-moment social behavior, individual differences in social behavior (i.e., personality traits), temporary social stimuli, and more stable qualities of social contexts and relationships (Smith, Gallo, & Ruiz, 2003). That is, affiliation and control can describe social responses and social stimuli in both their transient and stable forms.

In this framework, social interactions involve exchanges of two classes of social resources (Wiggins & Trapnell, 1996). *Status* (i.e., esteem, prestige) corresponds to the vertical dimension and is claimed when one behaves in a dominant or controlling manner and is granted to others when one is deferential. Broadly defined, *love* (i.e., acceptance, liking, inclusion) is the resource corresponding to the horizontal dimension. It is granted to others through warm behavior and denied or withdrawn in cold or hostile behavior. The IPC also describes social motivation (Wiggins & Trapnell, 1996). Corresponding to affiliation, *communion* refers to motives to form, maintain, or enhance social ties and the quality of relationships. Corresponding to the control dimension, *agency* refers to motives involving separateness from others and the acquisition, enhancement, and protection of status, power, achievement, and control over others (Bakan, 1966; Helgeson, 2003).

The best-established psychosocial risk factors for CVD include social isolation or low social support, conflict in personal relationships, personality traits reflecting anger and hostility, and other negative emotions such as anxiety and depression (Smith et al., 2010). These risk factors are related to the

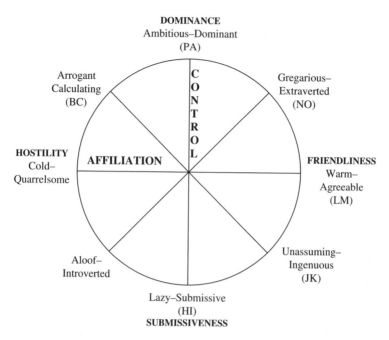

Figure 14.1. The interpersonal circumplex. Adapted from "Interpersonal Circumplex Descriptions of Psychosocial Risk Factors for Physical Illness: Application to Hostility, Neuroticism, and Marital Adjustment," by T. W. Smith, E. Traupman, B. N. Uchino, and C. A. Berg, 2010, *Journal of Personality, 78,* p. 1014. Copyright 2010 by Wiley-Blackwell. Reprinted with permission.

affiliation axis of the IPC. For example, trait anger and hostility involve a generally cold and quarrelsome interpersonal style, social support reflects perceptions of others as warm, and conflict in relationships reflects experiencing partners as hostile and quarrelsome (Smith et al., 2010; Trobst, 2000).

However, the vertical axis is also important. As components of the Type A behavior pattern, hostility and a socially dominant or controlling interactional style (i.e., emphatic speech, "talking over" others) are independent predictors of coronary heart disease and premature mortality (Houston, Babyak, Chesney, Black, & Ragland, 1997; Houston, Chesney, Black, Cates, & Hecker, 1992). Dominant personality traits predict development of coronary heart disease (Siegman et al., 2000) and coronary atherosclerosis (Smith et al., 2008). In animal models of CVD, dominant male monkeys respond to recurring social reorganization (i.e., unstable housing with repeated exposure to unfamiliar macaques) with greater development of atherosclerosis than do subordinate macaques (Kaplan & Manuck, 1998). These effects can be prevented by administration of beta-blockers (Kaplan & Manuck, 1998), dampening sympathetic nervous system input to the heart, a major influence on CVR (e.g., see Chapter 2, this volume).

Low socioeconomic status (SES) also confers risk of CVD. This may, in part, reflect the fact that low SES is associated with increased exposure to stressors and lower levels of psychosocial resources (e.g., social support; Matthews, Gallo, & Taylor, 2010). Low SES is associated with greater hostility from others during everyday interactions, less exposure to warmth, and greater exposure to displays of dominance (Gallo, Smith, & Cox, 2006). That is, low SES individuals are more likely to feel "put off" and "put down" during typical daily social interactions. Overall, studies of SES and socially dominant personality traits suggest that the second axis of the IPC is associated with CVD risk. If CVR links psychosocial risk factors to CVD development, the vertical dimension of our social lives is an important focus for research on this psychophysiological response.

CONCEPTUALIZING SPECIFIC ASPECTS OF THE VERTICAL AXIS OF SOCIAL LIFE

Before examining associations between CVR and the vertical axis, it is important to clarify similarities and distinctions among various constructs it comprises, such as status, dominance, power, prestige, control, and agency (Magee & Galinsky, 2008; Newton, 2009). Each of these terms relates to *social hierarchy*, an implicit or explicit, formal or informal rank ordering of individuals within groups with respect to a valued social dimension. Such hierarchical stratification is a ubiquitous, seemingly relentless, and often motivating part of social life (Magee & Galinsky, 2008). Position or rank within a hierarchy is usually conferred through two mechanisms: power or status. *Power* refers to control over resources and thus the relative capacity to grant or withhold rewards and punishment; *status* refers to the amount of respect or deference shown to an individual (Henrich & Gil-White, 2001; Magee & Galinsky, 2008). Power and status in a social hierarchy are often correlated, but power is more a function of formal social roles whereas status is less formally granted to the individual by other group members.

There are two sources of status. Individuals may actively assert their status during social interactions. That is, the individual may directly assert *dominance*, control, or influence over others, often in a competitive or agonistic process. When these efforts are successful, the individual is granted respect and/or deference by others. In contrast, *prestige* refers to respect and deference that is freely bestowed on the individual by other group members through the acknowledgment of the individual's valued skills, abilities, qualities, or accomplishments (Barkow, 1989; Henrich & Gil-White, 2001). Hence, asserting, seeking, or maintaining status through dominance is a direct and effortful process, whereas status based on prestige typically involves less direct action.

Individuals often gain prestige by exerting considerable effort in domains valued by the group, but such efforts are not primarily or immediately directed toward controlling others. Prestige is usually the more common source of status in human hierarchies, although we retain many social cues and behaviors from the agonistically negotiated, dominance-ordered nonhuman primate hierarchies (Barkow, 1989). It is notable that individual differences in aggressive behavior that predict CVD relate positively with dominance but negatively or not at all with prestige (Johnson, Burk, & Kirkpatrick, 2007).

In animal research, dominance refers to either hierarchy rank or aggressive behavior through which rank is achieved and maintained. In human research, dominance has been conceptualized as specific expressive behavior, personality traits, social rank, and social motives (Newton, 2009). These motives involve either achievement in competition with others or exertion of power. Dominant behaviors include vigorous vocal stylistics, direct eye contact, quickly taking charge in group interactions, and firmly asserting opinions. Personality measures of dominance include descriptors of these behaviors, such as assertiveness, forcefulness, and vigor. As a trait, dominance involves more frequent and pronounced displays of these behaviors, underlying motives to obtain status and exert influence and control, and the perceived ability in assertiveness and influencing others (Locke & Sadler, 2007). These constructs could have quite different effects on CVR.

INTERPERSONAL CIRCUMPLEX AS A NOMOLOGICAL NET FOR STUDYING CARDIOVASCULAR REACTIVITY

As we have discussed (Smith & Cundiff, 2011; Smith et al., 2003; Smith, Glazer, Ruiz, & Gallo, 2004), the IPC provides an integrative framework for a social psychophysiology of CVR and CVD risk. Effects on CVR of expressing various behaviors described in the IPC can be examined, as can the effects of exposure to these stimuli. Similarly, associations of CVR with individual differences in these interpersonal styles can be catalogued, as can associations with stable aspects of social contexts or relationships that vary on the IPC dimensions.

For the affiliation axis, hostile social stimuli heighten CVR (e.g., Gallo, Smith, & Kircher, 2000), and warm or supportive stimuli reduce it (Uchino, 2006), unless the presence of supportive others poses an evaluative threat (Taylor et al., 2010). Personality traits that reflect the horizontal axis (e.g., hostility) are positively related to CVR in response to social stressors (e.g., Christensen & Smith, 1993). Personal relationships or relationship interactions that are quarrelsome or unsupportive as opposed to neutral or supportive heighten CVR (Smith et al., 2009; Uchino, 2006). When positive and negative aspects of affiliation are assessed separately rather than as opposite ends of a continuum, their combination (i.e., ambivalence) is associated with particularly high levels of CVR (Holt-Lunstad, Uchino, Smith, Olson-Cerny, & Nealey-Moore, 2003), suggesting an important alternative to the usual IPC structure. In general, CVR is inversely associated with affiliation. In contrast, for our main focus here, associations between the vertical axis and CVR are more complex.

Expressing Interpersonal Influence, Dominance, and Other Agentic Concerns

In an early study of one form of interpersonal control or dominance (i.e., social influence; Smith, Allred, Morrison, & Carlson, 1989, Study 1), pairs of unacquainted undergraduate men participated in a debate task. Half were asked to simply discuss issues of public interest at the time (e.g., "Should Utah attempt to host the Winter Olympics?"), whereas half were given a financial incentive to persuade their partners. Compared with participants who simply discussed the issues, those trying to be persuasive displayed larger increases in systolic blood pressure (SBP) and diastolic blood pressure (DBP) and HR. It is notable that these effects were not attributable to speech rate or loudness. In a study of undergraduate men and women (Smith et al., 1989, Study 2), participants displayed greater increases in SBP and DBP while preparing and delivering a persuasive speech when they had been given a financial incentive to influence observer ratings, compared with subjects without an incentive. Further, this effect was greater for participants given a larger versus smaller incentive to exert influence (see Figure 14.2) and again was not due to speech artifacts.

CVR varies with the effort required to achieve desired outcomes (Wright & Kirby, 2001); increases in difficulty evoke greater effort-related CVR, up to the point that tasks are perceived as impossible or success is seen as not worth the effort required. At this motivational limit, effort is withdrawn and CVR is reduced. In another early study, this pattern was seen in a social context. Incentives to persuade observers again increased SBP, DBP, and HR reactivity while participants prepared and delivered speeches (Smith, Baldwin, & Christensen, 1990). Further, SBP, DBP, and HR reactivity varied in a curvilinear manner with task difficulty; a moderate level of persuasive task difficulty evoked greater CVR than did easy or nearly impossible tasks (see Figure 14.3).

Subsequent studies have replicated this general effect of incentives to influence others on CVR (Smith, Limon, Gallo, & Ngu, 1996; Smith, Nealey, Kircher, & Limon, 1997; Smith, Ruiz, & Uchino, 2000), even in the context of close relationships. Brown and Smith (1992) found that husbands given an incentive to influence their wives displayed larger increases in SBP before and during a discussion than did husbands without this incentive. Incentives to influence their husbands did not heighten wives' CVR. These results are con-

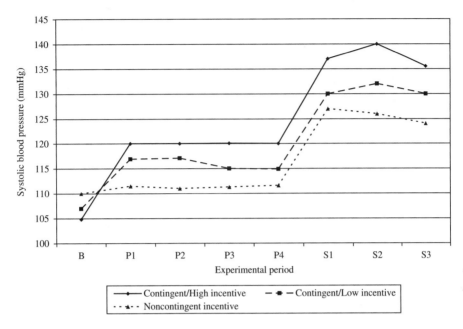

Figure 14.2. Raw baseline (B) and covariance-adjusted preparation (P) and speaking (S) period systolic blood pressure values as a function of incentive contingency and magnitude. Adapted from "Cardiovascular Reactivity and Interpersonal Influence: Active Coping In a Social Context," by T. W. Smith, K. D. Allred, C. A. Morrison, and S. D. Carlson, 1989, *Journal of Personality and Social Psychology, 56,* p. 215. Copyright 1989 by the American Psychological Association.

sistent with studies in which challenges to control in marriage increase men's risk of CVD (Carmelli, Swan, & Rosenman, 1985; Smith et al., in press).

CVR reflects several underlying physiological mechanisms (see Chapter 2, this volume). Increases in cardiac output or peripheral resistance can raise blood pressure. Sympathetic activation of the heart reflected in shorter pre-ejection periods (PEP) or decreases in parasympathetic inhibition of the heart reflected in reduced respiratory sinus arrhythmia (RSA) can raise heart rate. Among men, incentives to exert social influence raised SBP and DBP through cardiac output rather than peripheral resistance and raised HR through both PEP and RSA (Smith et al., 2000). In contrast, among women a closely related agentic stressor—debate—raised SBP through increased peripheral resistance rather than cardiac output (Nealey, Smith, & Uchino, 2002). Thus, mechanisms underlying effects of the vertical IPC axis on CVR can reflect distinct underlying processes, perhaps reflecting agentic challenges (i.e., opportunities to influence others and gain status) or threats (i.e., possible failure or loss of status; Scheepers, 2009).

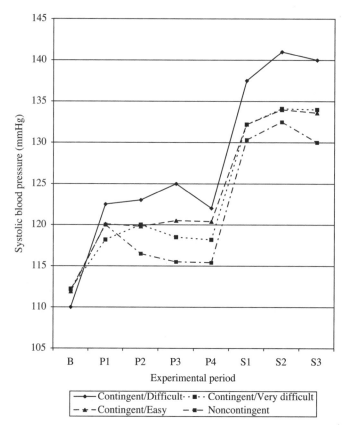

Figure 14.3. Raw baseline (B) and covariance-adjusted preparation (P) and speaking (S) period systolic blood pressure values as a function of incentive contingency and difficulty. Adapted from "Interpersonal Influence As Active Coping: Effects of Task Difficulty on Cardiovascular Reactivity," by T. W. Smith, M. Baldwin, and A. J. Christensen, 1990, *Psychophysiology, 27,* p. 433. Copyright 1990 by Wiley-Blackwell. Adapted with permission.

In an experimental manipulation of enacting dominant versus deferential behavior (Smith et al., 1996), a mock job interview required participants to enact a dominant and cold interpersonal style appropriate for a sales management position or a deferential and accommodating style for a customer relations position. Men displayed greater SBP, DBP, and HR reactivity in the more agentic compared with the communal role; women displayed the opposite pattern. Hence for men but not for women, enacting dominant behavior evoked greater CVR. Behavioral measures of dominance during marital interaction are positively associated with SBP for men but not women (Brown & Smith, 1992; Smith et al., 2009). However, in previously unacquainted mixed sex dyads, behavioral measures of dominance expression have been associated with increased CVR in women but not men (Newton & Bane, 2001).

Sex differences in the effects of the two IPC dimensions on CVR are also evident during marital interaction. As noted previously, incentives to exert social influence toward the spouse evoked greater SBP reactivity for husbands but not wives (Brown & Smith, 1992). A second study assigned married couples to a task requiring spouses to present either opposing or concurring positions on current events (Smith, Gallo, Goble, Ngu, & Stark, 1998). Half the couples were told that their remarks would be evaluated for verbal intelligence, whereas the others were simply asked to speak clearly. Hence, couples participated in a marital discussion under a condition that activated agentic motives (i.e., achievement-related evaluative threat) or communal motives (i.e., disagreement). Evaluative threat evoked greater SBP, DBP, and HR reactivity among men but not women, whereas disagreement evoked greater SBP, DBP, and HR reactivity for women but not men.

Evaluative threats concerning competence, task performance, and achievement activate agentic motives broadly related to status and can take the form of either challenges (i.e., opportunities to demonstrate valued competencies) or threat (e.g., fear of failure). Evaluation of this type generally evokes greater CVR for both men and women (Gendolla & Richter, 2006; Smith et al., 1997), especially when the evaluators are presented as high in status (Wright, Killebrew, & Pimpalapure, 2002). Overall, these findings suggest that arousal of agentic motives and engagement in related effort, as in response to evaluative threats and incentives to influence others, heighten CVR. Further, these effects are moderated by the magnitude of the importance of success and perceived task difficulty. This is generally true for men and women, but sex roles in marriage and elsewhere may moderate effects of manipulations of agentic and communal motives.

Exposure to Dominant Behavior and High Status in Others

Interacting with high as opposed to low status experimenters evokes greater CVR (Kleinke & Williams, 1994; Long, Lynch, Mancharian, Thomas, & Malinow, 1982), as does evaluation by high status observers (Wright et al., 2002). Interacting with individuals displaying dominant versus submissive behavior and having partners high rather than low in the personality trait of dominance have also been found to evoke greater CVR and delayed recovery of these responses (Gramer & Berner, 2005; Newton & Bane, 2001; Newton, Bane, Flores, & Greenfield, 1999).

In an attempt to test effects of low social rank on CVR among young women, Mendelson, Thurston, and Kubzansky (2008) manipulated a confederate's dominant versus submissive behavior during a joint problem-solving task. Those interacting with a dominant as opposed to a submissive partner displayed increased SBP reactivity. This was interpreted as analogous to effects of low rank in social hierarchies or low SES on CVR (Mendelson et al., 2008), but it is perhaps more parsimoniously seen as reflecting the effects of exposure to dominant behavior during social interaction.

Individual Differences in Dominance and Agency

At the level of personality traits, several characteristics related to the vertical axis have been examined as correlates of CVR. Trait dominance and competitiveness are the most obvious, but masculinity, social anxiety, and fear of negative evaluation have been examined as well. Masculinity reflects a dominant interpersonal style, whereas social anxiety and fear of negative evaluation reflect a submissive and somewhat cold style (Wiggins & Broughton, 1991). Trait dominance and competitiveness correlate positively with CVR during social stressors (Harrison, Denning, & Easton, 2001; Newton et al., 1999), although these findings are often moderated by gender and features of the social context. Among women, for example, low masculinity or agency has been found to be associated with greater DBP and HR reactivity and with larger decreases in RSA and PEP (Nealey et al., 2002). However, other measures of trait dominance have been found to be positively associated with women's CVR during social stressors such as job interviews (Sieverding, Weidner, & von Volkmann, 2005), debates (Rejeski, Parker, Gagne, & Koritnik, 1990), and speeches (Hughes & Callinan, 2007).

In a study of social interactions in same sex dyads, trait dominance was positively associated with CVR in men interacting with other dominant men but not among men interacting with submissive men or in women's dyads (Newton, Watters, Philhower, & Weigel, 2005). Other studies have found positive associations between trait dominance and CVR among men (Sieverding et al., 2005), but still others have found inverse associations (Gramer, 2003; Hughes & Callinan, 2007; Rejeski et al., 1989). Some studies have reported positive associations with SBP reactivity but inverse associations with DBP (Gramer, 2003; Gramer & Berner, 2005), perhaps reflecting different underling cardiac versus vascular bases of CVR.

The various positive and inverse associations could reflect differing levels of task difficulty or effort across studies. At low levels of difficulty, dominant individuals could find the task easier or less engaging than submissive participants, resulting in less effort and an inverse association between trait dominance and CVR. At higher difficulty or with higher levels of incentives that appeal particularly to dominant individuals (e.g., interacting with other dominant males), trait dominance would be associated with greater effort, resulting in a positive association with CVR (Wright & Kirby, 2001).

These effects of difficulty, incentives, and effort on CVR could also account for varying associations between the submissive interpersonal style in social anxiety and CVR. Positive associations likely indicate that socially anxious persons are more fearful of evaluation and loss of status, resulting in greater effort and CVR. Inverse associations could occur when socially anxious persons withdraw effort once they perceive such negative outcomes as likely (Gramer & Saria, 2007; Gramer & Sprintschnik, 2008).

Dominance as a Stable Feature of Social Contexts

In further analyses of the Brown and Smith (1992) study on influence attempts during marital interaction, Brown, Smith, and Benjamin (1998) modeled the difficulty of such social influence attempts by assessing perceptions of relative spouse dominance. High levels of spouse dominance indicate that the individual perceives his or her spouse as more dominant or controlling during typical marital interactions than they see themselves to be; low levels mean the individual sees the spouse as relatively less controlling. Presumably, trying to influence a more dominant spouse is perceived as more difficult than attempting to influence a less dominant spouse. Hence, relative spouse dominance is a stable feature of the marital context clearly related to the vertical axis of the IPC.

In these analyses, perceptions of spouse dominance were positively associated with SBP and DBP reactivity while anticipating and engaging in the interaction task (Brown et al., 1998). At high levels of spouse dominance this reactivity was attenuated, presumably because effort was reduced when the task was seen as nearly impossible or not worth the required effort. Contingent incentives for successful influence prevented this decrease in reactivity at the highest levels of spouse dominance. Hence, hierarchical differences between members of established relationships moderated the general effect of efforts to exert social influence on CVR.

CONCLUSION AND FUTURE DIRECTIONS

Compared with the consistent inverse association between the affiliation axis of the IPC and CVR, effects for the control axis—the vertical dimension of social life—are more complex. Yet, there are important points of consistency. First, efforts to influence and control others or obtain increased status through competitive or evaluated tasks generally increase CVR. This effect is greater with larger incentives, and incentives evoke greater effort-related CVR up until the point where success is seen as unlikely or not worthwhile. Decisions about when efforts are worthwhile may involve the impact of further agentic striving (e.g., greater efforts to achieve status or control others) on co-occurring communal concerns (i.e., maintaining relationship quality). The point where this tradeoff is reached may explain moderators (e.g., sex differences, couples vs. unacquainted dyads) of effects of efforts to achieve status and influence others on CVR. Second, threats of negative evaluation and potential loss of status consistently evoke greater CVR, likely reflecting effects of potential failure and loss on negative emotion and on the activation of efforts to avoid them. Third, exposure to expressions of dominance or higher status during social interaction also tend to evoke greater CVR, perhaps by increasing concerns about negative evaluation and potential loss of status but also by increasing the difficulty of efforts to influence the outcome of the interaction.

Our prior presentation of the interpersonal perspective as a guide to the social psychophysiology of CVR (Smith et al., 2003) emphasized the need to examine effects on CVR of expression of and exposure to various types of social behavior described in the IPC, in both transient and more stable forms. The present discussion makes clear that motivational perspectives presented in this volume and elsewhere have much to offer in this regard. The interpersonal perspective identifies two broad classes of social resources—status and love—and two related, broad classes of social motives—agency and communion—as animating interpersonal processes (Wiggins & Trapnell, 1996). The arousal of status-related motives can heighten CVR by evoking effort to influence and control others (Wright & Kirby, 2001). Individual differences in the strength of these motives (i.e., personality traits) can influence the magnitude of CVR, as can individual differences in self-perceptions of one's ability to influence others (Wright & Dismukes, 1995). Aspects of the social context (e.g., power, relative dominance or prestige) can moderate this effort-related CVR by altering the availability and importance of status-related incentives or altering the difficulty of acquiring or protecting status (Wright et al., 2002).

The model proposed by Blascovich (2008) suggests that an appraisal of situations involving status motives as a challenge will increase cardiac output; an appraisal of threat of impending status loss will increase peripheral resistance. These different processes could alter relative effects on SBP and DBP. This challenge versus threat pattern occurs when individuals make downward versus upward social comparisons with lower versus higher status targets, respectively (Mendes, Blascovich, Major, & Seery, 2001). Further, possessing higher social status or being presented with the opportunity to gain it evokes a challenge response, whereas having low status or facing possible status loss evokes a threat response (Scheepers, 2009). Consistent with models of achievement goal orientation (Elliot, 2005), agentic evaluation evokes a challenge response when it is framed as an opportunity to demonstrate high competence but a threat response when presented as potentially revealing incompetence (Chalabaev, Major, Cury, & Sarrazin, 2009).

These perspectives may also clarify the inconsistent associations between trait dominance and CVR. As a source of increased incentive to acquire or maintain status, the motivational component of this trait should increase effort-related CVR. However, by reducing the perceived difficulty of such tasks, the ability or self-efficacy component of trait dominance should sometimes lower CVR. Further, trait dominance should predict SBP and cardiac output in contexts evoking difficult or important status challenges, but it should predict DBP and peripheral resistance under status threats. Positive associations between trait dominance and CVR should occur at higher levels of perceived importance or difficulty of status threats and challenges, whereas inverse associations are likely at lower levels.

However, these perspectives mostly provide predictions regarding reactions to specific situations. Trait dominance may also be associated with poor health outcomes because it is associated with increased exposure to situations involving agentic motives. That is, dominant individuals may be at increased risk of CVD in part because they choose and create more frequent and stressful social interactions involving contested control and status. Less dominant persons may be protected because they avoid such situations and accept rather than contest lower status roles (Schmid Mast & Hall, 2003).

These motivational perspectives could also clarify the complex influences of social rank on stress and health. When status and power aspects of social hierarchies are clear and stable, high rank (i.e., power, dominance, prestige) should be consistently associated with reduced CVR and risk of CVD, through less exposure to perceived evaluative threat, less frequent exposure to higher status or dominant others during social interaction, and lower difficulty in meeting such challenges when they do occur. Under conditions of ambiguity or instability in hierarchies, all but the lowest ranks face increased threat of status loss, increased exposure to others' effort to rise in the hierarchy, and increased incentives to protect status. Such conditions could also heighten CVR by prompting increased vigilance regarding social interactions (Smith et al., 2000). Shifting or ambiguous status hierarchies may be particularly taxing for trait-dominant individuals who are more likely to see, choose, and create status-related challenges and threats.

Given that social connections are an essential part of human nature, it is perhaps not surprising that aspects of affiliation represented in personality traits and the quality of personal relationships are such potent influences on physical health. However, a second near universal trait of human groups—hierarchical organization—is also an important influence. Further consideration of this vertical dimension can add to the development of a more complete and useful social psychophysiology of everyday life.

REFERENCES

Bakan, D. (1966). *The duality of human existence*. Chicago, IL: Rand McNally.

Barkow, J. H. (1989). *Darwin, sex, and status: Biological approaches to mind and culture*. Toronto, Canada: University of Toronto Press.

Blascovich, J. (2008). Challenge and threat. In A. J. Elliott (Ed.), *Handbook of approach and avoidance motivation* (pp. 431–445). Mahwah, NJ: Erlbaum.

Brown, P. C., & Smith, T. W. (1992). Social influence, marriage, and the heart: Cardiovascular consequences of interpersonal control in husbands and wives. *Health Psychology, 11,* 88–96. doi:10.1037/0278-6133.11.2.88

Brown, P. C., Smith, T. W., & Benjamin, L. S. (1998). Perceptions of spouse dominance predict blood pressure reactivity during marital interactions. *Annals of Behavioral Medicine, 20,* 286–293. doi:10.1007/BF02886378

Carmelli, D., Swan, G., & Rosenman, R. (1985). The relationship between wives' social and psychologic status and their husbands' coronary heart disease: A case-control family study from the Western Collaborative Group Study. *American Journal of Epidemiology, 122,* 90–100.

Chalabaev, A., Major, B., Cury, F., & Sarrazin, P. (2009). Physiological markers of challenge and threat mediate the effects of performance-based goals on performance. *Journal of Experimental Social Psychology, 45,* 991–994. doi:10.1016/j.jesp.2009.04.009

Chida, Y., & Steptoe, A. (2009). The association of anger and hostility with future coronary heart disease: A meta-analytic review of prospective evidence. *Journal of the American College of Cardiology, 53,* 936–946. doi:10.1016/j.jacc.2008.11.044

Chida, Y., & Steptoe, A. (2010). Greater cardiovascular responses to laboratory mental stress are associated with poor subsequent cardiovascular risk status: A meta-analysis of prospective evidence. *Hypertension, 55,* 1026–1032. doi:10.1161/HYPERTENSIONAHA.109.146621

Christensen, A. J., & Smith, T. W. (1993). Cynical hostility and cardiovascular reactivity during self-disclosure. *Psychosomatic Medicine, 55,* 193–202.

De Vogli, R., Chandola, T., & Marmot, M. G. (2007). Negative aspects of close relationships and heart disease. *Archives of Internal Medicine, 167,* 1951–1957. doi:10.1001/archinte.167.18.1951

Elliot, A. J. (2005). A conceptual history of the achievement goal construct. In A. Elliot & C. Dweck (Eds.), *Handbook of competence and motivation* (pp. 52–72). New York, NY: Guilford Press.

Gallo, L. C., Smith, T. W., & Cox, C. (2006). Socioeconomic status, psychosocial processes, and perceived health: An interpersonal perspective. *Annals of Behavioral Medicine, 31,* 109–119. doi:10.1207/s15324796abm3102_2

Gallo, L. C., Smith, T. W., & Kircher, J. C. (2000). Cardiovascular and electrodermal responses to support and provocation: Interpersonal methods in the study of psychophysiological reactivity. *Psychophysiology, 37,* 289–301. doi:10.1111/1469-8986.3730289

Gendolla, G. H. E., & Richter, M. (2006). Ego-involvement and the difficulty law of motivation: Effects on performance-related cardiovascular response. *Personality and Social Psychology Bulletin, 32,* 1188–1203. doi:10.1177/0146167206288945

Gramer, M. (2003). Cognitive appraisal, emotional and cardiovascular response of high and low dominant subjects in active performance situations. *Personality and Individual Differences, 34,* 1303–1318. doi:10.1016/S0191-8869(02)00121-6

Gramer, M., & Berner, M. (2005). Effects of trait dominance on psychological and cardiovascular response to social influence attempts: The role of gender and partner dominance. *International Journal of Psychophysiology, 55,* 279–289. doi:10.1016/j.ijpsycho.2004.08.006

Gramer, M., & Saria, K. (2007). Effects of social anxiety and evaluative threat on cardiovascular responses to active performance situations. *Biological Psychology, 74,* 67–74. doi:10.1016/j.biopsycho.2006.07.004

Gramer, M., & Sprintschnik, E. (2008). Social anxiety and cardiovascular response to an evaluative speaking task: The role of stressor anticipation. *Personality and Individual Differences, 44,* 371–381. doi:10.1016/j.paid.2007.08.016

Harrison, L. K., Denning, S., & Easton, H. (2001). The effects of competition and competativeness on cardiovascular activity. *Psychophysiology, 38,* 601–606. doi:10.1111/1469-8986.3840601

Helgeson, V. S. (2003). Gender-related traits and health. In J. Suls & K. Wallston (Eds.), *Social psychological foundations of health and illness* (pp. 367–394). Malden, MA: Blackwell. doi:10.1002/9780470753552.ch14

Henrich, J., & Gil-White, F. J. (2001). The evolution of prestige: Freely conferred deference as a mechanism for enhancing the benefits of cultural transmission. *Evolution and Human Behavior, 22,* 165–196. doi:10.1016/S1090-5138(00)00071-4

Holt-Lunstad, J., Uchino, B. N., Smith, T. W., Olson-Cerny, C., & Nealey-Moore, J. (2003). Social relationships and ambulatory blood pressure: Structural and qualitative predictors of cardiovascular function during everyday social interactions. *Health Psychology, 22,* 388–397. doi:10.1037/0278-6133.22.4.388

Houston, B. K., Babyak, M. A., Chesney, M. A., Black, G., & Ragland, D. R. (1997). Social dominance and 22-year all-cause mortality in men. *Psychosomatic Medicine, 59,* 5–12.

Houston, B. K., Chesney, M., Black, G., Cates, D., & Hecker, M. (1992). Behavioral clusters and coronary heart disease risk. *Psychosomatic Medicine, 54,* 447–461.

Hughes, B., & Callinan, S. (2007). Trait dominance and cardiovascular reactivity to social and non-social stressors: Gender-specific implications. *Psychology & Health, 22,* 457–472. doi:10.1080/14768320600976174

Johnson, R. T., Burk, J. A., & Kirkpatrick, L. A. (2007). Dominance and prestige as differential predictors of aggression and testosterone levels in men. *Evolution and Human Behavior, 28,* 345–351. doi:10.1016/j.evolhumbehav.2007.04.003

Kaplan, J. R., & Manuck, S. B. (1998). Monkeys, aggression, and the pathobiology of atherosclerosis. *Aggressive Behavior, 24,* 323–334. doi:10.1002/(SICI)1098-2337(1998)24:4<323::AID-AB7>3.0.CO;2-J

Kiesler, D. J. (1983). The 1982 Interpersonal Circle: A taxonomy for complementarity in human transactions. *Psychological Review, 90,* 185–214. doi:10.1037/0033-295X.90.3.185

Kleinke, C. L., & Williams, G. (1994). Effects of interviewer status, touch, and gender on cardiovascular response. *The Journal of Social Psychology, 134,* 247–249. doi:10.1080/00224545.1994.9711389

Locke, K. D., & Sadler, P. (2007). Self-efficacy, values, and complementarity in dyadic interactions: Integrating interpersonal and social–cognitive theory. *Personality and Social Psychology Bulletin, 33,* 94–109. doi:10.1177/0146167206293375

Long, J. M., Lynch, J. J., Mancharian, N., Thomas, S., & Malinow, K. (1982). The effect of status on blood pressure during verbal communication. *Journal of Behavioral Medicine, 5,* 165–172. doi:10.1007/BF00844806

Magee, J. C., & Galinsky, A. D. (2008). Social hierarchy: The self-reinforcing nature of power and status. *The Academy of Management Annals, 2,* 351–398. doi:10.1080/19416520802211628

Matthews, K. A., Gallo, L. C., & Taylor, S. E. (2010). Are psychosocial factors mediators of socioeconomic status and health connections? A progress report and blueprint for the future. *Annals of the New York Academy of Sciences, 1186,* 146–173. doi:10.1111/j.1749-6632.2009.05332.x

Mendelson, T., Thurston, R. C., & Kubzansky, L. D. (2008). Affective and cardiovascular effects of experimentally induced social status. *Health Psychology, 27,* 482–489. doi:10.1037/0278-6133.27.4.482

Mendes, W. B., Blascovich, J., Major, B., & Seery, M. (2001). Challenge and threat responses during downward and upward social comparisons. *European Journal of Social Psychology, 31,* 477–497. doi:10.1002/ejsp.80

Nealey, J. B., Smith, T. W., & Uchino, B. N. (2002). Cardiovascular responses to agency and communion stressors in young women. *Journal of Research in Personality, 36,* 395–418. doi:10.1016/S0092-6566(02)00003-X

Newton, T. L. (2009). Cardiovascular functioning, personality, and the social world: The domain of hierarchical power. *Neuroscience and Biobehavioral Reviews, 33,* 145–159. doi:10.1016/j.neubiorev.2008.07.005

Newton, T. L., & Bane, C. M. (2001). Cardiovascular correlates of behavioral dominance and hostility during dyadic interaction. *International Journal of Psychophysiology, 40,* 33–46. doi:10.1016/S0167-8760(00)00124-0

Newton, T. L., Bane, C. M., Flores, A., & Greenfield, J. (1999). Dominance, gender, and cardiovascular reactivity during social interaction. *Psychophysiology, 36,* 245–252. doi:10.1017/S0048577299971986

Newton, T. L., Watters, C. A., Philhower, C. L., & Weigel, R. A. (2005). Cardiovascular reactivity during dyadic social interaction: The roles of gender and dominance. *International Journal of Psychophysiology, 57,* 219–228. doi:10.1016/j.ijpsycho.2005.03.001

Rejeski, W. J., Gagne, M., Parker, P. E., & Koritnik, D. R. (1989). Acute stress reactivity from contested dominance in dominant and submissive males. *Behavioral Medicine, 15*, 118–124. doi:10.1080/08964289.1989.9934574

Rejeski, W. J., Parker, P. E., Gagne, M., & Koritnik, D. R. (1990). Cardiovascular and testosterone responses to contested dominance in women. *Health Psychology, 9*, 35–47. doi:10.1037/0278-6133.9.1.35

Scheepers, D. (2009). Turning social identity threat into challenge: Status stability and cardiovascular reactivity during intergroup competition. *Journal of Experimental Social Psychology, 45*, 228–233. doi:10.1016/j.jesp.2008.09.011

Schmid Mast, M., & Hall, J. A. (2003). Anybody can be boss but only certain people make good subordinants: Behavioral impacts of striving for dominance and dominance aversion. *Journal of Personality, 71*, 871–892. doi:10.1111/1467-6494.7105007

Siegman, A. W., Kubzansky, L. D., Kawachi, I., Boyle, S., Vokonas, P. S., & Sparrow, D. (2000). A prospective study of dominance and coronary heart disease in the normative aging study. *The American Journal of Cardiology, 86*, 145–149. doi:10.1016/S0002-9149(00)00850-X

Sieverding, M., Weidner, G., & von Volkmann, B. (2005). Cardiovascular reactivity in a simulated job interview: The role of gender role self-concept. *International Journal of Behavioral Medicine, 12*, 1–10. doi:10.1207/s15327558ijbm1201_1

Smith, T. W., Allred, K. D., Morrison, C. A., & Carlson, S. D. (1989). Cardiovascular reactivity and interpersonal influence: Active coping in a social context. *Journal of Personality and Social Psychology, 56*, 209–218. doi:10.1037/0022-3514.56.2.209

Smith, T. W., Baldwin, M., & Christensen, A. J. (1990). Interpersonal influence as active coping: Effects of task difficulty on cardiovascular reactivity. *Psychophysiology, 27*, 429–437. doi:10.1111/j.1469-8986.1990.tb02339.x

Smith, T. W., & Cundiff, J. M. (2011). Risk for coronary heart disease: An interpersonal perspective. In L. M. Horowitz & S. Strack (Eds.), *Handbook of interpersonal psychology: Theory, research, assessment, and therapeutic interventions* (pp. 471–489). Hoboken, NJ: Wiley.

Smith, T. W., Gallo, L. C., Goble, L., Ngu, L. Q., & Stark, K. A. (1998). Agency, communion, and cardiovascular reactivity during marital interaction. *Health Psychology, 17*, 537–545. doi:10.1037/0278-6133.17.6.537

Smith, T. W., Gallo, L. C., & Ruiz, J. M. (2003). Toward a social psychophysiology of cardiovascular reactivity: Interpersonal concepts and methods in the study of stress and coronary disease. In J. Suls & K. Wallston (Eds.), *Social psychological foundations of health and illness* (pp. 335–366). Oxford, England: Blackwell. doi:10.1002/9780470753552.ch13

Smith, T. W., & Gerin, W. (1998). The social psychophysiology of cardiovascular response: An introduction to the special issue. *Annals of Behavioral Medicine, 20*, 243–246. doi:10.1007/BF02886373

Smith, T. W., Glazer, K., Ruiz, J. M., & Gallo, L. C. (2004). Hostility, anger, aggressiveness, and coronary heart disease: An interpersonal perspective on personality, emotion, and health. *Journal of Personality, 72*, 1217–1270. doi:10.1111/j.1467-6494.2004.00296.x

Smith, T. W., Limon, J. P., Gallo, L. C., & Ngu, L. Q. (1996). Interpersonal control and cardiovascular reactivity: Goals, behavioral expression, and the moderating effects of sex. *Journal of Personality and Social Psychology, 70*, 1012–1024. doi:10.1037/0022-3514.70.5.1012

Smith, T. W., Nealey, J. B., Kircher, J. C., & Limon, J. P. (1997). Social determinants of cardiovascular reactivity: Effects of incentive to exert influence and evaluative threat. *Psychophysiology, 34*, 65–73. doi:10.1111/j.1469-8986.1997.tb02417.x

Smith, T. W., Ruiz, J. M., & Uchino, B. N. (2000). Vigilance, incentive, and cardiovascular reactivity in social interactions. *Health Psychology, 19*, 382–392. doi:10.1037/0278-6133.19.4.382

Smith, T. W., Traupman, E. K., Uchino, B. N., Berg, C. A. (2010). Interpersonal circumplex descriptions of psychosocial risk factors for physical illness: Application to hostility, neuroticism, and marital adjustment. *Journal of Personality, 78*, 1011–1036.

Smith, T. W., Uchino, B. N., Berg, C. A., Florsheim, P., Pearce, G., Hawkins, M.,. . . Yoon, H.-C. (2008). Self-reports and spouse ratings of negative affectivity, dominance and affiliation in coronary artery disease: Where should we look and who should we ask when studying personality and health? *Health Psychology, 27*, 676–684. doi:10.1037/0278-6133.27.6.676

Smith, T. W., Uchino, B. N., Berg, C. A., Florsheim, P., Pearce, G., Hawkins, M.,. . . Olsen-Cerny, C. (2009). Conflict and collaboration in middle-aged and older married couples: II. Age, sex, and task context moderate cardiovascular reactivity during marital interaction. *Psychology and Aging, 24*, 274–286. doi:10.1037/a0016067

Smith, T. W., Uchino, B. N., Florsheim, P., Berg, C., Hawkins, M., Henry, N.,. . . Yoon, H. C. (in press). Affiliation and control during marital disagreement, history of divorce, and asymptomatic coronary artery clarification. *Psychosomatic Medicine*.

Taylor, S. E., Seeman, T., Eisenberger, N., Kozanian, T., Moore, A., & Moons, W. (2010). Effects of a supportive or an unsupportive audience on biological and psychological responses to stress. *Journal of Personality and Social Psychology, 98*, 47–56. doi:10.1037/a0016563

Trobst, K. K. (2000). An interpersonal conceptualization and quantification of social support transactions. *Personality and Social Psychology Bulletin, 26*, 971–986. doi:10.1177/01461672002610007

Uchino, B. N. (2004). *Social support and physical health: Understanding the health consequences of physical health*. New Haven, CT: Yale University Press.

Uchino, B. N. (2006). Social support and health: A review of physiological processes potentially underlying links to disease outcomes. *Journal of Behavioral Medicine, 29*, 377–387. doi:10.1007/s10865-006-9056-5

Wiggins, J. S., & Broughton, R. (1991). A geometric taxonomy of personality scales. *European Journal of Personality, 5*, 343–365. doi:10.1002/per.2410050503

Wiggins, J. S., & Trapnell, P. D. (1996). A dyadic-interactional perspective on the five-factor model. In J. S. Wiggins (Ed.), *The five-factor model of personality* (pp. 88–162). New York, NY: Guilford Press.

Wright, R. A., & Dismukes, A. (1995). Cardiovascular effects of experimentally induced efficacy (ability) appraisals at low and high levels of avoidant task demand. *Psychophysiology, 32*, 172–176. doi:10.1111/j.1469-8986.1995.tb03309.x

Wright, R. A., Killebrew, K., & Pimpalapure, D. (2002). Cardiovascular incentive effects when challenge is unfixed: Demonstrations involving social evaluation, evaluator status, and monetary reward. *Psychophysiology, 39*, 188–197. doi:10.1111/1469-8986.3920188

Wright, R. A., & Kirby, L. D. (2001). Effort determination of cardiovascular response: An integrative analysis with applications in social psychology. *Advances in Experimental Social Psychology, 33*, 255–307. doi:10.1016/S0065-2601(01)80007-1

15

SOCIAL INFLUENCES ON CARDIOVASCULAR PROCESSES: A FOCUS ON HEALTH

GREG J. NORMAN, A. COURTNEY DEVRIES, LOUISE HAWKLEY,
JOHN T. CACIOPPO, AND GARY G. BERNTSON

The purpose of the present chapter is to highlight recent empirical and theoretical developments in the study of social interactions and their influence on health, with a particular emphasis on perspectives that integrate across multiple levels of analysis. We first consider some aspects of evolutionary neurodevelopment and neuraxial organization that provide a framework for the integration of social and biological levels of analysis in the study of social motivation and cardiovascular health. We then consider the implications of this general approach and discuss some of the potential mechanisms that allow for the translation of complex social information into physiological and molecular signals relevant to cardiovascular health.

To be human is to be social. Much of the richness in life, from the joys of love to the agony of the loss of loved ones, can be directly linked to our interactions within a social network. The most stressful experiences people endure are typically those that strain or break social connections. The importance of social life is not restricted to humans. Numerous social creatures devote extraordinary amounts of time maintaining and building social relationships. Indeed, wild baboons spend the majority of their waking hours maintaining and building social relationships (Sapolsky, 2001). Relatively speaking, an isolated primate is a rather helpless animal, possessing only a fraction of the physical and sensory repertoire (e.g., speed) of animals occupying similar status within the food network. With that said, it is not surprising that the majority of primates, including humans, rarely operate in isolation and are highly motivated to integrate within cohesive groups. This strategy serves to overcome individual weaknesses and allows individuals to thrive in otherwise inhospitable environments. Superficially, this profound devotion to social interaction may seem more than what is necessary for procreation. A more comprehensive analysis, however, reveals that for many species, inclusion in a social group is necessary for survival, and its absence represents a threat to existence and as such engenders large neurobiological, cardiovascular, and psychological responses. Such processes are likely the result of ancestral humans who were inclined to form social connections, communicate, share food and defense, and retaliate in the face of threat, likely leading to a selective advantage to survive and pass on their genes (Cacioppo et al., 2006; Cacioppo & Patrick, 2008).

In this chapter, we first consider some aspects of evolutionary neurodevelopment and neuraxial organization that provide a framework for the integration of social and biological levels of analysis in the study of social motivation and cardiovascular health. We then consider the implications of this general approach for understanding how social processes influence cardiovascular health.

A particular consequence of a brain so highly tuned to social information is the pronounced cardiovascular reaction to social isolation from, or social disruption of, the group. The need to belong to a social group is so strong that its absence engenders rather remarkable changes in both physiology and behavior. Indeed, affiliation and nurturing social relationships within humans are essential for physical and psychological well-being across the life span (Cacioppo, Berntson, Sheridan, & McClintock, 2000; Cacioppo & Patrick, 2008). When individuals perceive that their particular social needs are not adequately met, a complex set of feelings (e.g., loneliness) are enacted that serve to motivate the resolution of these needs (Cacioppo & Patrick, 2008; Weiss, 1973). Consistent with the view that evolutionary developments tend to develop in layers, the motivational and affective aspects of loneliness may operate, in part, through the co-option and activation of more primitive aversive (pain) and appetitive (reward) systems (Cacioppo & Hawkley, 2003; Cacioppo et al., 2006; Lieberman & Eisenberger, 2009). Through the modulation of operating systems already highly adept at promoting or preventing particular behaviors, loneliness may motivate individuals to avoid the phylogenetically and ontogenetically dangerous state of social isolation, whereas the social reward of connecting with others promotes individuals to repair and maintain social connections.

The complexities inherent in attempting to mine behavioral and physiological signals for their social significance have likely placed a great deal of selective pressure on the evolution of higher level brain structures. With the increasing pressure to successfully adapt within a complex social environment, there has emerged the evolutionary development of specialized neural circuits underlying many of the behavioral and affective processes of the human mind. Many of these circuits overlap with, and were likely co-opted from, networks regulating metabolic and visceral functions, including respiratory and cardiovascular states that provide the energetic and physiological support for social and motivational processes. When the need to belong to a social group goes unfulfilled, organisms ranging from drosophila to humans undergo rather remarkable changes in both behavior and physiology (Cacioppo & Patrick, 2008), a topic discussed in further detail next.

LEVELS OF REPRESENTATION AND CARDIOVASCULAR TONE

An understanding of the underlying neurobiological architectures that govern cardiovascular processes is essential for the investigation of how and why social factors influence cardiovascular health. In this section, we briefly discuss the role of neurobiological organization and its influence of multilevel representation on cardiovascular output.

John Hughlings Jackson, an influential 19th-century neurologist, observed that the nervous system is organized in a hierarchical fashion, with multiple but interactive levels of processing characterized by an evolutionary re-representation of functions at progressively higher levels of the brain (Jackson, 1884). Jackson's work highlighted the fact that evolution results in a progressive neurological layering, or multilevel re-representation of functions. The higher level functional re-representations are characterized by elaborated networks with progressively greater flexibility and sophistication. Rather than replacing lower mechanisms, re-representative systems extensively interact with, and depend on, lower level substrates in a hierarchical-like fashion. This re-representation of function across levels of the neuraxis has important implications for the study of social influences on physiology and health.

Neural Hierarchy

The nervous system is characterized by a hierarchical organizational pattern comprising simple reflex-like circuits at the lowest levels (brainstem and spinal cord) and broadly distributed neural networks for more integrative processing at higher levels (for reviews, see Berntson, Boysen, & Cacioppo, 1993; Berridge & Kringelbach, 2008; Cacioppo et al., 2000). Examples include the pain-withdrawal reflex at the spinal level and homeostatic baroreceptor reflexes at brainstem levels. The former organizes a rapid protective withdrawal response to painful or damaging stimuli, and the latter provides a homeostatic regulatory adjustment to perturbations of blood pressure. For example, increases in blood pressure activate specialized cardiovascular mechanoreceptors, which then feed back into brainstem reflex circuitry leading to reciprocal increases in vagal cardiac output and decreases in sympathetic cardiac and vascular tone. These responses collectively lead to decreases in heart rate, cardiac output, and vascular tone, which synergistically compensate for the blood pressure perturbation (see Figure 15.1). Through parallel processing at multiple levels of the neuraxis, these interacting hierarchical structures allow neural systems to rapidly respond to adaptive challenges through low-level processing (e.g., startle reflex, increased blood pressure), whereas more rostral neural substrates permit elaborated processing of potential outcomes and future responses. Indeed, neural processing at progressively more rostral regions of the frontal cortex is distinguished by its ability to support more abstract representations and more complex rules (Badre & D'Esposito, 2009).

Based on hierarchical interconnections, higher level systems are routinely dependent on lower level systems for the transmission and preliminary processing of stressful stimuli. In neural hierarchies, the processing accomplished within lower level structures is crucial because it represents the basic means through which higher level systems, including those processing social information, achieve the expression of behavioral and physiological output. In addition to subserving higher level processes, lower level substrates have an inherent functional capability. Indeed, the distinct advantages and disadvantages associated with higher level (integrative, flexible, but capacity limited) and lower level (rapid, efficient, but rigid) processing was a likely source of evolutionary pressure for the preservation of lower level substrates, despite higher level elaborations and re-representations. The ability to strategically avoid potential danger on the basis of memory and reasoning would confer tremendous adaptive advantage. At the same time, rapid low-level processing (e.g., pain-withdrawal reflexes) may serve to sustain survival in the short term, so that higher level strategies can develop.

Neural Heterarchy and Cardiovascular Control

Additional complexities exist beyond strict hierarchical organization patterns. Descending projections from the highest levels of the neuraxis (e.g., cortical and limbic structures) are able to bypass intermediate levels and directly synapse onto lower level structures with direct input to cardiovascular control nuclei (Critchley et al., 2003; Wakana, Jiang, Nagae-Poetscher, van Zijl, & Mori, 2004). This organizational pattern, previously described as a *neural*

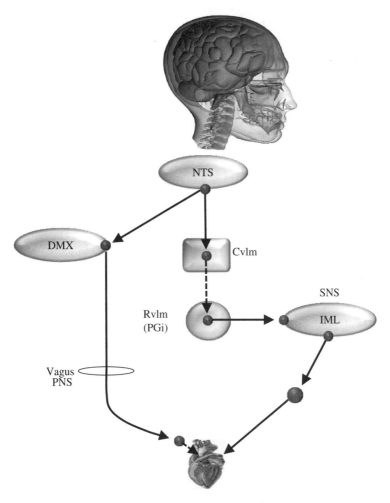

Figure 15.1. Summary of brainstem systems underlying the baroreceptor cardiac reflex. Baroreceptor afferents project to the nucleus tractus solitarius (NTS), which in turn leads to activation of parasympathetic motor neurons in the dorsal motor nucleus of the vagus (DMX). The NTS also activates the caudal ventrolateral medulla (Cvlm), which in turn inhibits the rostral ventrolateral medulla (Rvlm), leading to a withdrawal of excitatory drive on the sympathetic motor neurons in the intermediolateral cell column of the spinal cord (IML). PGi = paragigantocellularis; PNS = parasympathetic nervous system; SNS = sympathetic nervous system.

heterarchy (Berntson & Cacioppo, 2000), contains the components of hierarchical systems, because higher levels are in continuous communication with lower systems via intermediate levels, but it has the additional capacity to interact over widely separated levels through direct connections with the lowest levels. The capacity for direct interactions across widely separated organizational levels appears to be a progressive evolutionary development. Recent reports have demonstrated a "new" area within the primary motor cortex, present only in higher primates, that in conjunction with the well-described cortical projections to spinal motor interneurons in mammals entirely bypasses spinal cord reflexes and directly accesses spinal motor neurons, a process that facilitates the coordination of the skilled movements (Rathelot & Strick, 2009).

Similarly, autonomic control of cardiovascular tone is under sustained inhibitory control by the prefrontal cortex, which tonically inhibits activity within subcortical structures such as the amygdala and brainstem (Thayer, Yamamoto, & Brosschot, 2009). With descending heterarchical control, higher level brain structures, such as the anterior insula, receive afferent information regarding cardiovascular and visceral processes that is then used to modulate motivational states (Craig, 2002). This heterarchical ascending signaling pathway has been proposed as a mechanism through which the re-representation of peripheral states becomes the substrate for conscious feeling states (Craig, 2002, 2003). Thus, the highest and most recently developed levels of the cerebral cortex are able to directly interact with the lowest and most primitive levels, allowing for novel patterns of motor and cardiovascular control that are essential for complex, highly flexible output (Rathelot & Strick, 2009; Thayer et al., 2009).

It is notable that many of the same neural structures that provide monosynaptic input into lower level neurons controlling peripheral physiology are involved in the processing of social–affective information. For example, the anterior cingulate has received increasing attention for, among other things, partially mediating the aversive emotions that follow social rejection (Lieberman & Eisenberger, 2009) and perception of social status (Gianaros et al., 2007) while simultaneously controlling autonomic (Critchley et al., 2003) and neuroendocrine activity (MacLullich et al., 2006). Thus, it is partially through the evolutionary re-representation of function, described by Jackson over a century ago, that highly abstract and complex information from the social environment is able to alter cardiovascular processes, a topic further discussed in the sections to follow.

The evolutionarily driven heterarchical "design" has important theoretical and empirical implications for cardiovascular research. For example, traditional views of the sympathetic and parasympathetic branches of the autonomic nervous system, particularly influenced by the writings of Walter Cannon (1939), have typically been described as subject to reciprocal central control, with activation of one branch associated with inhibition of the other (see Berntson & Cacioppo, 2000). This bipolar conceptualization arose largely out of research on basic autonomic reflexes, which are rather rigid and lack the range and flexibility of control characteristic of higher level cerebral systems. The efferent arm of the baroreceptor heart rate reflex, for example, entails a notable reciprocal regulation of the parasympathetic and sympathetic nervous systems. Baroreceptor afferents increase their rate of firing in response to mechanical distortion associated with an increase in blood pressure, and this afferent signal is conveyed to the nucleus tractus solitarius (NTS) in the medulla, which is the primary visceral receiving area of the brain. The NTS subsequently issues direct and indirect excitatory projections to vagal motor neurons in the nucleus ambiguus and dorsal motor nucleus, leading to a reflexive increase in parasympathetic outflow. This yields a decrease in heart rate and a reduction in cardiac output, which tends to normalize or oppose the pressor perturbation. Projections from the NTS also indirectly suppress sympathetic outflow through inhibition of the sympathoexcitatory neurons in the rostral ventrolateral medulla. This sympathetic withdrawal acts to further slow the beat of the heart as well as to decrease myocardial contractility. Thus, the reciprocal actions of the individual branches of the autonomic nervous system synergistically contribute to the homeostatic regulation of blood pressure. This reflex represents a prototypic, reciprocally regulated system, having a bipolar action disposition extending from sympathetic to parasympathetic dominance. Although descriptive of some basic autonomic reflexive circuits, this characterization misconstrues the true complexity of autonomic control of cardiovascular function.

Higher level brain structures are capable of bypassing lower level structures and directly driving autonomic output through direct projections from forebrain structures, such as the cingulate cortex (Critchley et al., 2005), amygdala (LeDoux, 2003), and insular cortex (Cechetto & Shoemaker, 2009) to source nuclei controlling cardiovascular tone (see Figure 15.2). Stimulation and lesion studies of higher neural systems demonstrate their ability to facilitate, inhibit, and even bypass basic brainstem autonomic reflexes, thereby modulating autonomic outflow directly (Buchanan et al., 2010; Sévoz-Couche, Comet, Hamon, & Laguzzi, 2003). As discussed previously, many of the same brain structures that drive higher level autonomic and neuroendocrine control also serve as the substrates for higher level processing of social information. These descending pathways are the conduit by which psychological stressors can yield antihomeostatic effects on the cardiovasculature, including concurrent increases in blood pressure and heart rate (in opposition to baroreflex control), effects that likely have implications for cardiovascular health.

As discussed previously, the involvement of higher level neuraxial structures in the regulation of cardiovascular processes can result in greater

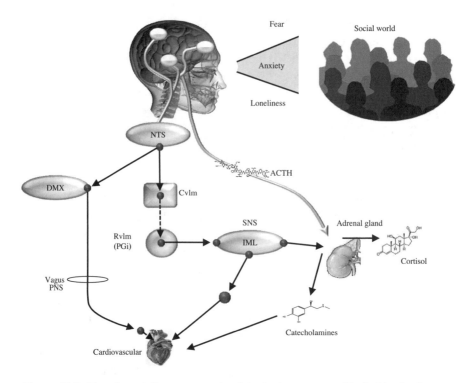

Figure 15.2. Top-down influences on physiological processes. Rostral brain structures influence autonomic output through projections to the nucleus tractus solitarius
(NTS) and rostral ventrolateral medulla (Rvlm). The NTS subsequently projects to
the dorsal motor nucleus of the vagus (DMX; parasympathetic control) and the Rvlm
to the intermediolateral cell column (IML; sympathetic control). Sympathetic activation at the adrenal medulla results in systemic catecholamine release. Rostral brain
structures influence neuroendocrine control through the hypothalamus. Activation
of hypothalamic neurons through corticotropin-releasing hormone results in systemic release of adrenocorticotropic hormone (ACTH). When ACTH reaches the
adrenal cortex, it induces the release of glucocorticoids. Cvlm = caudal ventrolateral
medulla; PGi = paragigantocellularis; PNS = parasympathetic nervous system;
SNS = sympathetic nervous system.

individual differences in autonomic responses. At a group level, the heart rate
responses of human subjects to orthostatic stress and to standard psychological stressors (mental arithmetic, speech stress, reaction time tasks) are similar
(Berntson et al., 1994; Cacioppo et al., 1994). Analyses of the separate contributions of the two autonomic branches by the use of single and dual pharmacological blockades have revealed that orthostatic stress (transition from
sitting to standing) yields consistent reflex-like responses characterized by a
highly correlated sympathetic activation and parasympathetic withdrawal. In
contrast, psychological stressors yield a more varied pattern of response across
subjects, with no overall correlation between the responses of the autonomic

branches. Some subjects showed a predominant sympathetic activation, others a predominant parasympathetic withdrawal, and others varying combinations of these responses (Berntson et al., 1994).

Extending such findings into the realm of cardiovascular health outcomes, Berntson, Norman, Hawkley, and Cacioppo (2008) derived two distinct metrics of autonomic control, based on two models of cardiac regulation. Both metrics used high-frequency heart rate variability (HF) and pre-ejection period (PEP) as measures of parasympathetic and sympathetic control. Based on bipolar measures of autonomic control, a cardiac autonomic balance (CAB) metric was derived as a scale extending from maximal sympathetic activation on one end of a continuum to maximal parasympathetic activation at the other extreme (i.e., along the reciprocity diagonal of Figure 15.3a). Although this

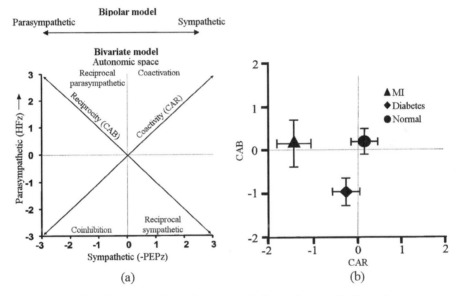

Figure 15.3. Bipolar versus bivariate representations of sympathetic and parasympathetic control (a). Cardiac autonomic regulatory capacity (CAR) and cardiac autonomic balance (CAB) in disease states (b). Data points illustrate means and standard errors of CAR and CAB as a function of participant group, relative to the population. Compared with other participants, subjects with a prior myocardial infarction (MI) had lower CAR scores, indicating lower overall cardiac regulatory capacity, but were not highly deviate on CAB. In contrast, those with diabetes showed a lower CAB score, reflective of a predominant sympathetic balance, but were not highly deviant on CAR. Adapted from "Cardiac Autonomic Balance Versus Cardiac Regulatory Capacity," by G. G. Berntson, G. J. Norman, L. C. Hawkley, and J. T. Cacioppo, 2008, *Psychophysiology, 45,* p. 649. Copyright 2008 by Wiley-Blackwell. Adapted with permission.

index was not correlated with most aspects of health and disease in a population-based sample (Chicago Health and Social Relations Study; Hawkley et al., 2008), it was predictive of diabetes mellitus, independent of demographics and health behaviors (Figure 15.3b). In contrast to bipolar models of autonomic control, recent conceptualizations of psychosomatic relations have emphasized the overall capacity for autonomic control as indexed by autonomic flexibility and variability (Friedman, 2007; Friedman & Thayer, 1998; Hoehn-Saric & McLeod, 2000; Thayer & Sternberg, 2006). This concept, together with the demonstration of the basic bivariate structure of autonomic control, provided an alternative metric to CAB. An index of cardiac autonomic regulatory capacity (CAR) was derived as the sum of activities of the autonomic branches, again based on normalized HF and PEP measures. In contrast to the reciprocal diagonal represented by CAB, CAR is a metric that captures the coactivity diagonal of Figure 15.3a. Analysis of the Chicago Health and Social Relations Study sample revealed that CAR was a better predictor of overall health status and a significant predictor of the occurrence of myocardial infarction, whereas the reciprocity metric (CAB) was not (Figure 15.3b). These results suggest that distinct patterns of autonomic control may be associated with distinct health dimensions.

IMPLICATIONS FOR CARDIOVASCULAR HEALTH

As would be expected from the work mentioned in the previous section, social stress has important implications for health. Stress deriving from the social world has effects above and beyond what might be expected from traditional animal models of stress and disease. For example, physical and psychological stressors yield comparable elevations in glucocorticoid levels, but physical stressors have been shown to have much less potent effects on disease (Padgett et al., 1998). It is notable that the cardiovascular consequences of social stress appear to covary with the animal's social status, with symptomology differing greatly depending on the particular species and individual levels of dominance (Sapolsky, 2005). Within groups of wild baboons, the individuals occupying the lowest ranks within their social hierarchy have chronically elevated glucocorticoid levels (Sapolsky, 1989). Similarly, destabilization of the social hierarchy within macaque monkeys promotes coronary atherogenesis, primarily due to heightened activity of the sympathetic nervous system (Kaplan & Manuck, 2008). Animals deprived of social contact show decreased ability to heal wounds (Detillion, Craft, Glasper, Prendergast, & DeVries, 2004) and diminished autonomic cardiac control (Grippo, Trahanas, Zimmerman, Porges, & Carter, 2009). In these latter two studies, the effects of social interaction were reversed by direct manipulation of brain levels of oxytocin, a neuropeptide associated with social interaction that will be discussed in the following section. Social isolation increases neuroendocrine proinflammatory cytokine and cell death responses in animal models of cardiovascular and cerebrovascular diseases, including cardiac arrest and stroke (Weil et al., 2008). In the latter study, it was determined that that brain interleukin-6 (IL-6) levels were different among socially isolated and paired animals. Although IL-6 has typically been viewed as a proinflammatory cytokine, recent evidence has suggested the situation is far more complex, with central IL-6 levels having neuroprotective and anti-inflammatory properties in the brain (Ali et al., 2000; Hawkley, Bosch, Engeland, Marucha, & Cacioppo, 2006). It is notable that Karelina et al. (2009) found that blockade of central IL-6 signaling entirely removes the effect of social housing on stroke outcome, suggesting a powerful role for neuroimmune signaling in the mediation of social influences on cerebrovascular health.

As discussed previously, various aspects of social behavior, including perceived and objective social isolation, social support, and social rejection, have been shown to affect physiological processes. Indeed, social isolation increases the risk of mortality and morbidity on par with other well-known risk factors (e.g., obesity, hypertension), even after statistically controlling for known biological predispositions and baseline measures of health (House, Landis, & Umberson, 1988). Indeed, social status strongly predicts well-being, morbidity, and mortality in both healthy (Sapolsky, 2005) and medically compromised individuals (Cohen & Syme, 1985). Similarly, social support predicts lower overall cortisol levels (Turner-Cobb, Sephton, Koopman, Blake-Mortimer, & Spiegel, 2000) and underlying atherosclerosis (Angerer et al., 2000; Knox et al., 2000; Wang, Mittleman, & Orth-Gomer, 2005). In addition, socially isolated individuals display increased levels of cholesterol and blood pressure reactivity (Grant, Hamer, & Steptoe, 2009). Similarly, perceived social isolation has been shown to be significantly associated with higher systolic blood pressure (Hawkley et al., 2006). It also predicts greater increases in systolic blood pressure over time (Hawkley, Thisted, Masi, & Cacioppo, 2010) and predicts incident coronary heart disease (Thurston & Kubzansky, 2009).

The aforementioned benefits of social integration and, conversely, the health risks of social isolation are not simply related to the presence, absence, or number of social ties but rather include an important determinant related to satisfaction with social relationship (Cacioppo & Patrick, 2008). The valuation of one's social network is particularly dependent on higher level neuronal structures. Indeed, the perception of explicit social dominance engages dorsolateral prefrontal cortex with additional structures recruited, including amygdala and prefrontal cortex, when status is not so apparent (Zink et al., 2008). Thus, the evolutionary re-representation of function, where higher level neuraxial structures process abstract social information and transduce this information to physiological signaling, represents an important modulator of health deserving of further attention.

These examples demonstrate the powerful influence of social relations on autonomic regulation of the cardiovascular, endocrine, and immunological processes and immunological outcome and illustrate how research conducted at the level of the physiological, pharmacological, or immunological analysis may not fully explicate complex data. Rather, comprehensive accounts of psychophysiological relation will likely require multiple analyses across distinct levels of functional organization.

OXYTOCIN AS A POTENTIAL MECHANISM

Although the association between social interaction and health likely consists of numerous psychological and physiological pathways, recent evidence has suggested that the neuropeptide oxytocin (OT) may play an important role in transducing social information to physiological processes. Work in animals has provided strong evidence that OT is essential in the processing of social information (Carter, DeVries, & Getz, 1995; Ferguson et al., 2000; Insel & Young, 2000). Furthermore, OT has powerful effects on autonomic and neuroendocrine output that has been previously suggested to mediate the salubrious effects of social interaction on health (Uvnäs-Moberg, 1998). Indeed, positive social interactions, such as social support, lead to increased levels of OT (Heinrichs, Baumgartner, Kirschbaum, & Ehlert, 2003).

Experimental work in animals has suggested that many of the effects of OT are a consequence of its actions within particular limbic structures, which subsequently modulate descending control of neuroendocrine and cardiovascular variables (Pyner, 2009; Uvnäs-Moberg, 1998). Within humans, intranasal OT attenuates amygdala activity and reduces amygdala–brainstem coupling in response to threatening social stimuli (Kirsch et al., 2005). The biological effects of OT on neural structures translate into observable changes in behavior. Intranasal OT increases trust, independent of risk taking (Kosfeld, Heinrichs, Zak, Fischbacher, & Fehr, 2005) and improves the ability to correctly infer the mental state of others (Domes et al., 2007). In addition to its effects on psychological processes, OT has potent effects on various factors that modulate cardiovascular tone. Indeed, OT has potent anti-inflammatory actions following endotoxin administration (Clodi et al., 2008) and decreases neuroendocrine stress reactivity (Heinrichs et al., 2003), both important contributors to cardiovascular health (Thayer et al., 2009). Similarly, OT administration significantly increases parasympathetic cardiac control (Grippo et al., 2009) and has been shown to modulate other cardiovascular variables, such as blood pressure and peripheral resistance (Gutkowska, Jankowski, Mukaddam-Daher, & McCann, 2000; Petersson & Uvnäs-Moberg, 2007). Within animals, centrally released OT significantly reduces the cardiovascular responses to acute stress following myocardial ischemia (Wsól, Cudnoch-Je drzejewska, Szczepanska-Sadowska, Kowalewski, & Dobruch, 2009) and improves ischemic outcome (Authier et al., 2010). Moreover, pharmacological blockade of brainstem OT receptors increases exercise-induced tachycardia (Higa-Taniguchi, Felix, & Michelini, 2009). Rodent studies have indicated that the most likely central sites of action would be the preganglionic sympathetic neurons (Gilbey, Coote, Fleetwood-Walker, & Peterson, 1982) and the parasympathetic neurons of the dorsal motor nucleus of the vagus (Higa, Mori, Viana, Morris, & Michelini, 2002). Treatment with OT following myocardial ischemia improves left ventricular functioning through the modulation of cell survival and angiogenesis signals (Kobayashi et al., 2009). Moreover, OT attenuates vascular oxidative stress and inflammation, which are both related to pathophysiological processes associated with atherosclerosis and cardiovascular disease (Szeto et al., 2008). Consistent with the animal data discussed previously, preliminary data from our laboratory have suggested that intranasal OT elevates autonomic cardiac control and that this effect is dependent on the individual's perceived level of social isolation. Therefore, OT may represent a pathway that translates social–motivational processes into physiological signals, including autonomic, neuroendocrine, and immune function, which are important for cardiovascular health.

CONCLUSION

The modern biomedical strategy of treating individuals irrespective of the social and cultural environment in which they are embedded has particular disadvantages. To be human is to belong to a social group and to send large amounts of neural energy to central networks dedicated to processing the computational demands of complex social life. These same structures are directly connected to lower level structures that directly control homeostatic autonomic and neurohormonal processes such as blood pressure and metabolism. Higher level modulation of these structures allows for nonhomeostatic regulation of cardiovascular processes, which can allow for the development or worsening of health conditions equal in magnitude to other well-known risk factors such as smoking and obesity. Thus, the social world has a profound influence on all levels of physiological function and, as such, should be recognized as one of the more important modulators of health and disease.

REFERENCES

Ali, C., Nicole, O., Docagne, F., Lesne, S., MacKenzie, E. T., Nouvelot, A.,. . . Vivien, D. (2000). Ischemia-induced interleukin-6 as a potential endogenous neuroprotective cytokine against NMDA receptor-mediated excitotoxicity in the brain. *Journal of Cerebral Blood Flow and Metabolism, 20,* 956–966. doi:10.1097/00004647-200006000-00008

Angerer, P., Siebert, U., Kothny, W., Muhlbauer, D., Mudra, H., & von Schacky, C. (2000). Impact of social support, cynical hostility, and anger expression on progression of coronary atherosclerosis. *Journal of the American College of Cardiology, 36,* 1781–1788. doi:10.1016/S0735-1097(00)00944-X

Authier, S., Tanguay, J. F., Geoffroy, P., Gauvin, D., Bichot, S., Ybarra, N.,. . . Troncy, E. (2010). Cardiovascular effects of oxytocin infusion in a porcine model of myocardial infarct. *Journal of Cardiovascular Pharmacology, 55,* 74–82. doi:10.1097/FJC.0b013e3181c5e7d4

Badre, D., & D'Esposito, M. (2009). Is the rostro-caudal axis of the frontal lobe hierarchical? *Nature Reviews Neuroscience, 10,* 659–669. doi:10.1038/nrn2667

Berntson, G. G., Boysen, S. T., & Cacioppo, J. T. (1993). Neurobehavioral organization and the cardinal principle of evaluative bivalence. *Annals of the New York Academy of Sciences, 702,* 75–102. doi:10.1111/j.1749-6632.1993.tb17243.x

Berntson, G. G., & Cacioppo, J. T. (2000). From homeostasis to allodynamic regulation. In J. T. Cacioppo, L. G. Tassinary, & G. G. Berntson (Eds.), *Handbook of psychophysiology* (2nd ed., pp. 459–481). Cambridge, England: Cambridge University Press.

Berntson, G. G., Cacioppo, J. T., Binkley, P. F., Uchino, B. N., Quigley, K. S., & Fieldstone, A. (1994). Autonomic cardiac control: III. Psychological stress and cardiac response in autonomic space as revealed by pharmacological blockades. *Psychophysiology, 31,* 599–608. doi:10.1111/j.1469-8986.1994.tb02352.x

Berntson, G. G., Norman, G. J., Hawkley, L. C., & Cacioppo, J. T. (2008). Cardiac autonomic balance versus cardiac regulatory capacity. *Psychophysiology, 45,* 643–652. doi:10.1111/j.1469-8986.2008.00652.x

Berridge, K. C., & Kringelbach, M. L. (2008). Affective neuroscience of pleasure: reward in humans and animals. *Psychopharmacology, 199,* 457–480. doi:10.1007/s00213-008-1099-6

Buchanan, T. W., Driscoll, D., Mowrer, S. M., Sollers, J. J., III, Thayer, J. F., Kirschbaum, C., & Tranel, D. (2010). Medial prefrontal cortex damage affects physiological and psychological stress responses differently in men and women. *Psychoneuroendocrinology, 35,* 56–66. doi:10.1016/j.psyneuen.2009.09.006

Cacioppo, J. T., Berntson, G. G., Binkley, P. F., Quigley, K. S., Uchino, B. N., & Fieldstone, A. (1994). Autonomic cardiac control: II. Noninvasive indices and basal response as revealed by autonomic blockades. *Psychophysiology, 31,* 586–598. doi:10.1111/j.1469-8986.1994.tb02351.x

Cacioppo, J. T., Berntson, G. G., Sheridan, J. F., & McClintock, M. K. (2000). Multilevel integrative analyses of human behavior: Social neuroscience and the complementing nature of social and biological approaches. *Psychological Bulletin, 126*, 829–843. doi:10.1037/0033-2909.126.6.829

Cacioppo, J. T., & Hawkley, L. C. (2003). Social isolation and health, with an emphasis on underlying mechanisms. *Perspectives in Biology and Medicine, 46*(3, Suppl), S39–S52. doi:10.1353/pbm.2003.0049

Cacioppo, J. T., Hawkley, L. C., Ernst, J. M., Burleson, M., Berntson, G. G., Nouriani, B., & Spiegel, D. (2006). Loneliness within a nomological net: An evolutionary perspective. *Journal of Research in Personality, 40*, 1054–1085. doi:10.1016/j.jrp.2005.11.007

Cacioppo, J. T., & Patrick, B. (2008). *Loneliness: Human nature and the need for social connection.* New York, NY: Norton.

Cannon, W. B. (1939). *The wisdom of the body.* New York, NY: Norton.

Carter, C. S., DeVries, A. C., & Getz, L. L. (1995). Physiological substrates of mammalian monogamy: The prairie vole model. *Neuroscience and Biobehavioral Reviews, 19*, 303–314. doi:10.1016/0149-7634(94)00070-H

Cechetto, D. F., & Shoemaker, J. K. (2009). Functional neuroanatomy of autonomic regulation. *NeuroImage, 47*, 795–803. doi:10.1016/j.neuroimage.2009.05.024

Clodi, M., Vila, G., Geyeregger, R., Riedl, M., Stulnig, T. M., Struck, J., . . . Luger, A. (2008). Oxytocin alleviates the neuroendocrine and cytokine response to bacterial endotoxin in healthy men. *American Journal of Physiology: Endocrinology and Metabolism, 295*, E686–E691.

Cohen, S., & Syme, S. L. (1985). *Social support and health.* Orlando, FL: Academic Press.

Craig, A. D. (2002). How do you feel? Interoception: The sense of the physiological condition of the body. *Nature Reviews Neuroscience, 3*, 655–666.

Craig, A. D. (2003). Interoception: The sense of the physiological condition of the body. *Current Opinion in Neurobiology, 13*, 500–505. doi:10.1016/S0959-4388(03)00090-4

Critchley, H. D., Mathias, C. J., Josephs, O., O'Doherty, J., Zanini, S., Dewar, B. K., . . . Dolan, R. J. (2003). Human cingulate cortex and autonomic control: Converging neuroimaging and clinical evidence. *Brain, 126*, 2139–2152. doi:10.1093/brain/awg216

Critchley, H. D., Rotshtein, P., Nagai, Y., O'Doherty, J., Mathias, C. J., & Dolan, R. J. (2005). Activity in the human brain predicting differential heart rate responses to emotional facial expressions. *NeuroImage, 24*, 751–762. doi:10.1016/j.neuroimage.2004.10.013

Detillion, C. E., Craft, T. K., Glasper, E. R., Prendergast, B. J., & DeVries, A. C. (2004). Social facilitation of wound healing. *Psychoneuroendocrinology, 29*, 1004–1011. doi:10.1016/j.psyneuen.2003.10.003

Domes, G., Heinrichs, M., Glascher, J., Buchel, C., Braus, D. F., & Herpertz, S. C. (2007). Oxytocin attenuates amygdala responses to emotional faces regardless of valence. *Biological Psychiatry, 62*, 1187–1190. doi:10.1016/j.biopsych.2007.03.025

Ferguson, J. N., Young, L. J., Hearn, E. F., Matzuk, M. M., Insel, T. R., & Winslow, J. T. (2000). Social amnesia in mice lacking the oxytocin gene. *Nature Genetics, 25,* 284–288. doi:10.1038/77040

Friedman, B. H. (2007). An autonomic flexibility-neurovisceral integration model of anxiety and cardiac vagal tone. *Biological Psychology, 74,* 185–199. doi:10.1016/j.biopsycho.2005.08.009

Friedman, B. H., & Thayer, J. F. (1998). Anxiety and autonomic flexibility: A cardiovascular approach. *Biological Psychology, 49,* 303–323. doi:10.1016/S0301-0511(97)00027-6

Gianaros, P. J., Horenstein, J. A., Cohen, S., Matthews, K. A., Brown, S. M., Flory, J. D., . . . Hariri, A. R. (2007). Perigenual anterior cingulate morphology covaries with perceived social standing. *Social Cognitive and Affective Neuroscience, 2,* 161–173. doi:10.1093/scan/nsm013

Gilbey, M. P., Coote, J. H., Fleetwood-Walker, S., & Peterson, D. F. (1982). The influence of the paraventriculo-spinal pathway, and oxytocin and vasopressin on sympathetic preganglionic neurones. *Brain Research, 251,* 283–290. doi:10.1016/0006-8993(82)90745-4

Grant, N., Hamer, M., & Steptoe, A. (2009). Social isolation and stress-related cardiovascular, lipid, and cortisol responses. *Annals of Behavioral Medicine, 37,* 29–37. doi:10.1007/s12160-009-9081-z

Grippo, A. J., Trahanas, D. M., Zimmerman, R. R., II, Porges, S. W., & Carter, C. S. (2009). Oxytocin protects against negative behavioral and autonomic consequences of long-term social isolation. *Psychoneuroendocrinology, 34,* 1542–1553.

Gutkowska, J., Jankowski, M., Mukaddam-Daher, S., & McCann, S. M. (2000). Oxytocin is a cardiovascular hormone. *Brazilian Journal of Medical and Biological Research, 33,* 625–633. doi:10.1590/S0100-879X2000000600003

Hawkley, L. C., Bosch, J. A., Engeland, C. G., Marucha, P. T., & Cacioppo, J. T. (2006). Loneliness, dysphoria, stress and immunity: A role for cytokines. In N. P. Plotnikoff, R. E. Faith, & A. J. Murgo (Eds.), *Cytokines: Stress and immunity* (2nd ed., pp. 67–85). Bocan Raton, FL: CRC Press.

Hawkley, L. C., Hughes, M. E., Waite, L. J., Masi, C. M., Thisted, R. A., & Cacioppo, J. T. (2008). From social structural factors to perceptions of relationship quality and loneliness: The Chicago Health, Aging, and Social Relations Study. *Journal of Gerontology: Social Sciences, 63,* S375–S384.

Hawkley, L. C., Thisted, R. A., Masi, C. M., & Cacioppo, J. T. (2010). Loneliness predicts increased blood pressure: Five-year cross-lagged analyses in middle-aged and older adults. *Psychology and Aging, 25,* 132–141.

Heinrichs, M., Baumgartner, T., Kirschbaum, C., & Ehlert, U. (2003). Social support and oxytocin interact to suppress cortisol and subjective responses to psychosocial stress. *Biological Psychiatry, 54,* 1389–1398. doi:10.1016/S0006-3223(03)00465-7

Higa, K. T., Mori, E., Viana, F. F., Morris, M., & Michelini, L. C. (2002). Baroreflex control of heart rate by oxytocin in the solitary-vagal complex. *American*

Journal of Physiology: Regulatory, Integrative and Comparative Physiology, 282, R537–R545.

Higa-Taniguchi, K. T., Felix, J. V., & Michelini, L. C. (2009). Brainstem oxytocinergic modulation of heart rate control in rats: Effects of hypertension and exercise training. *Experimental Physiology, 94,* 1103–1113. doi:10.1113/expphysiol. 2009.049262

Hoehn-Saric, R., & McLeod, D. R. (2000). Anxiety and arousal: Physiological changes and their perception. *Journal of Affective Disorders, 61,* 217–224. doi:10.1016/S0165-0327(00)00339-6

House, J. S., Landis, K. R., & Umberson, D. (1988, July 29). Social relationships and health. *Science, 241,* 540–545. doi:10.1126/science.3399889

Insel, T. R., & Young, L. J. (2000). Neuropeptides and the evolution of social behavior. *Current Opinion in Neurobiology, 10,* 784–789. doi:10.1016/S0959-4388(00)00146-X

Jackson, J. H. (Ed.). (1884). *Evolution and dissolution of the nervous system (Croonian Lectures).* New York, NY: Basic Books.

Kaplan, J. R., & Manuck, S. B. (2008). Status, stress, and heart disease: A monkey's tale. In F. Kessel, P. L. Rosenfeld, & N. B. Anderson (Eds.), *Interdisciplinary research: Case studies from health and social science* (pp. 74–102). New York, NY: Oxford University Press.

Karelina, K., Norman, G. J., Zhang, N., Morris, J. S., Peng, H., & DeVries, A. C. (2009). Social isolation alters neuroinflammatory response to stroke. *Proceedings of the National Academy of Sciences, 106,* 5895–5900. doi:10.1073/pnas.0810737106

Kirsch, P., Esslinger, C., Chen, Q., Mier, D., Lis, S., Siddhanti, S., . . . Meyer-Lindenberg, A. (2005). Oxytocin modulates neural circuitry for social cognition and fear in humans. *The Journal of Neuroscience, 25,* 11489–11493. doi:10.1523/JNEUROSCI.3984-05.2005

Knox, S. S., Adelman, A., Ellison, R. C., Arnett, D. K., Siegmund, K., Weidner, G., & Province, M. A. (2000). Hostility, social support, and carotid artery atherosclerosis in the National Heart, Lung, and Blood Institute Family Heart Study. *The American Journal of Cardiology, 86,* 1086–1089. doi:10.1016/S0002-9149(00)01164-4

Kobayashi, H., Yasuda, S., Bao, N., Iwasa, M., Kawamura, I., Yamada, Y., . . . Shinya, M. (2009). Postinfarct treatment with oxytocin improves cardiac function and remodeling via activating cell-survival signals and angiogenesis. *Journal of Cardiovascular Pharmacology, 54,* 510–519. doi:10.1097/FJC.0b013e3181bfac02

Kosfeld, M., Heinrichs, M., Zak, P. J., Fischbacher, U., & Fehr, E. (2005, June 2). Oxytocin increases trust in humans. *Nature, 435,* 673–676. doi:10.1038/nature03701

LeDoux, J. (2003). The emotional brain, fear, and the amygdala. *Cellular and Molecular Neurobiology, 23,* 727–738. doi:10.1023/A:1025048802629

Lieberman, M. D., & Eisenberger, N. I. (2009, February 13). Pains and pleasures of social life. *Science*, *323*, 890–891. doi:10.1126/science.1170008

MacLullich, A. M., Ferguson, K. J., Wardlaw, J. M., Starr, J. M., Deary, I. J., & Seckl, J. R. (2006). Smaller left anterior cingulate cortex volumes are associated with impaired hypothalamic-pituitary-adrenal axis regulation in healthy elderly men. *The Journal of Clinical Endocrinology and Metabolism*, *91*, 1591–1594. doi:10.1210/jc.2005-2610

Padgett, D. A., Sheridan, J. F., Dorne, J., Berntson, G. G., Candelora, J., & Glaser, R. (1998). Social stress and the reactivation of latent herpes simplex virus type 1. *Proceedings of the National Academy of Sciences of the United States of America*, *95*, 7231–7235. doi:10.1073/pnas.95.12.7231

Petersson, M., & Uvnäs-Moberg, K. (2007). Effects of an acute stressor on blood pressure and heart rate in rats pretreated with intracerebroventricular oxytocin injections. *Psychoneuroendocrinology*, *32*, 959–965. doi:10.1016/j.psyneuen.2007.06.015

Pyner, S. (2009). Neurochemistry of the paraventricular nucleus of the hypothalamus: Implications for cardiovascular regulation. *Journal of Chemical Neuroanatomy*, *38*, 197–208. doi:10.1016/j.jchemneu.2009.03.005

Rathelot, J. A., & Strick, P. L. (2009). Subdivisions of primary motor cortex based on cortico-motoneuronal cells. *Proceedings of the National Academy of Sciences of the United States of America*, *106*, 918–923. doi:10.1073/pnas.0808362106

Sapolsky, R. M. (1989). Hypercortisolism among socially subordinate wild baboons originates at the CNS level. *Archives of General Psychiatry*, *46*, 1047–1051.

Sapolsky, R. M. (2001). *A primate's memoir: A neuroscientist's unconventional life among the baboons*. New York, NY: Scribner.

Sapolsky, R. M. (2005, April 29). The influence of social hierarchy on primate health. *Science*, *308*, 648–652. doi:10.1126/science.1106477

Sévoz-Couche, C., Comet, M. A., Hamon, M., & Laguzzi, R. (2003). Role of nucleus tractus solitarius 5-HT3 receptors in the defense reaction-induced inhibition of the aortic baroreflex in rats. *Journal of Neurophysiology*, *90*, 2521–2530. doi:10.1152/jn.00275.2003

Szeto, A., Nation, D. A., Mendez, A. J., Dominguez-Bendala, J., Brooks, L. G., Schneiderman, N., & McCabe, P. M. (2008). Oxytocin attenuates NADPH-dependent superoxide activity and IL-6 secretion in macrophages and vascular cells. *American Journal of Physiology: Endocrinology and Metabolism*, *295*, E1495–E1501. doi:10.1152/ajpendo.90718.2008

Thayer, J. F., & Sternberg, E. (2006). Beyond heart rate variability: Vagal regulation of allostatic systems. *Annals of the New York Academy of Sciences*, *1088*, 361–372. doi:10.1196/annals.1366.014

Thayer, J. F., Yamamoto, S. S., & Brosschot, J. F. (2009). The relationship of autonomic imbalance, heart rate variability and cardiovascular disease risk factors. *International Journal of Cardiology*, *141*, 122–131.

Thurston, R. C., & Kubzansky, L. D. (2009). Women, loneliness, and incident coronary heart disease. *Psychosomatic Medicine, 71,* 836–842. doi:10.1097/PSY. 0b013e3181b40efc

Turner-Cobb, J. M., Sephton, S. E., Koopman, C., Blake-Mortimer, J., & Spiegel, D. (2000). Social support and salivary cortisol in women with metastatic breast cancer. *Psychosomatic Medicine, 62,* 337–345.

Uvnäs-Moberg, K. (1998). Oxytocin may mediate the benefits of positive social interaction and emotions. *Psychoneuroendocrinology, 23,* 819–835. doi:10.1016/ S0306-4530(98)00056-0

Wakana, S., Jiang, H., Nagae-Poetscher, L. M., van Zijl, P. C., & Mori, S. (2004). Fiber tract-based atlas of human white matter anatomy. *Radiology, 230,* 77–87. doi:10.1148/radiol.2301021640

Wang, H. X., Mittleman, M. A., & Orth-Gomer, K. (2005). Influence of social support on progression of coronary artery disease in women. *Social Science & Medicine, 60,* 599–607. doi:10.1016/j.socscimed.2004.05.021

Weil, Z. M., Norman, G. J., Barker, J. M., Su, A. J., Nelson, R. J., & Devries, A. C. (2008). Social isolation potentiates cell death and inflammatory responses after global ischemia. *Molecular Psychiatry, 13,* 913–915. doi:10.1038/mp.2008.70

Weiss, R. S. (1973). *Loneliness: The experience of emotional and social isolation.* Cambridge, MA: MIT Press.

Wsól, A., Cudnoch-Je drzejewska, A., Szczepanska-Sadowska, E., Kowalewski, S., & Dobruch, J. (2009). Central oxytocin modulation of acute stress-induced cardiovascular responses after myocardial infarction in the rat. *Stress, 12,* 517–525. doi:10.3109/10253890802687688

Zink, C. F., Tong, Y., Chen, Q., Bassett, D. S., Stein, J. L., & Meyer-Lindenberg, A. (2008). Know your place: Neural processing of social hierarchy in humans. *Neuron, 58,* 273–283. doi:10.1016/j.neuron.2008.01.025

16

INDETERMINATE MOTIVATIONS: CARDIOVASCULAR HEALTH COSTS OF LIVING IN A SOCIAL WORLD

BRITTA A. LARSEN AND NICHOLAS J. S. CHRISTENFELD

Stress is as ubiquitous as it is unpopular. It has been identified as a major risk factor for a wide range of diseases, from fatal heart attacks (Trichopoulos, Zavitsanos, Katsouyanni, Tzonou, & Dalla-Vorgia, 1983) to the common cold (Cohen, Tyrrell, & Smith, 1991). It is generally seen as an unwanted hazard of the modern world, and most people feel their lives would improve if they experienced less of it.

Although stress has a pernicious reputation, the fact that it is a universal, basic response suggests that it does—or did, at some point—serve a useful purpose. Stress is, in fact, very much a motivational phenomenon, facilitating the accomplishment of the most primitive goal of surviving. Although stress has become synonymous with discomfort, it is better thought of as a response to it. We feel stress when we perceive a threat, not as a punishment but ultimately to initiate a response that will enable us to do something about it. However, the form of modern stress—diffuse in time, social in nature, and often without clear resolution—may change the value of the stress response and render aspects of the process, such as the rate of recovery or the impact of anticipation, especially important.

It seems likely that, because the threats facing our ancient ancestors were primarily immediate and physical such as being chased by a predator, we respond to stress in an immediate and physiological way (Sapolsky, 1998). The physiological changes that accompany stress are meant to offer protection and enable actions that facilitate escape from physical harm. Immune changes coincident with acute stress, for example, include an influx of leukocytes from the bloodstream to the skin, lymph nodes, and mucosal linings, places where pathogens are most likely to be encountered (Dhabhar, 2000). Increases in heart rate and blood pressure allow for faster delivery of blood to long muscles, enhancing strength and endurance. Although in modern times these physiological changes are often regarded as hazardous to one's health, in primitive times they could have been the difference between surviving and perishing.

Modern stress is generally thought of in terms of the affective response that accompanies it, yet stress is primarily meant to influence not just emotions but also behavior. Although negative emotions accompany threatening experiences, stress is meant to facilitate behavior that will resolve those threats. This is supported by the fact that not all physiological responses to stress are equal; rather, the body's response depends, at least to some extent, on the nature of the threat. Physiological patterns differ based on the emotions we feel in response to a situation, such as anger or sadness (Schwartz, Weinberger, & Singer, 1981). It does not seem to be simply that physiological changes associated with affective states differ because one emotion is more or less "upsetting" than another but rather that they differ because the behaviors associated with each emotion also differ. Changes associated with anger, for example, seem best suited to provide strength, which may be needed in fighting an enemy, whereas fear leads to physiological changes that facilitate endurance, which is likely more helpful when fleeing something dangerous. This specificity reinforces the notion that stress is ultimately meant to enable task accomplishment.

There is a large body of experimental evidence connecting the stress response to preparation for appropriate action. Blascovich and colleagues have done extensive work distinguishing the physiological patterns that accompany tasks we believe we can accomplish and those we feel we are not able to manage (Tomaka, Blascovich, Kelsey, & Leitten, 1997). Participants in these studies were presented with identical tasks, but instructions were phrased in a way that either presented the participant with an opportunity to stretch their abilities and excel (challenge) or lead them to believe the task would be very difficult (threat). Cardiovascular reactivity (CVR) increased in both groups, yet those presented with a challenge showed physiological patterns, such as greater cardiac output, that better suited them for physical activity.

Wright and colleagues have also shown that cardiovascular reactivity increases commensurate with the effort needed to obtain success (Wright, Tunstall, Williams, Goodwin, & Harmon-Jones, 1995). In a series of studies, they presented subjects with one of two different sorts of tasks. In one, individuals were presented with an unfixed task, that is, one for which rewards increase incrementally with effort. In the others, individuals faced an easy fixed task, in which a low threshold of performance had to be met to receive a fixed reward. They found that blood pressure and heart rate increased more in individuals presented with unfixed tasks. This suggests that, in these stressful situations, CVR did not necessarily respond to the affective component of the tasks but to the level of activity needed to achieve success. With a fixed task, a high degree of CVR would be excessive because only a moderate amount is needed to pass a given threshold. In unfixed tasks, however, greater activation, and accompanying CVR, could produce greater rewards. Similarly, these authors found that CVR increases in the face of an audience but only for tasks that are moderately difficult. Overly simple tasks that did not require much effort did not result in increased CVR (Gendolla & Richter, 2006; Wright, Dill, Geen, & Anderson, 1998), nor did seemingly impossible tasks, in which case increasing reactivity would be futile (Wright et al., 1998).

Finally, studies have also shown that recovery from psychological stressors can be expedited when these tasks are followed by physical exercise (Chafin, Christenfeld, & Gerin, 2008), suggesting that, at some level, we may not feel a threat has been addressed until we have performed a physical task. The stress response appears often to be tailored to action. This emphasizes yet again that the stress response is meant to enable physical activity. The research cited previously further underscores that this response is not merely tailored to action in general but to specific actions that will fit the situations, such as fleeing, fighting, or exerting the effort needed to maximize rewards.

The physical enabling of the stress response, however, must come with metabolic costs. Mobilization of energy through so many bodily changes imposes costs on the systems involved. These costs are justified, however, by the great value of survival. The net value is positive, however, only if there are benefits to the activation of the stress system that are sufficient to offset the costs or, roughly, if the behaviors being enabled are actually performed. With threats for which no action is taken, or for which no concrete course of action exists, stress incurs all the metabolic costs with none of the benefits. Stress will therefore be most beneficial in situations with concrete attainable goals that can be met by clear courses of immediate action.

EFFECTS OF SOCIAL EVALUATION

A central goal for many people is gaining, or keeping, the approval of others. Situations that include the possibility of social evaluation, then, are likely to be stressful. Supporting such a view, cardiovascular reactivity during tasks is generally higher when there is evaluation by others (Smith, Nealey, Kircher, & Limon, 1997; Wright et al., 1995). Social evaluation can clearly affect one's task goals—both how they are appraised and how they are accomplished.

Research has shown that an audience can markedly affect task performance and that such effects are not confined only to humans. Social facilitation (Zajonc, 1965), a phenomenon in which the dominant response is enhanced in the presence of social evaluators, has been found in chickens, rats, and even cockroaches, as well as in humans (Zajonc, 1965; Zajonc, Heingartner, & Herman, 1969). Research in this field has shown that simple or well-practiced tasks are enhanced by the presence of others, whereas more complex ones, or those that are novel, are impaired. Some of this effect seems to be derived from the mere presence of others, though the effect does seem magnified when the audience is in a position to evaluate performance (Cottrell, 1968). This effect is thought to be arousal driven, which is supported by the finding that CVR in the face of an audience differs as a function of task familiarity. Those performing previously learned tasks have been found to show "challenge" CVR patterns, whereas those performing unlearned tasks show "threat" CVR patterns (Blascovich, Mendes, Hunter, & Salomon, 1999). This suggests that the presence of an audience can enable action, though only for tasks we know how to perform.

The addition of an audience can, as suggested by Hull-Spence models (Spence & Spence, 1967), create additional drive and thus have social facilitation effects. However, it can have other sorts of effects as well, including changing the set of relevant goals in the situation. That is, in addition to the accomplishment of the concrete goal, one also has the added goal of doing so in a way that wins the approval of an audience. It is likely that success in survival goals remains unaffected by an audience; when fleeing a predator, one's success is likely measured entirely by one's survival. When diffusing a bomb, it is unlikely that one cares about whether an audience was impressed by performance. In situations in which one's well-being is not immediately threatened, however, there is room to care about social approval. As a result, many modern stressors have become less concrete, with both the goal itself and one's success in its accomplishment becoming relatively ambiguous. Although survival could reasonably be seen as the mark of success for most primitive stressors, indicators of success for modern social stressors are more difficult to pinpoint and are not always immediate.

Giving a public speech, for example, could be seen as a stressor with a relatively concrete goal, namely, to deliver information to an audience. However, the goal is, of course, more complicated than that because one tends to not only wish to complete giving the speech but also to win the approval of the audience. Approval, however, is multidimensional and difficult to assess.

It is likely that each audience member will have different criteria by which to judge performance, and it is also likely that approval will lie on a spectrum rather than be dichotomous. In addition, there is no standard means by which an audience member concretely communicates approval. Even applause can be ambiguous—one can be left wondering whether the applause was loud enough, genuine, or unanimous.

This ambiguity of success could apply also to stressors that are not fundamentally social by nature. Kicking a field goal, for example, is a very concrete task, yet one can imagine that attempting it without an audience is a very different experience from doing it with social evaluators present. Even if the ball is successfully kicked through the uprights, it is likely one would likely feel less than completely successful if an audience watching the feat did not respond with applause.

Uncertainty of successful completion could also apply to situations with an informal audience. Social others need not be watching from bleacher seats to be evaluative. Indeed, the majority of social evaluators in our lives are much less formal: in-laws sitting across the dinner table, a colleague looking over your work, or a blind date seeing you for the first time. In such cases, success is even more difficult to measure because there is no standard response, nor a standard time to give it, to indicate approval. The most inherently social goals, therefore, are also the goals whose completion is most difficult to determine.

The presence of an audience, therefore, whether it is formal or informal, can turn even concrete stressors with clear courses of action into ambiguous goals with no clear measure of success. This type of stressor leads to net metabolic losses in terms of the stress response because we experience physiological activation but receive no concrete benefits from that activation in addressing the threat. We refer to these goals as *indeterminate goals* because both their nature and duration are uncertain. This uncertainty, as discussed in the following section, can prevent goal completion, which will potentially carry steep cognitive, affective, and physiological costs. These, in the long run, can carry serious consequences for cardiovascular health.

THE IMPORTANCE OF GOAL COMPLETION

Goal completion is important not only for self-esteem but also for returning to baseline—both physically and emotionally—after facing a task. Task completion affects the way we think about and remember the task. This classic phenomenon, known as the *Zeigarnik effect*, was first described in 1927 by Russian psychologist Bluma Zeigarnik when she noticed that waiters had a better memory for orders that were not yet completed. Although this improved memory may seem beneficial and can be used in the right contexts to improve learning or bring the right entrée, these lingering memories can also be dissonant and intrusive. Generally, this phenomenon suggests that the tension accompanying incomplete tasks solidifies them in our memories, and the completion that erases such memories is alleviating rather than destructive (Lewin, 1927).

It is possible that the notion of task completion will be sensitive to social feedback rather than just to the overt nominal goals related to the task. A lack of proper applause from an audience, or even a lingering question of whether the given applause was sufficient, could lead to pervasive intrusive memories by leaving one feeling that the given task was not actually completed. That is, the nominal task itself may be completed, but the social task remains an active challenge until one receives a clear indication of success.

Lack of completion of unpleasant tasks can lead not only to remembering them but also to rumination or intrusive thoughts. *Rumination*, or mentally dwelling on and reliving experiences, has been found to predict depressive episodes (Nolen-Hoeksema, 2000) and to worsen depression (Nolen-Hoeksema, 1991), whereas learning not to ruminate has been found to prevent depression (Morrow & Nolen-Hoeksema, 1990). Fixation on social failures, then, could significantly alter mood, turning a nominal acute stressor into a chronic psychological one. One could finish kicking the field goal but still mentally relive the experience wondering what went wrong.

Rumination can also affect physiology. Several studies have found that, following a psychological stressor, physiological return to baseline is delayed by rumination (Gerin, Davidson, Christenfeld, Goyal, & Schwartz, 2006). Participants in one study (Glynn, Christenfeld, & Gerin, 2002) performed a mental arithmetic task with harassment, after which they were either given a distracting magazine to read or left to sit and ponder the prior task. For those given a mental distraction, blood pressure returned to baseline levels significantly more quickly than for those ruminating on the task. Immediate cardiovascular responses to indeterminate goals, therefore, may not be fundamentally different than to concrete goals, but levels can remain elevated because of cognitive processes that follow such tasks. This may occur particularly in the face of social failure.

Research and folk psychology have long linked stress with cardiovascular disease (CVD) (cf. Pickering, 2001; Rozanski, Blumenthal, & Kaplan, 1999). Although there is evidence that acute stressors can contribute to CVD over time, it appears that chronically elevated heart rate and blood pressure, which can be due to chronic stressors or chronically ruminating over a short stressor, is potentially most damaging to the heart (McEwen, 1997). Brosschot, Gerin, and Thayer (2006) investigated the role of rumination, or perseverative cognition, in the development of heart disease and concluded that this extended mental activation of stressors may be a critical and perhaps necessary component in the link between psychological disorders and CVD (see also Larsen & Christenfeld, 2009).

The link between rumination and heart disease is not entirely speculative. A longitudinal study investigating the health effects of worry found that, over 20 years, men who worried more had a higher chance of developing heart disease (Kubzansky et al., 1997). In fact, worry over social conditions was most predictive of poor future health: Those with the highest levels of social worry had a 50% increased risk in both fatal and nonfatal coronary heart disease (CHD). The potential for social worry in particular to negatively impact health is underscored by the fact that this increased the risk of CHD more than did worry over health conditions. Of course, many different pathways could explain the link between social worry and CHD. It is not unreasonable, however, to believe that extended worry and rumination over unfinished, or unfinishable, social tasks could directly affect the cardiovascular system by extending reactivity.

STRESS AND FAILURE COMPENSATION

Just as the knowledge that one must perform a task can be stressful and, ultimately, lead to physiological arousal, failing a task can likewise be stressful and perhaps produce even greater arousal. This principle is likely what drives the effectiveness of laboratory tasks such as mental arithmetic with harassment, in which participants are repeatedly told they are not performing subtraction problems quickly or accurately enough. This task routinely produces spikes in blood pressure, likely because the participants not only are faced with a very difficult task but are also led to believe that they are not doing it well.

From a viewpoint of stress being enabling, it is easy to understand why this enhanced arousal would occur. If, for example, one's attempt to escape a predator is unsuccessful, greater mobilization of energy would be useful indeed. The added stress in this situation is not so much a sign that one has failed but an attempt by the body to enable compensation for the previous failure. Although it is possible that these physiological changes could have health consequences later on, it is unlikely that this stress will be chronic and continue after one has successfully escaped the predator.

Here again, however, social stressors are different from concrete survival tasks. That one feels added stress by failing in front of an audience is unquestioned. This stress, however, is not particularly enabling because there is rarely a clear course of action for compensating for social failures. Knowing that the speech you just delivered failed to impress the audience, for example, could be extremely stressful and physiologically arousing, yet that arousal would not necessarily facilitate actions that would improve your reputation among the audience. There is often nothing one can do to address the damage caused by social failures and if there is, it is rarely immediate and physical and rarely enhanced by marked physiological arousal. An audience, therefore, could be particularly damaging to health when one is not especially prone to success. The added stress incurs greater costs on the body, with few, if any, of the intended benefits.

SOCIAL SUPPORT

The preceding sections suggest a negative outlook on the social world and its effects on goal attainment and the cardiovascular system. Of course, this cannot be the whole story because research has shown time and again that social networks are beneficial for mental and physical health (see Uchino, Cacioppo, & Kiecolt-Glaser, 1996). Darwin (1871) actually suggested that our social nature was the most important adaptation of human beings, promoting survival rather than threatening health. Although the effects of audiences may suggest that social isolation would be safer for cardiovascular health, social isolation has actually been identified as a key risk factor for heart disease (House, Landis, & Umberson, 1988). How, then, can these two accounts of the social world be reconciled?

Clearly there is a marked difference between social evaluation and social support. Although social evaluation can be threatening and enhance stress, social support can be calming and decrease stress levels. Supporting the latter view, the *buffering hypothesis* (Cohen & Wills, 1985) suggests that social support enhances health by making stressful experiences less distressing. Although there is evidence that social support has a positive main effect on health regardless of stress level (Cohen & Wills, 1985), the buffering hypothesis has also received empirical support. In one of the most convincing studies, men in Sweden were followed for 7 years, during which they recorded health status, life stressors, and social support (Rosengren, Orth-Gomer, Wedel, & Wilhelmsen, 1993). Those with more life stressors had a higher mortality rate, unless they had sufficient social support. Mortality for the latter looked similar to those who had not faced significant stressors, supporting the idea that social support buffered the effects of stress.

Although a social audience can increase stress by making goal completion more ambiguous, the presence of others can sometimes counteract this stress by disambiguating our goals, the paths to be taken to accomplish them, and our degree of success along the way. Previous research has found that CVR during stressful tasks is decreased when friends are present (Gerin, Milner,

Chawla, & Pickering, 1995; Kamarck, Manuck, & Jennings, 1990) but only when those friends were in a nonevaluative position (e.g., were distracted with another task or given headphones). This line of research has suggested that friends buffer stress particularly when they cannot be evaluative (Kamarck, Peterman, & Raynor, 1998; Kors, Linden, & Gerin, 1997).

It is unlikely, however, that friends not being in a position to evaluate is necessary to their being beneficial. Surely if the threat inherent to social evaluation is that of being evaluated unfavorably, receiving favorable evaluations should eliminate the effects of negative evaluation or even reverse them. Research in fact has suggested this is true. In one study, participants were assigned to give a public speech either alone, with a supportive audience member, or with a nonsupportive audience member (Lepore, Allen, & Evans, 1993). While anticipating and giving the speech, those with a nonsupportive audience member showed significantly higher increases in blood pressure than those who were alone or supported. The smallest increases in blood pressure, however, were found in those with a supportive audience member who nodded and smiled as they delivered their speech. These results underscore the potential hazards of social evaluation when a social audience is nonresponsive, yet also show that positive social feedback can be cardioprotective, even compared with being alone. Further investigation of this effect has replicated these results (though emphasized that cardiovascular benefits may partially depend on qualities of the audience; Christenfeld et al., 1997; Glynn, Christenfeld, & Gerin, 1999). These results show that social support need not merely provide a calming effect of having a nonevaluative friend nearby but that social support can buffer stress by disambiguating indeterminate goals. Because one of the key sources of stress in these tasks is determining success, concrete indications of success provided by a social audience can decrease stress, suggesting that one is achieving both the nominal and social goals involved.

Using other people as sources of information can confer marked health benefits in situations outside the lab as well. In a classic study, Kulik, Mahler, and Moore (1996) examined recovery times for coronary bypass patients on the basis of their experience with their effectively randomly assigned preoperative roommates. They found two main effects: First, those who roomed with other cardiac patients were discharged from the hospital sooner; second, patients left sooner if their roommates were postoperative rather than preoperative, regardless of the type of surgery. Moreover, these effects were additive, so that those with the shortest recovery time in the hospital were those whose roommates were postoperative bypass patients. People with such roommates were also found to be more ambulatory following surgery. They affiliated with their roommates as much as patients with other types of roommates but received more "cognitive clarity" about their operations. This provision of information was found to reduce anxiety leading up to surgery. Those in a room by themselves without access to such information took significantly longer to recover and were less ambulatory following surgery than those with roommates. There was no significant difference in recovery time, however, between those rooming alone and those whose roommates were preoperative and non-cardiac—those providing the least amount of pertinent information. This suggests that the benefits of a roommate did not come from simple companionship but from the information roommates could provide.

Social others, therefore, can be valuable sources of information during stressful times. This can reduce stress through several mechanisms. First, it can reduce the perception of a threat, referred to by Lazarus as *primary appraisal* (Lazarus & Folkman, 1984). Those anticipating major surgery, for example, were likely reassured by seeing postoperative patients who had made it through the surgery relatively unscathed, and they may have perceived the process as less threatening. Second, social others could reduce stress through offering concrete ways to deal with the threat, thus affecting *secondary appraisal* (Lazarus & Folkman, 1984). This may include performing tasks that directly address the threat or simply providing information about such coping mechanisms. As suggested earlier, this could include providing concrete suggestions of behaviors that would reduce recovery time or increase comfort after surgery. In these cases postoperative stress, to some degree, could be considered beneficial because it could enable these coping behaviors, particularly those that are primarily physical. By directing behavior, social others could thus play the role of funneling diffuse stress-induced arousal into targeted survival-enhancing behaviors. Of course, with the work on postoperative recovery, the stressor itself is clear, immediate, and nonsocial. Impressing one's roommate is likely to be rather subordinate to surviving the surgery.

THE IMPORTANCE OF SOCIAL GOALS

When discussing the effects of success in social goals, it seems worth exploring how important and prevalent such goals actually are. Should they be inconsequential, it is unlikely that the introduction of social goals would significantly change a concrete task. Similarly, should these goals be infrequent, it is unlikely that the stress arising from their ambiguity could actually affect health in any significant way. Of course, it is difficult to quantify just how often we encounter social goals; as described previously, many nonsocial goals can become quasisocial just with the introduction of an observer. At the extreme, one could perhaps argue that anytime one performs a task outside of total isolation, the task carries a social goal.

That social goals are important to us is underscored by the fact that CVR increases in the face of an audience, particularly for tasks in which we feel we could impress social evaluators (Wright et al., 1998). Furthermore, although CVR has been shown to increase commensurate with monetary rewards offered for completing a task, reactivity also shows similar parallel increases when the status of a social evaluator increases (Wright, Killebrew, & Pimpalapure, 2002). Gaining social approval, then, may be both essential and quotidian, much like earning a paycheck.

The importance of social goals is highlighted in Maslow's famous hierarchy of needs (1970). This theory posits that after basic physiological and safety needs are met, our next most important goals are feeling loved and belonging, followed by receiving respect and esteem. This suggests a critical role for social goals. One could also argue that receiving social approval could also significantly contribute to the more basic physiological and safety needs. It is likely that when Darwin touted the advantages of the social nature of humans, he was focusing on the increased likelihood of finding food and protection when one is part of a group (Darwin, 1871). Gaining approval from others, then, is not necessarily a peripheral goal but directly or indirectly tied to the majority of goals necessary to surviving and feeling happy and fulfilled. It should not seem so surprising, then, that the potential for social failure can be so distressing or that indications of success from social others should be calming.

Social goals, and people's sensitivity to social feedback, have a number of effects on stress responses, many of which serve to reduce the adaptive advantages of that physiological activation and also serve to exacerbate its negative effects. Social goals are rarely achieved with immediate action and so do not generally require the mobilization of energy and rarely involve physical wounds; thus, activation of the immune system is also generally unwarranted. Furthermore, and perhaps most critically for disease, they tend not to have clear endpoints. A bad boss, needy children, and a failing marriage can certainly involve periods of acute stress, but these factors are mostly associated with generalized, chronic stress. It is not necessarily the activation that occurs during the actual interaction with the boss that is damaging but the fact that it can linger indefinitely, spurred by rumination. This can multiply the negative health ramifications of stress. There are certainly times when the presence of other people is desirable and promotes health, especially when the stressor is concrete and they can offer direct coping assistance. However, Sartre (1944) captured something essential about the long-term health consequences of vague, indeterminate, stress-prolonging effects of social goals when he wrote, "L'enfer, c'est les autres" [Hell is other people].

REFERENCES

Blascovich, J., Mendes, W. B., Hunter, S. B., & Salomon, K. (1999). Social "facilitation" as challenge and threat. *Journal of Personality and Social Psychology, 77,* 68–77. doi:10.1037/0022-3514.77.1.68

Brosschot, J. F., Gerin, W., & Thayer, J. F. (2006). The perseverative cognition hypothesis: A review of worry, prolonged stress-related physiological activation, and health. *Journal of Psychosomatic Research, 60,* 113–124. doi:10.1016/j.jpsychores.2005.06.074

Chafin, S., Christenfeld, N., & Gerin, W. (2008). Improving cardiovascular recovery from stress with brief poststress exercise. *Health Psychology, 27*(1, Suppl), S64–S72. doi:10.1037/0278-6133.27.1(Suppl.).S64

Christenfeld, N., Gerin, W., Linden, W., Sanders, M., Mathur, J., Deich, J. D., & Pickering, T. G. (1997). Social support effects on cardiovascular reactivity: Is a stranger as effective as a friend? *Psychosomatic Medicine, 59*(4), 388–398.

Cohen, S., Tyrrell, D. A. J., & Smith, A. P. (1991). Psychological stress and susceptibility to the common cold. *The New England Journal of Medicine, 325,* 606–612. doi:10.1056/NEJM199108293250903

Cohen, S., & Wills, T. A. (1985). Stress, social support, and the buffering hypothesis. *Psychological Bulletin, 98*(2), 310–357. doi:10.1037/0033-2909.98.2.310

Cottrell, N. B. (1968). Performance in the presence of other human beings: Mere presence, audience, and affiliation effects. In E. C. Simmel, R. A. Hoppe, & G. A. Milton (Eds.), *Social facilitation and imitative behavior* (pp. 91–110). Boston, MA: Allyn & Bacon.

Darwin, C. (1871). *The descent of man.* London, England: J. Murray.

Dhabhar, F. S. (2000). Acute stress enhances while chronic stress suppresses skin immunity: The role of stress hormones and leukocyte trafficking. *Annals of the New York Academy of Sciences, 917,* 876–893. doi:10.1111/j.1749-6632.2000.tb05454.x

Gendolla, G. H. E., & Richter, M. (2006). Cardiovascular reactivity during performance under social evaluation: The moderating role of task difficulty. *International Journal of Psychophysiology, 62,* 185–192. doi:10.1016/j.ijpsycho.2006.04.002

Gerin, W., Davidson, K. W., Christenfeld, N. J. S., Goyal, T., & Schwartz, J. E. (2006). The role of angry rumination and distraction in blood pressure recovery from emotional arousal. *Psychosomatic Medicine, 68,* 64–72. doi:10.1097/01.psy.0000195747.12404.aa

Gerin, W., Milner, D., Chawla, S., & Pickering, T. G. (1995). Social support as a moderator of cardiovascular reactivity in women: A test of the direct effects and buffering hypotheses. *Psychosomatic Medicine, 57,* 16–22.

Glynn, L. M., Christenfeld, N., & Gerin, W. (1999). Gender, social support, and cardiovascular responses to stress. *Psychosomatic Medicine, 61,* 234–242.

Glynn, L. M., Christenfeld, N., & Gerin, W. (2002). The role of rumination in recovery from reactivity: Cardiovascular consequences of emotional states. *Psychosomatic Medicine, 64*, 714–726. doi:10.1097/01.PSY.0000031574.42041.23

House, J. S., Landis, K. R., & Umberson, D. (1988, July 29). Social relationships and health. *Science, 241*, 540–545. doi:10.1126/science.3399889

Kamarck, T. W., Manuck, S. B., & Jennings, J. R. (1990). Social support reduces cardiovascular reactivity to psychological challenge: A laboratory model. *Psychosomatic Medicine, 52*, 42–58.

Kamarck, T. W., Peterman, A. H., & Raynor, D. A. (1998). The effects of the social environment on stress-related cardiovascular activation: Current findings, prospects, and implications. *Annals of Behavioral Medicine, 20*, 247–256. doi:10.1007/BF02886374

Kors, D. J., Linden, W., & Gerin, W. (1997). Evaluation interferes with social support: Effects on cardiovascular stress reactivity in women. *Journal of Social and Clinical Psychology, 16*, 1–23. doi:10.1521/jscp.1997.16.1.1

Kubzansky, L. D., Kawachi, I., Spiro, A., III, Weiss, S. T., Vokonas, P. S., & Sparrow, D. (1997). Is worrying bad for your heart? A prospective study of worry and coronary heart disease in the Normative Aging Study. *Circulation, 95*, 818–824.

Kulik, J. A., Mahler, H. I., & Moore, P. J. (1996). Social comparison and affiliation under threat: Effects on recovery from major surgery. *Journal of Personality and Social Psychology, 71*, 967–979. doi:10.1037/0022-3514.71.5.967

Larsen, B. A., & Christenfeld, N. J. S. (2009). Cardiovascular disease and psychiatric comorbidity: The potential role of perseverative cognition. *Cardiovascular Psychiatry and Neurology, 2009*, 1–9. doi:10.1155/2009/791017.

Lazarus, R. S., & Folkman, S. (1984). *Stress, appraisal, and coping*. New York, NY: Springer.

Lepore, S. J., Allen, K. A., & Evans, G. W. (1993). Social support lowers cardiovascular reactivity to an acute stressor. *Psychosomatic Medicine, 55*, 518–524.

Lewin, B. D. (1927). A study of the endocrine organs in the psychoses. *American Journal of Psychiatry, 7*, 391.

Maslow, A. H. (1970). *Motivation and personality*. New York, NY: Harper & Row.

McEwen, B. S. (1997). Stress, brain, and behaviour: Life-long effects of upon health and disease. In J. M. Kinney & H. N. Tucker (Eds.), *Physiology, stress, and malnutrition. Functional correlates of nutritional intervention* (pp. 113–130). Philadelphia, PA: Lippincott-Raven.

Morrow, J., & Nolen-Hoeksema, S. (1990). Effects of responses to depression on the remediation of depressive affect. *Journal of Personality and Social Psychology, 58*, 519–527. doi:10.1037/0022-3514.58.3.519

Nolen-Hoeksema, S. (1991). Responses to depression and their effects on the duration of depressive episodes. *Journal of Abnormal Psychology, 100*, 569–582. doi:10.1037/0021-843X.100.4.569

Nolen-Hoeksema, S. (2000). The role of rumination in depressive disorders and mixed anxiety/depressive symptoms. *Journal of Abnormal Psychology, 109*, 504–511. doi:10.1037/0021-843X.109.3.504

Pickering, T. G. (2001). Mental stress as a causal factor in the development of hypertension and cardiovascular disease. *Current Hypertension Reports, 3*, 249–254. doi:10.1007/s11906-001-0047-1

Rosengren, A., Orth-Gomer, K., Wedel, H., & Wilhelmsen, L. (1993). Stressful life events, social support, and mortality in men born in 1933. *British Medical Journal, 307*, 1102–1105. doi:10.1136/bmj.307.6912.1102

Rozanski, A., Blumenthal, J. A., & Kaplan, J. (1999). Impact of psychological factors on the pathogenesis of cardiovascular disease and implications for therapy. *Circulation, 99*, 2192–2217.

Sapolsky, R. M. (1998). *Why zebras don't get ulcers*. New York, NY: Friedman.

Sartre, J.-P. (1987). *Huis clos* [No exit] (K. Gore, Ed.). Oxford, England: Routledge.

Schwartz, G. E., Weinberger, D. A., & Singer, J. A. (1981). Cardiovascular differentiation of happiness, sadness, anger, and fear following imagery and exercise. *Psychosomatic Medicine, 43*, 343–364.

Smith, T. W., Nealey, J. B., Kircher, J. C., & Limon, J. P. (1997). Social determinants of cardiovascular reactivity: Effects of incentive to exert influence and evaluate threat. *Psychophysiology, 34*, 65–73. doi:10.1111/j.1469-8986.1997.tb02417.x

Spence, K. W., & Spence, J. T. (1967). *The psychology of learning and motivation*. New York, NY: Academic Press.

Tomaka, J., Blascovich, J., Kelsey, R. M., & Leitten, C. L. (1997). Subjective, physiological, and behavioral effects of threat and challenge appraisal. *Journal of Personality and Social Psychology, 73*, 63–72. doi:10.1037/0022-3514.73.1.63

Trichopoulos, D., Zavitsanos, X., Katsouyanni, K., Tzonou, A., & Dalla-Vorgia, P. (1983, February 26). Psychological stress and fatal heart attack: The Athens (1981) earthquake natural experiment. *The Lancet, 321*, 441–444. doi:10.1016/S0140-6736(83)91439-3

Uchino, B. N., Cacioppo, J. T., & Kiecolt-Glaser, J. K. (1996). The relationship between social support and physiological processes: A review with emphasis on underlying mechanisms and implications for health. *Psychological Bulletin, 119*, 488–531. doi:10.1037/0033-2909.119.3.488

Wright, R. A., Dill, J. C., Geen, R. G., & Anderson, C. A. (1998). Social evaluation influence on cardiovascular response to a fixed behavioral challenge: Effects across a range of difficulty levels. *Annals of Behavioral Medicine, 20*, 277–285. doi:10.1007/BF02886377

Wright, R. A., Killebrew, K., & Pimpalapure, D. (2002). Cardiovascular incentive effects where a challenge is unfixed: Demonstrations involving social evaluation, evaluator status, and monetary reward. *Psychophysiology, 39*, 188–197. doi:10.1111/1469-8986.3920188

Wright, R. A., Tunstall, A. M., Williams, B. J., Goodwin, J. S., & Harmon-Jones, E. (1995). Social evaluation and cardiovascular response: An active coping approach. *Journal of Personality and Social Psychology, 69*, 530–543. doi:10.1037/0022-3514.69.3.530

Zajonc, R. B. (1965, July 16). Social facilitation. *Science, 149*, 269–274. doi:10.1126/science.149.3681.269

Zajonc, R. B., Heingartner, A., & Herman, E. M. (1969). Social enhancement and impairment of performance in the cockroach. *Journal of Personality and Social Psychology, 13*, 83–92. doi:10.1037/h0028063

Zeigarnik, B. (1927). Über das behalten von erledigten und unerledigten handlungen [On the memory for completed and uncompleted tasks]. *Psychologische Forschung, 9*, 1–85.

17

EFFORT MECHANISMS LINKING SEX TO CARDIOVASCULAR RESPONSE: TOWARD A COMPREHENSIVE ANALYSIS WITH RELEVANCE FOR HEALTH

REX A. WRIGHT AND PATRICIA BARRETO

For some time now, research scientists have explored the possibility that sex might play an important and decipherable role in determining cardiovascular (CV) responses (i.e., elevations above baseline) in people confronted with performance challenges (Lash, Gillespie, Eisler, & Southard, 1991; Leinwand, 2003; Matthews, Davis, Stoney, Owens, & Caggiula, 1991). They have done so primarily for reasons related to health. Specifically, they have speculated that an improved understanding of sex influence on CV response might lead to an improved understanding of documented sex disparities in negative health outcomes, such as increased mortality from coronary artery disease in men (e.g., Saab, 1989).

A common assumption has been that chronically exaggerated CV responses predispose people to negative health outcomes (Glass, 1977; Surwit, Williams, & Shapiro, 1982; see also Chapters 11 and 14, this volume; cf. Chapter 12, this volume). Initially, this led investigators to search for main effect sex influences (Stoney, Davis, & Matthews, 1987). However, literature reviews and emerging studies uncovered a full range of CV sex effects, including ones that showed stronger responses in men, ones that showed stronger responses in women, and ones that showed equivalent responses between the

343

sexes (Atienza, Henderson, Wilcox, & King, 2001; Brown & Smith, 1992; Davis & Matthews, 1996; Jorgensen & Houston, 1981; Matthews & Stoney, 1988; Smith, Limon, Gallo, & Ngu, 1996; Stroud, Niaura, & Stoney, 2001; Van Egeren, 1979; van Well, Kolk, & Klugkist, 2008). Collectively, the CV sex effects provided the suggestion that sex does not exert a simple influence on CV responses but a complex one that varies with the performance context and personal characteristics (apart from sex) of the performer.

In this chapter, we examine the issue of sex influence on CV response from the perspective of an integrative analysis of ability, effort, and CV response that has long guided research in our laboratory (Wright & Kirby, 2001). We examine this issue with the goal of drawing attention to the potential of the analysis for explaining a variety of sex effects that have been observed and for anticipating new ones. Other articles have considered the sex influence issue from this perspective (e.g., Wright, Murray, Storey, & Williams, 1997). However, they have not done so as inclusively as we do here. We begin our presentation by describing the integrative analysis and considering some of its general effort and CV response implications. We then spell out implications of the integrative analysis for CV sex influence, review evidence relevant to them, and make several observations of theoretical and practical interest.

THE INTEGRATIVE ANALYSIS

The *integrative analysis* is an amalgam of ideas proposed decades ago by Paul Obrist and Jack Brehm. It is concerned with predicting CV responses in people who are invited or allowed to act in some fashion. In making predictions, the analysis distinguishes between situations in which performance challenges are fixed and ones in which they are unfixed. *Fixed challenges* are conceived as ones that call for a particular level of performance. *Unfixed challenges* are conceived as ones that do not. Predictions in both situations have implications for sex influence on CV response. However, in the interest of brevity, we focus here on the fixed challenge circumstance.

The Obrist component of the integrative analysis consists of what many refer to as his *active coping hypothesis* (Obrist, 1981), the idea that sympathetic nervous system influence on the CV system increases with effort or task engagement—what Obrist termed *active coping*. The Brehm component is Brehm's theory of motivation intensity (Brehm & Self, 1989; see also Chapter 6, this volume). *Motivation intensity theory* identifies conditions under which people should exert more and less effort. Consequently, when married with Obrist's hypothesis, it constitutes a framework for predicting sympathetic CV effects.

Effort as a Function of Difficulty

Motivation intensity theory holds that effort (i.e., motivation intensity) is not determined by needs and incentives directly, as motivation theorists traditionally have assumed. Rather, it is determined by the difficulty of imminent or ongoing behavior. If little effort is required to meet a performance challenge, then little should be exerted. As the difficulty of the challenge increases, so should effort up to one of two points: (a) that at which success appears excessively difficult, given the available "payoff" (i.e., is "too difficult") or (b) that at which success appears impossible. Once these challenge difficulty points have been reached, then effort should drop to a low level and remain low at all difficulty levels thereafter. Thus, a core proposition of the integrative analysis is that effort and associated CV responses should rise with the difficulty of a performance challenge until success appears impossible or calls for more effort than performers are willing to exert, and then fall sharply.

Upper Limit of Effort

In theory, the upper limit of what people will be willing to do in a performance situation should be determined by their perception of how important it is to succeed. Perceived success importance, in turn, should be determined by two things: (a) the value that performers place on the available incentive (e.g. food) and (b) the performers' expectancy of obtaining the incentive if behavior is performed successfully. The latter construct has been discussed variously over the years (see Heckhausen, 1991; Vroom, 1964) but most often in terms of the expression *outcome expectancy* (Maddux, 1995). Consequently, we refer to it as outcome expectancy here. The greater the value placed on the incentive and the higher the expectancy, the higher should be importance appraisals and, ultimately, the upper effort limit.

Notably, the value a performer places on an available incentive should be a function of two factors as well: the character of the incentive and the performer's need for the incentive. To illustrate, consider a pharmaceutical representative who is provided the chance to win a holiday cash bonus by selling 500 units of a product. Presumably, the value the representative would place on the bonus would be determined by its amount (i.e., its character) and the representative's current financial situation (i.e., his or her need). The higher the amount offered and the direr the representative's situation, the more value the representative should place on the bonus.

Also notably, the preceding reasoning should apply where incentives are aversive (avoidant) as well as where they are attractive (approach). Just as people can be driven to attain outcomes, they also can be driven to avoid outcomes. The importance of avoidance should be a function of the negative value placed on the outcome to be avoided and performers' expectancy of avoiding the outcome if required behavior is performed successfully. The negative value placed on the outcome, in turn, should be a function of the character of the outcome and the performers' need to avoid it. Thus, a boy on the beach might negatively value a potential back slap from his buddy to the extent that (a) he expects the slap to be forceful and (b) his skin has been burned from the sun. A more forceful slap would have an especially aversive character, and the boy would have a greater need to avoid all slaps the more burned his skin has been.

Some Implications

An important implication of these ideas is that people should sometimes show marked variations in what they are willing to do in a performance context because of variations in their appraisal of the available incentive's value and their confidence that they will secure the incentive if they meet the performance challenge (i.e., their outcome expectancy). Consider here, for example, students in a private school given the chance to win a well-crafted King James Bible by earning an A in an academic term. If some students were Christian and others were not, the students could vary sharply in how hard they were willing to work. As a group, the non-Christian students presumably would have a limited need for the incentive. They also might not fully appreciate the incentive's quality (i.e., its physical character) because of a lack of familiarity with this type of text and—depending on their circumstance—could doubt that their parents would allow them to accept the Bible if they won it.

Another implication is that group differences in the willingness to exert effort in a performance situation should not necessarily be manifested in actual effort and associated CV responses. In theory, effort should be proportional to challenge difficulty—not appraisals of success importance—so long as performers view success as possible and worthwhile. This means that so long as a possible performance challenge does not call for more effort than a less willing group can or will expend, then effort and CV responses for the less willing group should be equivalent to corresponding responses of a more willing group. Also in theory, effort should be low irrespective of success importance where success appears impossible and too difficult, given the contingent benefit (i.e., incentive). Thus, where a challenge calls for more than either a less or a more willing group can or will do, then effort and CV responses should be low for both groups. Following the integrative analysis logic discussed thus far, one would expect a variation in willingness to affect effort and CV responsiveness only where it leads some to conclude that success on a possible task is worthwhile and others to conclude that it is not. In such a circumstance, the more willing group should evince effort and CV responses that are proportional to difficulty, whereas the less willing group should evince minimal effort and CV responsiveness (for further relevant discussion, see Chapter 4, this volume).

Perceived Ability

The integrative analysis considers not only the roles that challenge difficulty and success importance play in determining effort and associated CV responses but also the role that ability perception plays in determining them. It does so by way of the assumption that people who view themselves as relatively incapable (relatively unable) with respect to a performance challenge should perceive success as harder than people who view themselves as relatively capable (relatively able) with respect to the task. If this is true, a number of additional implications ensue, including the following:

- Effort and associated CV responses should be greater for low- than for high-ability people so long as those with low ability view success as possible and worthwhile. This is because low-ability people should have to expend more effort to compensate for their lack of ability.
- Effort and associated CV responses should peak at a lower challenge difficulty level for low- than for high-ability people. This is because low-ability people should attain more quickly that difficulty level at which success requires more than they can or will do.
- Effort and associated CV responses should be low for both low- and high-ability people where challenge difficulty is high enough to cause success to appear impossible or excessive to both groups. This is because effort would not be justified, regardless of ability.
- Success importance should set the upper limit of effort and associated CV responses for all performers so long as they view success as possible. Thus, for example, high-ability people who place low value on an available incentive should withhold effort at a lower difficulty level than high-ability people who place high value on the incentive.

Taking into account ability perception, the integrative analysis provides an even richer framework for anticipating CV responses. It also highlights the theoretical point that ability appraisals do not exert simple effort and CV response effects but rather exert complex ones that are dependent on the level of challenge difficulty and success importance.

IMPLICATIONS FOR CARDIOVASCULAR SEX INFLUENCE

The preceding integrative reasoning highlights three ways in which sex could influence CV response in a performance circumstance. One is by affecting the value that performers place on available incentives. Another is by affecting performers' outcome expectancy. The third is by affecting ability perception with respect to the performance challenge. In the sections that follow, we consider each of these paths of influence in turn.

Value Appraisals

It is reasonable to assume that men and women sometimes differ in the value they place on available performance incentives. Differences in valuing could emerge for numerous reasons, including social, evolutionary, and constitutional ones. Thus, for example, men could be socialized to evaluate more favorably the character of certain types of clothing (e.g., trousers), whereas women could be socialized to evaluate more favorably the character of other types of clothing (e.g., skirts). Men also could be socialized to especially value accomplishment in certain career realms (e.g., firefighter), whereas women could be socialized to especially value accomplishment in others (e.g., kindergarten teacher). Evolutionary forces could have pressed men to evaluate more favorably certain mate characteristics (e.g., physical beauty) and women to evaluate more favorably others (e.g., wealth; Buss & Schmitt, 1993). These forces also could have pressed men to especially value outcomes associated with aggression (e.g., justice) and women to especially value outcomes associated with altruism (e.g., nurturance; Wood & Eagly, 2002). Regarding constitution, sex-specific physical vulnerabilities could lead men to value certain protective devices (e.g., athletic supporters) and women to value others (e.g., sports bras). Similarly, sex-specific physical attractiveness concerns (i.e., ones related to secondary sex characteristics) could lead men to value some grooming products (e.g., beard trimmers) and women to value others (e.g., lipstick).

Regardless of why sex differences in valuing might emerge or the form that they might take (i.e., greater for men or women), their presence should inject potential for sex differences in effort and CV response. Whether the potential is realized should depend on the character of the performance situation. Specifically, the integrative analysis implies the following:

- So long as success appears possible and worthwhile to both sexes, both should exert effort in proportion to difficulty and display corresponding levels of CV response. Thus, under these performance conditions, there should be no sex difference in effort-related CV response.

- If difficulty is high enough that success on a possible task appears worthwhile to the sex that values the incentive more (the "high-value" sex) but not worthwhile to the sex that values the incentive less (the "low-value" sex), then effort and CV responsiveness should be proportional to difficulty for the high-value sex but low for the low-value sex. Thus, in this situation, there should be a sex difference in CV response, with effort and CV responsiveness being greater for the sex that places more value on the incentive.
- If difficulty is so high that success appears impossible or not worthwhile to the high-value sex, then effort and CV responsiveness should be low for both sex groups. Thus, in this case, there should again be no sex difference in effort-related CV response.

Figure 17.1a illustrates the implied interaction between sex and difficulty under conditions where success is possible and one sex places greater

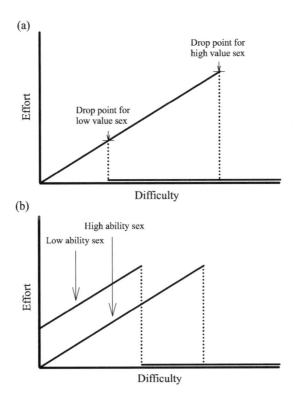

Figure 17.1. Relation between effort and challenge difficulty for the low and high value sex (a). Relation between effort and challenge difficulty for the low and high ability sex (b).

value on the performance incentive. It shows that for the low-value sex, effort and CV response should rise to a relatively low difficulty level before dropping. By contrast, for the high-value sex, effort and CV response should rise to a relatively high level of difficulty before dropping. Thus, CV sex differences should tend to be present in the middle difficulty range but not in the lower and higher difficulty ranges. Further, the size of the differences should increase as difficulty within the middle range rises. Naturally, the exact drop points for the low- and high-value sexes should depend on the exact value the sexes place on the incentive. Thus, precise predictions could be made only with precise knowledge of incentive value appraisals.

Outcome Expectancy

Just as it is reasonable to assume that men and women sometimes differ in the value they place on available performance incentives, it also is reasonable to assume that they sometimes differ in their expectancy of obtaining an incentive if they execute required behavior successfully. In a fantasy world, benefits might flow equally to all performers who meet performance standards. However, in real-world circumstances, benefits frequently flow differently depending on trait considerations, including sex.

At least two features of sex differences in outcome expectancy are worth noting. One is that they can go either way, that is, they can reflect higher expectancies in men or women. To envision a case in which expectancies might be higher in men, imagine a corporation that has never had a female chief executive officer. To envision a case in which expectancies might be higher in women, imagine a university that has never allowed a man to teach women's studies.

The other feature is that the differences can occur whether performance benefits are allocated socially or nonsocially. Many difference examples involve circumstances in which a social entity (i.e., a person or a group) determines what performers receive once they have met a standard. But social allocation is not necessary for differences to be present. Consider, for example, an aerobic exercise class in which students believe that, for biological reasons, exercise is especially likely to produce weight loss in men. In theory, the men should have higher outcome expectancies with respect to the weight loss incentive.

Regardless of where sex differences in expectancy might come from or the form that they might take, the differences should have potential for producing sex differences effort and CV response. Implications of the integrative analysis parallel those delineated in relation to sex differences in value appraisals. First, so long as success appears possible and worthwhile to both sexes, both should exert effort proportional to difficulty and display corresponding CV response levels. Second, if difficulty is high enough that success on a possible task appears worthwhile to the sex that has the higher outcome expectancy (the "high-expectancy" sex) but not to the sex that has the lower outcome expectancy (the "low-expectancy" sex), then effort and CV response should be proportional to difficulty for the high-expectancy sex but low for the low-expectancy sex. Third, if difficulty is so high that success appears impossible or not worthwhile to the high outcome expectancy sex, then effort and CV response should be low for both sexes. These effects can be seen in Figure 17.1a by simply replacing the labels "low-value sex" and "high-value sex" with the labels "low-expectancy sex" and "high-expectancy sex."

Ability

Our third path of CV sex influence is ability perception. It is self-evident that men and women sometimes view themselves as having different performance capacities with respect to different tasks. In some circumstances (e.g., ones involving strength), men tend to feel more capable; in others (e.g., ones involving child care), women do. Sex differences in ability perception are frequently illusory, having resulted from erroneous learning. However, they can be grounded in fact (Halpern, 2000). Where sex differences in ability perception are factually based, they can be so either for enduring constitutional reasons or for training reasons. To illustrate, consider a woman who has less upper body lifting capacity than her brother. Her diminished ability could be a function of her (enduring) skeletomuscular structure. However, it also could be because she was raised to view muscles as "masculine" and, as a result, has avoided activities that would develop hers (i.e., has avoided training).

Once again, the source and form of a sex difference should be unimportant. If the difference exists, it should have potential for producing sex differences in effort and CV response. Implications here are different from those in the value appraisal and outcome expectancy cases. First, effort and associated CV responses should be greater for the sex that feels less capable (the low-ability sex) than for the sex that feels more capable (the high-ability sex) so long as the low-ability sex perceives success as possible and worthwhile (see Figure 17.1b). Second, effort and associated CV responses should peak at a lower challenge difficulty level for the low-ability sex. Third, effort and associated CV responses should be low for both sexes where challenge difficulty is high enough to cause success to appear impossible or excessive to both groups. Fourth, success importance should set the upper limit of effort and associated CV responses for all performers so long as they view success as possible.

EVIDENCE

Of course, it is one thing to hypothesize and another to document. Fortunately, there is empirical support for the sex implications. Much is indirect, coming from studies that created groups with different incentive value appraisals, outcome expectancies, and ability perceptions. However, some is direct, coming from studies in which value appraisals and ability perceptions should—or might—have varied with sex. We now consider briefly this evidence.

Value Appraisal and Outcome Expectancy Implications

Implications related to sex differences in value appraisals and outcome expectancies are conceptually identical and are related to the broad success importance construct. Consequently, we consider them together. Indirect support comes from studies that have confirmed the implied interactional influence of challenge difficulty and importance factors, including incentive character, need, and outcome expectancy. There are numerous studies of this type (e.g., Gendolla & Richter, 2006a, 2006b; Gendolla, Richter, & Silvia, 2008; Wright, Williams, & Dill, 1992), most of which have been reviewed elsewhere (e.g., Gendolla & Wright, 2005; Chapter 4, this volume). Therefore, here we discuss only two.

One such study is an experiment that operationalized importance in terms of outcome expectancy (Wright & Gregorich, 1989). Participants were provided a low (1/15) or high (14/15) chance of winning a modest prize by succeeding on an easy (two-trigram) or moderately difficult (five-trigram) memorization task. Analysis of CV responses assessed just prior to the task revealed Difficulty × Chance (i.e., importance) interaction patterns for systolic blood pressure (SBP) and heart rate (HR), both CV response parameters that are sometimes affected by sympathetic nervous system activation (Brownley, Hurwitz, & Schneiderman, 2000; Richter & Gendolla, 2009; see also Chapter 2 and Chapter 3, this volume). Among the high chance (importance) participants, responses were proportional to difficulty; among the low chance (importance) participants, the responses were low regardless of difficulty. As would be expected, the chance (importance) manipulation affected SBP and HR responses where difficulty was high but not where it was low.

More fully illuminating is an experiment that varied importance by way of a social evaluation manipulation and included more difficulty levels (Wright, Dill, Geen, & Anderson, 1998). It operationalized importance in social evaluation terms on the assumption that evaluation affords performers the opportunity to favorably impress observers and, thus, frequently increases the incentive to do well. Over a series of work periods, participants were presented five versions of a memory task, ranging in difficulty from very low to very high. Specifically, they were presented computer recognition memory challenges involving two, four, six, eight, and 10 characters. Half were led to believe their responses would be public to a senior graduate student, and half were led to believe their responses would be private. Once again, difficulty interacted with importance to determine SBP and HR responses, this time assessed during the task. When performance was public (i.e., importance was high), the responses increased with difficulty to a point and then fell. They fell after a point presumably because success at the highest difficulty levels required more than the participants could or would do. When performance was private (i.e., importance was low), the responses were low at all difficulty levels. Comparisons at each difficulty level indicated that the evaluation (importance) manipulation affected SBP and HR responses only in the mid-difficulty range.

Direct support for the value appraisal and outcome expectancy sex implications comes from a study designed to examine the value appraisal path of sex influence (Frazier, Barreto, & Wright, 2008). As in the first study just described, participants were told that they could earn a chance to win a prize by meeting an easy (two trigram) or moderately difficult (six trigram) memory challenge. However, in this case the probability of winning was constantly modest, and, more important, the incentive was traditionally feminine (a fragrant body lotion). Investigators assumed that women would tend to place greater value on the incentive. In light of this, they predicted that effort and associated CV responses during the memory period would be proportional to difficulty among women but low under both difficulty conditions among men. Results for HR were supportive. A planned 3 versus 1 contrast confirmed that responses were stronger under difficult rather than easy conditions among women but low regardless of difficulty among men. The residual sum of squares did not approach significance, indicating that the contrast accounted for all reliable variance. Findings for SBP and diastolic blood pressure (DBP) also showed a difficulty effect among women but not men. However, for reasons that are unclear, they showed relatively elevated responses in men under both difficulty conditions.

Direct support also comes from a study that was not designed to examine the value appraisal path but that can be interpreted in value appraisal terms (Wright, Tunstall, Williams, Goodwin, & Harmon-Jones, 1995, Experiment 1). Participants were presented an easy (three character) or difficult (eight character) version of the memory task used in the second study described previously and told that their responses would be either public to "people in the control room" or private. The prediction was that effort and associated CV responses during the memory period would be proportional to difficulty where responses were public, but low irrespective of difficulty where responses were private. However, analysis confirmed this 3 versus 1 pattern for SBP only among women. Among men, SBP responses were relatively low in all conditions.

The preceding 3 Versus 1 Contrast × Sex interaction must be interpreted cautiously for two reasons. First, it was not expected. Second, it appears to conflict with results from the second study described previously, which showed no sex effects. Nonetheless, it could be taken to indicate that the study's men placed less value on favorably impressing potential observers in the public conditions than the study's women did. If the men had lower value appraisals, those in the difficult condition could have concluded that the requirements of their task were excessive and, as a result, withheld effort. An explanation for the conflict between study results could lie in the specifics of the purported audience. In the study described earlier, the audience was a senior graduate student—someone with relatively high status. In the present study, it was "people in the control room," who were likely to be low status junior assistants. It is possible that men in the difficult/public condition would have exerted strong effort—and evinced strong CV responses—if an audience of higher status had been used.

In summary, there is both indirect and direct empirical support for the sex implications related to value appraisals and outcome expectancies. Indirect support comes from studies that have documented the implied interactional effects of difficulty and success importance factors. Direct support comes from studies that have documented implied CV sex effects where men and women should or might have placed different value on available performance incentives.

Ability Implications

Indirect empirical support for the implications related to sex differences in ability appraisals comes from studies that have confirmed the implied interactional influences of challenge difficulty, ability, and success importance. Just as there are numerous studies that have confirmed the implied interactional influence of importance and difficulty, there are also numerous studies of this type (e.g., Wright, & Dill, 1993). Moreover, many have been reviewed in detail elsewhere (e.g., Wright & Kirby, 2001). Therefore, we again discuss only two cases for purposes of illustration.

An early ability study was concerned with naturally occurring ability appraisals (Wright, Wadley, Pharr, & Butler, 1994). The investigators first identified undergraduates who viewed themselves as having either low or high math ability. They then invited the undergraduates to participate in a study that gave them the chance to avoid a blast of noise by meeting a performance standard on math problems described as easy, difficult, or extremely difficult.

Analysis of CV responses measured immediately prior to performance showed a Difficulty × Ability interaction for SBP. Among high-ability participants, responses rose steadily with difficulty. By contrast, among low-ability participants, responses were higher roughly by a constant at the easy and high difficulty levels but low at the highest difficulty level.

A later study examined ability as a manipulated (rather than a measured) variable (Wright & Dismukes, 1995). Investigators first led participants to believe that they had low or high ability with respect to a scanning task. They then told participants that they could avoid noise by attaining a low (20th percentile) or high (95th percentile) performance standard on a version of the task. Results indicated a crossover response pattern for HR and, to a lesser degree, SBP and DBP. Among high-ability participants, responses were or tended to be stronger under difficult conditions. Among low-ability participants, the reverse was true. Whereas ability tended to be negatively associated with CV responsiveness when difficulty was low, it was positively associated with CV responsiveness when difficulty was high.

Direct support for the ability–sex implications has come from three studies that led participants to believe an experimental task was an activity at which men or women were especially adept (Wright et al., 1997). The earliest two (Experiments 1 and 2) used the recognition memory task used in two of the success–importance studies described previously. In the first of these ability–sex studies, participants performed with instructions that (a) men were better (masculine task) or women were better (feminine task) and (b) they could avoid noise by attaining a low or high performance standard (a score of 30 or 90, respectively, on a 100-point scale). The prediction was that participant sex would combine with task type (masculine vs. feminine) and standard (low vs. high) to determine effort and associated CV responses, with the responses forming a double crossover pattern across task type levels. Where the task was masculine, women were expected to be more responsive than men under low-standard conditions but less responsive than men under high-standard conditions. Where the task was feminine, women were expected to be less responsive than men under low-standard conditions but more responsive than men under high-standard conditions. SBP responses assessed during performance were broadly, but not perfectly, consistent with expectations. An a priori contrast corresponding to the predicted double crossover pattern was reliable. However, it yielded a significant residual sum of squares, reflecting the lack of a sex difference when the task was feminine and the standard was high.

In the second ability–sex study (Wright et al., 1997, Experiment 2), investigators used a similar procedure but offered participants the chance to win a prize (their choice of a pen, pencil, notebook, or folder). More important, they compared CV sex effects obtained under high-standard conditions with those obtained under extreme-standard conditions, with the goal of evaluating the idea that both sexes should evince reduced CV responses where both view success as impossible or excessively difficult, given the contingent benefit. The investigators created extreme-standard conditions by requiring a performance score of 95 and providing even more negative information about the low-ability sex's capacity to perform. As before, the expectation was that sex would combine with task type and standard to determine effort and associated CV responses. However, here, the prediction was for a pair of 3 versus 1 response patterns. Where the task was masculine, CV responses were expected to be greater for men than women under high-standard conditions but low for both sexes under extreme-standard conditions. Where the task was feminine, CV responses were expected to be greater for women than men under high-standard conditions but low for both sexes under extreme-standard conditions. SBP responses assessed during performance comported with expectations. An a priori contrast comparing responses of masculine/high-standard men and feminine/high-standard women with responses of other participants proved reliable. A test of the residual did not approach significance, confirming that the contrast accounted for all variance.

The third study that provided direct evidence for the ability sex implications is one that used a scanning task similar to the one used in the second ability study described previously (Wright & Lockard, 2006). It led participants to believe that men had special ability with respect to this task and that they could secure a low or high (1/15 vs. 14/15) chance of winning a prize by meeting a modest (40th percentile) standard. The prediction was that women would have stronger effort and associated CV responses than men when outcome expectancy (and thus success importance) was high but not when it was low. Women were expected to try harder than men in the high-expectancy condition because they were expected to view success as especially difficult but possible and worthwhile. They were expected to exert little effort in the low-expectancy condition because they were expected to view success as excessively difficult, given the chance of winning. Men were expected to exert low effort in this condition because little was required of them (given their ability) and little was warranted. SBP and DBP responses assessed during performance matched the implied 3 versus 1 pattern.

In summary, there is both indirect and direct empirical support for the integrative analysis implications related to sex differences in ability perception. The indirect support comes from studies that have documented the implied interactional effects of difficulty, ability, and success importance factors. The direct comes from studies that have documented implied CV sex effects under conditions in which men and women should have had disparate ability appraisals.

CONCLUSION

We have examined the issue of sex influence on CV response from the perspective of an integrative analysis that has guided work in our laboratory for many years. The analysis highlights three ways in which sex could influence effort and associated CV responses in a performance circumstance. One is by affecting the value that performers place on available incentives. Another is by affecting performers' outcome expectancy. The third is by affecting ability perception with respect to the performance challenge.

Sex differences in value appraisal and outcome expectancy should translate into sex differences in perceived success importance that should sometimes—but not always—yield sex differences in effort and CV response. Sex differences in importance should yield sex differences in effort and CV response when they lead members of one sex to conclude that a possible challenge is worth meeting and members of the other sex to conclude that it is not. The sex differences yielded should reflect stronger responses in the sex with higher importance perceptions. By contrast, sex differences in importance should not yield sex differences in effort and CV response when they allow members of both sexes to believe a possible challenge is or is not worth meeting, nor should they yield sex differences in effort and CV response when members of both sexes believe that success is impossible. When men and women both believe success is worthwhile, their effort and CV responses should correspond to difficulty. When they both believe success is impossible or not worthwhile, given a contingent benefit, their effort and CV responses should be low.

Sex differences in ability perception should yield a qualitatively different set of effort and CV response sex effects that are also situation-specific. Where success appears possible and worthwhile to both low- and high-ability sex groups, the low-ability group should evince stronger effort and CV responsiveness. Where success seems possible and worthwhile to a high- but not a low-ability group, the high-ability group should evince stronger effort and CV responsiveness. Where both sex groups view success as either impossible or not worthwhile, no sex differences in effort-related CV response should be in evidence. Both these ability implications and the preceding value appraisal and outcome expectancy implications are supported by data from a variety of experiments.

Numerous observations could be made about this theoretical approach. However, for space reasons, we limit ourselves to three. One observation is that the approach does not assume that sex differences in value appraisal, outcome expectancy, and ability have to be grounded in fact. As noted already, men and women frequently hold misguided ability perceptions. In the same fashion, they could hold misguided value appraisals and outcome expectancies, for example, because of erroneous learning about a personal need or sex bias in an employer. What should be critical for determining men's and women's effort and associated responses is not their reality but rather their perception of that reality.

A second observation is that the approach does not assume that sex differences in value appraisal, outcome expectancy, and ability perception will always be present or always reflect nonoverlapping (i.e., polarized) and strongly divergent subjective assessments. Presumably, men and women have common value appraisals, outcome expectancies, and ability perceptions in many circumstances. Even when they differ in their value appraisals, outcome expectancies, and ability perceptions at the group level, variation within their groups could approach the variation between their groups and mean group differences could be small. There obviously should be no potential for sex differences in effort-related CV response when the sexes do not vary in their assessment of value, outcome expectancy, and ability. When the sexes differ on these assessment dimensions, the potential for sex differences in effort-related CV response should increase as polarization and the size of mean differences between the groups increase.

The final observation is that the approach can be used to understand not only sex disparities in CV response but also alternative group disparities in CV response, such as race disparities. Just as men and women can differ in their value appraisals, outcome expectancies, and ability perceptions, so presumably can other groups. Where other groups differ on these dimensions, they should evince the same effort and CV response patterns that sex groups should when they differ on the dimensions. Exploration of the implied alternative group effects could be an exciting avenue for new research, and we would be pleased if this chapter inspired someone to take it up as a cause.

REFERENCES

Atienza, A. A., Henderson, P. C., Wilcox, S., & King, A. C. (2001). Gender differences in cardiovascular response to dementia caregiving. *The Gerontologist, 41*, 490–498.

Brehm, J. W., & Self, E. (1989). The intensity of motivation. In M. R. Rozenweig & L. W. Porter (Eds.), *Annual Review of Psychology* (pp. 109–131). Palo Alto, CA: Annual Reviews.

Brown, P. C., & Smith, T. W. (1992). Social influence, marriage, and the heart: Cardiovascular consequences of interpersonal control in husbands and wives. *Health Psychology, 11*, 88–96. doi:10.1037/0278-6133.11.2.88

Brownley, K. A., Hurwitz, B. E., & Schneiderman, N. (2000). Cardiovascular psychophysiology. In J. T. Cacioppo, L. G. Tassinary, & G. G. Berntson, *Handbook of Psychophysiology* (pp. 224–264). New York, NY: Cambridge University Press.

Buss, D. M., & Schmitt, D. P. (1993). Sexual strategies theory: An evolutionary perspective on human mating. *Psychological Review, 100,* 204–232. doi:10.1037/0033-295X.100.2.204

Davis, M. C., & Matthews, K. A. (1996). Do gender-relevant characteristics determine cardiovascular reactivity? Match versus mismatch of traits and situations. *Journal of Personality and Social Psychology, 71,* 527–535. doi:10.1037/0022-3514.71.3.527

Frazier, B., Barreto, P., & Wright, R. A. (2008). Gender, incentive value appraisals, and cardiovascular response to a behavioral challenge. *Sex Roles, 59,* 14–20. doi:10.1007/s11199-008-9440-4

Gendolla, G. H. E., & Richter, M. (2006a). Cardiovascular reactivity during performance under social observation: The moderating role of task difficulty. *International Journal of Psychophysiology, 62,* 185–192. doi:10.1016/j.ijpsycho.2006.04.002

Gendolla, G. H. E., & Richter, M. (2006b). Ego-involvement and the difficulty law of motivation: Effects on performance-related cardiovascular response. *Personality and Social Psychology Bulletin, 32,* 1188–1203. doi:10.1177/0146167206288945

Gendolla, G. H. E., Richter, M., & Silvia, P. J. (2008). Self-focus and task difficulty effects on effort-related cardiovascular reactivity. *Psychophysiology, 45,* 653–662. doi:10.1111/j.1469-8986.2008.00655.x

Gendolla, G. H. E., & Wright, R. A. (2005). Motivation in social settings: Studies of effort-related cardiovascular arousal. In J. P. Forgas, K. Williams, & B. von Hippel (Eds.), *Social motivation: Conscious and nonconscious processes* (pp. 71–90). Cambridge, England: Cambridge University Press.

Glass, D. C. (1977). *Behavior patterns, stress, and coronary disease.* Hillsdale, NJ: Erlbaum.

Halpern, D. F. (2000). *Sex differences in cognitive abilities.* Mahwah, NJ: Erlbaum.

Heckhausen, H. (1991). *Motivation and action* (P. K. Leppman, Trans.). Berlin, Germany: Springer-Verlag.

Jorgensen, R. S., & Houston, B. K. (1981). The Type A behavior pattern, sex differences, and cardiovascular response to and recovery from stress. *Motivation and Emotion, 5,* 201–214. doi:10.1007/BF00993884

Lash, S. J., Gillespie, B. L., Eisler, R. M., & Southard, D. R. (1991). Sex differences in cardiovascular reactivity: Effects of gender relevance of the stressor. *Health Psychology, 10,* 392–398. doi:10.1037/0278-6133.10.6.392

Leinwand, L. A. (2003). Sex is a potent modifier of the cardiovascular system. *The Journal of Clinical Investigation, 112,* 302–307.

Maddux, J. E. (1995). Self-efficacy theory: An introduction. In J. E. Maddux (Ed.), *Self-efficacy, adaptation, and adjustment: Theory, research, and application* (pp. 3–33). New York, NY: Plenum Press.

Matthews, K. A., Davis, M. C., Stoney, C. M., Owens, J. F., & Caggiula, A. R. (1991). Does the gender relevance of the stressor influence sex differences in psychophysiological responses? *Health Psychology, 10,* 112–120. doi:10.1037/0278-6133.10.2.112

Matthews, K. A., & Stoney, C. M. (1988). Influence of sex and age on cardiovascular responses during stress. *Psychosomatic Medicine, 50,* 46–56.

Obrist, P. A. (1981). *Cardiovascular psychophysiology: A perspective.* New York, NY: Plenum Press.

Richter, M., & Gendolla, G. H. E. (2009). The heart contracts to reward: Monetary incentives and pre-ejection period. *Psychophysiology, 46,* 451–457. doi:10.1111/j.1469-8986.2009.00795.x

Saab, P. G. (1989). Cardiovascular and neuroendocrine response to challenge in males and females. In N. Schneiderman, S. M. Weiss, & P. G. Kaufmann (Eds.), *Handbook of research methods in cardiovascular behavioral medicine* (pp. 453–481). New York, NY: Plenum Press.

Smith, T. W., Limon, J. P., Gallo, L. C., & Ngu, L. Q. (1996). Interpersonal control and cardiovascular activity: Goals, behavioral expression, and the moderating effects of sex. *Journal of Personality and Social Psychology, 70,* 1012–1024. doi:10.1037/0022-3514.70.5.1012

Stoney, C. M., Davis, M. C., & Matthews, K. A. (1987). Sex difference in physiological responses to stress and in coronary disease: A causal link? *Psychophysiology, 24,* 127–131. doi:10.1111/j.1469-8986.1987.tb00264.x

Stroud, L. R., Niaura, R. S., & Stoney, C. M. (2001). Sex differences in cardiovascular reactivity to physical appearance and performance challenges. *International Journal of Behavioral Medicine, 8,* 240–250. doi:10.1207/S15327558IJBM0803_6

Surwit, R. S., Williams, R. B., & Shapiro, D. (1982). *Behavioral approaches to cardiovascular disease.* New York, NY: Academic Press.

Van Egeren, L. F. (1979). Cardiovascular changes during social competition during a mixed motive game. *Journal of Personality and Social Psychology, 37,* 858–864. doi:10.1037/0022-3514.37.6.858

van Well, S. V., Kolk, A. M., & Klugkist, I. G. (2008). Effects of sex, gender role identification, and gender relevance of two types of stressors on cardiovascular and subjective responses. *Behavior Modification, 32,* 427–449. doi:10.1177/0145445507309030

Vroom, V. H. (1964). *Work and motivation.* New York, NY: Wiley.

Wood, W., & Eagly, A. H. (2002). A cross-cultural analysis of the behavior of women and men: Implications for the origins of sex difference. *Psychological Bulletin, 128,* 699–727. doi:10.1037/0033-2909.128.5.699

Wright, R. A., & Dill, J. C. (1993). Blood pressure reactivity and incentive appraisals as a function of perceived ability and objective task demand. *Psychophysiology, 30,* 152–160. doi:10.1111/j.1469-8986.1993.tb01728.x

Wright, R. A., Dill, J. C., Geen, R. G., & Anderson, C. A. (1998). Social evaluation influence on cardiovascular response to a fixed behavioral challenge: Effects across a range of difficulty levels. *Annals of Behavioral Medicine, 20,* 277–285. doi:10.1007/BF02886377

Wright, R. A., & Dismukes, A. (1995). Cardiovascular effects of experimentally induced efficacy (ability) appraisals at low and high levels of avoidant task demand. *Psychophysiology, 32*, 172–176. doi:10.1111/j.1469-8986.1995.tb03309.x

Wright, R. A., & Gregorich, S. (1989). Difficulty and instrumentality of imminent behavior as determinants of cardiovascular response and self-reported energy. *Psychophysiology, 26*, 586–592. doi:10.1111/j.1469-8986.1989.tb00715.x

Wright, R. A., & Kirby, L. D. (2001). Effort determination of cardiovascular response: An integrative analysis with applications in social psychology. In M. Zanna (Ed.), *Advances in experimental social psychology* (Vol. 33, pp. 255–307). San Diego, CA: Academic Press.

Wright, R. A., & Lockard, S. (2006). Sex, outcome expectancy, and cardiovascular response to a masculine appetitive challenge. *Psychophysiology, 43*, 190–196. doi:10.1111/j.1469-8986.2006.00384.x

Wright, R. A., Murray, J. B., Storey, P., & Williams, B. J. (1997). Ability analysis of gender relevance and sex differences in cardiovascular response to behavioral challenge. *Journal of Personality and Social Psychology, 73*, 405–417. doi:10.1037/0022-3514.73.2.405

Wright, R. A., Tunstall, A. M., Williams, B. J., Goodwin, J. S., & Harmon-Jones, E. (1995). Social evaluation and cardiovascular response: An active coping approach. *Journal of Personality and Social Psychology, 69*, 530–543. doi:10.1037/0022-3514.69.3.530

Wright, R. A., Wadley, V. G., Pharr, R. P., & Butler, M. (1994). Interactive influence of self-reported ability and avoidant task demand on anticipatory cardiovascular responsivity. *Journal of Research in Personality, 28*, 68–86. doi:10.1006/jrpe.1994.1007

Wright, R. A., Williams, B. J., & Dill, J. C. (1992). Interactive effects of difficulty and instrumentality of avoidant behavior on cardiovascular reactivity. *Psychophysiology, 29*, 677–686. doi:10.1111/j.1469-8986.1992.tb02045.x

C. WORK AND ACHIEVEMENT

18

CARDIOVASCULAR MEASURES IN HUMAN FACTORS/ ERGONOMICS RESEARCH

RICHARD W. BACKS, JOHN LENNEMAN,
AND NICHOLAS CASSAVAUGH

Human factors, also known as *ergonomics* (hence the abbreviation HF/E), is the science of people at work. HF/E is such a broad area that it is difficult to find a concise definition that covers all its different aspects and also distinguishes it from related fields such as industrial and organizational psychology. However, the goal of HF/E researchers and practitioners is usually to optimize the performance and/or to maximize the safety of a human–technology system. That is, HF/E researchers and practitioners are concerned with maximizing the strengths and minimizing the limitations of both human operators and the technology that they use. Thus, the emphasis in HF/E is on understanding how human operators (whether as individuals or groups) and technology can be best melded to produce optimal system performance.

Often the operators of human–technology systems have a high degree of expertise that has been acquired over years of training and practice (e.g., pilots, process-control plant operators, drivers). Thus, a key characteristic of operators is that they are highly motivated to acquire the needed expertise, regardless of whether that expertise is obtained through a process of self-selection or through a rigorous formal selection and training program. Further, these operators must maintain their motivation in order to keep system performance at or above some nominal level in the face of task, environmental, and physiological state stressors that would otherwise degrade performance with less motivated operators.

HF/E research has historically focused on what operators do and how they do it; why they do it (i.e., their motivation) has been largely ignored. Most of the existing literature on motivation in HF/E is borrowed from industrial and organizational psychology. In fact, Salas, Wilson, and Lyons (2008) noted that little HF/E research considers motivation and almost none attempts to assess it. Indeed, Salas and colleagues found only one article that discussed motivation from an HF/E perspective (Luczak, Kabel, & Licht, 2006). This lack of attention to motivation is perhaps not surprising given the historical focus on highly trained and motivated professionals in much HF/E research.

Motivation can be a difficult and time-consuming hypothetical construct to assess (Hoyos, 1987; Salas, Wilson, & Lyons, 2008), but it can also be an important factor in determining an operator's action in a given situation. The operator of a system has goals that center on attaining positive and/or avoiding negative outcomes. The actions of an operator are partly determined by the operator's assessment of the likelihood that an action will move the system outcome toward attainment of the goal. Consider the case, presented by Muir and Moray (1996), of supervising a milk processing facility. The operator supervising the milk pasteurization process system must monitor and control vat levels, flow rates, pump states, pressure levels, temperature levels, and output rate. The operator must exercise control over these factors to attain a balance between quality control and production rate. If, for instance, there is pressure to increase production because the input vat is reaching its capacity, the operator may choose to (a) increase the flow rate through the pasteurizer or (b) do nothing and leave the flow rate as is. In the first case, if the flow rate through the pasteurizer is too high, the milk may not attain the required temperature for pasteurization, resulting in a higher production rate at the expense of milk quality and possibly public health. In the second case, a considerable amount of milk may spoil or spill, resulting in lost production. Each action or inaction has an outcome (or range of outcomes) and possible consequences, and operators may differ in their expectations associated with the consequences. For example, if an operator expects to be disciplined or docked for the lost production, then he or she may risk the increased flow rate through the pasteurizer to avoid the negative consequences of inaction.

Mental workload assessment is one area where the concept of motivation has had a prominent role in HF/E theory and practice. It is also an area where psychophysiological measures have been widely used. In this chapter, we review some of our research using cardiovascular measures of mental workload and attention in the aviation and driving domains. We begin with a brief explanation of how we conceive of the concept of motivation within a model of mental workload. We then discuss how we use cardiovascular measures to obtain estimates of modes of cardiac autonomic control, which we believe are more sensitive and diagnostic of task demands on attentional processing resources than heart rate (HR).

MOTIVATION AND MENTAL WORKLOAD

One place where the concept of motivation has had a prominent role in HF/E theory and practice is in the assessment of mental workload. Gopher and Donchin (1986) described *mental workload* as the extent to which an operator's information processing abilities are actively engaged by tasks that he or she is motivated to perform. It is imperative to distinguish among motivation, stress, and effort and to understand the complex ways that they relate to each other. One representation of a human–technology system is presented in Figure 18.1. Although both mental workload and stress are related to balancing demands and resources, they differ in their sensitivity to different types of demands and in their scope (Gaillard & Kramer, 2000; Sanders, 1983). Mental workload is primarily determined by the cognitive demands of the task, the operator's individual differences in information processing ability, and the performance goal. *Stress*, however, is more broadly defined as a biobehavioral state that is determined by all aspects of the work environment, where mental workload is merely one of many possible stressors (e.g., physical conditions, social interactions). Further, not all aspects of a particular human–technology system will be affected by all types of stressors (Hockey, 1986).

Here we focus on the stress engendered by mental workload. Both low (underload) and high (overload) extremes of mental workload can be stressful. Under high workload, performance can be maintained by recruiting additional resources to increase the operator's effort in the task (Hockey, 1997). Perhaps surprisingly, low workload may also require effort to maintain performance, not to counter the negative effects of stress but to ensure that effort stays above a threshold (e.g., Dittmar, Warm, Dember, & Ricks, 1993). In both situations, an operator must be motivated to exert that additional effort to achieve his or her internal goal, such as a desire to perform well, or an external goal, such as maintaining safety. Further, only motivated operators will experience mental workload. If for any reason there is a breakdown of either the motivation–effort link or the performance feedback loop in Figure 18.1, then mental workload ceases to be a stressor. However, highly motivated operators can sometimes maintain system performance within an operational goal

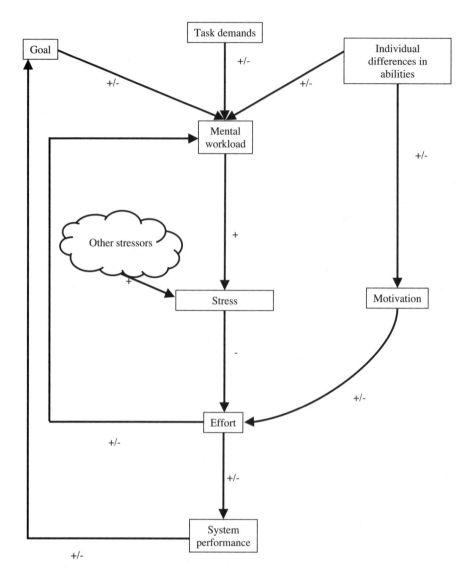

Figure 18.1. A schematic representation of the relations among workload, stress, effort, motivation and performance in a human–technology system.

under extremely stressful conditions by exerting more effort. These operators may provide little overt indication that they are overloaded until they are unable to respond to all of the demands placed on them or they lose their motivation to respond to those demands. Therefore, psychophysiological measures have often been used in HF/E to assess the status of the operator because they can indicate the effects of the task, environmental, and physiological stressors that may lead to reduced system performance before performance (or safety) begins to decline (Kramer, 1991).

USING CARDIOVASCULAR PSYCHOPHYSIOLOGY TO MAKE INFERENCES ABOUT MENTAL WORKLOAD

Although many central and autonomic nervous system responses have been used in HF/E research, cardiovascular responses obtained from the electrocardiogram (ECG) have been the most common psychophysiological measures used, for a number of reasons. First, they are among the least intrusive of the psychophysiological measures because only three electrodes (usually placed on the thorax) are needed, which rarely interfere with the ability of the operator to make responses. (In fact, with recent technology advances such as piezoelectric sensors and laser Doppler vibrometry, electrodes may not be needed at all.) Second, cardiovascular responses are robust and can be readily observed in the laboratory, in the simulator, and in the field. They also need minimal amplification and signal conditioning, and scoring and artifact rejection can be automated to a great extent. Third, ECG measurement is well tolerated by subjects, which is no small consideration for field studies using operators from a target population (e.g., pilots while they are in flight, drivers while they are on the road). Fourth, cardiovascular measures are sensitive to many aspects of the human–technology system that an HF/E researcher would be interested in. Finally, there is a wealth of empirical and theoretical research on cardiovascular responses in the area of mental workload assessment.

Mulder and colleagues (e.g., Mulder, 1986; Mulder, Meijman, Veldman, & van Roon, 2000) have written extensively on the relation between cognitive effort and HR and heart rate variability (HRV; usually computed as a sum of spectral power in the 0.1 Hz band from 0.06 to 0.12 Hz). For example, they have shown that HR increases and HRV decreases as cognitive effort increases to meet increased task demands but only while a person remains motivated to meet those demands. If the task becomes too difficult such that a person is no longer able to exert enough effort to adequately meet the demand, then the motivation to exert effort decreases, performance declines, and HR decreases and HRV increases back toward baseline levels (e.g., Mulder & Mulder, 1981).

Our research with cardiovascular measures of mental workload has attempted to move beyond end organ responses such as HR (Backs, 1995, 2001). We use the *autonomic space model* of Berntson, Cacioppo, and Quigley (1991; Berntson, Cacioppo, Quigley, & Fabro, 1994), which posits that organs such as the heart have multiple modes of control. The heart is dually innervated by the sympathetic and parasympathetic branches of the autonomic nervous system: Sympathetic activation increases HR, whereas parasympathetic activation

decreases HR. Historically, activity of these branches was thought to be reciprocal where change in HR was the result of activation of one branch coupled
with withdrawal of the other branch. However, Berntson and colleagues contend that in addition to the reciprocally coupled modes of control, the sympathetic and parasympathetic branches can be nonreciprocally coupled (i.e.,
coactivation or coinhibition) or even uncoupled (i.e., change in activity of one
branch occurs without change in activity of the other branch). Thus, instead
of a change in HR being due to activation of one branch and withdrawal of
the other, eight modes of autonomic control exist.

Figure 18.2 presents the eight modes of control for HR in "autonomic
space." Of course, noninvasive measures of underlying sympathetic and parasympathetic neural activity are needed to determine the mode of autonomic
control responsible for HR. Previous research using pharmacological blockades has shown that pre-ejection period and respiratory sinus arrhythmia
(RSA; usually computed as a sum of spectral power in the frequency band
from 0.14 to 0.40 Hz) can serve as valid indicators of cardiac sympathetic and
parasympathetic activity respectively (Cacioppo et al., 1994).

We have attempted to map these cardiac autonomic control modes to
the various attentional processing resources in Wickens's (1984) multiple-

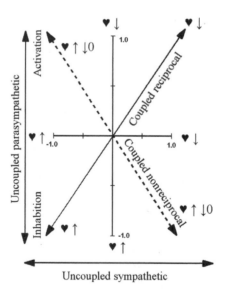

Figure 18.2. The eight modes of autonomic control of the heart in autonomic space.
The origin of the figure represents resting baseline, and the axes and vectors represent the control modes. Coinhibition and coactivation have multiple responses for
heart rate depending on the amount of activation or inhibition of the two autonomic
branches. ♥ = heart rate; ↑ indicates faster, ↓ indicates slower, and 0 indicates no
change in heart rate.

resource model of attention and performance (Backs, 2001). We believe that there is much promise to using cardiac modes of control to better understand the psychological processes responsible for an operator's HR change when engaged with human–technology systems. Unfortunately, little HF/E research using this approach has been conducted outside of our own laboratory. One major constraint is the requirement that the impedance cardiogram be collected along with the continuous ECG to obtain pre-ejection period (the sympathetic measure), which negates some of the advantages of using cardiovascular measures discussed previously. However, we have suggested elsewhere that residual HR can be used as an approximation for the sympathetic nervous system innervation of the heart to replace pre-ejection period in field studies (Backs, 1995). Residual HR is calculated by regressing HR on RSA (the parasympathetic measure) and then using the residual from the regression as the measure of sympathetic activity. We recommend that instead of using residual HR as the sympathetic index that factor analysis be used to form sympathetic and parasympathetic factors from the cardiovascular measures that are obtained from the ECG (i.e., HR, residual HR, HRV, RSA). Our validation studies indicate that the factor scores may be used when it is not possible to collect the impedance cardiogram (Backs, 1998; Lenneman & Backs, 2000).

CARDIOVASCULAR MEASURES OF MENTAL WORKLOAD IN AVIATION AND DRIVING DOMAINS

Our review is limited to HF/E research using cardiovascular measures for mental workload assessment. Further, we concentrate on research conducted in the field (i.e., in flight and on the road) or in the simulator as opposed to more conventional laboratory-based research. Although it has become more common to see basic psychophysiological science that is conducted outside of the laboratory, HF/E has long emphasized the need to observe "cognition in the wild" (Hutchins, 1995, p. xiii) to verify that the research conducted in the laboratory generalizes to the workplace. More comprehensive reviews of the psychophysiological HF/E literature can be found in Boucsein and Backs (2000, 2009).

Aviation

Cardiovascular measures have been used in HF/E studies in aviation for many years. Backs (1995) reviewed the earlier work on commercial and military pilots and found that HR increases during high-workload flight segments, such as takeoff, landing, and weapons delivery, as opposed to low-workload segments, such as cruise both in flight and during flight simulation. HR is faster for the pilot in control than for other crew members and during manual control than with an autopilot. Similar results have been found in more recent studies (e.g., Veltman, 2002; Wilson, 2002). However, Backs (1995) also noted that there were instances in which HR did not distinguish between flight conditions that appear to differ in mental workload and that would be expected to exhibit HR change such as between day and night flight or with greater landing approach angle. It was in part to explain these dissociations between HR and mental workload that led us to look beyond HR using Berntson et al.'s (1991, 1994) autonomic space model and to examine the modes of cardiac control that might underlie the HR observed in flight and during flight simulation. We use two examples to illustrate how the autonomic space approach can be applied outside of the laboratory, one using data collected from general aviation pilots in flight and the second using data collected from commercial pilots during high-fidelity flight simulation.

Hankins and Wilson (1998) collected cardiovascular response data and other psychophysiological and subjective mental workload measures from 15 instrument-rated general aviation pilots while they flew three flight profiles that differed in mental workload between the profiles and within the different flight segments of each profile. One profile was flown under visual flight rules (VFR), and the other two profiles were flown under instrument flight rules (IFR) while the pilot was wearing vision-restricting goggles. Psychophysiological data were collected during each flight. Consistent with the pattern described earlier, HR was highest for VFR takeoff, followed by VFR touch-and-go (a landing and takeoff practice technique where takeoff immediately follows the wheels touching down without completing the landing and coming to a stop), and then IFR missed approach and IFR–VFR landing, which were all higher than the cruise and air work segments. Hankins and Wilson concluded that the cardiovascular measures were sensitive to segments of high mental workload but that they were not diagnostic of which attentional resources were demanded in the segments.

Backs, Wilson, and Hankins (1995) used the cardiovascular data from Hankins and Wilson (1998) to compute residual heart period and the sympathetic and parasympathetic factors to estimate cardiac modes of control across the in-flight segments. In Figure 18.3, we have plotted the autonomic space for each of the three flight phases: VFR, IFR low airspeed, and IFR high airspeed. Within the autonomic space is plotted the sympathetic and parasympathetic factor scores for the sequence of flight segments, and the number plotted next to the segment is the heart period change from resting for that segment. (*Heart period* is the mean time between R-waves of successive heart beats across the segment; a shorter heart period is a faster HR, so negative heart period change means that HR in the segment is faster than baseline.)

What can be seen in Figure 18.3 is our estimate of the underlying cardiac mode of control responsible for the heart period change across the segments.

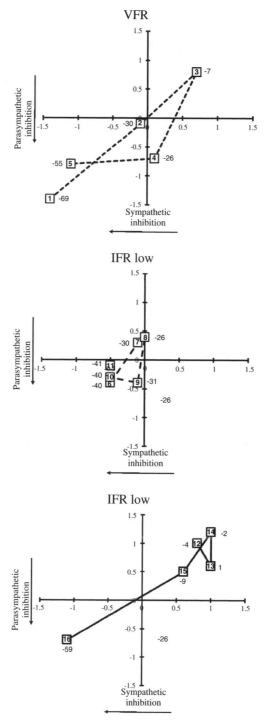

Figure 18.3. Autonomic space for each in-flight phase and segment. Mean heart period change from resting baseline is given next to each segment. Upper panel—visual flight rules (VFR) segments: 1 = takeoff; 2 = climb out; 3 = cruise; 4 = air work; 5 = touch-and-go. Middle panel—instrument flight rules (IFR) low airspeed segments: 6 = air work; 7 = hold; 8 = distance measuring equipment (DME) arc; 9 = ILS tracking; 10 = missed approach; 11 = climb out. Lower panel—IFR high airspeed segments: 12 = hold; 13 = DME arc; 14 = ILS tracking; 15 = IFR–VFR transition landing. Data from Hankins and Wilson (1998).

Several patterns are apparent in the figure. First, because the phases occur in succession, there is a general lengthening of heart period (slowing of HR) across the phases of the flight that is evident across the three panels of the figure. Second, we found that the slower HR across flight phases was due primarily to reciprocally coupled parasympathetic activation and sympathetic inhibition (along the positive diagonal of Figure 18.2) that our laboratory research has suggested occurred because of reduced perceptual and central processing demands. Although this conclusion is counter to the prediction that mental workload increases from the VFR to the IFR phases (which was found for the subjective mental workload measure that Hankins & Wilson, 1998, also collected), dissociations among subjective, psychophysiological, and performance measures of mental workload are common (Yeh & Wickens, 1988). In this case, we posit that the subjective measure was sensitive to the complexity of IFR flight but that added complexity was not particularly taxing on central processing resources for these experienced pilots.

The third pattern that is evident in Figure 18.3 is the consistency of the change through autonomic space within each flight phase. Takeoff, touch-and-go, missed approach, and landing have the largest reduction in heart period from baseline (fastest HR) and are located in the lower left quadrant along the positive diagonal, indicating a reciprocally coupled sympathetic activation and parasympathetic withdrawal mode of control. Then, during climb and cruise, heart period goes back toward baseline (HR slowing) along the positive diagonal indicating a reciprocally coupled parasympathetic activation and sympathetic withdrawal mode of control. The air work segments that follow cruise show reduced heart period (faster HR) but along the ordinate indicating an uncoupled parasympathetic withdrawal mode of control that our laboratory studies suggest is elicited by demands on response processing resources.

The second example to demonstrate the utility of the cardiac modes of control is taken from a flight simulation study conducted to identify valid and reliable mental workload measures that could be used to assess crew mental workload during the certification process for new flight deck designs (Corwin et al., 1989). This study examined a number of psychophysiological, subjective, and performance measures from 18 commercial airline pilots who flew two scenarios in each of two sessions: a low mental workload "nominal" flight in good weather with no equipment malfunctions and a high mental workload flight in poor weather with the autopilot inoperative and two equipment malfunctions (engine failure and loss of hydraulic pressure) along the route. Cardiovascular and the other measures were obtained during seven segments of each flight. The results are too extensive to summarize here, but the findings for HR were similar to the other studies, and HR was one of only three sensitive and reliable candidate measures that were recommended for use in aircraft certification.

However, as we have pointed out, HR alone is a sensitive, but not a diagnostic, mental workload measure. We were able to obtain the polygraph records from the Corwin et al. (1989) study and digitally scanned the records to measure the individual interbeat intervals in each flight segment. Although this method of data quantification only resulted in interbeat intervals with 12.5-ms resolution instead of the 1- to 2-ms resolution that is typical of a laboratory study, we were able to calculate the cardiovascular measures needed for computation of the sympathetic and parasympathetic factors. To simplify the results, we only present the data from the first session that was reported in Backs and Lenneman (1997).

The same general pattern across the flight segments that we observed in Figure 18.3 using the in-flight data in Backs et al. (1995) can also be seen in Figure 18.4. In the low mental workload scenario, heart period is shortest

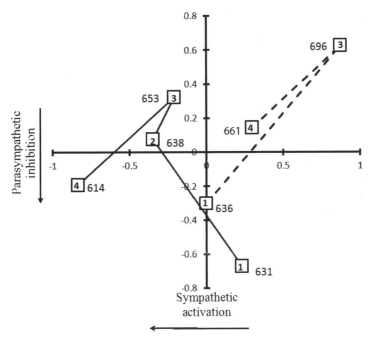

Figure 18.4. Autonomic space for Session 1 for the low (dashed line) and high (solid line) mental workload scenarios from Corwin et al. (1989). Mean heart period is given next to each segment. Segments within each scenario: 1 = takeoff; 2 = top of climb; 3 = cruise; 4 = landing approach. In the high mental workload scenario an unexpected engine failure occurs in Segment 2 and a hydraulic system failure occurs in Segment 3. Adapted from "Enhancing Cardiovascular Mental Workload Assessment in the Field Using Autonomic Components," by R. W. Backs and J. K. Lenneman, 1997, in D. Harris (Ed.), *Engineering Psychology and Cognitive Ergonomics: Vol. 1. Transportation Systems,* p. 266, Aldershot, England: Ashgate. Copyright 1997 by Ashgate. Adapted with permission. Data from Corwin et al. (1989).

(fastest HR) for takeoff and then significantly lengthens (slower HR) during cruise followed by significantly shorter heart period (faster HR) during approach for landing. The heart period change across these segments follows the reciprocally coupled mode of control pattern along the positive diagonal like they did in Figure 18.3. However, the pattern in autonomic space across flight segments is quite different in the high mental workload scenario. Heart period is not significantly different between the takeoff and the top-of-climb and cruise segments where the unexpected malfunctions occurred. Instead of following a pattern of change along the positive diagonal (reciprocally coupled modes of control) for these segments, the top-of-climb and cruise segments differ from takeoff along the negative diagonal, indicating a nonreciprocally coupled coactivation mode of control. Coactivation can occur across organ systems (e.g., bladder and bowel emptying during extreme fear; Berntson et al., 1991), but in this case the autonomic factors show that it can occur within the cardiovascular system in extreme mental workload conditions such as the loss of an engine and hydraulic system during simulated flight. Once the emergency conditions are handled, a significant shortening of heart period (faster HR) is observed for the landing approach segment that is again along the positive diagonal in autonomic space, indicating reciprocally coupled sympathetic activation and parasympathetic withdrawal.

We believe that the autonomic factors observed in the high mental workload flight in Figure 18.4 make a powerful case for the utility of the autonomic control mode approach to mental workload theory and application. If only HR had been observed, one might be led to conclude that there was no difference in pilot mental workload from takeoff to the emergency segments, because there was no significant change across these segments. However, as shown in Figure 18.2, the nonreciprocal control modes can result in an HR increase, decrease, or as in the present example, no change depending on the relative contribution of sympathetic and parasympathetic innervation. Therefore, the autonomic modes of control approach can not only be diagnostic of mental workload demands on attentional processing resources but also have the potential to be more sensitive than HR under extreme conditions.

Driving

Driver mental workload has also been examined in field studies using cardiovascular measures. In general, cardiovascular measures in on-road and driving simulator research converge with those obtained in flight and during flight simulation: HHR is sensitive to baseline-to-task mental workload changes as well as in within-task difficulty manipulations that require cognitive effort (e.g., de Waard, Kruizinga, & Brookhuis, 2008). Further, the autonomic mode of control results from our own driving simulation studies that have used pre-ejection period and RSA have been consistent with the aviation studies using autonomic factors discussed previously.

For example, Wetzel, Sheffert, and Backs (2004) conducted a simulated car-following task that required participants to maintain a target distance from the lead vehicle over a 10-min scenario. Driving mental workload varied between participants by the number of dimensions under the participant's control: one dimension, lateral control only (steering with cruise control), or two dimensions, lateral and headway control (steering and speed). The upper panel of Figure 18.5 shows the autonomic space for 15 participants in each driving condition. As can be seen, one-dimension and two-dimension control did not differ on heart period change from resting baseline, but they did differ in autonomic space. Both driving conditions elicited uncoupled parasympathetic withdrawal, but the vector for the two-dimension condition was significantly longer on the parasympathetic axis (RSA was more suppressed) than for the one-dimension condition. This finding supports our contention that primarily perceptual-response processing resources are required for driving and that making driving more difficult by adding another control dimension does not demand substantial central processing resources.

The lower panel of Figure 18.5 shows the autonomic space from Lenneman and Backs (2009), in which 32 participants drove one-dimension (lateral control) simulations with and without an n-back verbal working memory side task. In the zero-back dual task, drivers watched for letters presented on an overhead highway sign and decided whether or not the letter matched the first letter of the series, whereas in the three-back dual task, drivers decided whether or not the letter on the sign matched the letter that had been presented three signs previously. Heart period change from baseline was significantly shorter (faster HR) during the zero-back dual task compared with driving only, but both of these conditions elicited only uncoupled parasympathetic withdrawal, as in Wetzel et al. (2004). However, heart period change was significantly shorter (faster HR) during the three-back dual task compared with the other two conditions, and the three-back dual task elicited reciprocally coupled sympathetic activation and parasympathetic withdrawal that was significantly different from the other two conditions on both the sympathetic (pre-ejection period) and parasympathetic (RSA) axes.

We interpreted these results in the following way. HR during driving with the zero-back dual task differed from driving only because it was a dual task and required more effort. However, the zero-back task required little central processing because it is simply item recognition, which does not require working memory. Therefore, the attentional demands for driving with the zero-back task were primarily perceptual-response processing resources, as for driving only; and like driving only, it elicited uncoupled parasympathetic withdrawal. However, driving with the three-back task not only had faster HR associated with

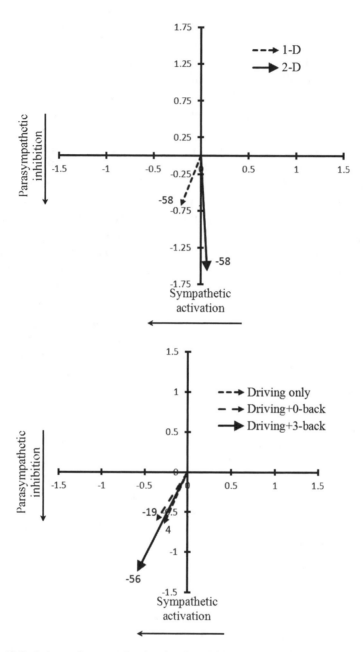

Figure 18.5. Autonomic space for the simulated driving conditions. Mean heart period change from resting baseline (the origin) is given next to each condition. Top panel: Data from Wetzel, Sheffert, and Backs (2004). Lower panel: Adapted from "Cardiac Autonomic Control During Simulated Driving with a Concurrent Verbal Working Memory Task," by J. K. Lenneman and R. W. Backs, 2009, *Human Factors, 51,* p. 414. Copyright 2009 by the Human Factors and Ergonomics Society. Adapted with permission.

additional effort but also elicited reciprocally coupled sympathetic activation and parasympathetic withdrawal, indicative of its intensive working memory requirement that is highly demanding of central processing resources.

CONCLUSION

As can be seen from our review, cardiovascular measures have been useful in HF/E research on mental workload. However, we believe that it is important to go beyond HR to fully realize the potential contributions of cardiovascular psychophysiology to the HF/E literature. We presented one approach in this chapter, cardiac modes of autonomic control, that we believe can be used in the laboratory, in the simulator, and in the field where HF/E research must ultimately be applied.

Recently, there has been a call to reconceptualize HF/E research around emerging theoretical and technological trends in neuroscience, termed *neuroergonomics* (Kramer & Parasuraman, 2007; Parasuraman & Wilson, 2008). We mention neuroergonomics here because we believe that it has the potential to bring powerful new technologies (e.g., functional magnetic resonance imaging, positron emission tomography, event-related optical signal, genetics) and theories derived from cognitive, social, and affective neuroscience to bear on fundamental issues in HF/E. Although neuroergonomics is almost always discussed in terms of integrating knowledge of the organizational and functional aspects of the central nervous system with HF/E, there is no reason that it could not be broadened to include the peripheral and autonomic nervous systems as well. In fact, we consider our mental workload research on understanding the structure of attentional processing resources using Berntson et al.'s (1991, 1994) autonomic space theory to be a prime example of the type of integrative research envisioned for neuroergonomics.

REFERENCES

Backs, R. W. (1995). Going beyond heart rate: Autonomic space and cardiovascular assessment of mental workload. *The International Journal of Aviation Psychology*, 5, 25–48. doi:10.1207/s15327108ijap0501_3

Backs, R. W. (1998). A comparison of factor analytics methods of obtaining cardiovascular autonomic components for the assessment of mental workload. *Ergonomics*, 41, 733–745. doi:10.1080/001401398186883

Backs, R. W. (2001). An autonomic space approach to the psychophysiological assessment of mental workload. In P. A. Hancock & P. A. Desmond (Eds.), *Stress, workload, and fatigue. Human factors in transportation* (pp. 279–289). Mahwah, NJ: Erlbaum.

Backs, R. W., & Lenneman, J. K. (1997). Enhancing cardiovascular mental workload assessment in the field using autonomic components. In D. Harris (Ed.), *Engineering psychology and cognitive ergonomics: Vol. 1. Transportation systems* (pp. 261–268). Aldershot, England: Ashgate.

Backs, R. W., Wilson, G. F., & Hankins, T. C. (1995). Cardiovascular assessment of mental workload using autonomic components: Laboratory and in-flight examples. In R.S. Jensen & L. A. Rakovan (Eds.), *Proceedings of the International Symposium on Aviation Psychology* (pp. 875–880). Columbus: Ohio State University.

Berntson, G. G., Cacioppo, J. T., & Quigley, K. S. (1991). Autonomic determinism: The modes of autonomic control, the doctrine of autonomic space, and the laws of autonomic constraint. *Psychological Review, 98,* 459–487. doi:10.1037/0033-295X.98.4.459

Berntson, G. G., Cacioppo, J. T., Quigley, K. S., & Fabro, V. T. (1994). Autonomic space and psychophysiological response. *Psychophysiology, 31,* 44–61. doi:10.1111/j.1469-8986.1994.tb01024.x

Boucsein, W., & Backs, R. W. (2000). Engineering psychophysiology as a discipline: Historical and theoretical aspects. In R. W. Backs & W. Boucsein (Eds.), *Engineering psychophysiology: Issues and applications* (pp. 3–30). Mahwah, NJ: Erlbaum.

Boucsein, W., & Backs, R. W. (2009). The psychophysiology of emotion, arousal, and personality: Methods and models. In V. G. Duffy (Ed.), *Handbook of digital human modeling for applied ergonomics and human factors engineering* (pp. 35-1–35-18). London, England: Taylor & Francis.

Cacioppo, J. T., Berntson, G. G., Binkley, P. F., Quigley, K. S., Uchino, B. N., & Fieldstone, A. (1994). Autonomic cardiac control. II. Noninvasive indices and basal response as revealed by autonomic blockade. *Psychophysiology, 31,* 586–598. doi:10.1111/j.1469-8986.1994.tb02351.x

Corwin, W. H., Sandry-Garza, D. L., Biferno, M. A., Boucek, G. P., Jonsson, J. E., Logan, A. L., & Metalis, S. A. (1989). *Assessment of crew workload measurement methods, techniques, and procedures* (Vols. 1 & 2, Tech. Rep. No. WDRC-TR-89-7006). Wright-Patterson Air Force Base, OH: USAF.

de Waard, D., Kruizinga, A., & Brookhuis, K. A. (2008). The consequences of an increase in heavy goods vehicles for passenger car drivers' mental workload and behaviour: A simulator study. *Accident Analysis and Prevention, 40,* 818–828. doi:10.1016/j.aap.2007.09.029

Dittmar, M. L., Warm, J. S., Dember, W. N., & Ricks, D. F. (1993). Sex differences in vigilance performance and perceived workload. *The Journal of General Psychology, 120,* 309–322. doi:10.1080/00221309.1993.9711150

Gaillard, A. W. K., & Kramer, A. F. (2000). Theoretical and methodological issues in psychophysiological research. In R. W. Backs & W. Boucsein (Eds.), *Engineering psychophysiology: Issues and applications* (pp. 31–58). Mahwah, NJ: Erlbaum.

Gopher, D., & Donchin, E. (1986). Workload: An examination of the concept. In K. R. Boff, L. Kaufman, & J. P. Thomas (Eds.), *Handbook of perception and human performance* (Vol. 2, pp. 1–49). New York, NY: Wiley.

Hankins, T. C., & Wilson, G. F. (1998). A comparison of heart rate, eye activity, EEG and subjective measures of pilot mental workload during flight. *Aviation, Space, and Environmental Medicine, 69,* 360–367.

Hockey, G. R. J. (1986). Changes in operator efficiency as a function of environmental stress, fatigue, and circadian rhythms. In K. R. Boff, L. Kaufman, & J. P. Thomas (Eds.), *Handbook of perception and human performance* (Vol. 2, pp. 1–44). New York, NY: Wiley.

Hockey, G. R. J. (1997). Compensatory control in the regulation of human performance under stress and high workload: A cognitive–energetical framework. *Biological Psychology, 45,* 73–93. doi:10.1016/S0301-0511(96)05223-4

Hoyos, C. G. (1987). Motivation. In G. Salvendy (Ed.), *Handbook of human factors* (pp. 108–123). New York, NY: Wiley.

Hutchins, E. (1995). *Cognition in the wild.* Cambridge, MA: MIT Press.

Kramer, A. F. (1991). Physiological metrics of mental workload: A review of recent progress. In D. L. Damos (Ed.), *Multiple-task performance* (pp. 279–328). London, England: Taylor & Francis.

Kramer, A. F., & Parasuraman, R. (2007). Neuroergonomics: Application of neuroscience to human factors. In J. T. Cacioppo, L. G. Tassinary, & G. G. Berntson (Eds.), *Handbook of psychophysiology* (3rd ed., pp. 704–722). New York, NY: Cambridge University Press. doi:10.1017/CBO9780511546396.030

Lenneman, J. K., & Backs, R. W. (2000). The validity of factor analytically derived cardiac autonomic components for mental workload assessment. In R. W. Backs & W. Boucsein (Eds.), *Engineering psychophysiology: Issues and applications* (pp. 161–174). Mahwah, NJ: Erlbaum.

Lenneman, J. K., & Backs, R. W. (2009). Cardiac autonomic control during simulated driving with a concurrent verbal working memory task. *Human Factors, 51,* 404–418. doi:10.1177/0018720809337716

Luczak, H., Kabel, T., & Licht, T. (2006). Task design and motivation. In G. Salvendy (Ed.), *Handbook of human factors and ergonomics* (3rd ed., pp. 384–427). Hoboken, NJ: Wiley. doi:10.1002/0470048204.ch15

Muir, B. M., & Moray, N. (1996). Trust in automation: Part II. Experimental studies of trust and human intervention in a process control simulation. *Ergonomics, 39,* 429–460. doi:10.1080/00140139608964474

Mulder, G. (1986). The concept and measurement of mental effort. In G. R. J. Hockey, A. W. K. Gaillard, & M. G. H. Coles (Eds.), *Energetics and human information processing* (pp. 175–198). Dordrecht, The Netherlands: Nijhoff.

Mulder, G., & Mulder, L. J. (1981). Information processing and cardiovascular control. *Psychophysiology, 18,* 392–402. doi:10.1111/j.1469-8986.1981.tb02470.x

Mulder, G., Mulder, L. J. M., Meijman, T. F., Veldman, J. B. P., & van Roon, A. M. (2000). A psychophysiological approach to working conditions. In R. W. Backs & W. Boucsein (Eds.), *Engineering psychophysiology: Issues and applications* (pp. 139–159). Mahwah, NJ: Erlbaum.

Parasuraman, R., & Wilson, G. F. (2008). Putting the brain to work: Neuro-ergonomics past, present, and future. *Human Factors, 50,* 468–474. doi:10.1518/001872008X288349

Salas, E., Wilson, K. A., & Lyons, R. (2008). Motivation and expertise at work: A human factors perspective. In R. Kanfer, G. Chen, & R. Pritchard (Eds.), *Work motivation: Past, present, and future* (pp. 560–567). New York, NY: Routledge.

Sanders, A. F. (1983). Towards a model of stress and human performance. *Acta Psychologica, 53,* 61–97. doi:10.1016/0001-6918(83)90016-1

Veltman, J. A. (2002). A comparative study of psychophysiological reactions during simulator and real flight. *The International Journal of Aviation Psychology, 12,* 33–48. doi:10.1207/S15327108IJAP1201_4

Wetzel, J. M., Sheffert, S. M., & Backs, R. W. (2004). Driver trust, annoyance, and acceptance of an automated calendar system. *Proceedings of the Human Factors and Ergonomics Society,* 2335–2339.

Wickens, C. D. (1984). Processing resources in attention. In R. Parasuraman & D. R. Davies (Eds.), *Varieties of attention* (pp. 63–102). Orlando, FL: Academic Press.

Wilson, G. F. (2002). An analysis of mental workload in pilots during flight using multiple psychophysiological measures. *The International Journal of Aviation Psychology, 12,* 3–18. doi:10.1207/S15327108IJAP1201_2

Yeh, Y. Y., & Wickens, C. D. (1988). Dissociations of performance and subjective measures of workload. *Human Factors, 30,* 111–120.

19

CLARIFYING ACHIEVEMENT MOTIVES AND EFFORT: STUDIES OF CARDIOVASCULAR RESPONSE

RÉMI L. CAPA

Achievement motivation may be defined as the energization and direction of competence-based affect, cognition, and behavior (Elliot, 1999). The concept of achievement motivation has been discussed in experimental psychology for over a century (e.g., James, 1890, pp. 309–311). Throughout the years, numerous theoretical conceptualizations of achievement motivation have been proffered. One of the most systematic analyses of achievement motivation, from both a theoretical and an empirical point of view, has been provided by the theory of achievement motives (Atkinson, 1957; McClelland, Atkinson, Clark, & Lowell, 1953). Achievement motives—the motives to achieve success and avoid failure—are conceived as general higher order motivational tendencies that energize individuals and orient them toward approach and avoidance behaviors. The first studies focused on the influence of achievement motives on risk preference (Atkinson, 1957), persistence after continual failure (Feather, 1961), future orientation (Raynor, 1970), and causal attributions (Weiner & Kukla, 1970; for a review, see Atkinson & Raynor, 1974). Throughout the 20th century and into the 21st, theories of motives have continued to diversify and broaden (Deci & Ryan, 2000). Intensive research continues to focus on the potential influence of achievement motives on other psychological factors, such as emotional well-being (Langens, 2007),

383

intention memory (Kazén & Kuhl, 2005), and creativity (Fodor & Carver, 2000). However, these studies reveal little about the link between achievement motives and effort.

The first section of this chapter presents the theory of achievement motives and its predictions. The second section discusses experimental studies evaluating the predictions derived from the theory of achievement motives, focusing on cardiovascular response as an index of effort mobilization (Obrist, 1981; Wright, 1996). The experimental studies and underlying theory of achievement motives use motivation intensity theory to guide effort predictions (Brehm & Self, 1989; Gendolla & Wright, 2005; Wright & Kirby, 2001).

ACHIEVEMENT MOTIVES THEORY

Atkinson (1957) and McClelland et al. (1953) conceived achievement-oriented behavior (T_A) as the result of a conflict between the strength of the tendency to achieve success (T_{AS}) and the strength of the tendency to avoid failure (T_{AF}; $T_A = T_{AS} - T_{AF}$). In any achievement situation in which it is apparent to people that their performance will be evaluated in reference to some standard, there is what we traditionally call an *approach–avoidance conflict*. The balance between these two factors determines the direction, intensity, and quality of achievement behaviors.[1]

It is assumed that the tendency to achieve success (T_{AS}) is a multiplicative function of three variables (Equation 1):

$$T_{AS} = M_{AS} \times P_S \times I_S \tag{1}$$

The motive to achieve success (M_{AS}) is defined as a relatively stable personality disposition to strive for success and the desire to work toward accomplishing challenging personal and professional goals. Two situational factors influence the approach of achievement activities: subjective probability of success (P_S) and incentive value of success (I_S). The incentive value of success is determined by the magnitude of the subjective probability of success and is inversely related to it ($I_S = 1 - P_S$). This assertion is based on the idea that one experiences more pride following success at a task perceived as difficult than after success at a task perceived as easy.

---

[1]The present chapter's focus is on the original theory of achievement motives (Atkinson, 1957; McClelland et al., 1953). Several elaborations of the original theory that include future goals, immediate consequences, or changes of tendencies over an extended period of time have been proposed. These elaborations do not concern effort mobilization and are not presented in this chapter.

The tendency to avoid failure (T_{AF}) is conceived by Atkinson (1957) as analogous to the tendency to achieve success and is a multiplicative function of three variables (Equation 2):

$$T_{AF} = M_{AF} \times P_F \times I_F \qquad (2)$$

The motive to achieve failure (M_{AF}) is defined as a relatively stable personality disposition to avoid and anticipate negative affects of failure outcomes in terms of shame, embarrassment, humiliation, and loss of status and esteem. Among the situational factors of avoidance behavior, P_F (subjective probability of failure) and I_F (incentive value of failure) are inversely related to the magnitude of the subjective probability of success ($P_F = 1 - P_S$) and the incentive value of success ($I_F = -P_S$).

Thus, after arithmetic substitution, the achievement-oriented tendency can be written as follows (Equation 3):

$$T_A = \left(M_{AS} - M_{AF}\right) \times \left[P_S \times \left(1 - P_S\right)\right] \qquad (3)$$

Predictions About Effort From the Achievement Motives Theory

As outlined in Equation 3, the dispositional tendency to achieve is determined by the strength of the motive to achieve success relative to the motive to avoid failure. Atkinson (1957) postulated that the two motives are independent factors. One implication is that persons high in the motive to achieve success and low in the motive to avoid failure are considered as approach-driven individuals. Conversely, persons low in the motive to achieve success and high in the motive to avoid failure are considered as avoidance-driven individuals. In accordance with the quadratic function established (Equation 3), Atkinson (1957) postulated curvilinear relationships between the subjective probability of success and the achievement-oriented tendency for approach-driven individuals (inverted U shape, Figure 19.1a) and for the avoidance-driven persons (U shape, Figure 19.1b). More precisely, it was predicted that approach-driven people have a greater achievement motivation and consequently invest more effort on tasks of intermediate difficulty than on easy and extremely difficult tasks. This should be especially the case if they are strongly approach-driven (Figure 19.1a). However, it was predicted that avoidance-driven participants have a greater achievement motivation and consequently mobilize more effort on easy and extremely difficult task than on intermediate difficult tasks (curvilinear function). This should be especially the case if they are strongly avoidance-driven (Figure 19.1b).

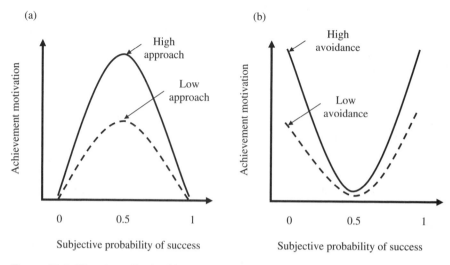

Figure 19.1. The strength of achievement motivation as a function of subjective probability of success and high or low approach-driven participants (a) and high or low avoidance–driven participants (b).

In conclusion, there are major predictions derived from achievement motives theory (Atkinson, 1957; McClelland et al., 1953) concerning effort mobilization:

- Incentive value is determined by the magnitude of the subjective probability of success and is inversely related to it ($I_S = 1 - P_S$ and $I_F = -P_F$). Within Atkinson's model, incentive value does not have independent operational existence and has not received much attention in most research on achievement motives theory. The first purpose is to clarify the effects of incentive value on effort mobilization.
- There are curvilinear relationships between subjective probability of success and effort mobilization for the approach-driven participants (inverted U shape, Figure 19.1a) and for the avoidance-driven participants (U shape, Figure 19.1b).

Evaluating the Predictions of Achievement Motives Theory

Motivational intensity theory (Brehm & Self, 1989) is a useful framework to explain the influence of incentive value on resource mobilization across difficulty levels. According to Wright's (1996) integration of motivational intensity theory (Brehm & Self, 1989) with Obrist's (1981) active coping approach, the impact of the sympathetic nervous system on the heart and the vasculature increases proportionally to the extent of subjective difficulty until the individual perceives the level of difficulty as impossible and disengages (Figure 19.2a). Especially, systolic blood pressure (SBP) responds sensitively to task difficulty (Wright, 1996). This is because SBP is strongly influenced by beta-adrenergic sympathetic discharge to the heart. Diastolic blood pressure depends more on vascular resistance and is unsystematically affected by beta-adrenergic sympathetic activation. Heart rate (HR) is determined by both sympathetic and parasympathetic activation and is not a reliable index of energy expenditure.

Cardiovascular reactivity related to effort is also determined by the maximal level of justified effort, or the peak of what an individual would be willing to do to succeed, which is potential motivation in terms of motivational intensity theory (Figure 19.2b). This upper limit of what an individual would be willing to do to succeed is determined by variables related to the importance of success and incentive value (e.g., Gendolla, Richter, & Silvia, 2008; Stewart, Wright, Hui, & Simmons, 2009; Wright, Killebrew, & Pimpalapure, 2002; Wright, Williams, & Dill, 1992). Participants in an easy task condition invested energy as a function of their level of subjective difficulty and not as a function of maximally justified effort. Participants mobilize the maximally justified effort only for very difficult tasks and also when task difficulty is unfixed (e.g., "Do your best"). Within this range (i.e., difficult tasks), energy expenditure is proportional to difficulty under high potential motivation and low under low potential motivation. When task difficulty is unfixed, individuals will strive for the highest possible performance level that is justified to be achieved to assure goal attainment (e.g., Gendolla & Richter, 2006). In that case, effort

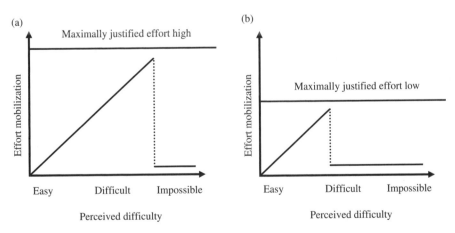

Figure 19.2. Mobilization of effort as a function of subjective difficulty and maximally justified effort high (a) and low (b).

mobilization is proportional to potential motivation. For impossible tasks, success is viewed as impossible and not worthwhile, even if potential motivation is high. Within this range (i.e., impossible tasks), effort investment is low irrespective of potential motivation.

Some studies investigated the influence of potential motivation on cardiovascular responses related to effort mobilization. In one of them, Gendolla et al. (2008, Experiment 2) invited participants to perform the d2 letter cancellation test in which they were assigned to press a "yes" response key if a letter d with two apostrophes appeared on a computer screen or a "no" response key if another stimulus appeared. In the difficult condition, each letter occurred for 600 ms. Stimuli were presented for 350 ms in the extremely difficult condition. In the unfixed difficulty condition, the letter disappeared after responding and participants received instructions to do their best. Participants in the high self-focus condition were exposed to their own face on a video monitor during the task. Conversely, they were not recorded in the low self-focus condition. According to self-awareness theory (Duval & Wicklund, 1972), focusing attention to the self induces a state of self-evaluation and thus makes success relatively important. Analyses revealed that greater cardiovascular reactivity was related to mental effort investment (stronger SBP) in the difficult task and in the unfixed difficulty task only when success was viewed as important (i.e., high self-focus condition). These results suggest that potential motivation directly determines mental effort mobilization only when task difficulty is extreme or unfixed.

In another study, Wright et al. (2002, Experiment 1) asked participants either to press a key once each time they heard a tone sound at 10-s intervals (fixed challenge condition) or to press the key repeatedly so long as each tone continued to sound, with the goal of pressing as many times as possible (unfixed challenge condition). Some participants were informed that their responses would be private (no-observer condition). In the observer condition, participants were told that their responses would be observed either by an undergraduate (low-status observer condition) or by a medical school professor (high-status observer condition). In accordance with the predictions of motivational intensity theory, SBP and HR responses in the unfixed and high-status observer condition were greater than those in the remaining conditions. As in the previous study (Gendolla et al., 2008), these results suggest that potential motivation is the upper limit of what an individual would be willing to do to succeed and determines mental effort mobilization only when task difficulty is extreme or unfixed.

To summarize, the incentive variable has been relatively ignored or at best crudely defined in most research on achievement motives theory. Atkinson's (1957) definition of incentive value of success as the inverse of probability of success provides a limited view of the possible influence of incentive value. However, considerable empirical support exists for the influence of incentive value on cardiovascular responses related to effort mobilization on approach and avoidance contexts in very difficult tasks and also when task difficulty is unfixed (e.g., "Do your best").

Testing the Curvilinear Relationships Between Achievement Motives and Effort

Karabenick and Youssef (1968) tested whether the curvilinear relationships between achievement motives and task difficulty has implications for effort mobilization operationalized indirectly as performance. Approach-driven participants learned word pairs of objectively equal difficulty faster when the word pairs were presented as intermediate difficulty compared with the easy and extremely difficult presentations. Inversely, avoidance-driven participants learned the words more rapidly when the task was easy or very difficult. Furthermore, participants high or low on both motives had the same level of performance across difficulty levels.

One main limitation of this study is that only one factor of performance (i.e., number of word pairs correctly recalled) was used as an index of effort mobilization. Because no result about the proportion of errors was presented, we could not determine whether the relationships between difficulty and performance for approach-driven and avoidance-driven participants were caused by an increase of mental effort or a change in strategy. In conclusion, there were no data that directly supported the curvilinear relationships between achievement motives and effort mobilization (Locke & Latham, 2002). However, that achievement motives influence effort mobilization in achievement situations seems to be a basic assumption. In the next paragraph, studies exploring this idea are reviewed.

Only four studies accounted for an influence of achievement motives and effort mobilization (Beh, 1990; Capa & Audiffren, 2009; Capa, Audiffren, & Ragot, 2008a, 2008b). Beh (1990) demonstrated that high achievers performed better (i.e., had shorter reaction times) and had higher HR than low achievers during the performance of a vigilance task. Analyses of the proportion of errors revealed no significant difference between groups, suggesting no speed–accuracy trade-off between groups. These findings are interpreted as indicating that high achievers expended greater mental effort than low achievers and obtained a better performance. However, these results do not address whether subjective probability of success mediates the relationship between achievement motives and mental effort mobilization. Moreover, participants were selected on the basis of their scores on the Edwards Personal Preference Schedule (Pietrofesa & Wurtz, 1970). This scale of achievement motivation was designed to measure 15 needs or motives (e.g., achievement, autonomy, affiliation, dominance, aggression). It is, consequently, difficult to determine which motives have influenced effort investment.[2]

More recently, Capa et al. (2008b) selected approach-driven and avoidance-driven participants on the basis of the two motives postulated by Atkinson (1957). A total of 710 participants filled out a measure of the motive to achieve success and a measure of the motive to avoid failure. The motive to achieve success subscale focused on the preference for difficult tasks. We referred to the corresponding subscale of the Achievement Motivation Inventory (Schuler, Thornton, Frintrup, & Mueller-Hanson, 2004), a multifaceted measure of achievement motivation, to construct items such as "I generally prefer difficult tasks more than easy tasks." We referred to the work of Hagtvet and Benson (1997) to build the motive to avoid failure subscale and formulated items such as "I dislike situations in which I am not sure of the result." Participants were classified as approach-driven if their score on the motive to achieve success was above the 80th percentile and if their score on the motive to avoid failure was below the 20th percentile, and conversely for the avoidance-driven participants. Subjective probability of success was manipulated by increasing task difficulty. Participants had to memorize one letter, two letters, or four letters in a memory set and compare the letters in a recognition set. They indicated whether any letter in the memory set was present in the recognition set by pressing a *yes* or *no* key. Difficulty was also manipulated by presenting the recognition set in two different colors (i.e., red and green). Participants were asked to count the number of red recognition sets. The three memory conditions with one, two, and four consonants were composed of 28, 32, and 44 red recognition sets, respectively. Midfrequency band of HR variability was used as an index of mental effort mobilization (Mulder, van Roon, Veldman, Elgersma, & Mulder, 1995). When people are confronted with performance challenges, an increase of sympathetic nervous system activity is related to task engagement (Obrist, 1981) and induces greater cardiac contractility and SBP reactivity (e.g., Richter, Friedrich, & Gendolla, 2008) and also a decrease of the midfrequency band (from .07 to .14 Hz) of HR reactivity (for a review, see Mulder et al., 1995). Fluctuations in this band are associated with short-term regulation of blood pressure, which causes a resonance in the veins with a frequency of about .10 Hz.

---

[2]McClelland et al. (1953) advocated the use of the Thematic Apperception Test (TAT), which involves coding the contents of people's imaginative stories about pictures for the presence of achievement-related thoughts. TAT-assessed motives have shown modest correlations with self-reported motives (Spangler, 1992). However, both implicit and self-attributed motives function to energize and direct behavior (e.g., Brunstein & Maier, 2005). Future studies are necessary to differentiate the influence of implicit and self-attributed motives on cardiovascular reactivity related to effort mobilization.

Approach-driven participants had a stronger decrease of midfrequency band HR variability (Figure 19.3a) and faster reaction times (Figure 19.3b) than avoidance-driven participants, especially during the difficult task (i.e., four letters to memorize). No group difference emerged for the proportion of errors in the recognition and in the counting tasks. The better performance obtained by approach-driven participants compared with avoidance-driven participants is interpreted as a higher investment of mental effort. Moreover, no group difference was found on the perceived difficulty scale. We concluded that there was probably no significant difference in perceived

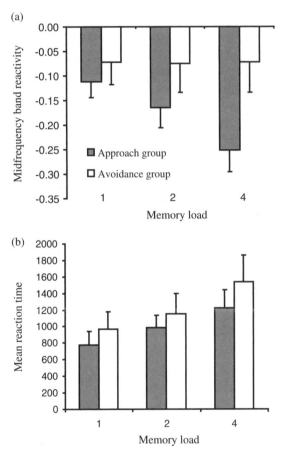

Figure 19.3. Cell means and standard errors of midfrequency band reactivity (a) and mean reaction time (b) as a function of approach-driven and avoidance-driven participants and memory load. Adapted from "The Interactive Effect of Achievement Motivation and Task Difficulty on Mental Effort," by R. L. Capa, M. Audiffren, and S. Ragot, 2008, *International Journal of Psychophysiology, 70*, p. 148. Copyright 2008 by Elsevier. Adapted with permission.

difficulty between groups. Contrary to other personality dispositions, such as dysphoria (Brinkmann & Gendolla, 2007) and extraversion (Kemper et al., 2008), the achievement motives influenced effort mobilization not by changing the perception of difficulty but by interacting with perceived difficulty.

To summarize, these results do not support a curvilinear relationship between subjective probability of success and effort mobilization. As in Beh (1990), approach-driven participants showed a better performance and had a stronger cardiovascular reactivity than avoidance-driven participants. No data support a curvilinear relationship between achievement motives and effort mobilization. By contrast, the linear relationship between task difficulty and effort-related physiological reactivity—until the individual perceives the level of difficulty as impossible and disengages—was confirmed in several studies (e.g., Fairclough & Houston, 2004; Richter et al., 2008). These results allowed the effect of achievement motives on this relationship between subjective difficulty and invested mental effort to be extended. However, the underlying cognitive mechanisms remain unknown.

How Do Achievement Motives Influence Effort Mobilization?

An interpretation of the results discussed so far is that achievement motives have influenced potential motivation (Figure 19.2). This interpretation accords well with studies on the relationships between motivational dispositions and affects. For example, Puca and Schmalt (1999) showed that approach-driven participants focused on the positive emotional consequences of success. However, avoidance-driven participants focused on the negative emotional consequences of failure. Gable, Reis, and Elliot (2000) found support for this idea in a study on motivational dispositions (i.e., behavioral activation system and behavioral inhibition system) and reactions to daily events. Achievement motives and the behavioral activation and inhibition systems are similar factors with probably similar influences on affect. Gable et al. found that strong behavioral inhibition system sensitivity was associated with more daily negative affect, and high behavioral activation system sensitivity was predictive of increased daily positive affect. Moreover, individuals with a more sensitive behavioral inhibition system reacted more strongly to the occurrence of negative events compared with individuals with more sensitive behavioral activation system.

In conclusion, one possible implication is that approach-driven participants have relatively high potential motivation. This hypothesis accords with the results presented earlier (Capa et al., 2008a). Approach-driven participants had a stronger decrease of midfrequency band reactivity when task difficulty increased. Potential motivation might have been so high that effort was justified even for the highest difficulty level. Another possible implication is that avoidance-driven participants have relatively low potential motivation. This hypothesis accords with the absence of a difficulty effect on the midfrequency band for the avoidance-driven participants. Potential motivation might have been so low that effort was not justified even for the lowest difficulty level.

Testing the Effect of Achievement Motives on Potential Motivation and Effort

Capa and Audiffren (2009) conducted another study to clarify whether the effect of achievement motives on mental effort is moderated by the level of maximally justified effort. Approach-driven and avoidance-driven participants were selected and first instructed to perform a reaction time task to the best of their abilities (i.e., "React as quickly as possible without making errors"). Next, participants were instructed to consistently beat their performance standard established in the first condition (i.e., "Beat your reaction time reference as often as possible without increasing your error rate"). Midfrequency HR variability and corrugator supercilii (i.e., facial muscle) responses were used as indices of mental effort mobilization (Mulder et al., 1995) and negative affects (Tassinary & Cacioppo, 2000), respectively. As in previous studies (Capa et al., 2008a, 2008b), approach-driven participants showed a stronger decrease of the midfrequency band of HR variability than avoidance-driven participants in the most difficult condition (i.e., second instruction condition). Moreover, avoidance-driven participants showed higher corrugator supercilii activity than approach-driven participants in the second instruction condition. As expected, results suggested that avoidance-driven participants experienced negative affect and decreased the level of maximally justified effort and their level of engagement, especially in the difficult condition.[3] These results accord with a more recent experiment in which participants in different mood conditions (negative mood, neutral mood, and positive mood) performed a memory task under conditions of unclear task difficulty (Richter & Gendolla, 2009). SBP reactivity during task performance increased from negative to positive mood. Negative mood has decreased the maximally justified effort and the level of engagement.

---

[3]Corrugator supercilii activity is also known as an index of general resource mobilization (van Boxtel & Jessurun, 1993). Corrugator supercilii activity related to effort is typically associated with high cardiovascular reactivity (Tassinary & Cacioppo, 2000), a pattern that we did not observe. For this reason, the greater corrugator supercilii reactivity of avoidance-driven participants was not interpreted as an index of effort.

CONCLUSION

Atkinson (1957) and McClelland et al. (1953) developed the first formal achievement motivation model incorporating achievement motives, expectancy, and incentive value constructs. Achievement motives theory (Atkinson, 1957; McClelland et al., 1953) has instigated intensive research; however, little of this research has focused explicitly on effort mobilization. In the present chapter, predictions of the achievement motives theory were confronted unsuccessfully with experimental arguments.

The findings by Capa and Audiffren (2009) suggest that avoidance-driven participants experienced negative affect decreasing the maximally justified effort and their level of engagement. A complementary interpretation is that avoidance-driven participants have poor emotion regulation. One main question is to determine why avoidance-driven participants may have a poor ability to regulate negative affects with the second set of instructions. Feedback should be the main factor. At the end of each trial, participants received performance feedback. In the second instruction condition, participants probably compared the reaction time achieved with their reaction time reference and their progress in relation to the goal assigned. This process of comparison has probably increased the development of negative affect when avoidance-driven participants achieved a reaction time inferior to their reaction time reference. Moreover, no significant interaction effect between achievement motives group and performance instructions was found. This suggests that those with avoidance-driven performance received the same amount of negative feedback (reaction time established inferior to the reaction time reference) and that they probably reacted more strongly to the occurrence of negative events. To test this prediction, further studies measuring event-related brain potential are necessary. When participants make an erroneous response in a choice reaction time task, an error negativity or error-related negativity has been described (Falkenstein, Hohnsbein, Hoormann, & Blanke, 1991), reflecting a motivational and emotional response (Bush, Luu, & Posner, 2000). We can expect that error-related negativity amplitudes would be larger after a feedback of failure for avoidance-driven participants than for approach-driven participants.

REFERENCES

Atkinson, J. W. (1957). Motivational determinants of risk-taking behavior. *Psychological Review, 64*, 359–372. doi:10.1037/h0043445

Atkinson, J. W., & Raynor, J. O. (1974). *Motivation and achievement.* Washington, DC: Winston.

Beh, H. C. (1990). Achievement motivation, performance and cardiovascular activity. *International Journal of Psychophysiology, 10*, 39–45. doi:10.1016/0167-8760(90)90043-D

Brehm, J. W., & Self, E. A. (1989). The intensity of motivation. *Annual Review of Psychology, 40*, 109–131. doi:10.1146/annurev.ps.40.020189.000545

Brinkmann, K., & Gendolla, G. H. E. (2007). Dysphoria and mobilization of mental effort: Effects on cardiovascular reactivity. *Motivation and Emotion, 31*, 71–82. doi:10.1007/s11031-007-9054-0

Brunstein, J. C., & Maier, G. (2005). Implicit and self-attributed motives to achieve: Two separate but interacting needs. *Journal of Personality and Social Psychology, 89*, 205–222. doi:10.1037/0022-3514.89.2.205

Bush, G., Luu, P., & Posner, M. I. (2000). Cognitive and emotional influences in anterior cingulate cortex. *Trends in Cognitive Sciences, 4*, 215–222. doi:10.1016/S1364-6613(00)01483-2

Capa, R. L., & Audiffren, M. (2009). How does achievement motivation influence mental effort mobilization? Physiological evidence of deteriorative effects of negative affects on the level of engagement. *International Journal of Psychophysiology, 74*, 236–242. doi:10.1016/j.ijpsycho.2009.09.007

Capa, R. L., Audiffren, M., & Ragot, S. (2008a). The effects of achievement motivation, task difficulty, and goal difficulty on physiological, behavioral, and subjective effort. *Psychophysiology, 45*, 859–868.

Capa, R. L., Audiffren, M., & Ragot, S. (2008b). The interactive effect of achievement motivation and task difficulty on mental effort. *International Journal of Psychophysiology, 70*, 144–150. doi:10.1016/j.ijpsycho.2008.06.007

Deci, E. L., & Ryan, R. M. (2000). The "what" and "why" of goal pursuits. Human needs and the self-determination of behavior. *Psychological Inquiry, 11*, 227–268. doi:10.1207/S15327965PLI1104_01

Duval, T. S., & Wicklund, R. A. (1972). *A theory of objective self-awareness*. New York, NY: Academic Press.

Elliot, A. J. (1999). Approach and avoidance motivation and achievement goals. *Journal of Personality and Social Psychology, 34*, 169–189.

Fairclough, S. H., & Houston, K. (2004). A metabolic measure of mental effort. *Biological Psychology, 66*, 177–190. doi:10.1016/j.biopsycho.2003.10.001

Falkenstein, M., Hohnsbein, J., Hoormann, J., & Blanke, L. (1991). Effects of crossmodal divided attention on late ERP components: II. Error processing in choice reaction tasks. *Electroencephalography and Clinical Neurophysiology, 78*, 447–455. doi:10.1016/0013-4694(91)90062-9

Feather, N. T. (1961). The relationship of persistence at a task to expectation of success and achievement related motives. *Journal of Abnormal and Social Psychology, 63*, 552–561.

Fodor, E. M., & Carver, R. A. (2000). Achievement and power motives, performance feedback, and creativity. *Journal of Research in Personality, 34*, 380–396. doi:10.1006/jrpe.2000.2289

Gable, S. L., Reis, H. T., & Elliot, A. J. (2000). Behavioral activation and inhibition in everyday life. *Journal of Personality and Social Psychology, 78*, 1135–1149. doi:10.1037/0022-3514.78.6.1135

Gendolla, G. H. E., & Richter, M. (2006). Ego-involvement and the difficulty law of motivation: Effects on performance-related cardiovascular response. *Personality and Social Psychology Bulletin, 32*, 1188–1203. doi:10.1177/0146167206288945

Gendolla, G. H. E., Richter, M., & Silvia, P. J. (2008). Self-focus and task difficulty effects on effort-related cardiovascular reactivity. *Psychophysiology, 45*, 653–662. doi:10.1111/j.1469-8986.2008.00655.x

Gendolla, G. H. E., & Wright, R. A. (2005). Motivation in social settings studies of effort-related cardiovascular arousal. In J. P. Forgas, K. D. Williams, & S. M. Laham (Eds.), *Social motivation: Conscious and unconscious processes* (pp. 71–90). New York, NY: Cambridge University Press.

Hagtvet, K. A., & Benson, J. (1997). The motive to avoid failure and test anxiety responses: Empirical support for integration of two research traditions. *Anxiety, Stress, and Coping, 10*, 35–57. doi:10.1080/10615809708249294

James, W. (1890). *The principles of psychology.* London, England: Macmillan. doi:10.1037/10538-000

Karabenick, S. A., & Youssef, Z. I. (1968). Performance as a function of achievement motive level and perceived difficulty. *Journal of Personality and Social Psychology, 10*, 414–419. doi:10.1037/h0026735

Kazén, M., & Kuhl, J. (2005). Intention memory and achievement motivation: Volitional facilitation and inhibition as a function of affective contents of need-related stimuli. *Journal of Personality and Social Psychology, 89*, 426–448. doi:10.1037/0022-3514.89.3.426

Kemper, C. J., Leue, A., Wacker, J., Chavanon, M.-L., Hennighausen, E., & Stemmler, G. (2008). Agentic extraversion as a predictor of effort-related cardiovascular response. *Biological Psychology, 78*, 191–199. doi:10.1016/j.biopsycho.2008.02.009

Langens, T. A. (2007). Congruence between implicit and explicit motives and emotional well-being: The moderating role of activity inhibition. *Motivation and Emotion, 31*, 49–59. doi:10.1007/s11031-006-9038-5

Locke, E. A., & Latham, G. P. (2002). Building a practically useful theory of goal setting and task motivation: A 35-year odyssey. *American Psychologist, 57*, 705–717. doi:10.1037/0003-066X.57.9.705

McClelland, D. C., Atkinson, J. W., Clark, R. A., & Lowell, E. L. (1953). *The achievement motive.* East Norwalk, CT: Appleton-Century-Crofts. doi:10.1037/11144-000

Mulder, L. J. M., van Roon, A. M., Veldman, J. B. P., Elgersma, A. F., & Mulder, G. (1995). Respiratory pattern, invested effort, and variability in heart rate and blood pressure during the performance of mental tasks. In M. Di Rienzo, G. Mancia, G. Parati, A. Pedotti, & A. Zanchetti (Eds.), *Computer analysis of cardiovascular signals* (pp. 219–233). Amsterdam, The Netherlands: IOS Press.

Obrist, P. A. (1981). *Cardiovascular psychophysiology: A perspective*. New York, NY: Plenum Press.

Pietrofesa, J. J., & Wurtz, R. E. (1970). *The Edwards Personal Preference Schedule*. Paper presented at the meeting of the American Personnel Guidance Association, New Orleans, LA.

Puca, R. M., & Schmalt, H.-D. (1999). Task enjoyment: A mediator between achievement motives and performance. *Motivation and Emotion, 23,* 15–29. doi:10.1023/A:1021327300925

Raynor, J. O. (1970). Relationships between achievement-related motives, future orientation, and academic performance. *Journal of Personality and Social Psychology, 15,* 28–33. doi:10.1037/h0029250

Richter, M., Friedrich, A., & Gendolla, G. H. E. (2008). Task difficulty effects on cardiac activity. *Psychophysiology, 45,* 869–875. doi:10.1111/j.1469-8986.2008.00688.x

Richter, M., & Gendolla, G. H. E. (2009). Mood impact on cardiovascular reactivity when task difficulty is unclear. *Motivation and Emotion, 33,* 239–248. doi:10.1007/s11031-009-9134-4

Schuler, H., Thornton, G. C., III, Frintrup, A., & Mueller-Hanson, R. (2004). *AMI: Achievement Motivation Inventory. Technical and user's manual*. Goettingen, Germany: Hogrefe.

Spangler, W. D. (1992). Validity of questionnaire and TAT measures of need for achievement: Two meta-analyses. *Psychological Bulletin, 112,* 140–154. doi:10.1037/0033-2909.112.1.140

Stewart, C. C., Wright, R. A., Hui, S.-K. A., & Simmons, A. (2009). Outcome expectancy as a moderator of mental fatigue influence on cardiovascular response. *Psychophysiology, 46,* 1141–1149. doi:10.1111/j.1469-8986.2009.00862.x

Tassinary, L. G., & Cacioppo, J. T. (2000). The skelemotor system: Surface electromyography. In J. T. Cacioppo, L. G. Tassinary, & G. G. Berntson (Eds.), *Handbook of psychophysiology* (pp. 163–169). New York, NY: Cambridge University Press.

van Boxtel, A., & Jessurun, M. (1993). Amplitude and bilateral coherency of facial and jaw-elevator EMG activity as an index of effort during a two-choice serial reaction task. *Psychophysiology, 30,* 589–604. doi:10.1111/j.1469-8986.1993.tb02085.x

Weiner, B., & Kukla, A. (1970). An attributional analysis of achievement motivation. *Journal of Personality and Social Psychology, 15,* 1–20. doi:10.1037/h0029211

Wright, R. A. (1996). Brehm's theory of motivation as a model of effort and cardiovascular response. In P. M. Gollwitzer & J. A. Bargh (Eds.), *The psychology of action: Linking cognition and motivation to behavior* (pp. 424–453). New York, NY: Guilford Press.

Wright, R. A., Killebrew, K., & Pimpalapure, D. (2002). Cardiovascular incentive effects where a challenge is unfixed: Demonstrations involving social evaluation, evaluator status, and monetary reward. *Psychophysiology, 39*, 188–197. doi:10.1111/1469-8986.3920188

Wright, R. A., & Kirby, L. D. (2001). Effort determination of cardiovascular response: An integrative analysis with applications in social psychology. In M. P. Zanna (Ed.), *Advances in experimental social psychology* (Vol. 33, pp. 255–307). New York, NY: Academic Press.

Wright, R. A., Williams, B. J., & Dill, J. C. (1992). Interactive effects of difficulty and instrumentality of avoidant behavior on cardiovascular reactivity. *Psychophysiology, 29*, 677–686. doi:10.1111/j.1469-8986.1992.tb02045.x

INDEX

Brain. *See also specific parts of brain*
diagram of, 250
levels of organization in, 232–234
Brain–behavioral level (CV response in emotion), 96
Brain–behavioral systems, 101–105
Branscombe, N. R., 123
Breathing rate, 67–69
Brehm, J. W., 9, 10, 82, 123, 201, 344
Brener, J., 6, 12, 44
Brenner, S. L., 56, 81, 82
Brinkmann, K., 149–151
Brosschot, J. F., 332
Brown, P. C., 292, 297
Buffering hypothesis, 334
Burns, J. W., 167

CAB (cardiac autonomic balance), 314–316
Cacioppo, J. T., 161, 315, 369
CAN (central autonomic network), 183, 192
Cannon, W. B., 95, 98, 162, 312
Capa, R. L., 390, 393, 394
CAR (cardiac autonomic regulatory capacity), 314, 316
Caramanos, Z., 24
Cardiac activity
conditions coupled with, 44
with increased SNS activity, 94
Cardiac autonomic balance (CAB), 314–316
Cardiac autonomic regulatory capacity (CAR), 314, 316
Cardiac chronotropy, 184
Cardiac contractility, 98
Cardiac death, 228
Cardiac disease, 35
Cardiac output (CO)
with anger, 127
and blood pressure, 310
and catecholamines, 99
with challenge, 111
and emotion, 101, 102
and interpersonal circumplex, 293
measuring changes in, 46
and social status, 298
with threat appraisal, 111
and vasoconstriction/vasodilation, 24

Cardiac reactivity
during active vs. passive coping, 44
and obesity, 249
Cardiac regulation, 183–184
Cardiac–somatic coupling
and emotion, 101
incentive effects on, 104
and "intake" tasks, 5
and task engagement, 82
Cardiography, 45–47. *See also* Electrocardiograms (ECGs)
Cardio–somatic coupling, 80
Cardiovascular behavior, 126–131
Cardiovascular disease (CVD)
agonistic striving as risk factor for, 281
and carotid intima–media thickness, 31
and depression, 247
and dominance, 299
endogenous opioid system and, 231
evidence linking reactivity to, 224–227
hypothalamic–pituitary–adrenocortical axis and, 225–226, 229–230
interpersonal circumplex framework for viewing, 291, 293
psychosocial risk of, 288–289
and social isolation, 317
and stress, 230, 245, 274, 332, 337
sympatho–adrenomedullary system and, 230–231
Cardiovascular reactivity (CVR)
during active vs. passive coping, 44
anger and, 224, 227–228
and beta-blockers, 289
and cardiovascular health, 224–227, 229–232
defined, 158, 224
and desired outcomes, 292
and dominance, 296–299
in dysphoric people, 149
to evaluative threats, 295
and incentives for influence, 297–298
integration of factors influencing, 232–234
interpersonal circumplex framework for viewing, 291–293
measures of, 45–46
in models of cardiovascular disease, 287

Control
cardiac modes of, 374
as dimension of interpersonal
relations, 288
and neural heterarchy, 310, 312–316
perceived, 111
Cook-Medley Hostility Scale, 163
Coping. *See also* Active coping; Passive
coping
defensive, 106–108
defined, 162
effortful, 170
and emotion, 101–102
emotion-focused, 162
problem-focused, 162
repressive, 164–165, 170, 171
Coping potential, 129
Coronary artery disease, 164, 228
Coronary heart disease (CHD), 332–333
and blood pressure, 225–227
dominant personality traits as
predictor of, 289
effect of worry on, 333
and social isolation, 317
Type A behavior as risk factor for, 163
Type D behavior as risk factor for, 164
Corr, P., 160
Corrugator supercilii activity, 393
Cortical areas, 126, 149
Cortical radiation, 31. *See also* Central
command theory
Corticosterone, 230
Corticotropin-releasing factor (CRF), 229
Cortisol, 230, 231, 252, 317
Corwin, W. H., 375
Costs, of mental effort investment, 62
CRF (corticotropin-releasing factor), 229
Critchley, H. D., 26, 35
CS (cingulate sulcus), 27
Cutaneous vascular beds, 24
CVD. *See* Cardiovascular disease
Cvlm (caudal ventrolateral medulla),
311, 315
CVR. *See* Cardiovascular reactivity;
Cardiovascular (CV) response
CVS (cardiovascular system), 94–95

Damasio, A. R., 160
Damasio, H., 160
Darby, D., 189

Darwin, C., 334, 337
Davidson, R. J., 164
DBP. *See* Diastolic blood pressure
Deactivating strategies, 165
de Burgo, J., 151
Decision making
ambivalence in, 161
and damage to insular cortex, 252
Defensive coping, 106–108
Defensive direction, 159–160
Defensive hostility, 163–164
Deferential behavior, 294
de Liver, Y., 161
Demand appraisals, 142–143, 146,
147, 229
De Morree, H. M., 207
Depletion. *See* Self-regulatory fatigue
Depression
ambivalence in, 159
and blunted reactivity, 247–248, 250
comorbidity with anxiety disorders,
152
motivational deficit in, 145, 146
PNS response to, 97
as risk factor for CVD, 288
and risk of cardiac event, 23
rumination linked with, 332
and social–emotional competence, 274
Depressive symptoms, 145–147,
149–150
Deterrence
in emotional intensity theory, 122–132
types of, 123
Diabetes mellitus, 316
Diastolic blood pressure (DBP)
and ability, 205, 355
agonistic striving's effect on, 278–282
anger's effect on, 227
and attachment, 165
and catecholamines, 99
and coronary heart disease, 225
counteracting perfusion with
increased, 106
and dominance, 292, 294
and emotional intensity theory, 125,
127–129
evaluative threat's effect on, 295
fatigue's effects on, 209, 211, 213
and low masculinity in women, 296
mood's effect on, 140, 144

Goldberg, D. E., 226
Gottman, J. M., 168
Gray, J. A., 80, 104, 105, 159, 160, 166
Gray, M. A., 35
Green, A. L., 32
Gross, J. J., 160, 162
Guilt
    and emotional intensity theory, 124
    and Type A behavior, 164

Habituation, 54
HACER (hypothalamic area controlling
    emotional responses), 233
Hagtvet, K. A., 390
Hankins, T. C., 372
Happiness, 123
Harm, 160
Harrison, N. A., 35
Hawkley, L. C., 315
Health. *See also* Cardiovascular disease
    (CVD); Social influences
    and blunted reactivity, 245–246
    and dominance, 299
    reactivity and cardiovascular,
        224–227, 229–232
Heart attacks, 327
Heartbeat evoked potential (HEP), 28
Heart contractility, 23
Heart disease. *See* Coronary heart
    disease (CHD)
Heart period (HP)
    and active vs. passive coping, 49
    and aviation mental workload, 374
    defined, 372
    and driver mental workload, 375, 377
    sympathetic and parasympathetic
        control of, 45
Heart rate (HR). *See also* Heart rate
    variability (HRV)
    and agonistic striving, 278
    anger's effect on, 227
    and aviation mental workload,
        371–372, 374–376
    and blood pressure, 310
    and catecholamines, 99
    and central command activity, 32
    changes in response to reward, 80–82
    cognitive effort's effect on, 369
    and dominance, 292, 294
    during driving tasks, 377, 378

in dual-system models, 103
and emotional intensity theory,
    125–129
and environmental stimuli, 5
evaluative threat's effect on, 295
fatigue's effects on, 208
and health, 224
incentives' effects on, 5, 56, 104
with increased effort sense, 33
with increased SNS activity, 94
and low masculinity in women, 296
marital conflict's effect on, 168
and mental effort investment, 65,
    68–70
mood's effect on, 140
nervous system's effect on, 369–370
observation's effect on, 54, 55, 388
outcome expectancy's effect on, 352
and parasympathetic efferents, 23
and passive coping, 101
performance challenge's effect on,
    390, 391
prior experience's effect on reactivity,
    51, 52
as psychophysiological measure, 45
with respiratory sinus arrhythmia, 293
response to orthostatic stress, 314
and reward, 84–87
and self-regulation, 184–186, 192
and stress, 328, 332
and task difficulty, 353, 387
and vasoconstriction/vasodilation, 24
Heart rate variability (HRV)
    cognitive effort's effect on, 369
    high-frequency component of, 104
    for measuring autonomic control, 315
    and mental effort, 65–70, 393
    with obesity, 248
    and pre-ejection period, 94
    and right insula cortex, 29
    during scanning tasks, 26
    and self-regulation, 183–185, 187–191
Hedonic affect regulation, 142, 147
Hedonic incentive, 143, 147–149
HEP (heartbeat evoked potential), 28
Hess, W. R., 97
HF/E. *See* Human factors/ergonomics
Hierarchy of needs, 337
High status, 295–296
Hockey, G. R. J., 61

Myocardial contractility
  inotropic measures of, 45
  mood's effect on, 140, 149
  in motivational intensity theory, 111
  and pre-ejection period, 94
  and relaxation, 102
Myocardial force, 101
Myocardial infarction
  anger as trigger of, 228
  and environmental stimuli, 23
Myocardial ischemia, 163–164, 318
Myocardial sympathetic activity, 81

NA. *See* Nucleus ambiguous
NA (noradrenaline), 99–101
Narcissism, 49
N-back working memory paradigm, 64
NE. *See* Norepinephrine
Needs
  hierarchy of, 337
  physiological, 21
Nervous system
  autonomic. *See* Autonomic nervous
    system (ANS)
  central. *See* Central nervous system
    (CNS)
  neural heterarchy in, 310, 312–316
  neural hierarchy in, 309–310
  parasympathetic. *See* Parasympathetic
    nervous system (PNS)
Neural heterarchy, 310, 312–316
Neural hierarchy, 309–311
Neuroendocrine system
  and cardiovascular activity, 158
  control of, 312, 313
  oxytocin's effects on, 317
  patterns of activity expressed
    through, 23
  and self-regulation, 183
Neuroergonomics, 379
Neurogenic bradycardia, 103
Neuroimaging research
  on cognitive–emotional functioning,
    23–36
  modern techniques for, 22
Neuromodulators, 100
Neuropeptide Y (NPY), 100–101
Neurotransmission, 100–101, 149
Nolte, R. N., 213
Noradrenaline (NA), 99–101

Norepinephrine (NE)
  and brain organization, 233
  and obesity, 248
  and pre-ejection period reactivity,
    46, 47
Norman, G. J., 315
Novelty, 43, 44, 50–52
NPY (neuropeptide Y), 100–101
NTS. *See* Nucleus tractus solitarius
Nucleus ambiguous (NA)
  and mental effort investment, 65
  parasympathetic efferents from, 23
  and social communication system,
    103
Nucleus tractus solitarius (NTS), 34
  and baroreceptor afferents, 311, 313
  and mental effort investment, 65
  projections to, 315

Obesity, 248–249
Obrist, P. A., 5, 6, 9, 12, 44, 46, 50, 82,
    139, 162, 192, 200, 344, 386
Observation, 52–56, 388. *See also*
    Audience presence
Occipital locations, 64
Öhman, A., 192
Oklahoma Family Health Patterns
    Project, 253
O'Leary, D. D., 34
Operant conditioning, 79
Opioid receptor blockade medications,
    231
OT (oxytocin), 316–319
Outcome expectancy
  sex differences in, 350–354
  and upper limit of effort, 345
Outcomes, 292
Overperfusion, tissue, 6, 12
Oxytocin (OT), 316–319

PAF (pure autonomic failure), 35
PAG. *See* Periaqueductal grey matter
Pain, 26
Palacios-Esquivel, R. L., 161
Paracingulate sulcus (PCS), 27
Paragigantocellularis (PGi), 311, 315
Parasympathetic nervous system (PNS)
  and achievement motives, 387
  and behavioral activation system, 81
  and cardiovascular arousal, 27

and pre-ejection period, 94
with sympathetic activation of heart, 293
Response modulation, 162
Resting conditions, 44
Reward, 79–88
   as direct determinant of CV response, 80–82
   and genual ACC, 26
   impact on human behavior, 79
   as indirect determinant of CV response, 82–86
   and mood, 145, 147–150
   and motivational intensity, 9
   and task difficulty, 82–84, 86–87
Richardson, J. E., 46
Richter, M., 50, 56, 85, 144, 151
Right insula cortex
   correlation between heart's function and, 29
   fMRI study on, 34
rMSSD. *See* Root mean squared successive differences
RN (red nucleus), 28
Roisman, G. I., 165
Romantic anger, 125
Root mean squared successive differences (rMSSD), 183, 185, 187, 190, 191
Rostral ventrolateral medulla (RVLM)
   inhibition of, 311
   and mental effort investment, 65
   projections to, 315
   sympathetic efferents from, 23
RSA. *See* Respiratory sinus arrhythmia
Rumination, 332–333
RVLM. *See* Rostral ventrolateral medulla
R-wave, 46, 47

Salas, E., 366
Salonen, J. T., 226
Sartre, J.-P., 337
SBP. *See* Systolic blood pressure
SC (superior colliculus), 28
SCAD (symptomatic coronary artery disease), 30
Scheier, M. F., 160, 167
Scherer, K. R., 109
Schirger, A., 227
Schmalt, H.-D., 392
Schmitt, M. T., 123

Schüpbach, L., 149, 150
Schwartz, G. E., 128, 164
SCI. *See* Social Competence Interview
SCL (skin conductance level), 185, 187
SCR. *See* Skin conductance response
Secondary appraisal, 160, 336
Self-awareness theory, 388
Self-control, 181
Self-improvement strivings, 268
Self-involvement, 111
Self-regulation, 181–193
   cardiac predictors of strength and fatigue, 184–189
   and cardiac regulation, 183–184
   defined, 181
   energy source for, 182
   and heart rate variability, 183–185, 187–191
   physiological profile of, 191–193
Self-regulatory competence, 274
Self-regulatory fatigue, 182–189
   cardiac predictors and correlates of, 184–189
   defined, 182
   and prefrontal cortex, 183–184
Self-regulatory strength, 184–189
Sensitization, 54
SES (socioeconomic status), 290, 296
Settels, J. J., 66
Sex differences, 343, 348–358
   in effects of IPC dimensions on CVR, 295
   in outcome expectancy, 350–354
   in perceived ability, 351, 354–356
   in value appraisal, 348–350, 352–354
Sheffert, S. M., 377
Sheldon, D. S., 227
Sheldon, K., 166
Shetler, S., 129, 131
Shoemaker, J. K., 34
Shortell, J., 125
Silvestrini, N., 149, 151
Single-photo-emission computed tomography (SPECT), 32, 33
Sinha, R., 127, 128
Sinotrial nodes, of heart, 23
Situation modification, 162
Situation selection, 162
Skeletal vascular beds, 24
Skin conductance level (SCL), 185, 187

Skin conductance response (SCR)
    and active vs. passive coping, 49
    with anger, 127
    and mood, 144
Smith, T. W., 292, 297
Smoking, 232, 252–253
SNS. *See* Sympathetic nervous system
Social action theory
    agonistic goals in, 271
    chronic interpersonal stress in, 268
    stress-related illness in, 274
Social and Personality Psychology Compass
        (journal), 4
Social communication system, 103–104
Social Competence Interview (SCI),
        268–270, 272, 273, 275, 276, 283
Social–emotional competence, 273–275
Social environments
    evolutionary development within, 21
    striving to alter, 270
Social evaluation
    effects of, 329–331
    sex differences in, 352
    social support vs., 334, 335
Social facilitation, 330
Social goals, 336–337
Social hierarchy, 290
Social influences, 307–319. *See also*
        Interpersonal circumplex
    and marriage, 295
    and neural hierarchy/heterarchy,
        309–316
    oxytocin and, 318–319
    research findings, 316–318
    social status, 290–291
Social isolation, 288, 317
Social–motivational model, 272–273, 282
Social rejection, 312, 317
Social skills, 274
Social status, 290–291
    defined, 288, 290
    exposure to, 295–296
    perception of, 312
    potential loss of, 298
    as predictor of morbidity and
        mortality, 317
Social support, 334–336
    as predictor of cortisol levels, 317
    reducing risk of CVD with, 287
    social evaluation vs., 334

Society for the Study of Motivation, 4
Socioeconomic status (SES), 290, 296
Somatic activity, 44
Somatizing disorders, 159
Specialized subsystems, 108–109
SPECT (single-photo-emission computed
        tomography), 32, 33
Spielberger, C. D., 164
Spinal motor neurons, 311, 312
Spinner, J., 166
Splanchnic vascular beds, 24
Sporting events, 23
SRS (superior rostral sulcus), 27
State–Trait Anger Expression Inventory,
        164
Statistical models, 36
Status. *See* Social status
Stemmler, G., 99
Steptoe, A., 228
Stewart, C. C., 212, 213
Stimulus–response, 159
Stoney, C. M., 54
Strange Situation studies, 165
Strength, 184–189
Stress. *See also* Motivational conflict
    acute, 23, 24, 244–245, 318
    and addiction, 250–253
    baroreceptor set point during, 24
    blood pressure reactivity to, 30
    and cardiac disease, 35
    chronic, 244, 268
    consequences of, 31, 271–272
    and CV adjustments, 157
    defined, 367
    and emotional intensity theory, 125
    environmental stimuli evoking, 23
    and epinephrine, 46, 231
    exposure to, 275–276
    and failure compensation, 333–334
    and health, 230–232, 234
    and immune function, 244–245
    and implicit goals, 268–269
    from marital conflict, 168
    mechanisms generating, 283
    and mental effort investment, 61–63
    from mental workload, 367, 368
    motivational profiles of psychological,
        269–271
    and myocardial ischemia, 163–164
    orthostatic, 314

ABOUT THE EDITORS

Rex A. Wright, PhD, is a professor of psychology at the University of Alabama at Birmingham. He received his BA at the University of Texas in Austin and his PhD at the University of Kansas, and he did his postdoctoral training at the State University of New York at Stony Brook. Dr. Wright's research is concerned chiefly with determinants and cardiovascular consequences of effort. He has authored numerous publications, including research articles, book chapters, and books. He also has held numerous visiting academic appointments, including ones at the Max Planck Institute (Germany), the University of Bielefeld (Germany), the University of Erlangen–Nuremberg (Germany), the University of Geneva (Switzerland), the University of Maryland at College Park, the University of Missouri at Columbia, and the University of Texas at Austin. Dr. Wright's visits have been supported in part by the Fulbright Program, the German Academic Exchange Service, and the Swiss National Science Foundation. His research has been supported by various granting agencies, most notably the National Science Foundation. Dr. Wright currently serves as an associate editor for the journal *Motivation and Emotion*.

Guido H. E. Gendolla, PhD, is a professor of psychology at the University of Geneva (Switzerland), where he holds the chair for motivation psychology and directs the Geneva Motivation Lab. He earned his diploma (corresponding to the MA) and his PhD in psychology at the University of Bielefeld (Germany). He earned his habilitation in psychology at the University of Erlangen–Nuremberg (Germany). Dr. Gendolla's research focuses on human motivation and affective states and is mainly concerned with psychophysiological processes. He has authored numerous publications, and his research has been supported by various grants from the Deutsche Forschungsgemeinschaft (DFG, German Research Foundation) and the Swiss National Funds.